The Culture of an Information Economy

The Culture of an Information Economy

Influences and Impacts in the Republic of Ireland

by

Eileen M. Trauth

College of Business Administration,
Northeastern University,
Boston, Massachusetts, U.S.A.

KLUWER ACADEMIC PUBLISHERS
DORDRECHT / BOSTON / LONDON

A C.I.P. Catalogue record for this book is available from the Library of Congress.

ISBN 0-7923-6555-0

Published by Kluwer Academic Publishers,
P.O. Box 17, 3300 AA Dordrecht, The Netherlands.

Sold and distributed in North, Central and South America
by Kluwer Academic Publishers,
101 Philip Drive, Norwell, MA 02061, U.S.A.

In all other countries, sold and distributed
by Kluwer Academic Publishers,
P.O. Box 322, 3300 AH Dordrecht, The Netherlands.

Printed on acid-free paper

Printed in the Netherlands.

This book is dedicated to four women who provided inspiration and motivation when I needed it: to my mother Martha Donelan Trauth for passing on to me her immense curiosity about our Irish heritage; to my sister Suzanne Trauth for encouraging me apply for the Fulbright Award that got me to Ireland; to Kathy Driehaus for her unwavering support throughout this journey; and to the memory of my sister Charlene Harvey who taught me more than I wanted to know about strength.

TABLE OF CONTENTS

Preface

The dialectic of the slow moving, traditional society actively engaging with the fast paced, state-of-the-art computer industry was apparent when I settled into Dublin in 1989. I had received a Fulbright Scholarship to study the impact of information technology on Irish society. Early on I noted the extent to which electronic business was conducted as a matter of course. The expected way to make automobile loan, insurance and television rental payments was to do so electronically -- albeit at the bank, not from home -- something that was not the case in the States at that time. Yet, at one of the two shops near my apartment where I would stop after work for a pint of milk or the *Irish Times* the proprietor always added up the bill by hand, writing with a pencil on the back of a brown paper bag. She said she preferred to calculate the bill herself because she did not trust the mechanical cash registers. I witnessed over and over the technological past and future living comfortably side by side, in Ireland.

As I draw this project to a close ten years later, much of the Ireland that I first encountered has disappeared. The effects of the information economy are apparent everywhere. The economy is booming as an ever larger part of the labor force turns to high tech employment. The information economy has, indeed, had a significant impact on Irish society. This apparent success makes my initial question all the more salient: What are the factors in Ireland's socio-cultural environment that help us to understand how Ireland has rapidly moved from a traditional, agrarian society to the modern information society it is fast becoming?

When I first came to Ireland I did not know that one year would turn into so many as I returned again and again in search of answers and explanations, for greater understanding about the societal transformation I was witnessing. As this has been a journey of understanding about the emergence of a particular information economy, it has also been a journey of self discovery as I navigated new methodological waters that placed me within the scope of my study.

Throughout the course of researching and writing this book, there have been scores of individuals who have made important contributions to its progress. There were the undergraduate students who, using my data management needs as a class project, designed and populated my respondent database. Graduate research assistants Chin-Fan Beckman, Pornpoj Chenkulprasutr, Cathy DiFonzo, Tony Dimichino, Jason Levy, Gretchen Snyder, Dave Stevens and Jon Thonet worked with my respondent data and the numerous documents I collected. Colleagues in the information systems community Allen Lee, Lynda Harvey, Mike Zack, Stephanie Collins and Dick Briotta helped me understand the nuances of my research methodology. My colleagues in the Irish studies community Ruth-Ann Harris, Rosemarie McDonald and Maurice Rahilly offered invaluable cultural insights and critique. My sisters Denise Trauth, Jeanette Trauth, Patricia Trauth and Kate Trauth patiently listened to me talk about this project for ten years.

Many members of the faculty and staff at Dublin City University helped guide my research as it was being conducted and gave feedback when I was writing this book. In particular, I would like to thank Barbara O'Connor, Stephanie McBride, Tanya Kiang, Paschal Preston, David Jacobson, Theresa Hogan and Brian Leavy. Various other people in Ireland helped me understand Irish history and culture: Rena Fleming, Michael and Jean Roberts, the Fanning family, Alma Clissman, Victor O'Reilly, Nora Norton, Marie Kennedy, Ann McCarthy, Mick Cunningham and the members of the American Women's Club Dublin. Julie Davenport and Stephen Odlum provided not only insights but also hospitality and warm conversation during my return visits to Ireland. American colleagues Rae Andre, Rob Kling, Linda Kuramoto, Marianne Murphy, Heidi Vernon and Judy Weisinger commented on drafts of my manuscript. Members of the Northeastern University, College of Business International Research Seminar helped me sculpt the final product. My colleagues at Griffith University in Brisbane, Australia, provided support and assistance during my Sabbatical as I completed the manuscript. Finally, Kathy Driehaus undertook the monumental task of turning my manuscript into this book.

While I have acknowledged by name the many friends, relatives, colleagues and students who have helped me, I would also like to acknowledge (but not by name) the representatives of the government agencies, and those workers and managers in Ireland's information-sector firms who participated in this study. Their observations about their work, their workplaces and their changing country formed the core of this book. To all those anonymous respondents I offer my heartfelt thanks for making this book possible. I still hear your voices as I read the words that appear on these pages.

Boston, Massachusetts

Part I
The Work

CHAPTER 1. INTRODUCTION

The radical changes in Ireland's economy during the last third of the twentieth century have been accompanied by a similar transformation in Ireland's society. As it discarded the image of a poor nation of small farmers it donned the mantle of a country with newfound economic health. Along with economic change came a change in attitude. Social commentators noted a psychological change that was occurring as Irish people who had always believed the worst about themselves were developing new pride in their small nation.[i] These economic and social changes have occurred alongside the growth of information technology (IT) industries in Ireland. These new industries now account for a significant part of Ireland's labor force and Gross National Product.[ii] Ireland is arguably an exemplar of economic development through information economy development.

As a heightened emphasis on information and information technology is transforming the world into a global information society, nations everywhere have begun to see opportunities for economic growth through the development of information-sector employment. But they have not all taken the same path. Leaders of the industrial era, such as the US, evolved their information sectors along with their gradual transition into a post-industrial society. Over the last two centuries the dominant forms of employment in such nations changed from agrarian to industrial to post-industrial. Along the way, they spawned the multinational IT companies which have facilitated the development of this global information society.

During the latter decades of the twentieth century, a second wave of countries, which were not dominant industrial nations, began to rapidly develop information-sector employment. Rather than developing an information economy on the shoulders of an industrial society, these countries have endeavored to achieve rapid development of their information sectors by importing both expertise and employment through inward investment by multinational firms. The global nature of the information sector is especially relevant for the case of Ireland where its outward approach was key to developing its information economy and realizing its economic growth.

As a result, a culturally diverse work environment has emerged in Ireland. It has resulted from the infusion of multinational information-sector firms reflecting a variety of cultures. This confluence of cultures -- multinational, indigenous, IT, and corporate -- is leaving its mark on the Irish information sector and influencing the way it is evolving. To the extent that Ireland's experiences represent the circumstances of other second wave countries, the lessons learned are extensible to indigenous and multinational managers as well as to government policy makers in other countries.

This book tells a story about Ireland's transition from a poor agricultural country to one whose economic health is due, in large part, to the development of its information sector. It does so by peeking inside the day-to-day work lives of the people who were bringing this transformation about. Their stories reveal the ways in which the different cultures have interacted to produce Ireland's information economy. In telling Ireland's story, this book also tells a larger story about how the change that is gripping all nations as they struggle to make sense of a new way of working and living is influenced by the cultural context within which it occurs.

1.   THE GLOBAL INFORMATION ECONOMY

There are several terms that endeavor to capture the cultural and economic shift that began during the second half of the twentieth century to transform the world. Daniel Bell (1973) described it as the movement to a *post-industrial society* in which knowledge replaces capital as the key resource much as capital in the industrial society replaced land, which had been the key resource of the agricultural society. When Daniel Bell wrote about the post-industrial society in the early 1970s he identified five dimensions of this emerging societal structure:

> *The change from a goods-producing to a service economy*
> *The pre-eminence of the professional and technical class*
> *The centrality of theoretical knowledge as the source of innovation*
> *The control of technology and technological assessment*
> *The creation of a new "intellectual technology"* (14)

The society he characterized was a marked departure from those that preceded it. In agrarian societies the focus of work was on *extraction*. As such, raw materials and land for farming were the key resources. In this society there was little social mobility. The source of power was fixed by birth order, gender and social class. In industrial societies the focus of work was on *fabrication* and the key resource needed to support manufacturing was capital. Power struggles between the bourgeoisie and the proletariat gave rise to the union movement that grew along with the industrial revolution. In the post-industrial society, the focus of work is on *service*. Rather than land or capital, the new key resource is knowledge. Thus, in this meritocracy, education and credentials rather than birth order or economic class create the route to power. Because information is the natural resource, countries that may have been "resource poor" in the industrial era have new competitive opportunities in the post-industrial age.

Peter Drucker (1969, 1993) characterized this societal shift as the movement to a *post-capitalist society* in which knowledge is the key resource.[iii] A range of political structures co-exists in this new society: transnational, regional and local. For industrial nations, this shift is evident in the decline of the power and pervasiveness of the proletariat. The decisive factor of production, the real controlling resource is neither capital nor land nor labor. It is knowledge. Replacing the landowner and farmer of the agricultural era, and the capitalist and proletarian of the industrial era, is the knowledge worker of the post-capitalist society. In this society there is a shift away from what had been considered to be the key wealth creating activities. Wealth in the post-capitalist society comes from the application of knowledge to productivity and innovation, rather than from the allocation of labor and capital to productive uses.

What these and other societal characterizations have in common is their recognition that the key resource of this new society is information. For this reason, some scholars have used the term *information society*[iv] to describe this societal transformation. By whatever name it is labeled, the engine of this new society is the *information sector*, which encompasses the work, and workers engaged in the processing of information and the production of information tools. Porat's (1977) analysis of the American information sector depicts an *information economy* that is divided into the primary information sector and the secondary information sector. The *primary information sector* produces information processing and communication hardware, the software and services which make it work, and the content which is its reason for being. It comprises those firms which are in the business of producing information and information tools.[v] The *secondary information sector*, on the other hand, consists of those organizations which process information in the course of accomplishing some other mission such as the provision of health care or transportation. Preston's (1998) analysis further refines Porat's primary information sector into four subcategories: information/communication technology (ICT), specialized information services, media and content, and hybrid professional information services. Kling (1990) defines the information sector as consisting of those jobs in which a significant portion of effort is devoted to recording, processing or communicating information. In all of these characterizations the terms information sector and information economy are used synonymously.

Those who proclaimed the societal transformation from industrialism to information during 1950s, 1960s and 1970s[vi] did so while the effects existed largely in potential. By the 1980s, however, the world's consciousness had been jarred by the introduction of the microcomputer. The ensuing "end user computing revolution" brought the computer's capability within reach of nonspecialists for the first time. The vision of an information society was becoming a reality. Twenty years after Bell's work was published another revolution -- the "Internet revolution" -- began to make this vision of an information society even more prominent. Throughout the 1980s and 1990s academic, management and popular literature have all taken up the banner of the information society or *information age*.[vii] Since the information economy is an important component of this emerging information society, the new rules for working in the information society apply very directly to those who are working to bring it about: those in the information economy.

Thurow (1999) has made an analogy between the current information revolution and other revolutions such as the one resulting from the invention of electricity. The availability of electricity brought new ways of working to the factory and significant changes in productivity. Electrification also brought profound changes in living habits, as people were no longer bound to the light cycles of the sun. Further, the opportunities for existing and new industries that resulted from electrification also brought new sources of wealth. In similar fashion, the information economy is a source of new wealth in the information age. The information economies of all nations are increasingly becoming both key to their economic health and a major source of employment.

This book focuses on a part of the information sector: companies and workers in the IT industries which produce hardware, software and information systems. In Preston's framework, this is the ICT subsector of the primary information sector. For convenience, I refer to it simply as the information sector or information economy.

1.1   Employment in the Information Economy

The pioneering American work on the information economy was carried out by Machlup (1962). In a seminal investigation of those engaged in the production and distribution of knowledge, he measured the expenditures on knowledge production and its importance to the US economy. Porat's (1977) follow-up study of the American information economy, which added greater refinement to this emerging concept, was repeated in other countries (Barnes and Lamberton, 1976; Katz, 1986; Lange and Rempp, 1977; OECD, 1981; and Wall, 1977).

When discussing employment in the information sector an important caveat is that work characteristics vary considerably depending upon whether one is engaged in hardware production, software development or information systems provision. Nevertheless, in totality, the characteristics described below are those found in the information-society workplace of which the information sector is a part. Therefore, some or all of these characteristics would apply to the information-sector workers and work considered in this book.

1.1.1   Information-sector Work

While the work of the agricultural society is based upon farming and that of the industrial society is based upon fabrication, the work of the information society is based upon information processing. The world economy is now dominated by *information capitalism* and the industries that have moved to the center of the world economy are in the business of producing and distributing *information* rather than *things*. In the information society the knowledge content of goods and services becomes ever more significant.

This focus on information has resulted from technological innovations, which are driving the convergence of information types. Print, voice and video data are converging into a single digital form. This, in turn, is motivating product innovations. The quickening speed of technological obsolescence places increasing emphasis on creativity as product life cycles shrink. Because of the pace of technological change, innovative responses to the marketplace are the hallmark of the information sector. New ways of thinking are needed to fuel the continuous search for new information products and services.

The focus on information has also resulted from corporate recognition that information is, indeed, an economically valuable resource. The terms, *intellectual capital* and *knowledge assets* signify the value placed upon information today. As the engine of the information society, the information economy is charged with providing the means by which organizations and individuals can acquire new and better types of information and ways to make better and quicker use of that information. The work of the information economy, thus, ranges from producing information content to producing information-processing tools.[viii]

An essential characteristic of this work is that it involves mental rather than physical labor. Work in the information sector is based around intellectual rather than physical activities and success is related to drive and determination the way farming is to the seasons and the sun. This type of work has several distinctive dimensions. Information-sector work requires the continuous acquisition of new knowledge. Consequently, the productivity of knowledge becomes an increasingly decisive factor in a country's economic and social success. The productivity of knowledge requires increased yield from what is known.

Information-sector work also requires that intelligence be incorporated into the tasks being carried out. With the commodification of information technology, the service component of information products increasingly becomes the key to competitive advantage. And it is intelligence that provides the value-added features of such service. The wealth of the agricultural society was in the hands of the landowners. The wealth of the industrial society was in the hands of steel barons. The new wealth of the information society is in the hands of those in the information sector: computer makers, software firms, information services providers, and those who organize their businesses around information.

Speed and flexibility are essential components of information-sector work. Information technology relaxes the constraints of time for all types of work, including information-sector work. And increased creativity demands reinforce the need for time flexibility. Rigid working hours may not be conducive to the generation of creative ideas. But while information-sector work can increasingly be done *any time* there is also the expectation that it be accomplished *faster*. Just-in-time approaches to the management of manufacturing and other aspects of business are shortening the time lag between demand for and provision of products and services, and the accompanying information.

Information-sector work is highly dynamic. The volatile nature of the sector and the need to keep up with the accelerating pace of change requires receptivity to new techniques. The constantly changing industry environment often means the need to work long and unpredictable hours. Further, because work in this sector moves into the unknown, it is not always possible to predict consequences. Therefore, coping with the unintended consequences of information/technology use requires constant adaptability.

1.1.2   Information-sector Workers

While the knowledge workers of the information economy had been recognized as such by a few prophets decades ago (Drucker, 1959; Machlup, 1962), the recognition of knowledge and information-sector work as a distinct class of employment is more typically a product of the 1980s and 1990s. As we enter the twenty-first century these people make up the largest portion of the labor force in developed nations and those that would become so. Because knowledge workers are the new "tools of production" by virtue of the knowledge that they possess, the productivity of these workers is increasingly the key to a society's economic health.

The information sector presents new challenges to its workers and those who manage them. The knowledge and skill requirements are both extensive and ever changing. Workers in the information economy need the intellectual capabilities to engage in work that is knowledge-intensive and creative but that also requires specialized skill and flexibility in carrying it out. The nature of the work demands a new definition of productivity; it requires that workers in the information economy be both adaptable and entrepreneurial about their jobs and their careers.

Because the knowledge possessed by its employees becomes the key asset in the information-age organization, the knowledge worker becomes the center of the information economy. The knowledge possessed by these workers can be broadly categorized into two types. One is specialized knowledge. In the information sector this means the technical know-how to create information tools, systems, services and content. The other type of knowledge is the generalized knowledge that has traditionally been associated with the liberally educated person. This latter type of learning helps one develop mental flexibility and the ability to quickly acquire new bodies knowledge. Together, these two types of knowledge enable the information-sector worker to possess the knowledge and skills necessary for a particular type of work but also to adapt to a rapidly changing and highly technical environment. Thus, this type of knowledge worker needs the tools to be able to see both the forest and the trees.

In addition to the base of technical knowledge needed for this work is the need to constantly keep up with new developments in order to remain at the technological forefront. But the need is more than simply continuous learning. In this domain significant changes in technology are a regular occurrence. Therefore, in order to remain on the leading edge of technological innovation, information economy workers need to not only keep up with the changes but also make the mental leaps into the new methods and approaches that accompany the new technology that is ever on the horizon.

Making these leaps requires the mental alertness to deal with unfamiliar situations, to recognize and respond to the ever-changing factors that enter the information sector. Workers must have flexibility as well as the ability to learn quickly. In addition to acquiring new knowledge, another reason for needing mental alertness is that information processing requires that intelligence be brought to bear on the task. There are two connotations of "intelligent," which are relevant to a discussion of knowledge-based work. One is the contextual understanding and critical thinking that is needed in order to process information. The other relevant connotation of "intelligent" is the general interest in and appreciation for liberal learning. The knowledge base needed for information-sector work varies with the subsector within which one works. But overall, a combination of both logical and technical, and liberal and interpersonal knowledge is needed. The former is required for one's specific job; the latter makes the information workers well rounded and enables them to respond to the contingencies of the workplace. Because of the pivotal role that knowledge plays in the information age, greater emphasis is placed upon formal education and credentials.

The nature of work in the information economy has produced changes in the measurement of the productivity of its workers. There has been a shift from the Tayloristic focus on the efficiency of repetitive tasks to a focus on the effectiveness of the output produced. Whereas productivity in the industrial society involved predetermined, machine-paced tasks in which the worker served the machine, productivity in the information society involves the machine serving the worker in carrying out tasks that are not a given but which must be determined. The ultimate productivity measure of information-sector workers is the quality of the product rather than the amount of time spent on the job. This change in the measure of productivity, therefore, brings with it a change in attitude toward time. Time flexibility is introduced as workers are expected to put in whatever amount of time is necessary in order to accomplish the job.

What is embedded in this work and demanded of its workers is another type of flexibility, as well. Information-sector work cannot be neatly segmented into rigid, unchanging job categories. The nature of work in the information sector is much less predictable. Neither the work nor the workers can be placed in boxes bounded by predetermined job descriptions. Workers are needed who can bring skills to a job that demands flexibility. People are not simply following a mechanical process and doing exactly what they are told. This type of flexibility is the willingness and ability to accomplish a range of tasks in order to get the job done. This means being a well-rounded worker who is willing to perform any task in pursuit of the goal.

A comfort level with risk is endemic to this sector and those working in it. This means that workers in the information economy need to adopt an entrepreneurial stance. They are both encouraged and forced to do so. Technological invention will yield great rewards to those who seize the opportunities it presents. However, even those who decline these opportunities must be entrepreneurial simply to stay employed. The constant change that defines the information sector and the incessant demand for new and different skills has brought an end to job stability. Having a single job throughout one's work life will be the exception rather than the rule. Information-sector workers may have several careers within the space of a lifetime of work.

In agrarian and industrial societies, information-intensive work is also carried out. The difference is that it is not the defining characteristic of the society, nor is it the type of work in which most of its citizens are engaged. It is largely the province of professional classes. In the information society, in general, and the information sector, in particular, information-intensive work is no longer the sole domain of the professional class of workers. It is also the work of the middle and working classes. This means that new classes of workers must receive formal education in order to have the general and specific skills needed for their work.

1.1.3   Information-sector Workplaces

A few key themes help to define the information-sector workplace: productivity of knowledge, working in teams and fluidity of work. In order for information-sector firms to be highly productive, they need to effectively utilize not only the knowledge possessed by their workers but also that knowledge which exists within the organization. In order to do this they need to foster a knowledge-producing environment. The information-economy workplace needs to foster both the specialized knowledge possessed by the individual workers and the knowledge they possess about the organization.

Three types of knowledge need to be fostered. The first is genuine innovation about the product or service. Innovation, the application of knowledge to produce new knowledge, is not best accomplished by loners. Rather, it requires organization and systematic effort. The second type of knowledge to be fostered is continuous improvement of the process, product or service. The third type of knowledge is the systematic exploitation of existing knowledge to develop new and different products, processes and services. Opportunities for change must be matched against the competencies and strengths of knowledge workers. While efforts are underway to capture their costs and economic impacts, some have argued that the real goal is not the quantitative measure of the amount of knowledge but rather the qualitative measure of the productivity of that knowledge.[ix]

A significant change in the nature of work in an information society is the shift in focus from individual to organizational productivity. Whereas the industrial society measured productivity in terms of the physical output of an individual worker, the information society requires productivity evaluated in terms of the quality of the good or service produced by a work unit. Therefore, workers in the information economy will increasingly be required to work in teams to accomplish their work. Doing so helps them to carry out specific tasks while maintaining a clearer picture of the whole.

Team-based work in the information sector is necessary because of the growth of knowledge. The accomplishment of a complete task with all the attendant knowledge can more easily be accomplished by a collection of individuals who, as a unit, possess more of the requisite knowledge than a single individual working alone. Along with the benefits of teams, however, come the challenges of working effectively. This requires the proper organization of work and its flow. Against the benefits of a larger skill set is the cost of greater coordination and communication among team members. Thus, the creation and facilitation of teams becomes an ever more important management task in information-sector workplaces.

There are several different models of how teams work and how information flows within them.[x] In one type of team the members work *on* the team but not *as* a team. Each worker has her or his specialized task to do; there is no cross training. This team model can be applied to mass production work that involves repetitive tasks. This type of team needs a controller. In another type of team the members interact to coordinate their individual specialized functions as they would on a soccer team or in a symphony orchestra. This type of team requires a coach or conductor. The members in the third type of team dynamically adjust to each other's strengths and weaknesses, and the contingencies of the moment. A sports analogy would be a doubles tennis team. This type of team is self-managed.

For the first type of team, control information flows in hierarchical form from the supervisor to the workers on the team. In the second type of team the coordination information of a predetermined fashion flows among team members who are jointly accomplishing some goal. In the third type of team the uncertainties of the situation require dynamic adjustment and unpredictable information flows among teams members in "real time." The demands of the information-sector workplace increasingly require this third type of team. Some interesting challenges for teamwork come from the technology itself. The virtual or distributed workplace is fast becoming the norm especially for multinational firms. Global teams may work on a single project in many different locations.

Just as change is the byword of information-sector work, fluidity is the byword of the information-sector workplace. It must be flexible and adaptable to changing technologies, consumer demands and competitors. Tapscott (1996) and others have described the enterprise in this new economy as a web of relationships whose boundaries are both permeable and fluid. Agility, flexibility and autonomy are paramount. The mindset of industrial-era work, whose workers' skills and knowledge were limited to predefined job categories, has little place in the information sector. Information-sector workers must be well-rounded individuals who will make the connections among disparate bodies of knowledge. The valued workers in the information economy are those who can bridge disciplinary boundaries in order to solve a problem.

Workplace fluidity also means transcending physical boundaries. Information technology frees the worker from location constraints.[xi] As is the case with time flexibility, creativity is supported by location flexibility as well. Especially for those engaged in the creative parts of the information sector, being "at work" occurs at home as well as in the office. Even for those who are not engaged in particularly creative work, telecommuting is breaking down the physical boundaries of the workplace. The global information economy further extends these bounds as job functions are disbursed around the globe. An information-sector worker may reside in one country while working on a computer in another.

Along with the changes that information-sector work has brought to the workplace has come a decline in the power of unions. The hierarchical organization structure, which has underlaid the role and behavior of unions, is being replaced by another ethic. The manager-as-overlord is replaced by the manager-as-coach. The rigid corporation of the industrial era is being replaced by an ensemble of individuals in a dynamic organization structure.

Thus, adaptability and openness describe both the management and the workers in the information economy. Because the nature of the work is often unpredictable, workers and their work cannot be programmed into rigid job categories. They are not simply following a set, mechanical process. Rather, workers must be self-directed. As the management function shifts from workers being told what to do to being asked how they do their jobs, workers begin to participate more in the management decisions about the organization of their job functions. In this way, information-sector workers are increasingly taking responsibility for their own productivity. This shift also has implications for what knowledge is valued. It means that the valued knowledge possessed by information-sector workers is not just their specialized knowledge but also their knowledge and understanding of organizational processes.

1.2   A Multinational Sector

A key characteristic of the information sector is its global nature. Information and knowledge know no boundaries and information technology promotes time and space independence. These factors have motivated multinational firms in the information sector to adopt a global perspective on work venues. New, global work teams co-produce information and information processing tools.

Because the information economy, like the economy in general, is global, a source of competitive advantage for a nation is openness to international interaction. But with this comes the need to work productively in the resulting cross-cultural workplace. Along with globalization the information-sector workplace is often influenced by the imported culture of some multinational information-sector firm. The national cultures of the multinational firms enter the country through the medium of corporate culture. While a firm's corporate culture -- its values, management style, methods of operation and work environment -- is, to a certain extent, unique to each particular firm, it also reflects the national culture in which it developed.[xii] The challenge is to balance this mixture of cultural influences.

While research in the information technology field has long considered the organizational context within which the information technology is used, the movement into a global economy has expanded the contextual boundaries of such research and practice to include societal context as well.[xiii] As the world comes closer together through transnational cooperation and political alliances, greater attention is being given to societal factors within a country, which may inhibit or enhance the information dimension of global endeavors. Such factors include political, cultural and economic characteristics as well as national infrastructure.

This new awareness has spawned several different areas of research into the global aspects of the information sector. An early stream of research was directed at studying information technology (IT) management issues in a transnational context and the aspects of the societal environment that must be taken into account.[xiv] A later stream of research has been directed at studying, within specific countries, the influence of societal context on IT development, diffusion and use.[xv] This book contributes to this second body of literature by providing primary-source information about the influence of socio-cultural factors in a particular information economy. However, it is different in that it is not focused on technology use but rather on those who are producing the technology. A third stream of relevant research has been concerned with IT and its role in economic development.[xvi] This book contributes to this body of literature as well by highlighting the human and management issues that arise in a nation endeavoring to use employment in the information economy as a vehicle for economic advancement.

These different streams of research support the argument that just as individual differences are incorporated into consideration of the organizational context of information systems and technology, differences among nations represented by factors in the societal context must be accounted for as well. Porter (1990) expressed this as understanding the role that national circumstances play in the development of a nation's competitive strategy. Understanding the influence of national circumstances enables managers at multinational firms to operate more effectively in countries other than their own.

Theories of contextualism (Pettigrew, 1987, 1990; Klein and Myers, 1999) which were originally developed for the study of organizational influences have been expanded in scope for the study of societal context as well (Walsham and Waema, 1994; Walsham and Sahay, 1999). The study of societal context also enables researchers, practitioners and policy analysts to better understand the factors at work in the successful introduction of new information technologies and practices in their own countries. The perspective taken in this book is that socio-cultural context is at the heart of the way in which an information economy develops. The influence can be felt in the way the work is done, in the way workers behave and in the atmosphere of the workplace.

2.   IN IRELAND

This book considers socio-cultural factors that have been significant in the evolution of Ireland's information economy during the closing decades of the twentieth century. It does so by exploring the thoughts, viewpoints and behaviors of particular people in certain firms at a specific point in time: information-sector workers and managers in selected Irish and American multinational IT firms in the early 1990s. The purpose is to examine the way that the various cultures -- the national culture of the multinational firms, the

IT industry culture, the corporate cultures of the individual firms, and the Irish culture -- interacted with each other. As they did so they influenced the development of the nascent information economy in Ireland just as the information economy was having an impact on Irish society and culture. The findings demonstrate the interaction between the cultural context, and the information-sector work, workers and workplaces in a given country.

The quantitative measures of economic change in Ireland are but the tip of the iceberg. Beneath the surface are deeper social and cultural changes that have been emerging alongside this transformation of employment. Until the onset of the multinational firms in the 1960s, Ireland had defined itself almost completely in relation to Britain. It looked to the UK as the source of both its problems and potential solutions. But as it developed its information economy, Ireland began to look to Europe and beyond. And it began looking inside itself as well. While Ireland's tradition of accepting authority whether exercised by the Church or the State made the rapid adoption of its new employment policy easier, this unquestioning acceptance also began to erode because of it. Accompanying the acceptance of authority had been deep conservatism, antipathy toward individualism, and clientelism, which had accompanied a lack of self-confidence and suspicion of success.[xvii] But these socio-cultural traits have been undermined as well. The result has not been a total redefinition of the Irish identity. Rather, multiple cultures like multiple economies coexist in Ireland.

What motivated this research project is an abiding interest in socio-cultural context as it relates to a nation's information sector. I was particularly interested in studying Ireland because of its conscious and deliberate creation of an information economy in recent years. It was a good laboratory for exploring the range of socio-cultural factors that come into play in shaping a nation's information sector. Ireland is, thus, a case study from which to consider broader themes about the cultural consequences of an information economy.

3.   A SELF-REFLEXIVE STUDY

3.1   Research Model

I had three goals in mind when I embarked upon this research project. The first was to explore an information economy while it was developing so that I could critically examine the influencing role of contextual factors. The second goal was to conduct such an investigation by using interpretive methods. The final goal was to extract from this particular case generalizable lessons that could be applicable to other regions, countries, states and cities which are engaged in creating an information economy.

Ireland was chosen for this study because it is representative of a group of countries which constitute a second wave of nations which are developing information economies.[xviii] Unlike first wave nations whose information-sector workers came from the ranks of industrialism, these countries are leapfrogging directly from agrarian to information-sector employment. Further, Ireland is an example of a country which has made a conscious and concerted effort to base its economic development, in large part, on the growth of its information sector. Such countries stand in contrast to countries such as the US and the UK whose information economies developed in the wake of their industrial economies. The two central questions that I wanted to answer in this research project were:

How does the socio-cultural context within which the information economy exists help to shape its structure?

How are the effects of an information economy manifested in a society?

The underlying theory reflected in these questions speaks to the interactive relationship between information technology and society.[xix] That is, societal factors influence the shape of the information sector that, in turn, has an impact on society. The research goals were addressed by examining the way in which aspects of Irish culture and society were influencing the structure and operations of certain information-sector firms, and the behavior of the people working in them. I also considered the impact of these information-sector firms on Irish society and culture. The information technology firms that were the focus of the research were both indigenous Irish firms and American multinational companies located in Ireland.

The research model governing this project is depicted in Figure 1. It illustrates the interaction between information technology and societal context: societal factors have an *influence* on the development and use of information technology; and the information technology has an *impact* on the society. In this research, I have employed the model to focus on ways in which a nation's socio-cultural characteristics influence the performance of information-sector work, and the reciprocal effects of such information-sector work on the society.[xx]

According to this model there are two forms of interaction between society and the information sector. First, societal context exerts an *influence* on the way in which the information sector develops and behaves. Second, there is a subsequent *impact* that the information sector has on society. This interaction is not linear, however. There is a constant interplay between society and the information sector. In this research model societal context is comprised of culture, economy, infrastructure and public policy. While the focus of this research project was on culture and was the source of primary data, aspects of the economy, infrastructure and public policy were also examined, to a lesser extent, through primary and secondary sources.

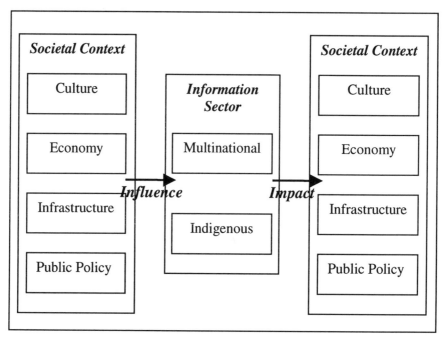

Figure 1. Influence-Impact Model

3.2   Research Method

In researching and writing this book about Ireland's information economy I wanted to uncover the story behind the statistics. I wanted to probe the subtle influences of an environment's culture, history and society on an emerging information sector. In order to do so, I interacted with both workers and managers who worked at information-sector firms in Ireland. During various phases of this research project I lived and worked in Ireland.[xxi] Thus, I learned about socio-cultural influences and impacts not only by talking about them, but by observing and experiencing them as well.

The research methodology that I employed to investigate these information-sector workplaces was ethnography. Ethnography is an anthropological method that relies on first-hand observations made by a researcher over the course of an extended period of time living and participating in a culture. I chose an ethnographic approach so that I could learn, first hand -- through discussions and observations -- about relevant dimensions of society and culture. My exploration was carried out at both the micro and the macro levels. At the micro level I learned from the people who worked in the information technology firms about the way in which socio-cultural factors were interacting with the work, the workers and the workplace. At the macro level, information obtained from participant observation along with interviews with cultural observers and government agents, and from analysis of public policy documents was used to explore the broader themes about the socio-cultural dimensions of Ireland's policy of economic development through inward investment by information technology firms.

3.2.1   Interpretive Research and Self-reflexive Writing

The use of interpretive methods in the conduct of information-technology research is a rather recent occurrence. While such methods have been used in Europe and elsewhere for a longer period of time they have only come into their own in the US since the 1990s.[xxii] Given the complexity and nature of this research project, the reflexivity[xxiii] that accompanies an ethnographic approach seemed the best way to enact the research model. The advantage of reflexivity was that it allowed for refocusing so that I could make changes as the research progressed. By using a reflexive approach, answers to questions could influence the direction of later questions by allowing me to alter them as I moved through my interviews.

A key dimension of the way in which I present this interpretive study is the *self-reflexive* stance that I have taken. I use myself and my learning process as a backdrop, if you will, against which to highlight the socio-cultural factors that became relevant in this study. I reveal my own discovery process and show how I came to understand the importance of these particular cultural factors. Many times I reveal how I came to recognize the importance of a certain factor or the contradictions that I saw. Being non-Irish enabled me to see things differently than Irish workers, managers or researchers might see them. Being in a non-American setting enabled me to see things that I might have overlooked had I conducted this research in America.

The explicit interjection of the self -- the researcher -- into the research is referred to as the "confessional" genre of ethnographic writing. In this genre, the researcher acknowledges her or his role in interpreting the data that she or he acquires through participant observation, interviews or documentary analysis. Van Maanen (1988) describes three conventions that are used in confessional writing and which are present in this book. The first is the depiction of the author as a personalized character who develops intimacy with the reader in showing how the work came into being. The second convention is the use of autobiographical detail to show the researcher's viewpoints and how they changed over the course of the study. The final convention -- naturalness -- consists of developing within the reader a sense of confidence in the cultural interpretations that are presented. Devices such as rich description and triangulation[xxiv] are used to show that the researcher did, indeed, uncover the relevant facets of a culture.

Recognition of this particular genre in social science research is evidenced by the growing number of studies employing this method (Behar, 1996; Rabinow, 1977; Whyte, 1996; and Wolf, 1992). The acceptance of this genre within the field of information systems is evidenced by the recent papers employing this method.[xxv] Indeed, one of the seven principles for conducting interpretive research in information systems put forth in a seminal paper on interpretive methodology (Klein and Myers, 1999) is critical reflection on how the research materials were socially constructed through the interaction between the researcher and the participants.[xxvi]

3.2.2   Data Collection and Analysis

Using open-ended interviewing techniques, I collected data from information-sector workers and their managers at 14 information technology firms in Ireland. Half were multinational (American) firms and half were Irish firms. Supplemental interviews were also conducted with selected individuals outside the information sector. These individuals were spouses of multinational executives, governmental officials and their spouses, and cultural commentators and researchers. These viewpoints provided background and contextual information about public policy. They also provided a counterpoint to the economic and cultural observations made by the information-sector workers.

Additional sources of data collected for purposes of triangulation were my participant observation (both in the firms and in Irish society) and document analysis. Transcripts of the interviews were open coded based on a content analysis schema developed in grounded fashion (Strauss, 1987). A database of respondent characteristics and comments was then created to facilitate retrieval and systematic analysis of data. More detail about my methodology is provided in the Appendix.

4.   ORGANIZATION OF BOOK

This book is organized into four parts. Part I introduces the concept of the information economy and Ireland's engagement with it. Chapter 1 has presented an overview of the changes in the meaning of work, workers and workplaces wrought by the emergence of an information economy. It has also presented the rationale for the research project and the methods employed in carrying it out. Chapter 2 provides the necessary historical background by tracing Ireland's journey from the isolated, agrarian society that it was in mid-twentieth century to the global information economy that it became at the dawn of the twenty-first.

Parts II and III consider specific socio-cultural factors which have influenced and been affected by Ireland's information economy. In presenting these factors I employ the voices of those information-sector workers and managers whom I interviewed. I also reflect the voices of researchers and government agents who have been helping to guide Ireland's economic transformation. Part II considers the characteristics of the information-sector workers in Ireland. Chapter 3 looks at this new breed of worker who is young, well educated and middle class. Chapter 4 examines issues about gender and family, and the ways in which these values influence the Irish information sector and its labor force.

Part III addresses the characteristics of the information-sector workplace in Ireland. Chapter 5 explores the effect of a small society, with social and interpersonal values, on the day-to-day work life of the information economy. Chapter 6 discusses the effect of Ireland's traditional agrarian and colonial past on productivity and behavior at work. Finally, Chapter 7 considers the management of an information-sector workplace that is both indigenous and multinational.

While this story about an information sector takes place in Ireland at a certain point in its economic development, the lessons are intended for all those who are engaged in constructing or studying information economies in any cultural context. Part IV considers these lessons for Ireland and beyond. Chapter 8 presents a critical examination of Ireland's information economy and the fit between cultural factors in Ireland and the characteristics of the information economy. It also considers those impacts that have already been felt. While the specific cultural factors may differ from country to country, what remains constant is that all information economies are situated within some cultural context. For this reason, Chapter 9 concludes this book by considering the broader themes about cultural context and the information economy.

Ireland has changed considerably in recent years. Some of the nascent impacts of 1990 were much in evidence or perhaps overturned in 1999 as this research project was coming to an end. For this reason the Conclusion to each chapter presents a commentary on the cultural themes which were discussed in the chapter from the vantage point of 1999.

---

[i] See, for example, Coogan's 1966 observation to this effect, cited in Jordan (1992), p. 81.

[ii] Between 1986 and 1996 Ireland saw a 20% increase in new job creation (Sweeney, 1998, p. 2). Between 1980 and 1996, non-agricultural employment grew 26%, compared with 7% and 15% percent growth in the European Union and the US, respectively, during this same period (ESRI, 1997, p. 39). Between 1986 and 1996 Ireland experienced an annual average GNP growth rate of 5% and a GDP growth rate of 5.4% (Sweeney, 1998, p. 44). These economic indicators are explained in greater detail in Chapter 2.

[iii] I use the term *information* in this book to characterize the work and the emerging economy while Drucker and others use the term *knowledge*.

[iv] See Webster (1995) for a review of prominent information society characterizations.

[v] Some might question the rationale for including hardware production in the category of information work. This has been done for two reasons. First, there has been a longstanding tradition of defining the information sector in this way (for example, Dordick and Wang, 1993; Machlup, 1962; Porat, 1977). Second, while hardware production is a form of manufacturing the line between hardware and software is often a fine one and the same firms often engage in both activities.

[vi] For example, Bell (1973, 1980), Drucker (1950, 1959), Toffler (1973) and Umesao (quoted in Ito, 1981).

[vii] See, for example, Buckholtz (1995), Castells (1996), Davenport (1997), Dordick and Wang (1993), Fukuyama (1999), Naisbett (1982), Nonaka and Takeuchi (1995), Norman (1993), Rifkin (1995), Schement and Curtis (1995), Tapscott (1996), Toffler (1981) and Webster (1995).

[viii] As noted earlier, this study was restricted to those engaged in producing information tools. Hence, companies and people engaged in producing and processing information content were not part of the study.

[ix] See, for example, Drucker (1993), Chapter 10.

[x] For further discussion of teams, see Keidel (1985) and Drucker (1993), Chapter 4.

[xi] This is a good example of the caveat about the information subsector. Hardware production is much more tied to a particular location than software and systems development, and information content creation might be.

[xii] Another point of view was expressed by Reich (1991) in his characterization of global managers as being devoid of national allegiance. While this may be true for some firms, the corporate cultures of the multinational firms in this study did reflect the national culture of their founders.

[xiii] See, for example, Kling (1996) for a survey of context issues. This recognition has also resulted in the codification of a body of theory and practice around the term "social informatics." See Kling (1999) for a discussion of the evolution and scope of social informatics.

[xiv] See, for example, Cash et al. (1992), Deans (1991), Ives and Jarvenpaa (1991), Keen (1992), and Steinbart and Nath (1992).

[xv] See, for example, Ang and Jiwahhasuchin (1998), Gan (1998), Hernandez, et al. (1996), Hill et al. (1998), Lally (1994), La Rovere (1996), Odedra-Straub (1993), Trauth, Derksen and Mevissen (1998), Van Rychegham (1996), Wilson and Meadows (1998) and Wong (1998).

[xvi] See, for example, Braa (1996), Burn, Ng Tye and Ma (1995), Cummings and Guynes (1994), Heeks (1996), Kedia and Bhagat (1988), Lopez and Vilaseca (1996), Nelson and Clark (1994), Neo (1991), and Walsham, Symons and Waema (1988). Books such as Palvia, Palvia, and Zigli (1992) address both country-specific issues and development/cross-cultural issues.

[xvii] See, for example, "Ireland Shines" (1997), and Schmidt (1973).

[xviii] See Dordick and Wang (1993) for an analysis of countries which were early and later developers of information economies.

[xix] For an application of this theory to the development of societal policies governing information technology and processing see Trauth (1979, 1986).

[xx] For further discussion of how this research model has been applied to specific aspects of this research see Trauth (1993a, 1995b, 1996a and 1999a) and for an example of how this research model has been applied in a different research setting see Trauth, Derksen and Mevissen (1993, 1998).

---

xxi I spent the 1989-90 academic year in Ireland during which I taught and conducted this research. After that initial period, I returned four more times -- 1992, 1993, 1995 and 1999 -- for shorter periods of time.

xxii See, for example, Walsham (1993). This is not to say that qualitative methods weren't used at all in previous decades. However, both the number of studies employing these methods and the recognition of this methodological approach has increased sharply in the 1990s. For example, a recent issue of an important journal in the field (*MIS Quarterly*) has been devoted to research employing such methods.

xxiii Reflexivity refers to research that reflects back upon itself such that both the data and the means of collecting it change as the research progresses and aspects of the phenomenon are better understood.

xxiv Triangulation refers to checking inferences drawn from one set of data sources by collecting data from other sources. See the Appendix for further discussion of triangulation.

xxv See, for example, Schultz (2000).

xxvi The confessional account in Trauth (1997) is used as the example of the application of this principle.

CHAPTER 2. THE TRANSFORMATION TO INFORMATION-SECTOR WORK

1. INTRODUCTION

[H]istory and culture are interleaved. In the late 1950s there was a government with vision and good planning. The questions they asked were, "What do we have to offer? How can we compete?" At the time it was an island economy, 90% dependent upon the UK. They saw that high tech was the future. [Seamus]

Few societies have changed as much as Ireland in the past 30 years. Prior to its transformation, Ireland was thought of as " . . . a rural, conservative and Catholic backwater of post-war Europe" (Breen et al., 1990, p. 1). One consistency since the founding of the Republic has been the tradition of an active role of government in economic stimulation. But Ireland's journey along this path has brought radical change. In order to understand the dimensions of the transformation that has occurred, it is necessary to understand the type of society from which the Ireland of today has emerged.

During its early years, the Irish Free State which was formed in 1922 was isolationist and strongly nationalistic. In an effort to reestablish Irish political and cultural sovereignty after centuries of colonial control, economic policies were directed at creating national self-sufficiency through protectionist policies.[i] This was not unlike other new states established in the early part of the twentieth century. This worldview, however, had important implications for industrial development. First, industrial development was expected to occur indigenously. Accompanying the intense nationalism and ambivalence toward foreigners the new country imposed severe restrictions on foreign investment. The second implication was that industrial development was shaped by both societal/nationalist and economic criteria. And the social objectives of the new state required that industrial development occur in such a way as to preserve the rural character of the nation (Daly, 1992).

The operating assumption in Ireland was that the nation would prosper by promoting the interests of small farmers and native industry serving local markets. The industrial policy at the time was two-pronged. Nonagricultural jobs could be found in the civil service or in a number of state-owned companies such as Bord na Mona (Irish Peat Board), CIE (Irish transportation company) or the Electricity Supply Board (ESB). In these state and semi-state organizations, attaining the social goals of employment and supporting rural Ireland were as important as being profitable. The remaining nonagricultural jobs came from Irish firms in the private sector, which were supported through tariffs and quotas. During this period of economic isolationism there was little incentive for involvement in international affairs. In such a society there was also little need for highly developed societal infrastructures associated with an industrialized society such as telecommunications, transportation and work-related education.

Agriculture was the dominant economic and societal organizing principle. In the 1920s farmers accounted for nearly half of the labor force (Rottman et al., 1982, p. 46). These farms were family-owned, generally small, and passed down from one generation to another. Society was organized around the activities and values associated with a stable, unchanging agricultural society. Land was the basis of social status. One's life chances generally depended on connections through marriage, the prospect of inheriting a family-owned business or farm, entering religious life or obtaining employment in the civil service.[ii]

Post-colonial Ireland sought to develop itself by looking inside itself. Foreign ownership of firms was discouraged.[iii] The ideal was economic and cultural self-sufficiency. The limited domestic market was seen as the sole outlet of industrial activity. Along with other founders of the new nation Eamon de Valera, the first President, believed that the primary goals of the nation should be the restoration of the Irish language and culture. In a famous St. Patrick's day radio speech in 1943, "The Ireland That We Dreamed Of," he presented his vision of Ireland as:

> . . . the home of a people who valued material wealth only as a basis of right living . . . who were satisfied with frugal comfort and devoted their leisure to things of the spirit; a land . . . bright with cozy homesteads, joyous with . . . the romping of sturdy children, the contests of athletic youth, the laughter of comely maidens; whose firesides would be forums for the wisdom of serene old age . . . the home of a people living the life that God desires men should live (Moynihan, 1980, p. 466).

The economic policies enacted as part of this vision attempted to foster tillage agriculture and a protected small industry to meet the limited needs of a national market in the effort to create a self-sufficient, bucolic, Irish utopia.

Ireland was one of the first nations in the twentieth century to shift from colonial to independent nation. Following the War of Independence the Anglo-Irish Treaty of 1921 divided the island into the independent Irish Free State and Northern Ireland. In 1949 the Free State became the Republic of Ireland. But partition of the island, which was the by-product of the Treaty, resulted in the absence of an industrial base in the new republic. O'Malley (1989) argues that the industrial revolution did not flourish in Ireland for three reasons. First, it lacked many of the natural resources needed to support heavy manufacturing industry. Second, its colonial status interfered with its participation in the industrial revolution that was occurring elsewhere. Finally, what little industrialization existed in Ireland at the turn of the twentieth century was located in Northern Ireland. The Irish economy outside Ulster was almost exclusively rural and had been ravaged by famine in the second half of the nineteenth century. Hence, the establishment of the Irish Republic moved the country away from its early industrialism and back toward agrarianism.

Because Ireland was not developing as an industrial society, it was not able to offset the declining agricultural jobs with industrial employment. In addition, there were historical and political factors that impeded Ireland's industrial growth. The colonial policies that favored Britain and kept the Irish economy dependent upon and vulnerable to economic forces in Britain, left a cultural legacy. Irish people adopted very cautious economic strategies that were designed to assure survival and avoid risk for family members. Further, for historical reasons, signs of enterprise or entrepreneurial activity were associated with the landlords, land grabbers and the hated gombeen man[iv] who were symbols of repression. Some argue that this conservatism was encouraged by the Catholic Church which feared that economic development would lessen its hold over the populace as it gave in to the corrupting influences of Britain and modernity.[v]

But the economic policy that favored an isolationist, rural Ireland was not working. Daly's analysis of industrial development in the first two decades of the new nation concludes that:

> The aspiration of a self-sufficient industrial sector under native control independent of international market forces was doomed to failure. Handicaps such as low incomes, a small market, lack of fuel and raw materials require little examination. The dual aims of self-sufficiency and native

control proved contradictory. Requirements of capital, technology, and expertise made employment and self-sufficiency possible only at the cost of admitting foreign industrialists, and a small market led firms to seek monopoly privileges as the price of investing in Ireland. . . [E]ven Irish shareholders, fitted uncomfortably with the vision of an egalitarian peasant society. . . In practice, self-sufficiency would have required monopoly powers and a level of state control unacceptable to Irish society (Daly, 1992, p. 102).[vi]

In 1961 after 115 years of steady rural depopulation, 36% of Ireland's labor force was employed in agriculture working on small, inefficient farms. Only 25% of the working population was employed in industry. The emigration rate in the 1950s rose to levels not seen since the waves of departure at the end of the nineteenth century: over 400,000 people left the country. Three decades after it had achieved independence from Britain, Ireland was unable to keep its people (Jordan, 1992, p. 79).

The response to this economic crisis was the radical change in industrial policy that occurred during the final decades of the twentieth century, the seeds of which were planted in the late 1950s. While there was early evidence of the wisdom of this new approach it, nevertheless, took several decades for the plan to come to complete fruition. The evolution from an agrarian into an information economy was both economic and societal; it was an evolution of employment as well as consciousness. The first evolutionary step, which lasted from the late 1950s through the 1960s, was Ireland's shift away from protectionist polices toward a focus on inward investment as a source of manufacturing employment. The second step, which occurred during the 1970s and 1980s, was the recognition that a particular sector -- information technology -- was outpacing others as a source of economic growth in Ireland. The third step in Ireland's evolutionary journey began in the 1990s with the acknowledgement of a diversified information economy that was crucial to the economic wellbeing of the country.

The remainder of this Chapter traces this evolution in employment, in economic growth and in thinking. The changes in industrial policy provide the backdrop against which the picture of the information economy emerges. Since the recognition of an information economy occurred within the context of industrial development, it becomes necessary to understand Ireland's developing information sector within the larger frame of industrial policy; these two things were occurring hand in hand.

2. INDUSTRIALIZATION BY INVITATION

We were going through a crisis point. We couldn't create enough jobs of our own, we needed an industrial environment. I think we would have taken any industry be it medical or anything. We tried the chemical and pharmaceutical industries and were reasonably successful. I think their first priority, irrespective of what the industry was, and even in a sense irrespective of how "clean" that industry was, was "Let's get them in. Let's get started. Let's take a short term viewpoint." And get employment for them.
[Robert]

By the late 1950s it was clear to Sean Lemass that the socio-economic vision of Ireland held by his predecessor, Eamon de Valera, was not viable. Some change in the course of action was needed. The change came in the form of the proposal by T. K. Whitaker, Secretary of Finance, to substitute planned economic development for cultural revival as the primary national imperative. Protectionism, Whitaker argued, fostered inefficiency. The role of the Irish State should shift from paternalism to encouraging risk taking and private initiative. His argument was laid out in *Economic Development* (1958), a document that marked a significant transition point in Ireland's economic history. The high emigration rate and economic decline evident in the 1950s had set in motion the forces that led to a new economic policy of industrialization by invitation. Thus, 1958 signaled the end of the post-independence search for a national identity and economy based on a conception of traditional, rural Ireland.

Whitaker's report became the basis for the White Paper, *Programme for Economic Expansion* published later that year. It embraced many of Whitaker's proposals and attempted to formulate them into government policy. By now Irish policy makers had come to believe that economic viability required that the country reverse its economic policy by opening the country up to foreign capital, technology and industry. The first of several industrial development plans to follow, the *Programme for Economic Expansion* represented a rupture from the past as it reversed the protectionist policies then in place. The assumption that Ireland would prosper by promoting the interests of small farmers and native industry serving local markets was cast aside. It was replaced with an agenda which opened wide the doors to foreign investment as Ireland began to participate fully in the world economy.[vii]

There were two key aspects of this new plan. The first was the mechanization and consolidation of farms so that Ireland could be more competitive in the European food market. Increased agricultural production at the expense of agricultural employment was to be the result. Between 1961 and 1981 the number of males employed in agriculture declined from 34% to 17% (Rottman et al., 1982, p. 46). The second aspect of the plan was replacing jobs lost in agriculture with those in industrial employment. This was to be accomplished by attracting foreign export-oriented manufacturing firms to Ireland. The hope was that foreign investment would provide not only the direct benefit of jobs but also the indirect benefit of a new business climate. It was hoped that these outside influences would help Ireland to more quickly develop an indigenous entrepreneurial capacity (O'Colla, 1967). This would come about through foreign influences that would counteract the protectionism and traditional conservatism which Irish society had fostered. Other aspects of the plan were to raise the level of education, to encourage initiative and enterprise and adopt improved management techniques. Thus, economic growth was envisioned as a process that also involved social, psychological and political change (Jordan, 1992; Whitaker, 1987).

The role of the State in this top-down approach was to provide capital, incentives and the proper infrastructure needed to attract industrial firms. Capital in the form of grants supported the development of export-oriented industry, particularly in advanced technology areas. These grants supported research that promoted new or improved industrial processes and increased employment. They were also available to facilitate acquisition of technology and to provide training in industrial processes. The main agency responsible for overseeing the implementation of this new industrial policy was the Industrial Development Authority (IDA). Originally established in 1949 to assist the efforts of private enterprise in industrial development, the IDA was reorganized and made an autonomous semi-state agency in 1970[viii] to promote industrial development throughout the country by stimulating job creation in manufacturing, and internationally traded and financial services. The IDA was interested in attracting small to mid-sized industrial plants that were clean and export-oriented. It also wanted the capability of establishing these plants away from traditional industrial centers to further Ireland's goal of avoiding traditional smokestack industries. Rather, it was looking for dynamic new industry that could help Ireland quickly change its economic profile from an agrarian to a leading-edge industrial nation. Another important dimension of the proper infrastructure that was being developed at this time was the educational infrastructure. In furtherance of the industrial plan, a significant change in educational funding occurred during this time. Prior to 1968 secondary education was private and funded by tuition. Educational policy at this time changed the funding of secondary education making it accessible to all citizens.

The industrial policy studies and plans that followed on the 1958 vision and the 1969 *Industrial Development Act*[ix] helped the Irish State respond by conscious design to this economic crisis. Ireland pursued a policy of industrialization by invitation from the late 1950s through the 1960s by offering substantial incentives to multinational companies to locate in Ireland. The goal was to generate cash and employment through export-led development. The attractions included low cost operations, an English speaking labor force, a location within the European Community (something especially attractive to American and Asian firms), and tax exemptions on export sales for companies that located in Ireland. The economic returns on this new policy were demonstrable. Between 1963 and 1973 manufacturing employment grew at an annual average rate of 1.7% which was nearly three times the OECD average (Fitzpatrick and Kelly, 1985, p. xviii).

As Ireland was stemming the tide of emigration and increasing the number of jobs for its people through its new industrial policy, it was also, albeit unintentionally, planting the seeds of its information economy.[x] Ireland's openness to the global economy through its invitation to multinational companies paved the way for a particular type of manufacturing -- electronics -- to grow and develop into a multifaceted information sector. The Metals sector,[xi] generally considered the most modern industrial sector, predominated from the early years of export-led industrialization in Ireland. Between 1959 and 1962 it accounted for nearly half of new foreign employment. While the mid-1960s brought the first electronics projects to Ireland, it was in the 1970s that electronics companies were the dominant multinational firms in the multinational Metals sector in Ireland (O'Hearn, 1987).

3.   THE RISE OF THE INFORMATION ECONOMY

The primary reason for [our firm] in coming to Europe was to better serve the customer, be closer to the customer to understand customer needs. Things are done differently in the US than they are here, and customers have different expectations. In many cases you can't appreciate those requests or the expectations or why they're being requested. But by being here we help on those, appreciate them, work on them. And also if there's any problems quality wise or errors

*or whatever, we're much closer, we're three thousand miles
closer. So that was the main reason for coming to Europe.
[Andrew]*

In considering which foreign industries to attract, Irish policy makers
identified three high growth industries that were not heavily dependent upon
the natural resources that Ireland lacked. They were pharmaceuticals,
chemicals and electronics. At this time electronics meant the manufacture
and/or final assembly of computer hardware for the European market. From
the point of view of foreign firms there was another reason for non-European
firms to locate in Europe in addition to being closer to the customer base.
With the European Union on the horizon in 1992, countries such as the United
States were interested in establishing manufacturing plants in Europe to
satisfy local content laws.[xii] Following its entry into the European Community
in 1973, Ireland recognized and exploited this additional attraction. American
information technology firms began coming to Ireland in the early 1970s.[xiii]

What was viewed as a promising type of manufacturing in the early 1970s
came to be recognized as a distinct sector by the end of the 1980s. This was
due to the combined effects of infrastructure development and serendipity.
The multinational IT firms which came to Ireland found both the place and the
people to be well suited to the work to be done. My discussions with
American managing directors, Irish managers, and policy makers consistently
indicated that the reasons for *coming* to Ireland derived primarily from the
economic incentives provided by the Irish government. However, the reasons
they gave for *staying* were unexpectedly found in the cultural, societal and
infrastructural aspects of the country.

The rapid globalization of the information technology industry that began
in the 1970s and significantly expanded in the 1980s was an important reason
that American computer firms were locating sites in Europe.[xiv] One key reason
was a desire to be closer to the customer. As the domestic market for large
computers was becoming saturated in the 1980s American IT firms were
increasingly looking abroad for new market opportunities. Europe was one
natural target. A second factor was the European Union. With the coming of
the European Union in 1992, American IT firms were looking to establish
bases inside the walls of Europe.

Recognizing the desire of multinational firms to locate subsidiaries in
Europe, the Irish government offered attractive financial incentives to
convince these firms to choose Ireland over some other European country.
These financial incentives included both tax relief and financial grants.
Depending upon when the firms came to Ireland and where they located, the
financial packages varied. But generally the firms were offered zero or low

tax rates for a certain period of time. In addition, they were offered grants for establishing and equipping their factories, and training their workforces. In some instances the Irish government through the IDA actually built the factories on greenfield sites.

A tax structure conducive to profitability became one of the key tangible attractions of Ireland. In the early years Ireland offered a 15 year full tax exemption on export sales for companies that located in Ireland. In 1981 this was replaced with a 10% corporate tax rate guaranteed until 2010 for all manufacturing companies and many export-oriented service companies. Other financial incentives included grants for capital equipment, training and product development. A final component of economic attractiveness was that the wage rates of Irish workers were lower than their American counterparts.

While attractive tax rates brought many firms to Ireland, it also made the country vulnerable to the commitment level of these mobile firms.

> *We've had a couple [multinational firms] here that locked the door and vanished. There was one company that at noontime management went out to lunch and didn't come back. It wasn't really funny, but I could imagine someone looking for whomever and the receptionist saying, "She'll be back, she'll be back." At [another company] people came to work in the morning and were simply told the plant was closed. [Kevin]*

While some early firms did leave Ireland once the tax and other financial advantages diminished, the ones who stayed did so because it made good business sense. And the reasons had to do chiefly with the labor force. A clear advantage that Ireland had over most other European countries was its English speaking population. Regions of England and Scotland were the only other contenders with Ireland in this regard.[xv] The language compatibility was the most attractive feature of the labor force for those US firms venturing abroad for the first time. Second, was the wage rate. Irish workers could be employed at a much lower rate than their American counterparts. Ireland's European competition in this regard was the Mediterranean region and countries such as Spain.

To keep these firms happy a variety of infrastructural improvements were needed including roads, utilities, a physical plant and telecommunications capability. Although Irish policy makers did not think in terms of an information sector at the time, they did recognize the importance of infrastructure as a necessary ingredient in attracting multinational firms. A key infrastructural change that was needed to support this industrial policy was the upgrading of Ireland's telecommunications system. As an agrarian society emphasizing small farming and local markets, sophisticated telecommunications was not an important priority. But the multinational firms Ireland was courting required the ability to move information quickly and efficiently. Consequently, during the 1970s and 1980s Ireland significantly upgraded its telecommunications network with the use of ISDN, satellite and fiber optic technologies. Ireland was assisted in this effort by its membership in the European Union which funded infrastructure projects for the country. The original motivation for heavy investment in education and telecommunications was to attract multinational investment. What resulted, however, was a labor force and communications infrastructure that enabled the expansion of the nascent information sector into new areas in the years to follow.

The remaining reasons for IT firms choosing and staying in Ireland had to do with the culture and society which produced these information-sector workers. If the economic incentives were the necessary conditions for coming to Ireland, the sufficient ones were an infrastructure supportive of the type of work to be done and a qualified labor force to do it. Multinational firms in the computer industry came to Ireland because they wanted a foothold in Europe and because Ireland provided the most competitive economic incentives. Once they arrived they found a national infrastructure being developed to keep them there. The crucial ingredient in this mix was the labor force. The availability of young, English speaking and well-educated workers was one of the main reasons that firms that came to Ireland remained there. By the late 1980s the quality of the education possessed by the labor force had risen to become a primary selling point of Ireland.

Ireland's homogeneous population was also seen as an attractive feature in that it was linked to political stability. American multinationals felt secure in their perception that Ireland was different from some other low wage countries in that there was little chance of violent political or societal change, which would disrupt operations. In addition, the quality of life in Ireland was both touted by the IDA and believed by American managers. As I probed this item, I came to see that this phrase had two different meanings. First, quality of life was meant to imply that the workers were happy and satisfied and, therefore, likely to be productive. Second, the quality of life feature was meant to serve as an attraction to firms who intended to send Americans to live in Ireland during the start up of their subsidiaries.

It was the decision to attract firms in the electronics industry -- such as Digital Equipment Corporation in 1971 -- that set Ireland on its path toward establishing an information economy. It is important to remember, however, that when these firms first began coming to Ireland during the 1970s and early 1980s Ireland did not think of itself as creating a separate information sector. To Irish policy makers, the computer and telecommunications industries were simply a form of manufacturing. But the combination of policy decisions and other infrastructural and societal changes resulted in the emergence of a diverse information economy that has become crucial to Ireland's economic health.

By the late 1980s the IDA had expanded its role to include the development and promotion of indigenous firms as well. Three other agencies provided support to the IDA in its efforts to promote new industry through selected activities. Coras Trachtala (CTT) the Irish export board was established in 1959 to promote and develop Irish exports. Foras Aiseauna Saothair (FAS) the training and employment authority was established in 1988 from the amalgamation of several existing labor force, youth employment and training agencies. Its purpose was to provide training and employment programs, and placement services for the new labor force, and advice to industry. EOLAS (Irish Science and Technology Agency) was created in 1987 from the merger of the Institute for Industrial Research and Standards and the National Board for Science and Technology. Its purpose was to develop, apply, coordinate and promote science and technology in Irish industry. An additional responsibility was to forge links between higher education and industry.

To facilitate the development of what was coming to be recognized as a distinct sector, further infrastructural activities were undertaken. Two new Irish universities were created. They were designed more in the American than in the classical European tradition. That is, the focus was on preparation for employment, specifically in business, science and technology rather than on liberal arts. Closely related to this effort was the establishment of University-research center collaborations. One was in Cork and the other in Limerick. However, a problem for the research and development initiative was that there wasn't enough R&D work coming from the multinationals to provide employment for all those qualified in this area. Consequently, there was a "brain drain" during the 1980s as well-educated but underemployed engineers flooded out of country.

The intangible attractions of Ireland -- the people, the culture and the values -- was also a source of concern as Ireland moved along its path of industrial development. Observers noted that those same values which were attractive to the American business community, also served to emphasize the dichotomy that was Ireland. Traveling alongside the high tech trajectory was

an "other worldly" orientation. As Jordan (1992) explains in his depiction of
Ireland as a "Silicon Valley":

> Ireland sells itself, currently balanced precariously between
> two worlds. Over the past 25 years, the nation has become a
> high-technology center with sophisticated road and
> telecommunication networks, modern financial institutions, a
> skilled and savvy workforce, and a government committed to
> business. Yet this is superimposed on a country that remains,
> in many ways, rural, slow, and cautious -- a country that is as
> much that of de Valera's vision as it is Whitaker's. (82)

Developing an economic vision of Ireland within the context of its cultural
values as well as it economic needs required adjustment and refocusing along
the way. Industrial policy documents[xvi] along with scholarly critiques of
public policy during this period[xvii] provided guidance as policy makers
analyzed, critiqued and sometimes redirected Ireland's industrial policy. As
previously noted, the development of a distinct information sector was not
anticipated at the outset; Ireland was simply looking for industrial
employment. Those IT firms which located in Ireland during the 1970s were
viewed as manufacturing firms that just happened to be producing computer
equipment. But after an examination of Ireland's industrial policy 20 years
into it, the perception shifted.

The decade of the 1970s revealed the structural changes that were
occurring in the industrial profile of Ireland as older, traditional industries
were declining in importance. In 1980 the indigenous sector of Ireland
represented about two-thirds of the total manufacturing employment, yet it
represented less than one-third of total exports of manufactured goods. Of the
1,262 indigenous companies created between 1973 and 1980, most were in
non-traded industries. At the same time those foreign-owned companies
producing the majority of the exports were those in the electrical engineering
industries.[xviii] By 1980 there were 70 multinational companies in the Electrical
and Electronics sector in Ireland, employing over 10,000 people. By 1982, the
electronics and chemicals sectors accounted for 90% of new foreign
investment (IDA, 1982). Nevertheless, the job gains and impressive output
performance in the new multinational firms was overshadowed by the job
losses in the indigenous sector.[xix] Between 1973 and 1984 while the output of
manufacturing industry rose in every year but three, employment in
manufacturing exceeded 1973 levels only once (Fitzpatrick and Kelly, 1985,
p. xix).

Foreign-owned companies, increasingly in the electronics sector, were being viewed by the IDA and other government agencies as the vehicle for economic deliverance. In some respects the hopes and goals of the IDA seemed to be coming to realization. The goal was to have a tax and grant environment that would make Ireland a target for electronic engineering firm site selection. The hope was that by attracting high growth firms, such as those in electronics, a skilled workforce would develop. This, in turn, would result in a spillover effect by producing a concentration of high tech firms as was the case in the Silicon Valley in California and Route 128 in Massachusetts. However, the first tenet ran into significant problems when the high tech firms chose Ireland as a site, not for decision making or development projects, but more as an assembly or manufacturing location. Where this was the case, the lack of high skill development precluded the second tenet of this plan. Because not enough workers were highly skilled, there tended to be minimal spin-offs from the foreign firms.

Consequently, concerns began to surface about the contribution of multinational firms in the electronics sector to Ireland's economic plan. Critics began to wonder about the extent to which this industry was truly rooted in Ireland. Besides concerns about the number of jobs in Ireland, there was also concern about the kind of employment available because of limited skill development and linkages. Although the electronics industry is a very high-skilled industry worldwide, the activities in Ireland's electronics industry did not always reflect this. Additional concerns arose from the low wage factor. The IDA acknowledged this vulnerability with respect to less developed countries that could consistently undercut wages. For this reason the IDA expressly stated its intention to move away from low wage business to prevent this type of competition. Finally, concerns were voiced about potential economic and political dependency resulting from this industrial policy (Girvin, 1982).

The joint concerns about economic dependence and vulnerability, and effective allocation of limited financial resources resulted in recognition of the need to take stock of Ireland's industrial policy, to see where the country stood on its road to economic development through inward investment. The Telesis Consultancy Group was commissioned by the National Economic and Social Council:

> . . . to evaluate existing industrial policies, and to make recommendations designed to ensure that the Irish Government's industrial policy is appropriate to the creation of an internationally competitive industrial base in Ireland

which will support increased employment and higher living standards (NESC, 1982a, p. i).

The resulting 1982 publication, *A Review of Industrial Policy: A Report Prepared by the Telesis Consultancy Group* (commonly referred to as the *Telesis Report),* was both comprehensive and critical. Evidence was given with respect to both multinational and indigenous parts of this sector. The report cited the high cost of government incentives, the low level of skills, a lack of R&D within plants, weak linkages to local suppliers, and the tendency of firms to leave Ireland once the tax incentives had expired. Further, it pointed out a widening income gap between Ireland and most other industrialized countries and the increasing dependence on foreign corporations for industrial jobs.

With respect to the indigenous side, it noted the few component suppliers to the multinational IT firms and the small size of the software sector. It seemed that the hoped for spin-off of Irish-owned firms was not happening. The *Telesis Report* recommended the creation of greater linkages between indigenous and multinational firms, providing greater support for the growth of local firms, and encouraging R&D and innovation. Despite these criticisms, however, it recommended a continuance of the industrial policy of job creation through inward investment by multinational firms.

The *Telesis Report* agreed with the goals of Irish industrial policy but concluded that the existing structure did not reflect those goals. There was a lack of high-skilled, high technology enterprises. Irish indigenous exports were limited in geographic scope. The indigenous companies were not successfully providing the sub-supplies necessary to foster the growth and attraction of foreign-owned industry. Small firms existed primarily in low-skilled, non-traded businesses. The spin-off, the "Route 128" phenomenon had not been realized. There had been minimal cooperation between primary producers and processors in raw materials-based industries. Foreign-owned industries had been unsophisticated and their evolution showed inadequate promise for substantial improvement, thereby limiting job defensibility.

In many ways, the assessment of the electronics industry served to illustrate the situation with respect to Irish industrialism as a whole.

> The electronics industry in Ireland is growing rapidly and many of the companies are highly profitable. The industry stands well in terms of viability in the near future. However, the industry has not so far provided the mechanisms for Ireland to move toward higher value-added businesses.

Companies have come primarily for tax concessions and other subsidies, and to enter the EEC. If present levels of skill development and sub-supply infrastructure are not improved, the industry's long-term future will be threatened (NESC, 1982b, p. 22).

The Irish government's response to the *Telesis Report* was presented in *The White Paper on Industrial Policy* published in 1984. It was intended to give a new impetus to industrial development at a time when the industrial plan was faltering. The rate of new job creation was not keeping up with the decline of older, labor-intensive industries during a time of fierce global competition for mobile investment. When a growing labor force was added to the mix, it resulted in the highest unemployment rate in post-war Ireland. The *White Paper* acknowledged that the policies that had served the country well during the 1960s were having less success in the 1970s and 1980s.

To correct this dilemma the Government endeavored to provide a more conducive environment for successful enterprise through tax incentives and other economic interventions. It also planned to act upon the recognition that a well-developed technological infrastructure is critical both for the development of indigenous industry and the attraction of manufacturing investment from abroad. The Minister of Energy was directed to bring energy prices in line with those in the rest of the European Community. Transport costs were to be reduced with a proposed liberalization of road freight haulage. In addition to improvements in the physical infrastructure of the nation, the human infrastructure was being addressed through education. The report recognized an urgent need to bring schools and industry closer together. Cooperation in technological activity at a national level between State agencies, industry and the higher education sectors had not yet been effectively developed. A proposal was given to make the specialists' technological skills in the higher education sector available to industry, and to make this sector more aware of and more responsive to the requirements of industry. Industrial training was to play an important role in Ireland's industrial development. The rate of technological change in industry was so rapid that in order to avoid worker obsolescence, ongoing or mid-career training was essential. To achieve this educational goal greater linkages with the educational system were required.

Finally, to bolster export performance of indigenous firms, the Government decided to introduce a range of initiatives to address identified weaknesses in Irish companies and to contribute to the improvement of their export performance. These included: a market entry and market development scheme to help offset costs related to travel, overseas warehousing, and promotion; market research initiated by the CTT; group marketing for small exporters sponsored by the CTT; building marketing strengths in firms; initiating the export of services; developing warehousing and distributor support programs supported by the CTT; and financing export credit insurance.

Specific to the development of the information technology sector were several initiatives. The government extended the 10% manufacturing tax to certain computer services. Programs for the provision of advanced business telecommunications systems were accelerated. The Government made a commitment to work with the educational sector to ensure that there would be a sufficient number of graduates in computer science and related disciplines who would be required by international service companies.

Two decisions made in this report were significant steps in moving Ireland into an information economy. One was to support not only computer manufacturing but also computer (i.e. information processing) services. The second was to support the development of software. By 1984 it was clear that Ireland's emerging IT sector needed diversification if it were to thrive in the uncertain times ahead.

> The decline of the cost of computer hardware (i.e. physical computer equipment) is placing increasing emphasis on software development which, because it relies on human intellectual capabilities, offers opportunities for employment creation in a country with an educated young population. We must ensure that we fill any gaps in our infrastructure and provide the facilities for both Irish and overseas software companies to develop in Ireland (White Paper, 1984, p. 69-70).

The software subsector was a later but natural addition to Ireland's information economy. One can work with software packages in any locale. There are several reasons why software development was a desirable subsector for Irish companies to pursue. Unlike firms in the hardware subsector, companies in the computer software subsector have very low startup costs, require limited capital resources and have lower overhead. Further, the availability of a young, skilled workforce -- increasingly with university credentials in engineering and computer applications -- promised a continuing supply of human resources.

This period of assessment in the early 1980s instigated by the *Telesis Report* and reinforced by the *White Paper* continued throughout the decade. When the decade began Irish policy analysts recognized the as yet unnamed sector as the type of industrial development Ireland sought; at its close they spoke in terms of an information sector that offered a range of economic and employment opportunities for Ireland and its people. Following these two industrial review reports a series of studies were published in the 1980s that were focused on redirecting the course of action. A short review of these plans highlights the decisions and actions taken along the way which served to nurture the evolving information economy in Ireland.

The Way Forward (1982) was a five year economic plan covering the time period 1983 to 1987. It was corrective in measure, emphasizing short term sacrifices for long term gain. Two components of this document related to the information economy. First, it identified electronics as the most promising source of new jobs in the overseas sector as well as a source of spin-off opportunities for indigenous firms. Second, it emphasized two aspects of infrastructure important to information-sector work: telecommunications and education. The Government's stated objective was to provide an efficient, modern telecommunications service that was adequate to the industrial, commercial, administrative and social needs of the country. A related objective was to assist Irish telecommunications and electronics manufacturing industry in the process of providing and maintaining a good telecommunications service. With respect to education, monies were targeted toward improvement of post secondary education in order to provide a supply of qualified workers for the new forms of employment. New educational institutions were created which had a particular orientation toward science and technology.

Building on Reality addressed the time period 1985 to 1987. The objective was to ensure that economic policy was developed within the context of a social policy consistent with Ireland's culture. The Plan addressed dual needs. One was to reverse the continuing upward spiral of unemployment. The second was to make certain that even in the face of scarce resources social policy in health, education, welfare and housing was continuously developed. This Plan emphasized the social dimension of Irish public policy, which needed attention even in times of grave economic difficulty. The central economic and social priority in the period of the plan was to tackle the unemployment crisis. To achieve rapid employment growth in Ireland, the Plan argued for establishing the conditions under which Irish workers could effectively achieve their productive potential. These were: encouraging initiative and managerial effectiveness; securing better industrial relations; improving wage-cost competitiveness; and breaking down artificial barriers at work (restrictive practices). But, it also acknowledged that it took time to develop the productive framework required to meet such an employment challenge.

The social policy guidelines employed in this planning document came from a 1981 report by the National Economic and Social Council that laid out Irish social policies according to the following viewpoint:

> [S]ocial policies are those actions of Government which deliberately or accidentally affect the distribution of resources, status, opportunities and life chances among social groups and categories of people within the country, and thus help shape the general character and equity of its social relations (NESC, 1981, p. 5).

Accordingly, the values underpinning the policy measures in *Building on Reality* were: the individual's dignity and right to personal development; the value of bonds of mutual obligation within society; the importance of fair shares within the community; and the securing of basic rights within a democratic framework. Social policy, it held, should seek to make progress even in times of severe financial constraint.

Two aspects of social policy particularly relevant to this discussion were education and gender equality. Having a well-educated population was stated as the highest priority of the government. It acknowledged a need for closer links between education and modern society. To that end plans were being made for university-level courses of study in computer services, microcomputer networks, office technology, and telecommunications. With respect to the second aspect, legislation for the implementation of the EEC directive on equal treatment between men and women in matters of social security would be introduced. The government would also make every effort to promote equality in the workplace. These two aspects of social policy had a significant influence on broadening the base of qualified workers for the emerging information sector. They also were directed at spreading the benefits of this economic sector more widely throughout Irish society.

Guiding the creation of economic plans were policy analysis documents such as the report produced by the Economic and Social Research Institute (O'Malley, 1987). It was a study of the Irish engineering industry focusing on its strengths and weaknesses. It also suggested the types of industry that might be most suitable for development in the future. Finally, it offered suggestions regarding policy measures that would be required in order to make further progress in these areas. It reinforced the importance to Ireland of the Metals and Engineering sector that contained electronic goods along with the manufacture of metals and automobiles. It noted, specifically, Office and Data Processing Machinery as the fastest growing subsector in Ireland. Within this subsector some issues were highlighted. While the skill level required of the work in Ireland was higher than that in some newly industrializing countries, R&D was more limited than in advanced economies. It also noted a pattern of employment decline in the multinational firms, which placed the burden of additional employment growth upon first-time arrivals in Ireland. The recommendation of this report was to focus greater attention on nurturing indigenous firms in targeted industries. In doing so, it recommended the avoidance of capital-intensive industries and those that would have a low wage advantage. It recommended that Ireland, instead, concentrate on industries in high demand, in a related industrial group to develop linkages and diversification opportunities, and for which there already existed relevant indigenous capabilities.

In a consistent message, *A Strategy for Development, 1986-1990* (NESC, 1986) argued that persisting with existing policies was no longer a viable option. This was an important turning point in Ireland's journey into the information economy because the report claimed that even a modest upturn in the world economy would not improve Ireland's prospects for economic growth under existing policies. More significant structural changes were needed. Several aspects of this plan had direct relevance to Ireland's emerging information sector. Reinforcement of the need to continue attracting overseas firms combined with the recognition that major change was needed in industrial policy provided impetus to expand beyond computer hardware into software and information services.[xx] Helping to provide the human resources to fuel this expanded information sector was the call for education policy to address social class and gender inequalities.

The 1980s saw an identifiable information sector emerge from an industrial policy aimed at attracting electronics firms within the Metals and Engineering sector of manufacturing. As the decade progressed and the challenges of an industrial policy based on inward investment became better understood, policy changes occurred which opened the door to other types of information-sector work including software development and information services.[xxi]

4.   THE INFORMATION ECONOMY: ENGINE OF THE INFORMATION SOCIETY

Throughout the 1990s industrial policy studies and recommendations continued to identify employment in Ireland's information sector as a key to the country's economic development. By the end of the decade Ireland publicly acknowledged a distinct information economy.[xxii] But neither the existence nor the significance of Ireland's information economy was apparent at first.[xxiii] Studies of employment growth (Gray, 1992; NESC, 1992) reinforced two important trends: the decline of agricultural employment and the inability of Irish industry to keep up with the numbers of well-educated young people entering the workforce. A result was the emigration of some of Ireland's best and brightest.[xxiv] These studies called for significant reevaluation of potential employment sectors and a more focused emphasis on those which exploited Ireland's strengths.

Building upon the *Programme for National Recovery*, the *National Development and Plan, 1989-1993* set out to address such issues in the context of preparing Ireland to compete within a single European market. Ireland was receiving assistance in this regard from European structural funds directed at peripheral locations within the European Community. This plan laid out the structural measures which Ireland proposed to implement in the first half of 1990s. Several of these directly influenced the development of Ireland's information economy. One was improved educational and training resources and programs in the areas of technology and business to ensure a supply of an appropriately trained labor force. Another was a shift in the allocation of resources so as to support those functions that could secure the long-term competitiveness of Irish industry in marketing, technology, productivity, management development and training. A final measure was the development of a service industry, particularly international services.

At the same time the Industrial Policy Review Group conducted a study of current industrial policy in Ireland for the Department of Industry and Commerce. The final report (commonly referred to as the *Culliton Report* after the Group's chairman) called for significant change. It concluded that there were no short-term solutions to Irish unemployment. Rather, Ireland's economic problems were deep-rooted and persistent. Hence, their resolution would require a fundamental reappraisal of the country's strengths and weaknesses and a proactive plan for the future:

> It is a time for change. . . Time to accept that the solutions to our problems lie in our own hands. We need to foster a spirit of self-reliance and a determination to take charge of our future. The next decade will provide greater opportunities for enterprise and initiative than we have ever seen before. The extent to which our community will accept this challenge will determine our future levels of employment and national wealth (Industrial Policy Review Group, 1992, p. 7).

A significant contribution of this study was its breadth of perspective. It called for industrial policy to move beyond departmental views to take into account the relationship among the relevant factors influencing industrial development in Ireland, namely, taxation policy, the societal infrastructure, and the relevance and effectiveness of education and training. It also encouraged greater focus in decisions regarding resource allocation. Agencies were encouraged to foster clusters of related industries that built upon areas of potential national competitive advantage. With respect to furthering Ireland's information economy, however, it took a critical stance. While acknowledging the considerable promotion of the high tech and pharmaceuticals sectors, it suggested that neither sector built on pre-existing Irish strengths or natural advantages (Industrial Policy Review Group, 1992, p. 74).

The information economy, nevertheless, grew and expanded during the 1990s as Ireland pursued a strategy of diversification and emphasis on building up indigenous industry. What emerged was the recognition of distinct subsectors of the information economy. One industry that emerged from this national self-examination was the software industry. In addition to the electronics (or computer hardware manufacture) subsector, industrial development agencies recognized other employment opportunities that were based upon the sophisticated telecommunications capability being installed in Ireland. One of these was software development. In the first wave of inward investment in the software subsector during the 1970s and 1980s, multinational companies such as Wang Laboratories, Digital Equipment Corporation and IBM located software development groups in Ireland. Later, firms such as Lotus and Microsoft set up in Ireland to carry out localization activities. [xxv]

The indigenous software subsector grew alongside the emergence of distributed computing and data communications, new fields that were easier to enter than the established desktop software market. The Industrial Development Authority established a National Software Centre to speed up the development of infrastructural support for this industry. The aims of this Centre were to increase the technical capability of Irish software companies and to improve the international image of the Irish software industry. The ultimate goal was to open up new export markets for Irish companies and make Ireland a more attractive location for overseas software companies (National Software Directorate, 1992). The software subsector was heavily export-oriented. According to a mid-decade assessment (National Software Directorate, 1995), two-thirds of indigenous software companies were producing actual products and exports grew from 41% of total revenues in 1991 to 58% in 1995.

Alongside the development of the software subsector of the information economy evolved a third subsector: information services. By taking advantage of time differences and less expensive real estate, Ireland was able to offer offshore information processing outsourcing services. Originally taking the form of low skilled data entry for American insurance companies in the 1980s, this subsector grew in sophistication and diversity in the 1990s. A more recent type of service that has evolved is call centre support. The creation of the International Financial Services Centre in the former docklands of Dublin in 1987 has become another new source of economic development and employment for Ireland as many American and European firms in the financial services and related industries have located offices there.[xxvi]

As agriculture has declined in Ireland during the second half of the twentieth century, industry and services have been on the rise. The parts of the industrial and services sectors, which comprise the information economy, have played a significant role in this societal and economic transformation. Ireland currently has a robust information economy which includes technology manufacture, software development and information services. In 1949, 43% of the labor force was engaged in agriculture while industry and service employed 21% and 36%, respectively (Department of Foreign Affairs, 1999). By the time this research began in 1989 the number employed in agriculture had shrunk to 15% of the labor force while employment in industry had grown to 28% and services to 57% (Central Statistics Office, 1992, p. 23). In 1995 agriculture declined further to 11%, industrial employment remained the same and the service sector grew to 61% (Department of Foreign Affairs, 1999).

Not only has the balance among agriculture, industry and services changed but the mix within the industrial sector has changed. In 1989 nearly a third of the industrial employment in Ireland was accounted for by the Metals and Engineering sector (Institute of Public Administration, 1989, p. 388). Electrical, electronic, chemicals and pharmaceuticals industries increased output by an average of 15% per year between 1975 and 1990. In contrast, the traditional, labor-intensive, low value-added industries suffered a decline in output of 2%. By 1990 Ireland was noteworthy within the European Union for having half of its total manufacturing output accounted for by these fast growing new technology sectors (Power, 1990).

As Ireland's information economy grew and diversified throughout the 1990s, it contributed to a more open economy and significant growth in exports. Exports of goods and services were 37% of GNP in 1973, 56% in 1983 and 90% in 1995 (Department of Foreign Affairs, 1999). High technology investment especially from the US has dominated Ireland's information economy since the beginning.[xxvii] In 1990 there were 13,700 first-time jobs in Ireland at over 1,000 foreign-owned firms for a total of 36,200 jobs created between 1987 and 1990. Of the 1,000 foreign companies, 309 were American (Jordan, 1992, p. 82).

Success breeds success as firms saw others in Ireland doing well. As a result, a self-sustaining cluster of related firms such as those in electronics worked to create a pool of suitably skilled labor. In 1997, electronics accounted for 30% of Irish exports while software accounted for 10% (O'Riain, 1997, p. 11). As the Irish information economy diversified beyond electronics to software and information services, Ireland became the European capital for software localization and production and hosted five of the world's top ten independent software companies (IDA Ireland, 1997a). In 1999 there were over 1,100 foreign-owned manufacturing and international services companies in Ireland -- nearly half of which were American -- employing 100,000 people and accounting for 70% of total manufactured exports (Department of Foreign Affairs, 1999).

5. CONCLUSION

In three important respects Ireland's path into an information economy represents a departure from the approach that had been taken by the first wave of countries to have done so. First, nations such as the United States moved gradually from an agrarian economy into an industrial one during a period which lasted over one hundred years before developing an information sector in mid-twentieth century. Second wave countries such as Ireland, however, began moving directly from a traditional, agrarian economy to a modern, information economy only at the end of the twentieth century.[xxviii] In doing so, they bypassed an industrial economy, for better and worse. The second difference is that Ireland and other such countries[xxix] have endeavored to accomplish this rapid transition by importing both information sector jobs and expertise. This is being accomplished through inward investment by multinational information technology firms. Finally, unlike the undirected evolution of the information economy in the first wave countries, there has been a "visible hand" guiding Ireland's economic progress. The multifaceted information economy that became evident by the end of the 1990s represented the culmination of conscious actions taken in previous decades. Ireland has achieved this economic transition by employing a comprehensive industrial policy framework to guide societal, industry and governmental behavior. The adaptive quality of this approach has enabled Ireland to alter its course as it responded to challenges and recognized opportunities on its way to creating its information economy.

Current economic evidence suggests that this approach has served Ireland well. de Valera's vision of rural Ireland has faded into the background, replaced by a new self image of Ireland as a modern, information society. But some have suggested that the price of such rapid economic development has been cultural dissonance. Writing in the *Irish Times* on the fiftieth anniversary of de Valera's "vision" speech, Waters (1993) suggested that:

> . . . [F]or the last 30 years, Ireland has been engaged in a war conducted in the heads of its people. . . There is a notion that has become entrenched in official thinking in Ireland that "the present" began with the 1960s. Prior to that was "the past," which is associated with backwardness, poverty, stagnation and failure. "The present," on the other hand, is associated with modernity, industrialisation, urbanisation and prosperity. . . Thus, the constant, dialectical evolution of a healthy society has not occurred. Instead, we adopted a rigid, ideological view which drew a line in the sand at the end of the de Valera era and resolved that, from that moment on, everything would be different. . . For 30 years we have . . . conducted in our heads a war against our past. This war has left hardly a sensible thought standing on the ideological landscape of modern Ireland. We have thrown out not merely the bath water and the baby, but the bath, the plumbing and the rubber duck as well. (10)

This "war against the past" could be detected in the comments of the people who were playing a large role in bringing about Ireland's future. It was evident in my observations and experiences as well. Perhaps it is this "war" that accounts for some of the contradictions I encountered as I explored what the emerging information economy was like in the day-to-day lives of those who were helping to create it. The remainder of this book explores the cultural dimension of Ireland's rapid evolution from a traditional, agrarian society on the periphery of Europe to a modern player in the global information economy.

---

[i] For greater analysis of Ireland's efforts to reclaim its sovereignty see Foster (1988), Chapter 21: In a Free State, and Chapter 22: The de Valera Dispensation.

[ii] Fukuyama (1999) characterizes the organization of pre-modern societies around the concept of local, unchanging community: " . . . the [community] that characterized a typical pre-modern European peasant society consisted of a dense network of personal relationships based heavily on kinship and on the direct, face-to-face contact that occurs in a small, closed village. Norms were largely unwritten, and individuals were bound to one another in a web

of mutual interdependence that touched all aspects of life, from family to work to the few leisure activities that such societies enjoyed. (57)

[iii] The *Control of Manufactures Acts of 1932-34* restricted ownership of manufacturing companies in Ireland (O'Malley, 1989, p. 63).

[iv] The gombeen man was a money-lending merchant. This concept is explored in greater detail in Chapter 8.

[v] See, for example, Jordan (1992), p. 80.

[vi] See also, Fitzpatrick and Kelly (1985), and McAleese and Foley (1991).

[vii] For further discussion, see Lee (1989), Chapter 5: Expansion: 1958-1969.

[viii] The *Industrial Development Act of 1969* facilitated this process by consolidating the *Industrial Development Acts of 1950* with the *Underdeveloped Areas Acts of 1952-1969*, and the *Industrial Grants Acts of 1959-1969*.

[ix] See, for example: *Economic and Social Development, 1969-72* and *Second Programme for Economic Expansion, 1964-70*.

[x] While not in a majority, there were some writers of the time who thought in terms of a recognizable information sector. See, for example, O'Donnell (1980a).

[xi] This sector includes traditional areas such as shipbuilding as well as more modern areas such as electronics.

[xii] The local content requirement holds that a certain percentage of the manufacturing of a product must be carried out within Europe's borders in order to avoid paying import duties.

[xiii] Some of the multinational companies that came to Ireland include: Amdahl, Analog Devices, Apple Computer, Dell, Digital Equipment Corporation, Gateway, Hewlett-Packard, IBM, Intel, Lotus, Microsoft, Motorola, Novell, Oracle, Prime Computer, Stratus Computer and Wang Laboratories.

[xiv] Some of the same comments could be said about Japanese firms, which also were setting up subsidiaries in Ireland. But because this study only included American multinational firms, I limit my comments to the American context.

[xv] One American firm mentioned The Netherlands as a contender. Despite the fact that English is not the primary language, the number who does speak English made this country attractive.

[xvi] Some of these industrial policy documents include the following:
A Review of Industrial Policy: A Report Prepared by the Telesis Consultancy Group, 1982.
The Way Forward: National Economic Plan 1983-1987.

White Paper on Industrial Policy, 1984.
Review of Industrial Performance, 1986.
Building on Reality, 1985-1987.
Industrial Development Act of 1986.
Programme for National Recovery, 1987.

[xvii] See, for example, Buckley (1974) and O'Donnell (1979).

[xviii] This was the term used to describe the nascent information technology sector at that time.

[xix] See, for example, McCabe (1984).

[xx] A study of the Irish software industry conducted in the late 1980s (Coopers and Lybrand, 1988) revealed the promise of this subsector of the information economy. It was a new industry: 95% of the companies had been in existence 15 years or less. There were opportunities for small, independent, indigenous software houses to exploit niche specializations. Finally, the overall market for software was expected to expand in the 1990s.

[xxi] Contemporary books such as Punset and Sweeney (1989) reflect this recognition.

[xxii] While Ireland didn't necessarily use the term information economy it did separate out the information subsectors: computer manufacture, software development and information services.

[xxiii] I experienced evidence of this in my efforts during the early 1990s to obtain statistics on the size of the information economy. I found that I had to infer the size of the information economy from the size of a variety of industrial categories including: Manufacturing, Commerce, Insurance and Finance, and Transport, Communication and Storage. (See, for example, Trauth, 1996a.)

[xxiv] Between 1986 and 1991 Ireland experienced a 5% decrease in its population (CSO, 1991, p. 11). These emigrants had a different profile from previous decades: they tended to be highly educated and often possessed underutilized information-sector skills.

[xxv] Localization refers to the adapting of software to specific national contexts. Key among the activities is the translation of software and documentation into other languages. (See, Jacobson and O'Sullivan, 1994).

[xxvi] See Financial Services Industry Association (1988) and Industrial Development Authority (1992, 1997b).

[xxvii] Since 1980 40% of all US new inward investment in European electronics has come to Ireland (Industrial Development Authority, 1997a).

[xxviii] In some respects, then, Ireland's experience can be compared with those of developing countries. For further discussion see Breen et al. (1990) and Trauth (1996a).

[xxix] For a general discussion of the information economy and economic growth see Dordick and Wang (1993), Chapter 6: How Does the Information Work Force Contribute to Economic Growth?

Part II
The Workers

CHAPTER 3. A NEW BREED

1. INTRODUCTION

Young workers have none of the habits of older employees. They have grown up in an open management situation. They are allowed to develop where they can contribute their best. Here, workers used to union settings wouldn't do as well. A union worker's attitudes and habits of work are not flexible enough for this industry. For these young people, there is no understanding of what's expected, what's the norm in other industries. [Eamon]

Firms in Ireland's information sector were fortunate in their human resource development efforts because, in many respects, they had a blank slate with which to work. That such a large segment of Ireland's population was young meant that a significant number of the workers entered the information sector with no previous work experience. When attempting to alter work culture and assumptions, inexperience can be a definite benefit. Accompanying their youth was their educational background. The group of young workers with whom I spoke represented the first cohort for whom secondary education was economically viable. They represented a definite break with the past. But though the economic barriers to education were crumbling, social class walls remained. I could see that the information sector in Ireland had the potential to both transcend and reinforce boundaries between the "haves" and the "have nots."

2. YOUNG

The average age of my clients is 45. They are the decision-makers in the companies. I find that the young people at the client sites show much greater willingness to accept new technology. Young people take 12 days to learn [about new

technology]; old people take 12 months. Young people are
also more excited about new things at work like technology.
[Tom]

The youth of the workers was an immediately noticeable feature of the Irish information-sector workplace. At the time of these interviews half the population was under the age of 27. One effect of Ireland's change in industrial policy, and the economic expansion that resulted, was the tide of emigration that was stemmed during the late 1960s and the 1970s. One consequence was a large increase in the number of Irish people who remained in Ireland to marry, raise families, and produce a population bulge. To put this demographic information in perspective, one older informant noted that 90% of his school classmates had emigrated.

When the Irish government was formulating its industrial policy, the large, young population was factored in as a highly valuable resource for Ireland. In the early years, workers were typically between the ages of 18 and 22 and in their first job. At one American firm in this study the average age of the workers was 26 (and 21when the firm first arrived in Ireland ten years before), while the average age of the firm's American workers in 1990 was 40. Because the information technology industry was relatively new in Ireland and because the bulk of the workforce was young, youth was a driving force in the industry in the early 1990s. Unlike America, which had a well-established information economy by the 1960s, Ireland did not have a generation of information professionals who had been working in the field for 20 or 30 years.

Such a large cohort of young people was viewed as a boon to the information industry in two ways. Companies could locate in Ireland knowing there were plenty of these young workers available. Alternatively, multinational firms could come to Ireland to recruit for positions in other countries.[i] However, the age divide also made it more difficult for older workers to obtain employment in the information sector. People over 40 were perceived as having old ways of thinking, old traditions, little inclination toward innovation, and reluctance to change. They were considered too expensive to hire and too old fashioned to work in high technology industries. Resistance to the new techniques which American firms were trying to introduce was perceived to be a function of age. Flexibility was highly valued and was associated with youth while resistance to change and modern ideas was associated with older workers. For example, Leo, who had recently arrived as the managing director of his firm's Irish site, found middle aged Irish managers reluctant to introduce flex time at the plant. However, he also acknowledged that aged-based resistance to new methods in a large manufacturing firm in America would also occur.

Margie, a middle aged worker at an American plant in the West of Ireland, observed that the youth of both the sector and its workers was evident in numerous ways. On the one hand, these workers possessed both enthusiasm and inexperience. On the other hand, people like her were changing as well. She found herself becoming more broadminded, more flexible. She also spoke of the effects on some quiet little towns whose population ranks were suddenly swelled by an influx of young IT workers. In one case the young Irish workers from the newly relocated multinational firm were barred from entering the local pubs because they were too rowdy. Some workers who were over 40 and were not managers often struggled to fit in with this younger crowd. Aine, who worked at an Irish software firm in Dublin, pointed to social examples of this struggle to fit in. She told me about playing softball on a recent Tuesday night when she'd rather have gone home to bed!

Perhaps it was the difference in the average age of workers that made the Americans with whom I spoke so acutely aware of the influence of the young workforce. They noted that along with youth comes inexperience but that having little or no exposure to the work environment and work ethic of other work sectors was generally preferred. Young workers who were not yet formed did not have the entrenched work habits of older workers. They did not need to unlearn attitudes that would be counterproductive in the workplaces of the information economy. They did not have "union habits"[ii] -- a euphemism for inflexibility -- which were perceived as incompatible with such work. Consequently, for many positions too much work experience was viewed in a negative light. In both the multinationals and large Irish companies a person with a breadth of work experiences was seen as less rather than more marketable.

A final dimension of the workers' limited work experience was the absence of experience in being held back. In contrast with their older counterparts, they knew no limits. The result was a large pool of malleable and intelligent workers. Among the American managing directors whom I interviewed, Eric had the shortest tenure in Ireland. He had only arrived to set up his firm's new plant a few months before we met. As he shared his first impressions about Ireland he expressed the opinion that, in many respects, Irish people were very set in their ways. Therefore, a company like his would be inclined to look for young workers who were *less* influenced by previous work experiences and at the same time were *more* knowledgeable about the outside world.[iii] The main disadvantage, in the perception of the older managers, was that these inexperienced workers would make more mistakes.

Hence, they would be learning by their mistakes as they worked through situations that arose.

Some argued that experience wasn't all that important anyway, that the high technology fields suited young people because age and experience did not give one an advantage. Because the industry changed so much it needed young and enthusiastic passion for the work in order to be able to evolve at this pace. Impatience -- a characteristic of youth -- had shaped the pace of the industry. What young people lacked in experience was compensated by enthusiasm. This kept them from seeing obstacles in their way. They had no set ideas of how things were done. They were very adaptable and interested in challenge. There was energy present in the workplace because everyone wanted to get on, and get promoted. They were impatient to get ahead.

Patrick -- who, in his late 40s, was considered old -- found the influence of young people on the workplace to be refreshing because of their ideas, enthusiasm and willingness to learn. They didn't approach a situation with an "I know this already" attitude. They were open to new ideas, to changes and were prepared to work. He spoke of the "buzz" that existed in the industry in Ireland that could not be sustained were it populated predominantly with older people. Those who had worked in the UK observed that the information industry seemed more dynamic in Ireland where the people were younger, and more settled in the UK where the people were older. The effect they observed was a freer and less cautious attitude. On the negative side, they noted a lack of discipline among young Irish workers.

In addition to inexperience and enthusiasm, this large cohort of young workers was having its influence felt on the emerging information sector in other ways. Having a team spirit at work was easier with the younger people who tended to identify more easily with a group. They were also more mobile, moving around and bumping into each other in different jobs. A final effect of the young workforce was that more emphasis was being placed upon training and development, and additional education.

This population bulge, as it aged, also challenged the promotion system. The cohort of workers who were 19 or 20 in the early 1980s had produced a large group of people at mid-level by the early 1990s that was creating a bottleneck in the advancement system. As more of these workers got married and started families they began to settle down. Consequently, the workplace had changed. There was a decline in workplace socializing, for example. One specific effect on the multinational firms was the reluctance to take transfers to America. Deirdre, a human resource manager at an American plant, noted that during the 1980s Irish workers would have jumped at the chance to take an assignment in America. Ten years later she noticed that several people had turned down these opportunities, citing family reasons.

The effect of an industrial policy that lowered emigration rates extended beyond the information sector. An indirect impact of the emerging information sector was the change in attitude about politics, economics, religion and gender that came about along with this cohort of young people who remained in Ireland. Whereas young adults used to vote the way their parents did, these young people made their own decisions. They were concerned about job stability, ecology, emigration and taxes. They wanted equitable personal taxes. They wanted more from politicians, beyond the old, traditional treatment.

3.   EDUCATED

> *ET: Do you think the growth of information work has had any impact on education?*
>
> *Well, because of job demands, [this firm's] factory workers, for example, now have to have the Leaving Cert.[iv] Forty years ago you would have left school at 13 or 14 to go work in a factory. You need more education because of the scarcity of jobs, but also because of the maturity you have based on having more education.*
>
> *ET: Do you think the kind of education students receive is changing?*
>
> *Yes. I think it is changing slowly from liberal arts which must take a second place to technical education. Liberal arts is now a luxury. But there is still snobbery about regional technical colleges. For a job interview you need a set of skills not general education. You must be able to do something. [Stephanie]*

Throughout Ireland's history both skills and attitudes, including the value placed upon education, itself, have been communicated through the educational system. Hence, education has played a pivotal role in the evolution of Ireland's information economy. Education became an important topic in this research for two reasons. First, by its nature, most of the work in the information sector requires specialized and often technical skills. Second, the "well educated Irish population" had been from the outset of this industrial policy one of Ireland's drawing cards in attracting the multinational firms. The educational infrastructure that was in place at the inception of this economic plan had a significant *influence* on Ireland's ability to attract foreign investment. It was considered a national resource which Irish policy makers leveraged to their advantage in the world labor market. Likewise, over the ensuing decades that this industrial policy has been in place the changes in the educational infrastructure also reveal the *impact* of this sector. Thus, education illustrates the mutual effects that the socio-cultural context and the information sector are having on each other.[v]

> *Education was seen as the route by which sons and daughters could actually stay in Ireland and join typical civil service employment, banks and insurance companies. Failing that, if they went abroad, education would be something that would be seen as standing them in very good stead. . . I think in the high tech area, it stood Ireland in good stead because . . . it is brain-power intensive. It's education intensive. I think that's now beginning to be fully recognized and it's certainly one of the reasons why Ireland was attractive to many multinational companies in software, for example, or electronics, or design activities. [Martin]*

When both Irish and American respondents spoke about the educational quality of the labor force they were more often than not speaking about the overall, general educational qualifications possessed by the labor force. Seamus, a human resources manager at an American firm, told me about his firm's experiences in hiring the initial workforce. The workers were, for the most part, from the farm and needed training. Some training came from the firms themselves while other training was provided by organizations like the Irish Management Institute. But this training was made significantly easier by the fact that many of these farmers had been to college. While there is a clear link between information-sector employment and education, I was curious to learn the origins of an attitude about education that predated the emergence of this employment sector.

The strong emphasis on education was linked, in part, to Ireland's colonial history. Like religion, some of the fierce commitment to education seemed to have stemmed from past attempts to suppress it. In response to seventeenth century penal laws which limited educational options to surreptitious "hedge schools,"[vi] education became a way of maintaining national and religious identity.

3.1 The Role of Education in Ireland's Industrial Policy

Irish policy makers recognized that the Irish population was a powerful resource, which could be leveraged to support the country's information economy. Not only was the substantial number of young people attractive but the way in which their mental capacities had been developed was also appealing. A culture that placed a value on getting an education and on continuous learning reflected a tradition of motivating people to use their brains to the fullest.

But while the educational attitudes and infrastructure that existed at the outset of the information economy had much to recommend them, providing a workforce capable of working in this new sector required certain changes in the content and structure of Irish education. Ireland's approach to educating people for employment in the emerging information sector was twofold. First, it identified those aspects of the existing educational system which were consistent with the new industrial plan. Second, it identified those changes in both educational content and infrastructure that needed to occur in order for the industrial policy to succeed. For this part of the discussion about education, I have drawn from three different perspectives on this topic: the educational "products" themselves (the Irish information-sector workers); American managers involved with the decision to come to Ireland and the initial hiring of information-sector workers; and representatives of the Irish government who were bringing foreign investment to Ireland.

These three groups held conflicting viewpoints regarding the appropriateness of the education possessed by the pool of potential workers. According to American managers, labor force qualifications was both a positive and a negative factor in the decision to come to Ireland. While the general literacy of Ireland's workforce was an attraction, the difficulty in finding enough specifically qualified people to fill the jobs that were being brought to and developed within Ireland was a detraction.

> *Finding experienced people, especially managers, is more difficult in Ireland. It was hard for us to find people with university degrees in electronic engineering who also had management experience because they usually emigrate. Companies like Philips or Siemens will hire an entire UCC [University College Cork] graduating class. [Andrew]*

Emerging from what appeared at first glance to be contradictory comments were three different types of knowledge or skill. Ireland had one in abundance and needed to develop the other two. All categories of respondents acknowledged the high educational quality of school Leavers and the consequent breadth of knowledge of university graduates. This type of knowledge and skill was already present in the worker pool when the information technology firms first started coming to Ireland. But the other two types of knowledge that were needed were technical skills and business knowledge. Because Ireland had little extant industrialism, these skills needed to be enhanced within the labor force.

3.1.1   General Knowledge

> *We are more versatile here, more adaptable. We have a broader perspective, like the colonial country. In the US there is a bigger emphasis on specializing. I have the impression that the people here are more intelligent than the [firm's] people in the US. [Deirdre]*

Deirdre captured a sentiment expressed by both Irish and American respondents about the Irish workforce. In addition to the technical skills required for the particular job, both groups found the Irish workforce to be broad based and flexible in its knowledge. The traits of broad, general knowledge combined with a willingness to be flexible and adaptable and a willingness to work at any task was repeatedly noted by American managers. Indeed, government representatives emphasized the worker flexibility as a significant contributor to productivity. Workers were described as having language facility, mental alertness and the ability to use intelligence in the workplace, the flexibility to deal with unfamiliar situations, and an interest in job variety coupled with an eagerness to learn quickly.

> *The people [at this Irish site of the firm] . . . have a better idea of how the company is run, they have a better idea of overall operations. Is this because it's a smaller operation or because of something about the Irish people? . . . You do have to be a jack of all trades here because it's part of the culture. Although you may not know the person, you tend to help them . . . to help people do other jobs. And . . . in general people tend to want to help. So by helping they get to expand their knowledge. If you were doing a job and if I offered to help, I would have to pick up your skills or part of your skills. So therefore it's part of the culture, which makes it happen. A willingness to help and not sit back. [Albert]*

A final dimension of general skills is social skills. In the hiring process, Aine told me, they didn't just look for technical skills; social interaction skills were also taken into account. Hiring managers asked themselves, "Could this person fit in?" The reason for seeking social as well as technical skills was that if someone failed in a technical job it would probably be for a nontechnical reason. During recruiting it was understood that the candidates, by virtue of their university degrees, knew the technical material; the recruiter, therefore, tried to get a feel for the person. Were the candidates happy with themselves? Did they have their lives sorted out?

The competition for these multinational plants was usually Scotland and England (and in one case, The Netherlands). While Scotland and England possessed the same basic attractions as Ireland, what repeatedly emerged as a determining factor during conversations with Americans was the well trained and available labor force. Some fundamentally attractive features of Ireland's educational system existed well before this industrial policy was enacted.

> *We chose Ireland for the following reasons. The educational system is the best in the world. I'm not talking about people that go to Trinity College but the general knowledge that people have with the Leaving Cert. The ones I'm impressed with are the rural and working class people. For example, when I was first here, one of our workers, a 19 year old with a Leaving Cert explained the five political parties in Ireland to me. He explained it with regard to who is on the left and who is on the right. I'm certain that an American high school graduate wouldn't be able to do such a good job. When I say this, I'm thinking of my high school daughter in [America]. The Irish system is much better. They are much more literate than other societies. [Eric]*

For their part, government representatives echoed the viewpoint of the American managers. Representatives of the Industrial Development Authority ranked the Irish labor force as the number one reason that firms came to Ireland. The qualities of this labor force, they said, were its youth and educational level. Other government representatives commented on the impact that the information sector was having on Irish education. More science and mathematics was being taught at the secondary level, especially in girls' schools. One official pointed out that there was a greater number of women in science and engineering than ever before.

Francis, who worked at an Irish firm in the Dublin area, made several interesting observations about the interaction of education and the labor force.

He believed that the educational process in Ireland brought out a person's natural intelligence to a much greater degree than might be the case elsewhere. His second observation pointed to the impact that the information economy was having on education in Ireland. Those in the information sector were seeing much better educated people working in jobs that previously would have been done by less educated people. Consequently, a manager could trust workers to do more, and to work with less supervision and less control than would have been possible before. However, his final observation was that the price of developing such a labor force was that salary expectations were also higher. If the job levels did not keep pace, these highly qualified workers would go off to the UK or some other place, as many had already done.

It is important to note that this abundance of well-educated young people was a fairly recent phenomenon in 1990. It had only been since the late 1960s when government support of second and third level education became available, that large numbers of the farming and working classes could afford to send their children on. Niall's background illustrates this point. When he was in primary school in the 1940s, he was the only one in his class to go on to second level and only one of three in the whole school to go on. He had to go to a boarding school, as there was no secondary school in close proximity to his town. In Dublin, working class jobs did not require third level education. One could work on the docks, in construction, at Guinness, even at a newspaper without a third level degree.

There was not complete unanimity on this topic, however. One camp held the view that people in rural Ireland have always placed a high value on attaining as much formal education as possible. The other camp argued that this was only fairly recently the case. To some extent, the resolution of this conflict lay in the meaning of formal education. To some, the term meant the second level boarding school; to others formal education meant going to university.

3.1.2   Technical Knowledge

> *Irish culture now places emphasis on careers in computing. Until the mid 1970s it was: "Become a teacher, doctor or work in the government." The idea was get one of these secure jobs. Now, the message is: "If you know anything about computers you are all set." [Dermot]*

The skill expectations of employers have grown along with the information economy. Initially, only a moderate level of skill was needed. An

American firm which started a plant in Ireland in the late 1970s required workers to have only moderate skill levels: the ability to read instructions and follow directions. Ireland's training at the secondary level more than adequately prepared a labor force for this type of work. But as more specialized jobs became available, greater specificity of skill became needed. While there was no disagreement that Ireland had a good, generally educated labor force, that portion which had a sufficient level of technical skill was another matter. These technical skills can be broadly placed into three categories: technician, programmer, and engineer.

When considering the skills required of workers in the information economy it becomes necessary to bear in mind the particular subsector in question. The hardware subsector, the original and intended object of Ireland's industrial policy, includes firms working with the physical information processing equipment. These firms are engaged with the production of component parts such as microprocessors, the manufacture of a particular line of computers, and the final assembly of individualized computers for clients in the European market. The majority of those working in this subsector were technicians. They typically had a third level degree from a technical college. American managers thought highly of the education and skill level of technicians finding some Irish technicians to be similar in technical background to an engineer in the US.

> *In the States a person out of high school can get a six months' certificate and qualify as a technician whereas here they have even more education. Here, they're almost engineers. They have two to three year programs that they're going through. [The technicians in the States] have a high school diploma, a lot of them -- at least at [our firm] -- and went to those, you know, [six months'] Technical Schools. . . So you won't see four year degrees [in the US site but] a smattering of two year degrees, and the rest with the certificate. [Ed]*

The software subsector, which was more recently recognized as a lucrative subsector to exploit, required a skilled workforce. Creating this labor force required that conscious attention be given to gaps in university education, particularly in the area of computer science. William, who worked at an American firm in the West of Ireland, commented that this region of Ireland was basically barren in terms of software until the local universities began to offer programs in computer science.

People were of two minds on the topic of the software business being a good opportunity for Irish start-up firms. Those supporting this view believed that one didn't need extensive experience in order to enter this business. The opposing viewpoint was that experience was, indeed, crucial and that while Ireland's educational institutions could provide one component of a qualified labor force -- education -- it could not sufficiently provide the other: experience. Somebody coming out of one of Ireland's computer science programs with no experience was not able to compete with a programmer in the States who might have been 20 years in a particular line of business. Programmers were typically in their mid to late 20s. Martin, a manager at an Irish firm, echoed this position. He said the difficulty for Irish graduates with high tech training was the lack of experience. Employers wanted graduates with the knowledge *plus* some work experience. The total package of qualifications, he repeated, included the education plus the experience.

3.1.3   Business Knowledge

Technical knowledge was necessary for successful companies and careers in the information economy, but it was not sufficient. Because those skills needed to be acted out within some context, business knowledge was necessary as well.[vii] The respondents' comments about this theme generally tended to be expressed in terms of skills that the Irish labor force lacked.

One of the legacies of being a nonindustrial society was the absence of a business class and business culture. And because of that, complained a minority of both Irish and American respondents, some people doing business in Ireland lacked sufficient attention to the organization of work and common business courtesies. Louise worked in marketing for an Irish software company. She explained that while on the surface a manager might appear quite organized and competent, in her experience they did not have the administrative backup to be able to ensure consistent execution of simple tasks such as remembering appointments. She would ring someone for an appointment only to arrive and find they had forgotten she was coming.

Robert, who worked for an American electronics firm, offered his insights on this topic. Such behaviors could be attributed to the absence of an understanding of "true capitalism." He had given considerable thought beforehand to what he would say in our interview and shared the results of that thought process.

> *Well, we have in Ireland these "cowboy operators". . . He*
> *goes out and sees a quick deal and makes a fast buck. And in*
> *Ireland for a long time he'd have been classed a "capitalist."*

And I think that's wrong . . . if you look at it, capitalism itself is not concerned about the well being of the individual but rather about the creation of the means of well being of all persons. . . If you take a guy who goes to school, right? Very brilliant student, works hard, gets interested in science, in the evening goes to college, studies for a doctor because he's interested in science. When he qualifies as a doctor he's probably still very academic, and decides that because the heart is such a unique organ he wants to study it. So he studies the heart and becomes a heart specialist. In time the guy becomes one of the world's leading heart surgeons. If you want him to do an operation on you, you're going to have to pay because of his skill and his ability. And as a result of all this experience he probably has or appears to have a tremendous life style as far as he has the trappings of wealth. He has a nice house with a swimming pool, the whole lot, the family needs nothing. If you look at him and ask yourself, "What made him have that life style? Was it his desire to have that life style that encouraged him to become a heart surgeon or was it his desire to study this particular aspect that intrigued his mind that led him to have that life style?" I would argue it was his desire to study and to use his brain power that led him to have that life style. I think I am lucky in that I've thought about what I want from life in that regard. I'm not driven by the desire to have a big house. But I am driven by the desire to do a good job and have the opportunity to work for myself. Whereas I have a brother who's a year older than me and financially far more successful who's constantly thinking, "I think I'll get into that activity next year because I can double my income level." I think the idea of the quality of life that I look for and that he looks for, it's a bankbook he looks for. Unfortunately I think true capitalism is very much a minority, a tiny minority here in Ireland. [Robert]

A final aspect of business knowledge that was brought up in our interviews was career management. This includes resume writing, interviewing and other job seeking skills. William, who graduated from a computer science program, complained about the lack of career guidance at his university and help in obtaining jobs. It was from the training course rather than his computer science degree that he obtained his job with the IT firm. In addition to learning software skills he also learned how to look for a job in the information sector. The consensus on this topic seemed to be that the third level institutions were not sufficiently marketing the jobs that existed within Ireland.

As these reflections and experiences point out, the appropriately educated workforce that was touted in 1990 was a relatively new phenomenon. Declan was working at an Irish firm when we talked but had started his career at a multinational firm. He suggested that the expectations of the foreign firms were low when then they first came to Ireland. He doubted that when his employer first came to Ireland in the early 1980s it had in mind to be doing such an extensive amount of manufacturing for the European market. He thought they wouldn't have trusted that sort of highly skilled work to the Irish. Rather, they would have intended to produce one of their simpler products. That both the reality and the attitude have changed so much is clearly attributable to the concerted effort to develop a technically qualified labor force in Ireland. Since the successful implementation of Ireland's plan hinged on the availability of a qualified labor force, industrial development policy has been a driving force behind the changes in Ireland's educational policies in recent decades.

3.2   Developing a Qualified Labor Force

I have a graduate diploma in computer science from University of Limerick. This is a one year, post graduate degree. Following that I did a six months course in expert systems and advanced programming at Nixdorf in Bray. It was run by FAS. FAS provides courses from basic computing up to advanced. The National Universities[viii] never helped you get a job and career guidance. Since 1986 UCG now has a guidance center. The private courses must produce. That is, Nixdorf won't get money from FAS unless 75% of the graduates get jobs. That was the course that got me my job here. In addition to programming, it taught me how to prepare a CV[ix] and interview techniques. In addition, there are currently some obstacles to getting into computer courses because of the demand in the form of the points system. In the last two to three years computer courses have really taken off. [William]

The role of education in the evolution of Ireland's information economy clearly demonstrates how aspects of the societal context both shaped and were shaped by the information sector. The abundance of highly educated young people at first in general, then later in a technical sense, furthered the information sector by becoming one of the strongest attractions to multinational IT firms. William's educational path to his position at an Irish software start-up firm illustrates the diverse avenues that were pursued in the effort to produce a qualified labor force. His comments also point to some of the stones in the road.

3.2.1 Secondary Education

Throughout the entire story of Ireland's march into the information age, what was perhaps the most significant educational influence was the policy change in 1968 which altered the source of funding for secondary schools. Before this time extensive formal education was not available to the general population. Since the nineteenth century, primary education had been provided through the free national school system. But until 30 years ago limited post-primary education was available in two forms. Free vocational schools were established in the 1930s with the mission of practical training in preparation for employment in the trades, manufacturing, agriculture and commerce.

The alternative form of post-primary education was the secondary school, a private, academically oriented institution generally run by priests and nuns.[x] The role of the secondary school was not to provide a skilled labor force. Rather, the focus was on

> . . . religious, moral and intellectual construction, and the products of this form of education were [if male] destined for jobs in professional and other white collar occupations, achieved in some cases via third level education (Breen, et al., 1990, p. 126).

Education beyond primary level was the province of the middle class and well to do farmers. It was generally not a vehicle for upward mobility. Rather, it was a refining process for those who were already members of the privileged classes (O'Toole, 1990a, p. 15). Therefore, children of poor farming or working class families typically received no more than a primary education. In some cases, they also attended a vocational school.

Those who could afford to send their children on had to send them to an available school. To families in the rural parts of Ireland this generally meant sending their sons and daughters away to boarding school. Hence, for middle-aged respondents the terms boarding school or convent school were synonymous with secondary school. The majority of workers[xi] whom I interviewed was part of the first generation to have secondary education financially available to everyone.

While it is clear that a large part of successfully rising to the challenge of the information economy is education, it is also important to note that these educational policy initiatives were not the orderly outgrowth of a grand vision. In the late 1960s nobody could have foreseen the ubiquity of computers today or the dominance of information technology in the global economy. Rather, educational reform occurred first; it was not until later that this group of educated young people was recognized as constituting an important national resource for the emerging information sector.

Following the changed educational policy religious orders continued to operate the secondary schools in an arrangement whereby the State paid the fees for the students. The influence of nuns and priests resulted in two noteworthy aspects of Irish secondary education. There was a strong emphasis on a well-rounded liberal arts education and it was carried out in a structured and disciplined environment. The result led American managers in Ireland to notice the quality of the overall education and, in particular, the analytical and communication skills possessed by workers who had the Leaving Certificate. The image of Irish secondary schools that was conveyed by those who discussed their own experiences -- and by Americans who reflected on the end product -- was of a disciplined setting from which an ethic of hard work and rigorous learning emerged.

Besides a strong emphasis on education in general, Irish secondary school graduates possessed a broad base of knowledge, which resulted from the breadth of their studies. In order to gain admission to Irish universities, students needed good marks in a wide range of subjects. The required number of points for admission to the university of choice as well as the desired degree program was a function of both the raw scores and the number of subjects tested. A very popular program of study in a university, for example, required top scores in five or six different subjects. In the case of degrees for the information professions, students often needed to have taken Honors sections of courses such as mathematics.[xii] Respondents noted how this broad educational base translated directly into benefits for the IT firms.

> *I think one of the important things about the Leaving Cert they're taking is they generally do seven or eight subjects, they have a rounded education. I came across one guy [in the UK] whom I knew reasonably well, had done history of art and Italian for his A levels. That was it. And that was good enough to get into college. He hadn't done math since he was*

16. And that is not atypical, I was told. When I expressed surprise, they expressed surprise that I was surprised! So I think one of the advantages we have is that we have a fairly rounded education through to the eighteenth year. But as a result of that, we're more able to respond to someone's request for change, I feel. We, in fact, have an understanding of the job. Instead of like the Charlie Chaplin of Modern Times, *movie where you're doing this, and twisting one note in one direction, you have an understanding of what you're doing, and because the more companies are prepared to explain to you what the result of those consequences are, you can see how it fits in. And as a result, if somebody comes along and says, "We want you to change, because . . . " you can understand that too. And you're more likely to change, happily. [Declan]*

A spillover effect of the change in funding for secondary education was the effect on attitudes about third level educational options. Free secondary education opened the door to greater participation in third level education. It was at this level that the most significant changes in Irish education in support of the information economy subsequently occurred. The concerted effort to provide education appropriate for work in the information sector involved several significant changes in post-secondary education.

3.2.2 Third Level Education

I think it's becoming almost de rigueur for young kids to be pointed towards third level education. It's a little cheaper, probably, or more people can afford it, might be a better way of putting it. There's more places of it. Secondary education is free, and third level was a little easier. See, the good thing about what's also happened here in the last 30 years was your night courses, where you can pick up degrees down here at the local university. Or you can pick up diplomas in the regional technical colleges. A good example is [a woman I know] with an interest in doing engineering, but didn't get enough points to get in here, into the local university. But now she's down in Tralee in the engineering school in the RTC [regional technical college] in the vision technical college. Picking up a diploma will take her two to three years which means that she can then go on to university at night,

do another two to three years and pick up her degree. More
and more people are doing that. [Michael]

While a generally literate workforce resulted from the changed educational policy which made secondary education free and available to all, the technical and business skill requirements for the information economy required that many if not most of these workers also receive some form of post-secondary training. Education in the form of a strong standing in the Leaving Cert was the goal of the majority in Ireland and a solid background in the form of a university degree had long been the expectation of many. However, there was also a change in the emphasis placed upon education. Whereas people had been expected to learn what was needed for the job *on the job,* that task was largely shifted to the university, something that made credentials ever more important.

Nevertheless, during the period from the early 1970s to the early 1990s the American multinational firms still found a less credentialed workforce than in the US.

> *. . . [W]e adjusted somewhat when we came over here in hiring. When we were writing the job specs, in the States [it was]: "Here's the description of the job, here's the type of diploma we're looking for, X amount of experience." By default, we carried that over here. But when you're looking through their resumes, some of them had school, some of them didn't. If you liked them on the interview and they had some experience you kind of forgot about: "Gee there's no college degree there." [Ed]*

Since post-primary education did not become freely available until 1968, only the younger respondents would have had advanced education practically available to them. Many of the older workers would have obtained their experience without the benefit of formal, advanced education. Further, it wasn't until the 1980s that a third level educational infrastructure in support of the information economy was in place. Therefore, only those attending college in the 1980s had had the opportunity to receive third level education appropriate to this work sector.

Irish managers responsible for hiring generally acknowledged that a college degree was fast becoming a prerequisite for employment. Some of this trend was attributed to the recession of the 1980s. People turned to school because jobs weren't available. Ronald, an Irish human resource manager at an American firm, pointed out that young workers in Ireland's information sector increasingly wanted the formal credential because of the added mobility it afforded them. He spoke about how the culture in his firm had been that one would learn the business better from within the company. However, he found that an increasing number of desirable employees wanted to improve themselves by obtaining an MBA, an externally recognized marker of their knowledge and skill.

For such reasons, developing a qualified labor force meant that some changes in orientation in the existing universities were needed. When Ireland embarked upon its journey into the information economy the only form of third level education in existence was the traditional university whose focus was classical not vocational. Courses of study were directed at producing a well-rounded individual, not responding to labor force requirements. Therefore, in order to have an appropriately educated workforce, one area that was addressed was the university itself. Changes were needed in both content and in orientation. They needed to place greater overall emphasis on science and technology, and specific emphasis on computer science, engineering and business. Along with changes in content, universities also needed to change their perception of the role of university education to include preparation for employment and linkages with industry.

But no matter how much or how quickly these schools could have changed, they would not have had sufficient resources to accommodate the number of people who needed access to higher education. Besides adding technical courses of study to the traditional universities, another effort was to create new universities with a specific focus on education for the information economy. The educational establishment rapidly accepted two new universities that reflected this changed mission. The University of Limerick was established in 1972 followed by Dublin City University in 1980. These universities were distinctly different from the traditional universities in several respects. First, their focus was technical and professional education. They were very directly oriented toward technology, science and business. They offered degrees in subjects such as computer science, business, communications and engineering. Further, they operated within the framework of links with industry. One key way in which this was done was through work placements or internships. They adopted the cooperative education model whereby students incorporated periods of work placement into their courses of study.

The relationship between these new universities and the information economy was graphically evident in the case of Wang Laboratories and the University of Limerick. Driving down the Limerick road one encountered a roundabout. The road in one direction would go to the University, the other to Wang Laboratories. This close physical relationship was symbolic of the close working relationship between the two institutions. When I asked representatives of Wang about their decision to locate software and hardware plants in Ireland and specifically Limerick they noted the availability of a well-trained labor force, mostly from the nearby University of Limerick.

Throughout the period of this research I witnessed the rapid acceptance of this new type of university. In 1990 during conversations with respondents about university education or with faculty from other Irish universities, I could detect in people's voices the perception that these universities were not quite "real universities" at the same level as the other Irish universities. However, by the time of follow-up visits in the mid 1990s, there was a noticeable change in perception. For example, during a conversation about careers, one woman expressed her relief that her daughter had achieved the points to gain admission to the prestigious and highly competitive Dublin City University.

While educational policy at the secondary level made it free, educational policy for third level education did not go that far. But comparatively speaking, Irish university education was affordable. In addition, grants were available based upon parental income. The creation of two new universities, the reorientation of others and the availability of grants all worked together to make it much easier for potential IT workers to obtain the kind of educational credentials they needed. In such ways Ireland quite consciously went about reshaping its educational infrastructure.

Over the course of this research project I found ample evidence that Ireland benefited from not having an industrial economy prior to establishing an information economy. The handling of the educational infrastructure is one such example. Because Ireland was not encumbered by work patterns suited to manufacturing and assembly line work, it also had not been burdened with an educational system oriented toward traditional, heavy industry. Therefore, Ireland could start with a clean slate to create educational programs and institutions oriented toward an information rather than a traditional industrial economy. One way it did this was by establishing additional types of third level institutions to supplement the universities. Consequently, a series of regional technical colleges (RTCs) were established in Dublin and throughout the country.[xiii] In this way, the type of education that was needed was brought to the people so that they were not forced to come to the few rapidly growing cities to obtain it.

The final component of the changed educational infrastructure related to adult education. While government programs for job training provided technical skills training, working adults also needed access to higher education. As competition for jobs grew and new entrants to the labor force increasingly had third level degrees, educational credentials became increasingly important. Many individuals who had been able to obtain positions with only the Leaving Certificate in 1980 needed a third level degree for career advancement and mobility in 1990. To provide for this, the universities began to offer both undergraduate and graduate degrees through evening school. Some multinational companies helped further this educational goal by paying the third level fees of their employees. Whereas it was quite commonplace in some other countries for adults to obtain part-time degrees, this was not the case in Ireland. In this culture, higher education had been the purview of the privileged. It was for young people who had the financial resources to attend school full-time before embarking upon their positions of leadership in society. Therefore, providing evening degree programs to working adults was truly opening education up to the masses.

3.2.3   Job Training

> *I'm an Arts graduate, in German and geography. I studied and worked three years in total in Germany. Then I went on a conversion course to computer science offered for grads in Cork FAS. The purpose was to have an understanding of the material covered in the computer science area. We used Pascal. The preparation was for both hardware and software jobs, to prepare you for a job in the industry. Your degree and aptitude were taken into account in this program. [Eileen]*

Technical education provided by the universities and technical colleges was supplemented by the efforts of government agencies, which provided training and employment. In 1988 several agencies were amalgamated into a single agency Foras Aiseauna Saothair (FAS), the Irish Training and Employment Authority. FAS training facilities were situated throughout the country to provide specific job training to young people following their formal education and to offer retraining to the existing labor force. These schemes trained school Leavers in computer technology, in the basics of computerization, office procedures and business operations.

Particularly because of the speed with which a trained labor force was needed, firms received government grants to train their workers as well. A typical incentive package for a multinational firm, for example, would include grants for training. One firm I visited received several thousand pounds per person to educate workers. In exchange the firm was required to show how it used the money.

While FAS provided training courses, the IDA provided grants to both multinational and indigenous firms to support in-house training. Another vehicle for training was government agencies such as EOLAS, the science and technology agency. With funding from the European Union, programs such as the TECHSTART scheme provided financial assistance to a company to employ graduate engineers in order to give them an opportunity to get work experience, thereby keeping them in Ireland. The money covered part of the engineers' salaries for the first few years when they were least productive and the firm was spending money training them. Another government-sponsored program was called the "Work Experience Program." In a fashion similar to TECHSTART, firms received financial assistance with the salaries of new secondary graduates. One Irish firm in my study took on ten people over the duration of this program; all ten either remained at that firm or found full-time employment elsewhere.

Much has been said about the educational quality of the information-sector workforce in Ireland. But it is important to temper these comments with some sensitivity to time. The firms at which I conducted interviews had been in Ireland anywhere from a few months to 20 years. Depending on when they came, the part of Ireland in which they located, and their subsector (i.e. hardware, software, and services), the perception of the respondents differed. For example, those who came around 1980 found a paucity of trained workers. Whereas Sean, an Irish human resources manager at an American firm, observed a substantial level of general education (to the point of some college) on the part of the farmers who were being recruited, these people did not have the specific technical skills that were needed. Hence the firm had to train the staff. This firm did a considerable amount of training because it believed in grooming its workers and promoting from within. Consequently, one influence of Ireland's young, inexperienced population on the information sector was the training that was emphasized a bit more than sites of these firms in other countries.

In examining the transformation of Irish education that accompanied the society's migration from an agricultural to an information economy, certain issues were identified. One significant challenge for both educators and policy makers was maintaining a balance between the kinds of IT jobs available and characteristics of the information-sector labor force emerging from the schools. An important motivator for the industrial policy was to stem the tide of emigration, which had long been a feature of Irish society. Historically, the ones who emigrated were those without employment options, the classic example being the sons who did not inherit the family farm. However, during the 1980s the emigration of Ireland's "best and brightest" became a cause of concern. In 1981 8.1% of Ireland's graduates had emigrated; by 1987 the proportion had risen to 25.6% (Higher Education Authority, 1988). These individuals emigrated for a variety of reasons. Some wanted to gain work experience abroad while they were young. Others left to avoid the high tax burden in Ireland. However, many left because there were not sufficient jobs suited to the type of education they had received. Electronic engineers complained that the multinational companies' failure to locate the research and development function in Ireland limited their employment prospects following graduation.

The country was loosing out in several respects when its well-educated graduates emigrated. First, Ireland lost the contribution that these young people could make to the information sector. Second, return on the State's investment in education was lost when graduates went abroad to work. Finally, many of the scarce spaces in the universities were being taken by students who did not remain in Ireland.

> *I think at the family level it has a certain tragedy because so many of those go overseas because there isn't enough growth in the economy, change in the economy to keep them at home. One impact is that a lot of youngsters who are well educated are leaving the country. That's generally accepted, I think, to be a loss to the economy. On the other hand, it's a boon to the high tech information sector. It's raw material, almost sitting here waiting to be employed. And the way it's employed is in two ways. Either by locating here or by coming here on very heavy recruitment contacts. Philips, for example, in The Netherlands, is renowned for coming over recruiting 50 to 80 technically qualified graduates in one swoop. I know people embellish the story a bit and suddenly there's a Boeing 747 full of the cream of our engineering graduates just queuing into Eindhoven. So the way those of us who live here would like to see it developing is more by investment, actually come and locate here. Leave these people in good living environments, good work environments. In doing so contribute to the economy's growth rather than seeing them do the same jobs effectively overseas. [Martin]*

For a country such as Ireland, where the industrial policy and its supporting infrastructure were enacted in the context of an overall plan, it would be consistent to conduct national monitoring of employment trends and maintain close coordination between industry and academe. Another response was attracting firms that required the kinds of skills that graduates possessed. Over the period of this industrial policy, high tech employment had migrated from lower level, minimally skilled jobs to more sophisticated work. This was evidenced in companies such as Intel, which came to Ireland in 1990 to produce its newest generation of microprocessor chips.

Part of the problem of matching educational qualifications with available employment was attributed to the reluctance of the universities to accept their new role as the bridge between education and employment. Several examples point this out. Liam, an executive at an indigenous firm complained about trying to recruit engineers from one of the universities. Because of the placement office's failure to adequately advertise the positions in his firm, he said, all the available graduates took positions with foreign firms never knowing about employment opportunities at home. Irish information-sector workers, in turn, complained that traditional universities did not introduce information technology courses soon enough. Some of them were forced to turn to programs provided by FAS following their formal education in order to acquire the needed skills.

Martin, who was a successful entrepreneur, believed that there were enough jobs for graduates with technological degrees; the problem, he said, was an insufficient number of young people with both *education* and *experience*. His recommendation was to emphasize cooperative education programs, which are ideally suited to provide this dual form of credentialing. Yet some of the schools had been reluctant to incorporate what they perceived to be such a blatantly vocational element into their curricula. In describing his own work history, Martin told me how he had to leave his university position after his start-up company was established. The concept of the "incubator"[xiv] did not exist in the early 1970s when he began his company. Such close ties between formal education and industrial application were resisted in academe by those who saw these linkages as somehow contrary to the educational mission.

The educational infrastructure in Ireland was undergoing a transformation no less dramatic than what was occurring in society as a whole. Many more students were obtaining a third level education. In 1986 25% of those who had obtained the Leaving Certificate entered institutions of higher education. There was a significant shift from an emphasis on traditional arts subjects like language, history and geography to science and technology. In 1986 41% of new entrants were studying science and technology and 22% were studying commerce (Clancy, 1988).

There was also a change in the educational qualifications of those who emigrated. In the latter part of the 1980s the educational attainment of the emigrants saw about one-third of them having third level education in comparison with less than 20% in the period from the 1960s to the late 1980s. Fitz Gerald (1995, pp. 5-6) found that while those with a good education were more likely to emigrate than those with only a primary education, they were also more likely to come back. In 1991 over a quarter of all those in the country who possessed third level qualifications had lived abroad for at least a year. This meant that when calculating the return on investment in education, Ireland needed to take a medium term view. Despite the outflow of graduates, their eventual return with additional experience from working abroad actually meant education had been enhanced by emigration.

4.   MIDDLE CLASS

> *The "us-them" doesn't apply to multinational IT firms. The Irish population would resist this sort of thing. Ireland is a classless society -- middle class. In Britain, on the other hand, people will or will not talk to you, depending upon your status. [Aidan]*

Social class stratification is one topic that interested me from the very beginning of this project because of the contradictions I experienced early on. At the start of my year in Ireland, during an orientation program for the Fulbright Scholars, an Irish historian who was characterizing Irish society made a point of emphasizing the absence of a strong class system in Ireland. However, what I had read, experiences I had had, and comments I had heard provided evidence to the contrary. A series of articles in the *Irish Times* about the class system noted that in Ireland the social class of one's parents was a predictor of one's own social class more than in any of the other western European societies with which it was compared (O'Toole, 1990b, p. 17).

Symbolizing the change in the type of work and the educational requirements for doing it was the transformation of the Customs House docks in Dublin which was underway as these interviews were being conducted. Long a source of employment which did not require formal education, the docks were being replaced by the construction of a new International Financial Services Centre. The children of generations of dockworkers would no longer be able to look to the docks for their livelihoods unless they became educated information services workers.

> *I drive past the financial sector where they're building the docks. I remember when I was going to school. One of my*

> *school pal's father used to work on that side, loading and
> unloading ships. It was all done by crane. It was all manual,
> and the containers were a novelty at that stage. Now that
> whole area is totally redundant. [Colin]*

What interested me was the connection between social class and
participation in the information economy. I wondered about the ease with
which individuals from different social classes would be able to participate in
the information economy and the middle class life that it allowed. Simple
reasoning holds that since work in the information sector generally requires
more skill than that of traditional industries, the main threshold is educational:
those who can obtain a third level education should be able to acquire the
necessary qualifications to become software developers, for example. But
what about working class people whose parents and grandparents had worked
in the trades or been laborers on the docks? I wondered what barriers might
exist for the working class people who would be shifting from manual to
intellectual work. Did one have to come from the middle class in order to
work in this sector? What effect was this sector having on social mobility
from working and agrarian classes to the middle class?

4.1   Signifiers of Social Class

Some of the indicators of social class initially escaped my understanding.
But through repeated exposure and reflection I came to identify four signifiers
of social class in Irish society: surname and family background, accent and
address, school and type of education, and religion.[xv]

> *[T]he thing I certainly noticed is that because people here
> are less anonymous and because they have predefined roles
> to play and characteristics because of where they come from
> and who they're known to be, that it's very difficult for them
> to make any kind of change or to break the mold. So, for
> example, if you have an employee who's trying to make the
> switch from being an employee to being a member of
> management, they will find it much harder than somebody in
> the States will have done to make that transition. Because
> everybody knows where they have come from and everybody
> knows who they're supposed to be and how they're supposed
> to behave. [Sue]*

This observation by Sue, an American woman who worked outside the IT
sector, sums up a sentiment that was repeatedly conveyed to me in a myriad of

ways: your family background places you in a certain social class within which you should remain. I was told that a person from modest circumstances might be perceived as a "young upstart" if he or she displayed too much inclination to improve her or his status. Various expressions were used to characterize the begrudging attitude toward those who attempted to move beyond their station.

> *In most other countries if you make it somewhere else you're accepted. Whereas here if you make it, people still say, "Yeah, well OK you're brilliant, but your father wasn't."*
> *[Cahal]*

Martin had done considerable business in the US. He noted a difference in that Americans didn't really want to know what your father did or whether you were monied or not before they engaged in a transaction with you. Basically, it was what you could do, or what you had done.

While the influence of family background was very strong in Ireland, the situation was not static. For example, the trend toward married women working outside the home was introducing cultural changes. Children who were attending day care centers in their formative years were acquiring attitudes, beliefs and traits not only of their parents but of the caregivers as well. Another factor was the growth of the locale where one lived. In places experiencing rapid growth there were so many newcomers that where a person's "people" came from was less relevant.

I was exposed to the second indicator of social class -- address -- before I even arrived in Ireland. While still in the States I met with some representatives of different Irish governmental agencies to collect background information about Irish culture. During our conversations about the practicalities of living in Dublin Barry, a trade representative, gave me consistent and sometimes not-too-subtle advice to live on the south side of the city and the River Liffy.[xvi] Once I got to Ireland I understood the reason. Going back to colonial times the Liffy River, running through City Centre, marked the economic and cultural divide in Dublin: the Anglo-Irish Protestant Ascendancy class lived on the south side while the Irish Catholic, working class lived on the north side.

The past lives into the present. The south side of the city became home to the professional and middle class neighborhoods while the north side remained largely working class neighborhoods. During interviews respondents frequently used address to convey social standing. When providing information about themselves or others, people would frequently make reference to postal code. This also occurred during informal conversations with both information-sector workers and other Irish people.

They live in Dublin 4.

When I inquired about barriers to working class people succeeding in Irish society, Julie, an Irish woman with working class roots, said that some employers were likely to use the return address of a job application as a screening device: the letter was automatically put in the trash bin if it was from the wrong side of town. Consequently, it was commonplace for job applicants to "borrow" someone's address. Closely related to the proper address was having the proper accent. However, it seemed that accent and address were having less of an effect on information-sector workers because of the strong emphasis on skills and experience.

> *You'll always hear things like, "Well, he has the wrong accent," [but] . . . you'll find that in IT it's not so bad because I've worked in places where you need staff, you just get them in. There's one girl who worked for me, she lived in an [underclass] area . . . which is the pits. It's an awful place. And the language she used, Jaysus! They didn't care, you just did your job. It's probably good, in a way, if you're so short of staff and you get somebody who has the experience, you'll take them on. [Cahal]*

The connection between education and social class had several dimensions. Whether one went beyond national school, whether one went to trade-oriented secondary school or boarding school, whether one acquired third level credentials and in which field, were all connected to social class. Nuala, a young programmer working at an Irish software firm, explained that whereas in Britain people had capital wealth to pass on to their children, the Irish had little of that. But what they could pass on was education. Consequently, in the post-independence class system in Ireland one's educational background became intimately connected to social standing.

I was provided with one unsolicited piece of information that I initially found peculiar. It was the name of the religious order of nuns, brothers or priests who taught the respondents. This information would be tacked on at the end of an answer about their educational backgrounds. Whereas I simply wanted to know if they had acquired the Leaving Cert or had attended third level education, they wanted to tell me who taught them.

It was a Jesuit school.

It became clear to me that religious order was yet another indicator of social class when I understood that different religious orders ministered to students of different social classes. For example, the Jesuits taught the sons of the middle class and Christian Brothers taught those in the working class.

A variation on the theme of education as a signifier of social class was the role of education in placing someone *in* a particular social class, whether in society in general or within a firm, in particular. Credentials, themselves, helped to reinforce a social divide. Margie spoke of the elitist attitude on the part of people who had university degrees toward those who did not, and the resentment toward those "graduates." In this particular American firm the divide reflected a cultural change. In the early days people were hired without formal credentials. But the shift toward recruiting workers with more formal credentials had caused a rift between long time and recently hired workers.

4.2 Social Class Attitudes and Behaviors

> *It is hard to get away, blood is thicker than water, you know?*
> *So, if you were raised in an environment -- you mightn't want*
> *to believe it, but -- you are influenced by your parents, the*
> *people that you've grown up with. They actually form the*
> *framework for, I think, a lot of your own personal standards.*
> *But, you can change it, it's up to yourself if you decide. Like,*
> *I could have been a farmer, right? Sometimes I wonder*
> *maybe I should have been but, financially, it's much better*
> *now than it was 20 years ago. But if you're convinced you*
> *want to try something else, I think you'll get all the*
> *encouragement in the world. The docker's son or something,*
> *if he really wants he can go to college at night because you*
> *can do some kind of classes, you want to give him a chance, I*
> *think. But there is a bit of status. [Jim]*

Jim was a software developer at a multinational firm. His comments suggest not only that different social classes have different attitudes but also that these attitudes were passed down from one generation to another.

4.2.1 Middle Class Attitudes[xvii]

A set of middle class attitudes that were reflected in the comments of the information-sector workers centered around being financially independent, confident in relationships with management and comfortable in the material world. Francis talked at length about the middle class value system he received from his parents. Prior to working in the information sector he had worked in a range of positions including traditional manufacturing. He spoke about the early years of his marriage and career. Though their income level would have qualified them for government-subsidized housing, Francis and his wife never considered that option. That wasn't the way he was brought up. Rather, he was reared to depend upon his own resources to get on in life, not to be dependent upon the government. Francis went on to talk about middle class attitudes in the workplace. At the Irish firm where he worked there was none of the "us-them" relationship between management and workers which he characterized as a working class attitude.

When Deirdre spoke of the middle class family in which she was raised, there was a noteworthy absence of status markers such as money or position or social standing. In fact, she said her parents were very contemptuous of those who were impressed by big cars and such things. Their evaluation of people was based upon whether or not they were enjoyable company. The worst thing that her parents could say about anybody was that "He's a bore." To them, the most important element in their evaluation of a holiday or a dinner party or people was simply, "Were they good fun?"

An attitude of self sufficiency, being comfortable in one's own skin and not overly concerned about material wealth stood in contrast with other middle class attitudes which I encountered. At the information-sector firms I visited these other attitudes were only rarely in evidence though respondents did mention them and I sometimes observed them in Irish society. What was emerging was a new breed of Irish who possessed both greater materialism and the earning potential to afford such comforts. For these young people, the information sector was an avenue for achieving their financial goals. On each successive visit to Ireland I witnessed increased evidence of the modern, material world.

A final middle class attitude that I encountered is part of the legacy of colonialism captured in the term West Brit. This label is applied to those who still adhere to the social class ethic of colonial Ireland. To be called a West Brit is to be perceived as a person who has or aspires to have the status held by the Anglo-Irish Ascendancy in colonial Ireland. These may be individuals possessing "old money" whose social and financial status derived from property, education and long established connections. Other times it applies to people who simply aspire to such a status. Julie expressed her feelings about such people.

> . . . *[A]n awful lot of people would treat Ireland as though it was part of England . [T]hey put ourselves and the country down. Put the people down. A lot of so-called Irish people.*

ET: The West Brits?

Yes. They say the worst trait we Irish have is putting ourselves down. We've been put down for long enough that we should be able to get away from that now and appreciate our own selves. I heard a very irritating comment on a TV program. They were talking about some English person who's been interviewed on Irish television. And they're saying, "Back on the mainland," which they mean, of course, to be Britain: England, Scotland and Wales. "Back on the mainland." And they probably could tie it down further, they probably really mean England. But they see this country as being still part of the United Kingdom. [Julie]

The general consensus among information-sector workers was that while many or most of them were middle class they were not West Brits. It may have been the case in the traditional Irish industries which were heavily influenced by England -- ship building, transport, the civil service -- but not in the information sector. The general consensus was that because information technology was newer it had different guiding rules, directives and patterns. The information sector was not completely immune from the influence of social status, however. Deirdre told me about an Irish IT manager whose influence within a professional association seemed to be derived more from his own social class than the status of his firm in Ireland.

[He] is a West Brit. Yet most are not his class. Even though [his firm] isn't big here, [he] is viewed as the head [of the association]. [Deidre]

4.2.2 Working Class Attitudes

The contradictory and perhaps ambivalent attitude about social class that was evident in discussions about the middle class was also evident during discussions about -- and in my observations of -- the working class. On the one hand, people wanted to downplay the importance of class differences.

There had never been an industrial revolution in Ireland. Therefore, there were no "bad habits" to overcome [regarding] how the working population was treated, like in the UK with the miners. There was no class system. There had been a leveling off, partly because of the famine and Ireland's colonial status. [Seamus]

On the other hand I witnessed educational and attitudinal barriers that kept working class people from moving up in society. Julie had made her way from her working class origins into a middle class life by working in the information sector. Because she got in on the ground floor, Julie's lack of formal education -- she stopped at the Inter Cert -- did not hold her back. But now that this information sector was maturer, employers were increasing their expectations about educational credentials, often requiring a university degree. Nevertheless, Julie told me that none of her younger cousins -- those who would need educational credentials in order to find the kind of employment she currently had in the information sector – were going to college. She thought the change in attitude and behavior would take more time. Each generation was going a step ahead of its parents. Her aunts and uncles stopped at age 14 with national school education and went straight to work. Her cousins were doing the Inter Cert and possibly the Leaving Cert. They were advancing their education by making one jump ahead in each generation. She thought that perhaps the sons and daughters of these cousins would then go a step ahead of their parents and on to college. It would be too big a jump for the parents who had received only primary education to have a son or daughter picking up a university degree

To parents who were able to obtain employment without much formal education, the notion of a child remaining out of the workforce until the age of 18 or 21 might seem wasteful, a loss of income to the family. These semi- or unskilled workers have historically worked as manual laborers on farms or in the cities. However, the need for this type of work in Ireland has sharply declined. Children of these workers are much less likely to find similar employment. Indeed, much of the impetus for a new industrial policy was to respond to this decline. The jobs that were replacing them required brain-rather than muscle-power, and some form of post-secondary education.

Another working class barrier that emerged was an attitude about remaining in one's place. Besides a mindset that did not make the link between education and social mobility was one that *resented* those who did.

> *. . . an example [is my husband] working in the ESB [Electricity Supply Board]. He didn't have a degree and he was very ambitious and very hard working. He was doing his part-time studies and picking up his certificates and diplomas, etc. One of the senior people in ESB talked to him at some point and said he shouldn't be getting ideas above his station concerning his career, that he was an electrician and he didn't have his degree, so he shouldn't expect to go*

any further than that. So in other words, "You have your
place. Now stay in it." [Julie]

In America, with its immigrant ethic, parents expect their children to do better
than they. This has not been the case in Ireland. If parents did have that goal,
they would probably have expected their children to go abroad to achieve it.
Further, the self-made person in Ireland was not always accepted, often
becoming a target of ridicule. As they put it, very often such people could not
hold up their heads and let success rest easily on their shoulders.

Some thought that barriers to social mobility were diminishing. But in
saying this, people always qualified their comments. While it was becoming
acceptable for one to be doing better for her- or himself, it was not becoming
acceptable to put on airs like the man who went off to London in search of a
better life.

He came back a regular Cockney. He made a fool of himself.
If he had gone over and become manager of the Bank of
England and come back talking normal, he would have been
accepted but the fact that he'd go out and try to be something
he wasn't [was not accepted]. Being hoity toity when really
they're not upper crust, that kind of thing. Certainly, people
would frown on that. People, I think, would like you to just be
yourself. [Charles]

They also said social mobility through employment depended upon what
type of employment it was and where it was located. In traditional sectors the
social class of one's parents might influence one's social standing even if two
people were doing the same jobs and earning the same money. In a small
town, there might be more class-consciousness than in the cities. The
information sector, however, seemed to be at the forefront of lowering
barriers. While these attitudes about strict social class boundaries may have
existed among their parents, it was less prevalent among the young workers in
the IT firms. The typical view among the IT workers was that if people
wanted to get ahead, they would. This viewpoint takes on added import as the
route to power becomes more dependent upon one's intellectual capital and
less on inherited capital.

Deirdre made a connection between openness to social mobility and
diversity. She talked about her firm's "valuing diversity" program and how
she initially saw it as an American issue: one of race and ethnicity. But once
her firm began to hold diversity workshops she began to understand it in
broader terms that included social class as well.

4.3   Social Class and Employment in the Information Economy

Programmers are young, well educated, from the middle class. [Dermot]

An initial question that I brought to my research was about the influence of social class on one's participation in the information economy. As my research progressed three questions about social class and the information economy emerged. The first question was: Why or in what way does information-sector work fit the criteria for middle class work? A derivative question was: Are the markers of this employment sector different from the markers of other types of middle class employment? The third question was: Is there any stratification within the information sector by social class?

There was a perception that employment in this sector provided a means of remaining in or entering the middle class. To understand why I considered the criteria for middle class jobs in other sectors in Ireland; there were five. The first criterion for middle class employment was some formal education followed, perhaps, by some additional qualification for admission. An example of the former was being a teacher; and example of the latter was being a solicitor. To the extent that information-sector employment required educational credentials to participate it satisfied this criterion. The second criterion, which more or less derived from educational qualifications, was that the position be a "white collar" job. This type of position would sit in contrast to a job in the trades, for example, or on a factory assembly line. Before Ireland's movement into the information economy a typical middle class position would be one in the civil service.

The third criterion was income. Work in this sector afforded one a level of material comfort sufficient to qualify for middle class status. This criterion, however, was not that prominent. In Ireland income, alone, did not qualify one for membership in the middle class. Another criterion for middle class membership was that the position conveyed some status or authority to the person holding it. I found that employment in the information sector was being added to the list of professions typically conferring status in Ireland. Others were education, medicine and law.

Because it's a high tech industry it has a certain mystique among friends and relations. Tell your granny you're working with computers and she's delighted at this and doesn't understand it but she's terribly proud of you sort of a thing. [Connor]

The final criterion for middle class membership was personal control over one's job and/or career mobility. There was a perception that while working class people in factories needed the help of unions, professional people in middle class offices did not need such protections.

> *ET: Well, do you think it's appropriate to have unions in high tech companies?*
>
> *I think a lot of the unions have very little actually to offer. Now I would totally defend trade unions as necessary tools to defend working class interests.*
>
> *ET: What about defending middle class interests? That's who tends to be working in the information technology industry.*
>
> *Yeah, that's why it's not as relevant in software development, in that kind of industry. It's not as relevant because people don't need protection. I don't need protection. [Nuala]*

Having identified the ways in which information-sector work fit the criteria for membership in the middle class, I also noted three characteristics of this sector that were different from traditional sectors in their definition of middle class and working class jobs. The first was that the boundaries were more permeable. The boundaries around the legal and education professions, for example, were clear. One had to obtain a certain degree, pass qualifying exams, etc. in order to enter. While the middle class position of manager was bounded to a lesser extent, the movement still existed within a rigid set of constraints. Ethna, an Irish woman who had worked in the Irish financial sector before coming to work at an American IT firm, explained this situation by describing the middle class position of bank manager.

> *In the bank you had to be under 21 to be hired. Therefore, if you are young you perceive it as a secure job with a good salary and a reputable position. You are socialized into the bank; you don't know anything else. You could move from lower middle to upper middle class through being at the bank. [Ethna]*

In contrast, one could enter the information sector by going through a variety of educational doors. Further, there were varying amounts of education required. While some certification exams existed, it was not universally required as it was in the professions of law, medicine and education, for example.

Another difference was that title and appearance could be deceptive. Whereas office workers in traditional industries would not be considered middle class, in the information sector they might. For example, since a computer programmer or system designer works at a desk in an office he or she could legitimately be classified as an "office worker." In a traditional sector one would have to be in a certain level of management in order to have a job considered middle class. However, in the information sector, one could be an individual contributor in an office and yet satisfy the criteria for middle class membership.

The final difference was perhaps the most noteworthy. It was that this line of work was generally considered a "technical position" something historically akin to a trade and, thus, considered to be a working class job. Nuala spoke to this point when she compared the status of engineers in Ireland and the UK.

> *In Britain engineers and people related to sort of engineering industries have a very low status. And this is definitely reflected in salaries there and here. [T]hey hired engineers and they treated them the same as they would craftsmen and that. Whereas here, we started off from more of an educational base. There was no real throwback to the seventeenth and eighteenth centuries here whereas you would have had in Britain. So we started off with a fresh educational system and people who could do the business technologically speaking but were well regarded for it. I think engineering types have a higher status here than they would in Britain as well. I don't think there's as rigid a class structure. [Nuala]*

The last sentence of Nuala's comments, notwithstanding, I did observe a stratification within the information sector by social class. I found that people working in software companies tended to be from the middle class whereas people working in the hardware companies tended to represent a combination of middle, working as well and agrarian classes. Both the firm nationality and the particular type of work helped to explain why this would be the case.

One big reason that working in the software subsector drew people from the middle class was that specific skills were needed to work as a programmer. Another reason was that software firms tended to be Irish. Being Irish they also tended to be smaller than the multinational firms. As such, they were less able to absorb the costs of training people. In the early years of the information sector -- when there were not enough qualified programmers to be found and the universities were not yet equipped to produce them -- it was easier to find employment in software after having taken a government-sponsored program of study such as those funded by FAS. However, in the latter part of the 1980s and certainly in the 1990s it became easier for these firms to hire people who were university graduates and already trained. Since working class youths were less likely to attend university than their middle class counterparts, it would be the exception to the rule for a working class person to attain a position in an Irish software firm.

> ET: *Would the people who work for this company or typically the other software companies, would they have middle class backgrounds?*
>
> *Yes. It's because people can afford to send their kids to college. It's a money and education thing. [We have] one of our chaps who didn't go to college, who would come from probably lower middle class, maybe, who had done a lot of his own self-development, but he's the exception. [Sean]*

Finally, Irish firms tended to be more influenced by social class signifiers in hiring than were multinational firms.

> *Well you do have things like working class people tend to live in certain areas for starters. And that would certainly go against children of working class people getting jobs. [Paul]*

On more than one occasion respondents working in software firms who *did not* have technical skills -- they worked in marketing or management capacities -- specifically told me that it was the high level of their general education, their breeding, and their accents which were important factors taken into account when they were hired.

In contrast, I found that workers in the hardware subsector were drawn from all three classes. A number of factors explained this. The hardware firms, being more multinational and larger, could more easily afford to train people who had not received the proper skills in school. In addition to being in a better position to train people, they also had a broader range of work to be done. The hardware firms had some work that was lower skilled. They were also located in regions all over the country whereas software firms tended to be in Dublin. Therefore, they could hire people from working class backgrounds if they were located in a city or from a rural background if they were located in the country. Finally, multinational firms were less influenced by social class signifiers. People at these firms did not seem to care that much about the part of town one was from or what one's father or grandfather did for a living. Neither did accent have much impact. The need to hire people who could or could not learn to do the job was the overriding consideration. Besides, the nuances of accent would probably have been lost on the non-Irish hiring managers at multinational firms. As a new industry, the information sector had less societal baggage; it relied more on education and skills. To the extent that one had those she or he could get on at the firm.

> *They are recruiting the sons and daughters of ordinary people, unlike [this other non IT firm] where you had to have clout to get an office job. So there is less snobbery in these new industries. I think some of this new management style is coming from the home country of the multinationals, but I also think it is coming from the educational system. It had an elitist background. Then it became available to ordinary people. [Brendan]*

As evidence of this, Ethna said workers at her firm came from both sides of the Liffy River. With respect to the necessary skills she said people in assembly did not need any special training while people from working class backgrounds who wanted to work in areas requiring specialized skills might take a few months' course or obtain a certificate from a third level technical institution. In addition, some of the firms would offer tuition reimbursement for individuals who would like to attend university part-time.

I found it noteworthy that the American multinational firms provided more evidence that the information economy was making a difference in class options and mobility. This was exemplified in the exercise Deirdre took me through. As I sat there she read through a list of the highest-ranking managers at her multinational firm. Their parents were shop clerks, bus drivers and small farmers.

> *None of them would probably have been able to achieve these jobs in a traditional firm. I'm amazed, but it always fascinates me, actually, to look at some of the senior people in [this firm]. I know what their background is, right. And if you look at the jump, right, in one generation, it is amazing. [Deidre]*

My interest in understanding the connection between working class people and the information technology sector had to do with the new types of employment that the information economy was bringing about. Working class people who had historically worked more with their hands than with their heads were having to change their orientation in order to find a place in this new economy. Some information-sector employment has characteristics that bear a resemblance to working class jobs as much as to middle class jobs. When this fact is added to the explosive growth of information-sector jobs since the 1970s it is not hard to conclude that there is, indeed, a place at the information table for people from all types of backgrounds.

In talking about information-sector work it is important to understand the range of different jobs that exist. Positions in software development houses are in line with professional positions in other sectors to the extent that educational credentials are required and workers have some personal power in the workplace. In contrast, production jobs at a hardware firm could have many of the characteristics of a manufacturing firm in any sector. Because the work done by these workers would be lower skilled and more easily replaceable, workers would have less personal power in the workplace.

Ironically, since some of the work required considerable technical skill, working class technicians had the advantage in the beginning over middle class people who wanted to enter the information sector. Some of the earliest IT workers came from technical colleges not universities. Consequently, many senior people in electronics were those who had been at the regional technical colleges not the universities.

They are the ones with skill, not the 'Rugby/bank' people.[xviii]
[Deidre]

4.4 Social Class in the Information Age

If you're a kid growing up in a poor housing estate in Galway, your father is unemployed, your mother has four or five kids, no education. Living there in 1977 it wasn't the done thing to go on to secondary school if you were a bright kid, and so you would drop out. My primary school was more working class than middle class -- a Christian Brothers school. . . Only one other guy went on to Inter Cert with me. [But] he was a "macho guy" who wouldn't consider college.
[William]

Whereas membership in a particular social class had derived from one's family (and the land and money they did or didn't have), the information economy was changing the basis of social class membership to intellectual capital. To a large extent, then, social mobility hinges on education. The social policy that developed in Ireland held that, theoretically, anyone in Ireland could attain any educational qualifications she or he chose as long as the person had the intellectual capacity for it. But reality interjects some complexities into this neat equation. There were several factors that influenced the ease with which someone from the working class was able to use employment in the information sector as a vehicle for social mobility.

I wondered about barriers to working class people gaining the education needed for employment in the information sector. It seemed that many of the barriers to upward mobility in Ireland were attitudinal. There were few absolute barriers. Just about anybody could actually progress up through Leaving Certificate without having barriers placed in their way. However, this theoretical situation had to be balanced against the reality of pressure on young people lower on the socio-economic ladder to start working as soon as they could. In addition to income lost to the family while a young person is in school instead of working, there was also the matter of the fees for attending university or other third level institution. Yet despite the changing employment landscape and the obvious advantages of obtaining educational credentials, there were still people who did not avail themselves of these opportunities.

> Why a working class kid can't make it in the post-industrial world is not because of lack of knowledge, but because of barriers to the source of knowledge, that is, from the lack of parental role modeling and lack of funds to go to the right schools. [Matthew]

Parental and family influence seemed to be the key. Some workers from uneducated families received little to negative reinforcement to obtain an education. There were others, however, whose parents may not have gone to college themselves but who had emphasized learning. Both cases serve to illustrate the important role of family support. Money wasn't the only barrier; desire was also needed. Similarly, to the extent that middle class people had computers in their homes and the children developed technological literacy at an early age, they had an advantage both in skill development and in knowing about the range of career options available to them.

Another dimension of the barrier discussion was the effect of free secondary education on the masses. Nuala, whose father was a secondary school teacher, noted that before secondary education was free, those few working class people who got scholarships were studying in an environment which valued education and reinforced the need to learn. But, once free education became available, these students were now mixed with people who had lower ambition, whose parents had lower educational ambitions. Consequently in schools located in working class communities it often became more difficult to teach the good students because of the resistance that was imparted to the students by their environment. In certain respects, then, the brightest working class students suffered from the policy of greater access.

> *There has traditionally been a rigid barrier between classes.*
> *I expect this to remain except for bright, educated*
> *individuals. Not-so-bright middle class kids go to college.*
> *Not-so-bright working class kids don't. [Eileen]*

Class divisions in the information sector were observable in several ways. One was simply the number of working class people who made their way into the multinational firms. Another was stratification based upon social class. Even though there was a wider range of social class backgrounds in the multinational firms, clouds were appearing on the horizon as the set of minimum credentials rose. The social class gap was most dramatic, however, upon examination of the labor force in Irish IT firms. These firms tended to emphasize the software rather than the hardware aspects of the field. However, this type of work required significantly more educational background than assembly work for computer manufacture. Consequently, the workers at indigenous firms were predominantly of the middle class.

However, despite any barriers to employment in Irish information-sector firms based upon social class, the respondents were unanimous that it was easier for working class people to work in an Irish high tech company than to achieve similar social status in another sector. There was agreement that the information economy was one of the places where working class people in Ireland could, indeed, move up. In order to obtain employment in the information sector one did not need contacts as one would in other fields such as medicine or law.

The Irish information industry was in a position to provide distinct benefits to the working class. In theory, working class people were able, in their jobs, to satisfy criteria for middle class positions. Because the work required skill, both the government and societal norms about the value of education were changing. Secondary education became available and free. Consequently, working class people began to obtain marketable qualifications in the information workplace. This "clean" work was being done in a positive work environment, which was financially rewarding.

> *Before we just used to be white collar worker, blue collar*
> *worker kind of thing. White collar would look down on blue*
> *collar, there was always that distinction. All of those things*
> *are changing now. Because obviously, the administrative*
> *kind of jobs are decreasing and technical jobs are coming to*

the fore, you know? But I think there would be still a sort of snobbish element about what a person does. Primarily, of course, based on what he can have, not what he does, I don't think [Irish people] would be terribly fussy about the position provided the position produces good money. [Stephanie]

Finally, because skilled positions in the information economy were in demand they conferred status and personal control over one's employment. Technical people continued to rise in status as their skills were sought.

There was one viewpoint about information-sector work and social mobility that I found particularly intriguing. It was that the path to becoming an information-sector worker was consistent with working class attitudes about the relationship between education and employment: one learned in order to obtain a job. This clear link between skill and craft has been extended to high tech work. Just as someone in the trades would do an apprenticeship to become a qualified plumber or electrician, in the information sector one studies computer science or engineering. In both cases education is tightly connected to employment. However, another piece of the educational role in social mobility introduced a different kind of skill development. Some of my respondents talked about the additional need to develop an overall sense of professionalism and the attendant skills for successful participation in middle class circles.

Throughout my interviews about social class I tried to resolve the discrepancy I had experienced early on: Irish people professing to live in a classless society while at the same time sending strong signals about class consciousness. I determined that some of this was the legacy of colonialism that produced a rigid "us-them" situation. The members of the upper class were the Anglo-Irish aristocracy. The Irish weren't well off enough to create their own individual classes until quite recently. It had only been in recent decades that Irish people had begun to be wealthy in their own right. In relative terms, then, Irish people could speak of their society as "classless." Perhaps this was why people did not speak of an upper class when delineating the class system in Ireland. Instead, people were stratified according to middle class, working class and agricultural class. After witnessing the ambivalence about the class system I concluded that people's comments about a classless society expressed wishful thinking about what *ought* to be the case.

5.   CONCLUSION

A leisurely walk through the Temple Bar section of Dublin on a Friday evening in summer 1999 provides, perhaps, the best evidence that Ireland has become even more of a young person's country than it was ten years ago. What had been a crumbling, artists' enclave with a few old pubs has been transformed into a modern, youth-oriented cultural mecca. In 1998 40% of Ireland's population was under 25 and 55% was under 35, making it the youngest population in Europe. What has added to the youth of this population is the recent trend of returning émigrés. A recent survey commissioned by Intel found that 80% of Irish graduates would return if they could secure a comparable job in Ireland. A June 1999 Irish job fair sponsored by Enterprise Ireland was held in Boston and other American cities in order to attract not only IT firms but also IT workers (from Ireland and other countries) to Ireland.

The youth of Ireland's population continues to be a significant cultural characteristic that is influencing the development of its information sector. The young workforce in Ireland makes it especially suited for the software subsector. Inexperience can be a drawback in another sector and had been a concern of some in the software subsector. However, the pace of innovation and the radical technological changes accompanying it obviate the need for experience with prior generations of software. In other industries or the trades age brings respect because of the connection between experience and skill. But in the software subsector the driving force is the energy and quickmindedness of the young people. The flexibility of the Irish workforce continues to be emphasized and valued.[xix] This helps to explain why the software subsector has taken off so explosively in Ireland. More than 60% of business application software sold in Europe is manufactured in Ireland and 300 indigenous software companies are servicing local and international markets from Ireland (Houston, 1999, p. 18).

As with the youth of the population, the education they possess continues to be a linchpin of Ireland's information economy. Secondary education has been adapted to support the direction of Ireland's employment market. In 1996, 77% of Irish students completed the Leaving Certificate (The Economist Intelligence Unit, 1998) and almost 40% of these graduates went on to third level education (IDA Ireland, 1997a), giving it one of the highest third level enrollment rates in the OECD (The Economist Intelligence Unit, 1998). Ireland now has the second highest proportion of the population aged 25 to 34 with a third level qualification in the EU (IDA Ireland, 1998). Over the past ten years the number of full time third level students in university has increased by almost 80% and the number of full time students in technical institutions has more than doubled (Enterprise Ireland, 1999). The policy change in 1996, which eliminated third level fees, has, no doubt, contributed to the large number of young people continuing their education.

Reflecting the impact of the information economy on Ireland's economic health and reinforcing the direct link between education and employment, there has been a dramatic shift in the focus of study at the third level. Sixty percent of Ireland's third level students are now majoring in engineering, science or business studies (IDA Ireland, 1997a). Ireland now produces more mathematics, science and engineering graduates as a proportion of all graduates than any other OECD country except Japan (The Economist Intelligence Unit, 1998).

To further align itself with the needs of the information economy, institutions of higher education have expanded their offerings on a number of fronts. In addition to enhanced university curricula in the areas of science, technology and business, there has also been an expansion of other forms of third level education. One-year conversion courses for graduates with qualifications in non-computing disciplines have been funded (National Software Directorate, 1998b) and a special Science and Technology Fund was created to finance training in the latest information and communications technologies. Much of this is to be allocated to vocational training in third level institutes of technology: the former RTCs (The Economist Intelligence Unit, 1998). In addition, close ties between industry and academe help to ensure that the human resources needed to fuel Ireland's information economy will continue to be available. For example, in 1998 IBM engaged in a project with local schools adjacent to its campus in Dublin to link the schools and libraries to the Internet to enable teachers, students and parents to explore the ways in which new technologies can support education and training (Houston, 1999, p. 13).

---

[i] In my interviews the Dutch company Philips was often given as an example of this trend.

[ii] The topic of unions is considered in greater detail in Chapter 7.

[iii] The topic of exposure to the outside world is considered in more detail in Chapter 6.

[iv] The Leaving Certificate is the Irish equivalent of a high school diploma.

[v] This section draws from a previously published work (Trauth, 1993a) which examined issues surrounding the education of information professionals in Ireland.

^{vi} The term "hedge school" refers to the way education was conducted in order to be away from the prying eyes of the colonial power structure: classes were typically conducted out doors in fields or behind a hedge.

^{vii} These findings are supported by those of an American study of the skills and knowledge required of information systems professionals (Trauth, Farwell and Lee, 1993).

^{viii} University College Dublin, University College Galway and University College Cork.

^{ix} Curriculum Vitae or resume.

^x The secondary school structure in Ireland is divided into two phases. The Junior Cycle lasting three years until the age of 14 or 15 culminates in a series of examinations on specific subjects for which one receives the Intermediate Certificate (Inter Cert). The Senior Cycle lasting two to three years, involves similar examinations, and results in the Leaving Certificate (Leaving Cert). Attaining certain points or exam grades on the Leaving Cert is the basis upon which admission to third level institutions and particular programs within them is determined.

^{xi} This meant people under the age of 35.

^{xii} I personally witnessed this emphasis on education in Ireland. Following completion of the Leaving Cert exams, the daily newspapers would publish the results and the points that would be needed for admission to the various programs and universities.

^{xiii} O'Riain (1997), p. 12.

^{xiv} An incubator is a supportive environment in which new high tech firms can develop. These are usually established in conjunction with one or more universities or research centers in a certain geographic location.

^{xv} Since religion is treated in Chapter 6, I do not discuss it here.

^{xvi} The well meaning advice, notwithstanding, I stayed with my initial inclination and lived on the north side of Dublin.

^{xvii} As an American I came to see that the definition of the middle class in Ireland is somewhat different from what I was used to in the United States. Individuals assigned to the middle class in Ireland would be in the upper middle or professional class in America.

^{xviii} In Ireland the sport of Rugby is associated with Anglo-Irish and/or upper middle class people, as is also the case for being a bank manager.

^{xix} In a chapter on job hunting, Houston (1999) instructs job applicants to highlight their flexibility and ability to cope with change in job interviews noting that: "The importance of these skills cannot be stressed enough." (136)

CHAPTER 4. A FAMILY MAN

1. INTRODUCTION

I was at a conference recently and was the only woman in a group of 30 fairly senior attendees. One man who was there said there were not enough women represented. There are lots of women programmers [but not that many women managers in this field]. This is a very traditional society. People are shocked that I am 34 and unmarried. I think the barrier to women's progress is inside women themselves. It is still frowned upon for a mother to work. [Patricia]

The argument that the information sector transcended traditional barriers to diverse employee participation was introduced in Chapter 3. In theory, anyone who could get the education could participate in the information economy because it was "brain not brawn" that mattered. But the ideal of a meritocracy is far different from the reality that is embedded in a particular socio-cultural context. In Ireland, family and gender are inextricably intertwined with each other and with the culture of the information sector. There was clear evidence that the emerging information economy was having an impact on both families and female participation in that workforce. However, I also found evidence that the Irish culture was exerting an influence on the makeup and behavior of the information-sector workforce.

2. MALE

I think the main barrier that I would be more concerned about is the barrier of male-female in society. There are a lot of people who are anti-female. Sometimes incredibly subtle.

ET: You mean in terms of the workplace?

In terms of what people can do, right? There's men's jobs, women's jobs, and women don't do certain things. Now, I think where I see a problem isn't so much that side of things because there is legislation. That is, if you've got enough neck you can get a radish. You can bash your way through because these things are wrong and you've got right on your side. If you're sufficiently determined to do it. But I certainly think that women in this country -- and this is going back into history and the matriarchy and everything else -- have got ability. Just like everybody else's ability. Where I always feel that women are letting themselves down, for want of a better term, is that they have been brainwashed into thinking they cannot do things. They've been brainwashed through all their childhood. It's not the man standing there saying, "No, you can't do that. You're a woman," It's much more subtle than that. The woman didn't just arrive at a particular stage in her life. She has been conditioned all the way along into thinking that "I'm only a woman. I can't do certain things." I see this particularly on my course [at university], for instance, where in the class which starts off, you've got 75 people. There were about eight or nine women. [Colin]

Women were definitely present in the information sector workforce and their voices were also present in this study.[i] However, while the information sector provided more opportunities for women than traditional industry and business, complete equality between the genders remained an elusive goal. Women did not have the same presence in the Irish information sector that they did in America, for example. This was particularly the case in the middle and upper management echelons of the firms in Ireland. Women tended to work at the lower levels in the corporate hierarchy and to work in hardware assembly rather than software development.

Gender in Irish society as it relates to the information economy particularly interested me for a couple of reasons. One was academic. I expected that the position of women in the IT sector in Ireland would be a good way to examine both the *influence* of socio-cultural factors on the structure of the emerging information sector in Ireland and the *impact* that this new sector was having on values and behaviors such as those associated with women working in a technical field. The other reason was personal. As a woman who grew up in an era when women in the US had more limited technical career opportunities than they do today, I was curious to explore this dimension in another society.

I ended up with four major observations about women in the information sector in Ireland.[ii]

First, as with social class, both men and women believed that the information technology field gave women greater opportunities than other sectors. Nevertheless, women were not equal participants in this emerging industry. Second, despite better career opportunities, the tension between career and family was holding most women back, in one form or another, in their careers. Third, barriers to women's advancement in the information sector were embedded in the institutions of Irish culture and in attitudes about women and their place in Irish society. My final observation was that in many instances the nationality of the employing information sector firm helped to explain differences in perceptions: people who worked at American multinational firms often had viewpoints which were different from those of workers at Irish IT firms.

2.1 Women in the Information Sector

The presence of multinational IT firms in Ireland has had a positive impact on women in the Irish labor force.[iii] There was general agreement that this industry was much better than traditional industries, had less discrimination than banks, for example, and was less male-oriented than the civil service.[iv] This positive perception existed along side the acknowledged stereotype of programming as a male activity.

If women found it easier to get on in the information industry, my question was: Why? I learned that part of the answer could be found in the nature of the work, itself, and part could be found in the way in which this sector was developing in Ireland. The information sector was a good work setting for women because it was a new industry and, as such, hadn't had as much time for the old, traditional, patterns to develop. There had been less time for traditions regarding gender-typed work to establish themselves. On numerous occasions women drew contrasts between high tech companies and banks, which they viewed as male domains. Since the computer field was wide open, they believed women would have more of a chance because there would be fewer prejudices. Further, because this industry depends upon intellectual not physical strength, women can theoretically compete equally with men. Skill was what counted.

The other reason for greater opportunity resulted from the way in which the IT field was developing in Ireland. Because the information sector was dominated by American multinational firms, values about gender that existed in America had been transmitted to Ireland through the medium of *corporate* culture. Since a firm's corporate culture derives, in part, from the national culture of the individuals shaping it, it is reasonable to expect American norms regarding gender to be reflected in management practices. Therefore, to the extent that the IT industry developed through the presence of American multinational firms, the accompanying values about gender roles would permeate the Irish IT industry, thereby influencing both men and women in the workplace. My research results show that this was occurring.

Irish women thought that greater gender diversity in the US made Americans more used to seeing women in important positions, as Elizabeth pointed out. However, as a middle aged woman who had worked at American firms in other industries before taking a job in the IT sector, she noted that there was a difference in the treatment of women at the multinationals depending on the industry. She gave as an example an early American multinational company in the chemicals industry. This firm came to Ireland before the IT firms. She said the strong, capable women working there were passed over for promotions. In her view, it was only American *information technology* businesses that were advanced with respect to women. She said the prevalent view was that if you were capable, and could improve yourself, and a job was open you might get it.

To underscore the influence of American culture on the corporate cultures of the multinational firms, it is noteworthy that all those women who believed that it was easier for women to get on in IT because of the American influence, worked at American firms. Deirdre spoke about this topic from her vantage point of working as a human resources manager.

> *ET: Do you think that it's easier for a woman to get on in the electronics than in traditional industry?*
>
> *Relatively speaking, yes. Definitely. Because there is a culture of equality, equal benefits, equal opportunities.*
>
> *ET: Do you think any of that has to do with the fact that it's an American based multinational?*
>
> *Yes, I do. Definitely, It has a lot to do with it. I think the whole equality thrust in the group, the same benefits for people is very much American initiated. And a single status [for everyone]. I mean, in [this American IT firm], for example, they will tell you the stories, [about an Irish non IT firm] in Cork, they had about four different dining rooms. They had the executive dining room, senior management dining room, middle management dining room. You know,*

they had special car park spaces. You know, this was one of the status symbols of how you got on. How well you were doing. All those are thrown out by companies such as [ours]. When [our firm] started, a lot of the things that they did -- single status, and similar benefits, one canteen, treating people on the floor, equal contribution -- was unique and it was radical in Ireland at the time. Now it's practically the norm. And you're out of date if you talk any different kind of language. [Deidre]

Because of the characteristics of the industry and the way in which it was developing, people perceived less gender discrimination at multinationals. Ethna worked in a middle management position at an American firm in Dublin. She was never conscious of being a female at her job where both the financial controller and the MIS manager were women. However, at the bank where she worked previously, she was well aware of discrimination against women.

The comments by Irish men working in American firms were strongly consistent with the view of females that this sector was much more welcoming to women.

I don't think the people are used to seeing women in traditional industry. I think that a lot of it is climatization. In the high tech industry, because, for instance in the electronics engineering sense you had a high proportion of female graduates who went on to become product engineers and designers and so forth. And some of whom went on to become engineering managers. That was acceptable. It was considered normal. If you look at the traditional engineering area, first of all, the environment tends to be more hostile. And you generally have not just the physical environment but the people there [as a deterrent]. [Brian]

American men working in and managing American firms also believed this sector to be more progressive than others.

Irish men working in Irish firms agreed as well. In the traditional work environments men tended to assume that work was their prerogative, it's what they should do and should achieve and the woman's place was in the home. In the high tech environment, they said, where women could use their intellectual skills without needing manual skills to go with it, things were working out particularly well for women. However, part of the problem was motivating schoolgirls to aim for such careers. There were still too many females aiming for such jobs as airhostess, jobs seen as having glamour but which were limited in terms of career advancement, or who planned to work in an office but did not plan to make it a career and become a manager. Too many went into clerical positions and were not actually managing and achieving.

Colin explained the plight of women in more traditional sectors like banking by telling me about his wife. It was taking them a long time to start a family. Because they didn't know whether they were going to be able to have children it seemed perfectly sensible to both of them that she pursue a career. When she applied to become an assistant manager, however, one manager was very happy to put her case forward while another was openly against and the third was decidedly indifferent. He and his wife found it frustrating that while she had been in the bank ten years and was meeting with this resistance, men who had been there half the time had already advanced past her to become assistant managers.

Sean, an Irish entrepreneur who ran a software firm, attributed the improved opportunities in the information sector to the emphasis on brainpower over physical power. Technical fields, which were stereotypically physical ones -- such as civil or mechanical engineering -- were predominantly male whereas computer science was more gender balanced in the schools. In his firm the head of software was a woman as was the lead programmer.

2.2   The Career - Family Dilemma

The other side of the opportunity coin was the set of barriers to women. These barriers existed both within women and within the larger society. A fundamental question that arose repeatedly during the interviews with both women and men was whether Irish women *wanted* to have careers. One group of Irish women thought that women did not see themselves having a career outside the home. They did not think there were many women who really wanted to rise up through the ranks to become managers. Julie, for example, commented that many women who thought they wanted a career changed their minds once they had children. These comments were equally divided among those who worked at American and at Irish firms. Another group of women believed that Irish women did want to have a career. In their view, the attitude had changed so that there were many more women looking for careers or wanting to work outside the home than in the past. Nearly all those who expressed this point of view worked at American firms.

Despite the tensions between work and family, the emerging reality in Irish society was that women with families did work outside the home. Only 36% of the women I interviewed were single. Fifty-two percent had children and 12% were married without children. This number of married women working was much higher than the population as a whole. The number of married women in the workforce had risen sharply from 5% of women in 1961 to 23% in 1989. The overall percentage of women who worked had remained constant since 1961 at 30% of all women. With the birth of each additional child, however, women's participation levels were halved (Callan and Farrell, 1991, pp. 31, 34).

Wickham and Murray's (1987) study of women in the Irish electronics industry revealed that over 50% of the workers in this industry were women (9). Age was an important factor in these considerations. Most of the workers in the information sector were under 35 and it was within this age cohort that working mothers were fast becoming the norm.

> *ET: Is it socially acceptable for a mother to work? Within the under 35 set?*
>
> *I would definitely say it would be.*
>
> *ET: What about the over 35?*
>
> *I would imagine it would be different. It's to do with the environment or the conditioning the people have been brought up to. I suppose you could say progress is a very questionable thing in relation to where we are at on the scale. We would be behind where America would be in the cycle, whether that's good, bad or indifferent is another question. What will be looked upon as the more traditional views would be more prevalent in Ireland than they are in the States. That's just a question of the development of the society. [John]*

But it appeared that financial rather than feminist motives were the reason. It was economic necessity that made it socially acceptable for a mother to work outside the home. If a woman had to work for economic reasons it was acceptable. However, if she worked because she chose to work, she received less approval. People recognized that an improved standard of living with the accompanying mortgages and bills often required the wife's financial input. As with the other viewpoints about women and work, most of the women who believed that it was socially acceptable for mothers to work were either American or worked in American firms.

This sentiment was echoed in the male perspective. Neil worked for an American firm. While he acknowledged that some people thought that a mother shouldn't work, he believed that pure economics drove the trend toward a two-income family. In contrast, Colm who was working at an Irish software start-up firm, contrasted the ethics of "work to live" and "live to work" when offering his thoughts on women and careers. In his view, the reason women worked after having children was that the family wanted to sustain a certain materialistic standard of living. He said many families' reluctance to "tighten the belt" a bit was the reason for a two-career family.

In the comments of men working in Irish firms there was no mention of personal fulfillment as a reason that women might want to have jobs outside the home or would want a particular career. Only those men working at American firms acknowledged that some of the motivation for women working outside the home might come from personal fulfillment needs. The male perspective also noted a shift in viewpoint about working women that coincided with the wave of high tech firms coming to Ireland in the early 1980s. Accompanying this change was the potential for husbands of working wives to take greater responsibility for the children. Men, for example, might have to leave work on time to pick up the children from day care, they said. Still, the working wife was not seen as the accepted norm among younger married people in Ireland.

More negative than positive comments were made during discussions with female respondents about mothers working outside the home. They talked about societal approval, the difficulties of returning to a technical field after maternity leave, and the day-to-day difficulties encountered by a mother with a job outside the home. The societal infrastructure as reflected in the operating hours of banks, stores and day care centers was not set up to accommodate women working outside the home. To some degree what was underlying all these views about married women working was the scarcity of jobs. There was a sentiment that a married woman who worked outside the home was taking a job away from some other family.

> *ET: What is the general societal attitude toward women working?*
>
> *It is that if jobs are scarce why have two partners working? "Isn't she married and her husband working?" If a married woman returns to work it's even worse. It's viewed as taking a job from a young, single girl. I think the underlying view is women should be kept with the menial jobs because they will be leaving them anyway. [Patricia]*

This attitude was reinforced by the companion belief that a child should be at home with its mother, not in some childcare facility. Some of the women admitted to feeling guilty about having jobs outside the home. The major complaint was the amount of time spent away from home. They complained that it was extremely difficult -- if not impossible -- to give the hours expected at work in order to get ahead and still have time for some meaningful family life. As a result, the working mothers believed, those women who stayed home were looked upon in society as better mothers. Anne who was from a farming background noted the irony. The issue was not a mother working; in rural Ireland mothers worked, she said. The difference was that they worked at home. She went on to say that by leaving the home to work, she felt torn and had a sense of guilt about leaving the children or not being there when they returned from school.

The women spoke in a rueful tone about balancing work and family. They acknowledge the societal views yet nearly all of them were working mothers. Mary, who was also from the agrarian West, talked about the trade-offs between agrarian and information economy work in terms of the quality of life. On the one hand, she had more money and the opportunity to get dressed up each day and go into the city. On the other hand, she thought it was definitely easier to be a working mother if the work was on the family farm rather than in an information technology firm. She thought it was easier to have a family life in a rural setting, despite the economic hardships. Working in these new industries was hard on families because it required that one leave the home to work and because of the long hours -- in some cases exacerbated by a long journey from the country into the city. The general conclusion was that families were not as close knit, as they had been when Ireland was a predominantly agrarian society.

A minority of women with whom I spoke had the opinion that women with children *should* stay home, that staying at home could be more rewarding than going out of the house to work.

> *I agree with the old idea about a mother's role being at home. About not divided loyalties. I have seen kids some of whose mothers work. Where the mother stays at home, the character of the kids is better. If I had a family and didn't need the money. I'd stay at home. I liked that my mother was always around when I was young. [Elizabeth]*

****

> *I don't understand the women who say, "I'd be a vegetable if I stayed at home. I would not have any adults to talk to. I*

*would go crazy with a child all day long." There is an
enormous amount of stuff that they could do. What is
intellectually stimulating about sitting at a typewriter all day
long? I remember talking to a woman at some point and
saying, "How could you choose to spend time in here as
against time with your child at home? Time at home with
your child? Spending time with it? Seeing its reactions,
seeing it taking its first steps?" Very shortly after that she did
pack it in and go home. I don't know whether I had anything
to do with that but I could not understand. The job she was
doing was not interesting. There was no way in the world she
was getting any stimulation from that. [Julie]*

The predominance of marriage and motherhood as the typical life
trajectory coupled with the ambivalence about mothers working outside the
home gave rise to a question: If women did not see themselves as having a
career, why was it that equal percentages of both female and male students
(25%) went on to higher education (Clancy, 1988, p. 53)? I learned that there
were, in fact, several answers to this question.

Many career-oriented women resolved this dilemma by marrying and
having children later. In this "early retirement" approach, many Irish women
had careers for about ten years following attainment of their university
degrees, which they then left upon the commencement of marriage or
motherhood. Patricia, who was in her late twenties, worked at an American
multinational firm recently arrived in Ireland. She noted that she was the only
one out of her eight school friends who was married yet did not have children.
I found it interesting that this was the case for women with professional
qualifications such as engineering, medicine and law as well as for those in
less skilled occupations. Eileen, who was a programming manager at an
American software firm, noted that her mother, a physician, stayed at home
while raising her family. This point of view was reinforced in interviews with
men. They talked about how the economics of parenthood favored even
women who were engineers quitting their jobs. Given the high taxes on wages
and the cost of childcare, an economic case could be made for the mother not
working outside the home.

This behavior provided partial explanation for the attitude in the workplace
that management should not invest many resources in women because they
would not be around "for the long haul." Both women and men held this view.
Kathleen, who worked at an Irish IT firm, spoke about the attitude in her
secondary school in the late 1970s. Girls were overtly encouraged to go to

university and get a job but the message behind all that was to marry and have children.

> *You were expected to be high achievers, yet fellow students thought it was weird that one of our classmates wanted to go into engineering. The general attitude in my age group is that we will work but deep down, we don't want to work until age 65. My father thinks I should be at home. He does not appreciate the independence I have by virtue of my job, that I have a say in [domestic] decision making. [Kathleen]*

Paul worked at a multinational plant and offered his explanation for why women's careers were abbreviated: women had to bear the children and, by implication, be the primary care giver as well.

> *And therefore I've heard people in here, one manager in here before said he wouldn't invest money in sending our female technicians on courses because all they're going to do eventually is get married anyway. Which I thought was a terrible thing for him to say. Even if he thought it, he really should have kept his mouth shut! I know a woman I am working with now on a project. She's not married, she has a boyfriend, her career seems to be very important to her. I don't know whether she wants to have children and settle down. But she would probably be the exception. [Paul]*

A second approach that women took was to attempt to retain their careers while rearing children. Some American respondents observed that Irish women resented the idea of being required to stay at home yet felt a conflict between career and home. When the topic of balancing career and family was raised, it was always women working at American companies who commented on this topic. Their comments centered around the heavy time demands imposed by their positions and the subsequent toll it might be taking on their families. They said the number of hours expected at work militated against women. They said women then backed away when they saw what was expected of them. In their view, men's perception that women were not ambitious was not accurate. The real reason, they said, was that it was difficult to give the hours demanded at work and still have time for family responsibilities. Thus, because family was so strong there was a reluctance to give total commitment to work. Deirdre summed it up.

> *Of course, there is that women are not putting themselves forward. But the real question is "Why?" That's the answer*

> *you always get from men. "They're not putting themselves forward," "They're not ambitious," "They will not do it." But, of course, we know that there is a complex set of reasons why that is the case. Some of it has to do with the amount of hours and commitment that is required in an industry such as ours. On personal choice they do not want to make that decision. I mean a lot of men here -- senior guys -- get strung up every now and then about how much time they're not spending with their families. If you really talk to them, and if you get them to open up, they are very worried about that. And they get a lot of grief at home about that, right. But they do not change. Ambition, I think, supersedes all that. That is simply not the case for women. I don't think we find it as easy to kind of toss it off. Most of the women that you talk to, mothers that I talk to, it's not about not wanting to work or not wanting to get on. Of course they want to get on, same as anybody else, and realize their potential. But they're very concerned and guilty about what effect that's having on their children, and they will pull back. That'll go on the back burner. [Deidre]*

The male perspective was not substantially different. A frequently expressed viewpoint was that whereas women with families sometimes stayed in the workforce they were not so inclined to want to move up through the ranks because they placed too much emphasis on life outside of work. Neil articulated the mindset that helped account for the minimal involvement of women in management positions in Irish industry. He said a lot of men had the attitude that the woman should be at home. They would employ her for a while but they expected her to eventually leave to get married and have children. Therefore, if there were a man and a woman up for promotion the inclination would be to give it to the man because the woman probably wouldn't be around in a few years' time anyway.

When giving his perception of the role of family in Ireland, Eric believed that family emphasis meant that the father provided for the children economically and the mother spent the actual time with them. This sentiment was echoed by Eugene, an Irish man whom I interviewed in the US before departing for Ireland.

> *Irish value their free time. There isn't "women's lib" as there is in the States. In Ireland men can go out for drinks after*

work. In the US they must get home to be with the family.
[Eugene]

When I began my on-site interviews and learned about the importance of the pub in social and work life I often reflected on Eugene's comment and wondered about the women workers. If they too went to the pub after work like their male counterparts who was at home minding the children? And if they did not go to the pub, would this impede their chances of getting on at the company?

Stephen, a young Irish entrepreneur, agreed with what seemed to be the prevailing view among members of both genders that it was easier for women to get on in the information sector than in others because it was new and expanding in Ireland. His take on why women didn't seem to progress as fast or as far as men was that this must be what women wanted, that this was the natural order of things. Tom was a young engineer working at an Irish firm. His response was somewhat contradictory. He started off by saying that people under 30 thought it was great for a woman to get on in her career. But, he then went on to observe that he never encountered women in his line of work. Further, he said that to be on maternity leave even for six months in a small company in an aggressive high tech area would be difficult. He, personally, thought a mother should stay home but only for a few years if she were an engineer. And if she were good, she might be able to get back into her career once again. The message written between the lines was that the cards would be stacked against such a woman as evidenced by the fact that he did not encounter any women in the course of his own engineering work.

Sean noted that the top two people in his company happened to be women. He then went on to share his perception that they both intended to pursue their careers to the exclusion of family, and explained why:

> *I think that in the IT industry where there is a strong demand*
> *for flexible time, sometimes very long working hours,*
> *practically speaking, it's difficult if it's working mothers with*
> *childcare duties. It's not as easy. For instance, Fiona is to be*
> *in the UK for the next three months. She couldn't do that if*
> *she has a family. She couldn't ring up the husband and say,*
> *"I'm going to the UK this evening for two days. I won't see*
> *you until Friday." The nature of the IT industry, I think, is*
> *that that happens. You have to respond, and you have to go.*
> *[Sean]*

On the other hand, several Irish men in speaking about redundancies in the multinational firms noted that the impact was lessened in Ireland because those taking the voluntary redundancies tended to be married women who wanted to leave the workforce anyway. Aidan, who worked at an American firm, explained that there were two types of women in IT and her type would determine her attitude toward her job and her behavior in it.

> *One is the minority [two women at his firm]. . . They are professional, often unmarried, career people and will make significant progress. The second type is the majority: 40 women at his firm]. They are the opposite. They will eventually leave work at a young age. . . Females have a difference in attitude, they are less committed. If they are made redundant then they will have more time with the kids. They have a "take the money and run" attitude. If they don't get chosen to be made redundant then they have bad morale. They see being made redundant as a reward. However, if a woman quits it's harder for her to get another job. Women come with a package of problems. Females are vastly less reliable, they are more temperamental than males. There is also a higher absenteeism due to family priorities. If the kids are sick the mother is out. Then there is the disruption caused when they go on maternity leave. Kids are a woman problem. [Aidan]*

The issue of childcare was closely linked to the decision about working outside the home. A minority of the women respondents believed that childcare was and should be provided by family members. Mary noted that she would only leave her child with another family member. While the majority of women noted that using a crèche[v] represents the most common form of childcare, they also observed that there were not enough, the cost was high, and that they were not coordinated with parents' work hours. A mother holding a job outside the home was sometimes not cost-justifiable.

A third option for resolving the dilemma was to make a mutually exclusive choice between either career or family.[vi]

> *I deal with mostly women in senior positions in [the US office of the firm]. They are all married with children. In contrast, in Ireland, senior position women are usually unmarried or have no children. Or they have their own company. [Eileen]*

During some of the interviews with older women who may have been obliged to make this difficult choice, a hint of resentment could be detected in discussions about career and family. Younger women respondents observed that these older women were sometimes difficult to work for. Perhaps because they had had to make a clear choice between career and family, they were not as sympathetic to the position of younger women attempting to have it all. The women also noted the obvious double standard in evidence. They noted that Irish men could have both a family and career advancement. Eileen cited her own situation as a case in point. All the other managers at her firm were men and were married as well. She was the only manager at the firm who was a woman and she was the only manager who was unmarried.

> *About women, 50% of my workers are women. I think they have more loyalty than men but then they aren't married. [Tom]*

Eric observed that at his firm the male workers on the factory floor assumed that the young, single women working in the factory would not marry. This was partly due to an assumption that women who wanted to work also wanted to remain single. Their evidence was that the women didn't try to make themselves look attractive at work. Tom explained that women who worked in engineering seemed to be less feminine

> *. . . wearing jeans instead of a dress and perfume. The field seems to attract that type of woman. [Tom]*

2.3   Gender Barriers and the Information Sector

Besides the career-family dilemma, other barriers that were preventing women from taking an equal place with men at the IT table were embedded in cultural attitudes and societal institutions. Women expressed a general feeling of inequality within Irish society. They believed there was discrimination both in obtaining and advancing in their jobs. Other barriers seemed to be embedded in Irish institutions. When asked about the current position of women in Ireland, half of the female respondents said women were losing their rights, that they were treated as second class citizens, and that married women were paid less than men. They also said women were stereotyped in the workplace, that they had to scream louder to get heard. As a result, they said, women who expected equal treatment were categorized as troublemakers or, like the woman at one firm, developed a reputation of always fighting to prove something.

Some male respondents agreed with these sentiments. Eric observed that everywhere he looked it was the mother who was taking care of the children. In his view, men would be threatened by married professional women who also had families. To bolster his opinion he gave some examples. At the time of the interview Eric had recently attended a European Union dinner in Ireland along with another man and a woman from his firm. He noted that there were two hundred people in attendance, ten of whom were women. Of the ten women in attendance, eight were waitresses. His other example was about society in general.

> *I was offered membership in an exclusive tennis club in Dublin. I commented on the long waiting list and they told me they would make an exception for me. Then the man said there are more and more female professionals and they are the ones put on the long waiting list. Whereas, as an American and a man I was instantly made a member of the club. [Eric]*

Dan was a programmer at an Irish firm. He thought that women in IT were on an equal level with men as far as official management practices went. He said that while he had never observed overt discrimination or sexual harassment, there was subtle bias beneath the surface. He said some older men -- those in their 50s -- looked down on women who worked in the information sector. He said some men had trouble accepting a woman as the boss. Men sometimes didn't quite know how to relate to a woman co-worker thinking they could "chat her up" as though they were in a pub.

Neil noted that the government was working against discrimination in areas such as pay because a woman still didn't earn as much as her male counterpart who was doing the same job. He said that while in his own work environment women were given the same opportunities and were treated the same as men, in other work environments in Ireland that was not the case. No matter what the work environment and no matter how open it was, in order for a woman to get on she always felt she had to be better than her male counterpart, said Nuala.

> *People wondered how I could advise people about computing since I was a woman. At [my firm] I was the only technical woman in the beginning. Boys are taught how to brag, to exploit and brag. There was a guy at work who would always hassle the women. No matter how I distinguish myself, I can never escape being a woman. My sister-in-law noticed that I am now more assertive, bragging about my skills now. Men have the confidence, will give "flyers"[vii] right away. [Nuala]*

The women viewed themselves as insecure, and the men as having confidence. My own experience in conducting this research bears this out. In more than half of the interviews with women there was some noticeable undercurrent. They were more reluctant than men to have the interviews tape-recorded. Those respondents who were the most defensive and least willing to open up tended to be women. These individuals' reactions ranged from aloof and noncommittal to resentful. For example, in contrast with interviews with men -- the vast majority of which occurred at the firm and during the workday, Nuala wanted the interview to be conducted after work hours and away from the workplace. When I arrived at the agreed upon location, I was met not only by her but also by her sister and two male colleagues from university. The circumstances of my interview with Fiona, a young, single woman who was marketing manager at an Irish firm, were similarly arresting. After both she and her boss agreed beforehand to a 90-minute interview, she made me wait for 30 minutes into my appointment before she would see me. When I finally was escorted into her office, she looked at her watch and said, "Well, I can spare 30 minutes to talk with you." Since I am a woman, this type of response from those of my own gender was unexpected. On the contrary, I had expected it to be easier to talk with women respondents. When I raised this issue with my university colleagues, one man quipped: "They're just not able to lie as well as men!" I understood his point to be that the men with whom I spoke had more confidence about and experience with managing a public persona.

At the same time that some women were citing examples of discrimination, a minority of them expressed the view that women *deserved* the treatment they got. Julie observed that women contributed to the lower status attributed to the homemaker role when they made disparaging comments like, "Oh, I'm just a housewife," when asked what she did. Stephanie, a middle aged, woman working at an American firm, expressed sentiments similar to those I heard from her male counterparts:

> *I am afraid I am "anti woman." I think they are too emotional and then there is the problem of pregnancy and guaranteed [four months] maternity leave. [Stephanie]*

Discrimination in employment has historically been both blatant and accepted in Ireland. Until the early 1970s a marriage bar was in effect whereby women working in the civil service were required to leave their jobs upon marriage.[viii] This policy was unofficially extended into other sectors to the extent that women employed in the service industries, banks, local authorities and semi-state bodies would resign from their employment upon marriage.[ix] Since the service sector has been the major source of employment for women in Ireland -- 62% of females employed in 1961 and 75% in 1981 were in the service sector with one-third to two-fifths of these in the public sector in these respective years -- the marriage bar limited a broad arena of opportunities to a certain type of worker: unmarried women or males (Pyle, 1990, p. 87).

Stephanie related her own personal story about the marriage bar. She was employed at Aer Lingus when she got married in April 1964. The marriage bar meant that she could not continue working. While there was no question of her returning to permanent work, she did manage to get hired on as a temporary summer employee in passenger handling, her old department. She thought she was probably one of the first married females to return, even on a temporary basis. She worked from May until October of that year. However, she went back to the minimum of the salary scale.

> *. . . despite the fact that I was coming back to do exactly the*
> *job I had left to change my name! [Stephanie]*

But she appeared to harbor no resentment. That was just the way things were. While there was a cultural rationale for this marriage bar, there was also a compelling economic reason: during the post war era of the 1950s when unemployment was very high, this measure was used as a way of increasing employment for young people. Once a woman got married it was assumed that her husband was responsible for her and the children, so she no longer needed a job.

In 1977 employers in all sectors were prohibited from discriminating against married women by the Antidiscrimination Act (Clancy et al., 1988, p. 301). But even though the marriage bar no longer existed, the underlying rationale remained. If jobs were scarce they should be rationed and shared. Consequently, there was a negative attitude toward married women working. Some of the women, themselves, said they thought that married women should not work in order that single people could have jobs.

Interestingly, the antidiscrimination legislation that was enacted largely in response to European Union requirements on gender equality had, in certain respects, an opposite effect. Since employers would be required to provide mothers with four months' paid maternity leave, some employers were reluctant to hire women in the first place. Stephanie agreed with this attitude.

> *Well, if I were in charge of human resources I'd probably*
> *discriminate against women too. You know, if I've got two*
> *candidates and one of them was always going to go off*
> *getting pregnant. . . [Stephanie]*

The women believed that the barriers to women advancing in their careers were not so much due to overt discrimination as to perceptions about the role of women in Irish society. Because of the early retirement phenomenon, there was perhaps unconscious discrimination born of the assumption that a woman was not interested in a job for the long haul. Further, it was difficult for a woman in IT because of the long hours and the dual roles that a working mother had to play in Ireland. Simply by extension, unmarried women or those without children got treated as less serious as well. They emphasized the fact that because women were not viewed as in it for the long term, they were kept at low level positions; it was expected that all women would eventually leave.

Leo offered his observation that the work environment at the Irish site of his firm was more sexist than what he was accustomed to. He cited an issue about a secretary who wanted to avail herself of some education benefits offered by the firm. There was resistance on the grounds that she didn't really need the education; one could get secretaries anywhere. The firm did not have to make an effort to retain women workers.

Views such as these suggest why it was uncommon for women to be holding senior positions in a company. But the majority of women respondents took pains to point out that the absence of women in senior positions was *not* due to a lack of qualified women interested in advancing. Rather, women simply moved up through the ranks very slowly. One woman who had been at a firm for quite a few years noted that several men who entered the company after her were at levels above her. While overt discrimination had diminished and legal sanctions existed, there was still discriminatory behavior that was an outgrowth of long held attitudes which some people were reluctant to give up.

Irish men tended to echo the sentiment of the women that it was easier for women to have careers in the information sector than in more traditional sectors. Given the proper credentials it had become relatively easy for women to find entry-level positions. The issue was progressing into senior positions. For example, at one of the Irish firms I visited 50% of the workers were women yet there were no women managers. When it came to discussing the reasons, male and female viewpoints began to diverge. While women claimed that qualified women did exist, men believed there was a shortage of women at this level rather than a desire to hold them back. In general, men expressed some consternation on this topic. They weren't quite sure if the paucity of senior women was attributable to a perception of limited opportunity that drove them away or to other factors. I asked for reaction to the conclusion I had drawn from my interviews with female respondents: women were able to get into the workforce but didn't seem to be able to progress. They agreed.

> *I think that's true, yes. And, if you look at the individual case, there is not an individual company that says, "Well we don't have [women] at that level to be promoted," but it's a cultural thing. If the women don't perceive that they have the opportunities then they lose interest or they leave or whatever. [Gerald]*

Tom gave an interesting response to the question about women in the information sector moving forward in their careers. His explanation for why the three women engineers who had worked at his firm had left was that they couldn't handle the intensive work schedule like the male engineers. However, later in the interview he pointed out that 50% of the male engineers had also left the firm.

2.3.1   Gender and Education

One institution that has had a definite influence on a women's position in the information sector is education. The success of Ireland's current industrial policy has depended heavily upon its educational system. Unlike agricultural or industrial work, companies in the information industry required employees with extensive, specialized skills and knowledge. And despite some traditionally held views about a woman's role, the tradition that girls don't go to college appeared to be gone, as both respondents' comments and statistics have born out. Parents wanted their daughters to be educated; most children were encouraged to go to college. In one sense, this was good news for women: the recognition that IT was a new industry where "brains not brawn" was needed. Therefore, if women could avail themselves of education and resolve the career-family dilemma, they could get on in this field.

However, to the extent that female students were unable to obtain the skills and knowledge needed in this industry, education represented a barrier to women. Indeed, some of the women gave examples from their own experience of these barriers. They said that when courses of study in computer applications were introduced in the secondary schools -- the vast majority of which were gender segregated -- girls were educated in a gender-stereotyped way, such as how to create a home budget. They were also hampered by the view that mathematics was a male subject. Nuala was particularly vocal about her views on gender and education. Among other things she spoke about her father's influence -- on her, personally, and on the school where he taught -- in changing that situation. It was the norm where he taught in the 1930s that girls were sent off to cooking classes while boys were studying maths. However, he used that time to teach the boys classics so that the girls could learn maths as well when they returned! She credited her father's enlightened view -- which also caused him to send his daughters to a school that offered the best maths curriculum at the time -- for her ability to enter the computer field. Kathleen recalled being told in 1976 in the convent school, "Now girls, this is very difficult," as the introduction to every maths instruction. In retrospect, she thought that this statement more accurately reflected the discomfort felt by the teachers who had no real qualifications to teach the subject than it did the students' feelings.

The reason for singling out mathematics is that attaining a certain level of competency in this subject in secondary school is a prerequisite to entrance into computer programs at the university. Therefore, to the extent that secondary schools provided unequal mathematics backgrounds to boys and girls, they served as a barrier to women's entry into the IT field. For example, some girls' schools were not offering the kind of mathematics background required for admission to the university computing and engineering programs. Nuala explained that honors maths was required for admission to the university program she wanted to attend, yet her secondary school did not offer it. Patricia noted that boys' schools offered honors maths and honors physics; girls' schools offered chemistry, biology and maths but not at the honors level. To her, girls were at a distinct educational disadvantage and were sent a clear message in the lack of honors maths. She observed that girls had internalized these constraints. When she was in university in the 1970s she said girls entering engineering would do so with as many as seven honors subjects on the Leaving Cert whereas boys would enroll with as few as two honors subjects. This was because it was an accepted thing for boys to do engineering whereas girls believed they had to be exceptional.

Male perception of this state of affairs was consistent. Paul recalled that in his cohort of students studying electrical engineering between 1972 and 1976 under ten percent were women. But even those women who overcame the maths hurdle[x] and made it to the university level experienced gender barriers.

> *[When we were presenting our final project] the lecturer asked who had done what. I started out talking first but the lecturer didn't seem to be paying any attention to me. He wasn't looking at me. He wouldn't make eye contact. It was going so bad that Sean jumped in and finished my statement to save our grade. Because of that, I almost didn't pass. I was told by the other students that Sean and Tom were "carrying*

> *me." And everyone believed these guys were doing all the*
> *work. [Nuala]*

Such anecdotes appear to be quite consistent with actual data about higher
education. In 1986, 40% of male entrants to higher education took up the
study of technology while less than 8% of female entrants did (Clancy, 1988,
p. 68), making technology the most gender-typed field of study in Ireland at
that time.

The male respondents offered a range of views on this topic. One
explanation was that men are more naturally suited to studying technical
topics. Paul suggested that the reason that only 20% of the workers at his firm
were women was that more skills were needed. He said that because 60% of
women in Ireland worked in unskilled work there would naturally be fewer
women in high tech. He also gave examples from his personal life. Despite his
wife's vociferous disagreement, his attitude was that men tended to take more
easily to technical things like engineering and electronics. "Now why that is, I
don't know," he said and then went on to observe that in interacting with his
wife he would joke with her saying, "Well that's too technical, I won't explain
it." While he said he was only joking, still, he found few women who were
very technical and were very good at engineering.

Another view held by some men was that there simply were not enough
qualified women around. Kevin, who worked at an American firm, believed
that there were definite differences in the position of women in IT as opposed
to other workplaces. In information technology, he said, there was equal
opportunity. Nevertheless, there were not that many women in electronics, but
not because the opportunity wasn't there, he insisted. There was equal
opportunity but there wasn't an equal number of women who *wanted* to be in
the industry.

In general, the men agreed that there were barriers to women participating
fully in the information sector and that a significant part of the reason lay in
the educational structures. But where the male and female viewpoints
diverged was their reaction to this reality. While men acknowledged that the
barriers and discrimination existed they were more sanguine about the
situation. For example, Paul acknowledged the paucity of technical women
and that the cause was societal barriers. However, he thought that if the
educational barriers had been removed when the information sector was first
being introduced in Ireland there would have been many more women going
to college. Hence, given increased opportunities for women since then, he was
a bit perplexed as to why there weren't more women in technical positions.

A typical male response was first to acknowledging that barriers existed,
and then to emphasize the fact that the situation was changing. For example,

Francis acknowledged that when Ireland had gender-segregated education the girls' schools tended to emphasize domestic science whereas the boys' schools would emphasize maths and science. But the trend toward more comprehensive and coeducational schools replacing religious secondary schools brought with it an introduction to a wider range of skills including wood working, metal working and commerce. It was no longer a situation in which the girls did domestic science and the boys did the physics and chemistry. Such a segregated educational setting was becoming less and less the norm. Nevertheless, Francis, who was in his mid thirties, agreed that those of his generation, those available to participate in the information sector, had been subject to gender-based educational discrimination. Change came slowly in Irish society, he said.

When discussing Ireland's industrial policy with official representatives before I began my on-site interviews, the topic of gender came up in the context of labor force characteristics. Barry confirmed Francis' perception that more science and maths was being taught in the secondary schools, especially in the girl's schools. He emphasized the increased number of women in science and engineering. One man's comment about his school-age daughter reinforced this claim. He said she wanted to go into business and that it was typical for girls her age to consider becoming an engineer or a doctor. One of her friends wanted to become a mechanic.

The effects of this change in educational policy seemed already to have been felt. Brian, who worked at a multinational electronics firm in the West, thought it was good for males and females to interact in the workplace, to be able to go to lunch together, to work side by side, to have platonic relationships. He saw this happening with the younger people. They seemed to mix more easily with the opposite sex. Several male respondents attributed to third level education the changing attitude about women working and the kind of work it was acceptable for a woman to do.

When I examined the responses of women on this topic I found that the nationality of their employing firms accounted for some differences in response. So I decided to see if that was also the case for the male respondents. I considered male responses according three categories: Irish men working at Irish firms, Irish men working at American firms and American men working at American firms. I wanted to know if the nationality of the firm or respondent had any influence on their views about women's position in the information sector in Ireland. I found that it did. The most dramatic influence was seen in the nationality of the respondents. American men believed it was easier for a woman to get on in the information sector than in other sectors in Ireland. American firms that had an American management team did not have the attitude that the women were not to be taken seriously because they would be going off and getting married. At one particular firm, the managing director informed me that seven out of the top ten workers were women.

The cohort of Irish men working in American firms agreed that the information sector was more progressive with respect to women and the opportunities for women were much better than in traditional industrial sectors. Nevertheless, they acknowledged that discrimination existed in the information sector. The men said women did not receive equal pay for the same work, they had to be better to get on, and they were not promoted as easily and were kept at lower levels because they were thought to be less committed to their careers. These men said the perception hadn't kept up with the reality. Among younger workers -- who represented those working in IT -- it was socially acceptable for married women and mothers to work. They also said that within the information sector it was easier for a woman to get on in a multinational firm because of the ideas imported from America. Several of these respondents pointed to the impact of the multinational firms when explaining how and why the attitudes about working women were changing.

Martin had considerable interaction with multinational firms both in Ireland and in the US. When he compared the status of Irish women in IT with American women in this industry he said the opportunities for Irish women were better than in other industrial sectors in Ireland but they fell well short of the opportunities that existed for women in America. He also observed a difference between the roles of women at Irish versus American sites in multinational companies. Men in Ireland held managerial positions that were frequently filled by women in the States. When I asked him to describe the attitude towards women in the workplace in Ireland he gave the following blunt reply:

> *In Ireland? By and large that they shouldn't be there. The family culture says they should be at home. It is much less progressive than the States. Or England.*
>
> *ET: Does that mean mothers or does it mean married women?*
>
> *It would tend to mean more mothers, in truth. It would be more accepted for married women [without children]. [Martin]*

Irish men working at Irish firms generally agreed with women that it was easier for a woman to get on in the information sector than in more traditional sectors. They were also in agreement that this generally meant getting hired but not promoted into the top management ranks. But whereas the female respondents might have attributed the reasons to discrimination (such as a general bias against women or the belief that they were not as committed as men), these men were a bit more vague. Some believed a woman's own priorities would keep her from moving forward in a company. Others believed that a mother needed to be at home with the children, and therefore she would stay at a lower position in a firm or would retire when she had children. A few men acknowledged that men might have difficulty reporting to a woman boss. They also expressed the viewpoint that the time and flexibility demanded in the information sector -- especially for small, Irish firms -- militated against women who had responsibilities at home. Finally, some just considered the lower position of women an immutable "cultural thing."

I then asked about cultural influences from American firms in Ireland with respect to the attitude toward women. I was interested in hearing thoughts about a value system and culture that the multinationals might be bringing to Ireland. I wanted to know if American values and attitudes were adapted to the Irish cultural context.

> *In that context it certainly does. Whether it just reflects the availability of labor supply and nothing more I don't know. It certainly imports a lot of its own culture. But if you go looking for ladies in the workplace and you looked in the workplace in Ireland you'd be horrified compared to the high tech sector in the States. If you took it to [one of the multinationals in the States] you'd be horrified. If I visit the States things always surprise me as to the portion of women I meet in the workplace. I will meet product managers and senior executives [who are women]. We rarely get that in Ireland. They are the exceptions. [Martin]*

In discussing changes in the acceptability of working women I sought, among other things, evidence of the impact of the multinational firms on societal views. While there was some correlation between the coming of the multinational firms and the increase in the number of working wives, I could not identify a direct impact. However, there were exceptions such as the one offered by John who had worked at an American multinational since the early 1980s.

> *I think American companies, certainly [in the mid 1970s to early 1980s] were setting up here, they would have influenced this because in the company's structures and*

*benefits [they were] making it a lot easier for working wives
to continue working in the work environment. There certainly
would have been an influence there, no question about that.
[John]*

Irish men working at American firms also noted the increased number of
women in management positions as evidence of acceptance of women in the
information workplace. After giving the caveat that like his father he is
nervous around women, Albert, an Irish worker at an American plant,
proceeded to explain the impact of the multinational IT firms on the status of
women. It was hard for Irish men to treat Irish women equally, he said,
because tradition held that the mother looked after the children. But exposure
to outside views coming from the media, education and the American
multinational firms was changing all that. Nevertheless, he concluded his
remarks on this topic by stating that the States had gone overboard about
women in the area of equality legislation.

A view about the increased role of the father in a two-income family also
came from workers at American plants. Paul mused about whether the person
earning the highest salary ought not to stay in the workplace even if it were
the woman. But, he said, there was no paternity leave available for fathers.
When discussing the topic of working women the Irish men quite often looked
to their own lives as a source of examples and issues. They noted the
problems their own wives had in education or in obtaining and progressing in
careers. So, for the majority of the respondents, this topic was not a theoretical
one; our discussions were grounded in reflection about personal experiences.

Women in the younger generation were most definitely different. Older
female respondents noted that women never used to go out with their friends
in the evenings. Men would go out with their friends but women would stay at
home. But things had changed, they said. As I examined responses on the
topic of gender and the information sector, firm nationality came through as a
significant influence. It was women working at American firms who tended to
believe greater gender diversity was on the horizon and attributed the greater
ease of getting on in the information sector to the American view of gender
equality. While they believed husbands shared domestic duties more when a
wife worked outside the home, they still acknowledged that the challenge of
balancing career and family demands fell primarily upon their shoulders.

Irish women participating in the information technology industry thought
this employment sector represented a mixed blessing for women. On the one
hand, there were clear economic benefits. Women had much greater career
opportunities than in traditional industrial areas. The influence of American
culture entering the country through the corporate cultures of the multinational

firms was welcomed and was bringing with it a greater openness to gender diversity. At the same time there was wistfulness in their manner. The old ways were fading. A family could not be as close, they believed, when both mother and father left the home to work. As employment opportunities took people to Dublin and other cities, extended families were breaking up. The women in IT had resolved the personal conflict between the demands of family and the demands of career in several ways. Some had foregone having families altogether. Others delayed marriage and childbearing, and retired from their careers at an early age. Still others pulled back from total commitment to career and did not advance the way they could. Deirdre summed up the complexity of the situation for women participating in Ireland's information sector:

> *You scratch the surface and we find that an awful lot of people disapprove, essentially [of mothers working outside the home]. I had an awful lot of thoughts because I thought you might ask about the role of women in high tech, and I would have said probably up until reasonably recently that it's had a very positive impact. I do not think that women have necessarily suffered, you know, have not suffered because they are women because it has been open and very accessible and so on. And I do think that is true. I do not think there is any overt discrimination as such or prejudice. But at the same time you cannot walk away from the statistics, right, which is that at the more senior levels there are fewer women. At junior levels there are more women. That's putting it crude, but that's the facts. Plus I think that the other thing that occurs to me is that the amount of hours that are expected does mitigate against women, right, in that they somehow choose to back off on the ambition trail, if you like, when they see what's involved and what's expected. [Deidre]*

3.   FAMILY-ORIENTED

> *The farm, itself, the piece of land is a very strong magnet. And what happens in the agricultural unit is that sons, particularly, and daughters, perhaps, end up with a few acres of the farm being theirs. They build a house they set up their family on that land and even if they're not working the land*

they may end up living on a piece of it. It keeps them very close together. And of course if their sons and daughters are working the land, they're there. Even if they're not they may end up building a house and raising a family right in the same area. The generations kind of stay together like that. It's good, I suppose, in that it builds up a caring infrastructure. The older generations are surrounded by younger relatives. I suppose that's an advantage for a way of life in some respects. [Gerry]

Family plays a very significant role in Irish society. And a strong thread running through the comments about the relationship between family and work is that the latter exists to support the former. Family was the object of very explicit attention by the participants in this study. Perhaps the origins of the family orientation are in Ireland's agrarian culture as suggested by Gerry, a young Irish man working in a Dublin firm. The degree of emphasis on the family was also related to the size of families. Families in Ireland were typically larger than in other European countries or America. Church influence contributed to this demographic trend, as well. Until the 1990s contraceptives were illegal in Ireland.[xi] Obtaining information about abortions was constitutionally prohibited. In a variety of ways, family was deeply embedded in the Irish culture. With this knowledge in mind, I was interested in knowing how the value placed upon family was influencing the development of the information sector. I also wanted to know if the growth of the information sector in Ireland was having any discernible impact on the institution of the family in Ireland.

3.1   Marriage and Family Life

All these girls in my class want to be married and most of them have been out of Ireland. They've come back because it's cheap to go to school here, for them. They've come back to get their degree here. And they're looking for husbands, basically! They want to get married. Their families want them to get married; they want to get married. Their friends are all married. There's not enough men for them, that's what they say. [Barbara]

Barbara, an American woman studying in an Irish university, offered observations about the centrality of marriage in Irish society that she learned from listening to her classmates. She had the impression that there was no lifestyle for unmarried people. She noted her classmates' willingness to move from Dublin to other parts of the country in order to improve their chances of finding a suitable husband. In a discussion about a mother working outside the home, Paul quipped:

> *There's no problem with that. The woman that doesn't have the children is probably the one that's sort of. . . You know, if a woman is 35 or 40 and has no children, that's probably the abnormal rather than the other way around. [Paul]*

But whether or not one had children, family in Ireland was viewed as the most fundamental institution, the conveyor of culture and the social glue that held the society together. Cahal, a young entrepreneur who owned an Irish software house, drew a comparison between his life and that of his older brother who lived in the UK. They came from a family of ten children from the West. His brother suffered, he said, from not having as much access to the family. Even though Cahal's brother had a wife and children of his own he missed the extended family. He spent all his holidays in Ireland rather than traveling to other countries. He wanted to spend all his time off in Ireland. The importance placed upon family was intimately linked to the importance of community, continuity and children in Ireland.

There was a very strong perception that in Ireland children were both sheltered and safe. Even more than with other topics, the discussion of children took the form of comparison with America. Mark was an expatriate whose two teenage sons were with him in the West of Ireland. In his observation Irish youth were more protected, less exposed, and did not grow up quite as fast as they did in America. His sons, he said, experienced less peer pressure with respect to drugs, sex, driving and clothing. He was happy that his sons were able to experience a few more years of youth as a result.

Irish respondents made consistent reference to Ireland as a better place than America to raise children. The term better was often synonymous with safer in our discussions. When they talked about emigrating to America or deciding to return to Ireland, the topic of children's welfare was always at the forefront. Some of those who made these comments had never experienced America directly; their knowledge of America came from imported television shows. However, the consistency of these comments across both groups revealed a fairly common perception of the difference in attitudes about children in the two countries. And in highlighting the difference with America, the Irish attitude about children came through.

Deirdre relayed the comments she had heard from emigrants to California and those who had returned. She said the people who had been to the US and had come back and talked about it, said California was a wonderful lifestyle because there were so many things to do. There were so many opportunities for people to really enjoy life, and their leisure life was much richer than it would have been in Ireland. But, she went on, there were issues with safety and freedom for children. She pointed out the difference between the two countries by relating a story about the differences in children's behavior in one particular family. In California, when the children came home from school they stayed in the house or the back yard. But the day they came home from California and arrived back at their own house, the children just scattered. The parents didn't see most of them for about four hours; they just got calls from parents in the neighborhood:

Oh, your son is staying in my house for tea

to which they comfortably replied:

Just send them off at bedtime.

For a variety of reasons -- key among them the number of mothers at home and the size of families -- there was a high level of social interaction in Irish neighborhoods. Children had many playmates in the neighborhood and parents did not worry about their children going into some neighbor's house.

They're in and out of each other's house and each other's garden all day long. [Michael]

As I reflected upon these comments about children I recalled an experience I had in America before I came to Ireland. Barry was working as a trade representative in Boston. He invited me to his house in order to discuss background information for my research project. Over dinner his wife related the following story. While she was shopping in an upper middle class suburban supermarket one of her children wandered off to another part of the store. A patron brought the child back and chastised Barry's wife for letting the child out of her sight explaining that in America, children can be stolen and parents, therefore, need to keep them always within sight. This story reflects the perception of my respondents about children and their safety in America versus Ireland.

The topic of childcare was the primary link between the discussions of gender and family life in Ireland as they related to the information sector. There was a diversity of sentiments about this topic. One view was that children needed to be under the direct care of the mother, and if not her, then another family member. Those holding this view expressed reservation about crèches as a viable mechanism for childcare. Some said not enough facilities existed in Ireland. Others simply believed crèches were not an appropriate way to care for children; someone should be at home with the children. Colin expressed the view that men ought to be able to serve in that role.

> *My wife certainly enjoyed her work. She was very involved in her work. [But] I think both her and myself value parenthood very highly. Given the choice I'd stay home with the kid. One of us has to work, and financially it was better that I go and work. If I had the money, I'd be home with my kid. I totally understand somebody wanting a career and have great admiration for people who can bring up children and work, because I find it hard enough being a working parent. I don't know how people can cope when there are two working parents. It would seem that a lot of the family time would have to be sacrificed. [Colin]*

With more women entering the workforce -- IT and otherwise -- the role of fathers was shifting as well. Where women worked outside the home some fathers were taking a more active role. The mother historically dominated the home and family life, especially when she did not work outside the home. However, even when women worked outside the home, they bore the bulk of domestic responsibilities and seemed to willingly take on this dual responsibility of children and job as illustrated by Deirdre's experiences at her daughter's school:

> *He takes time off if I can't get time off to go see the teacher, for example. I'll give you an interesting example. You know, once a year you get invited down to meet the teacher. We've had three years now of this. It's [our daughter's] third year of primary school. Every single year my husband has come with me, and every single year he's been the only male. When we go in the teacher invariably has one chair. She expects the mother and she has to scramble around to find a second chair because there's two of us. [Deidre]*

Whether or not the father was an active participant in the day-to-day aspects of the family, it was clear that one's family played a significant role in shaping the priorities of both women and men. Workers clearly wanted to derive from their jobs sufficient income to satisfy their requirements for food, clothing and shelter. But material benefits, alone, were not sufficient. People wanted enough income to cover their needs but they saw a breakeven point at which more money would mean less time for family and socializing -- oftentimes, the same thing -- which would be unacceptable. Therefore, a high standard of living combined a level of financial security with the time and a safe environment in which to enjoy oneself and one's family. There was a strong desire to maintain a balanced life. Several Irish workers told me they would turn down an opportunity to come to America even if it meant a job promotion because work-related benefits would not make up for the expected losses in personal and family life.

3.2   Family Life in the Information Economy

The institution of the family had both influenced the evolution of the Irish information sector and felt its impact. There were four ways in which family was exerting an influence on the information sector. The first was through attitudes about education. There was tremendous sentiment in Ireland for education. Relative to the individuals' wealth and origins the Irish family would make considerable sacrifices in order to educate their children, to send them to secondary school and possibly to university. The emphasis on education reflected the value that the family placed on it. This was also why émigrés returned to Ireland. The family influence on education was not always a positive one, however. I spoke with more than one individual in the information sector whose families were not particularly encouraging about education. Charles, who worked for an American firm in the West, recounted how there was nobody telling him he had to go to secondary school, save an aunt who once promised to pay for his education if he went and then reneged when he did! No one else gave him direction one way or the other.

> *If I happened to take offense at staying home at the farm, that would have been fine. If I decided to go to the university, that would have been fine. There was no pressure involved. No guidance either. A lack of direction. [Charles]*

A second way in which family was influencing the information sector was in the extent of family pressure in the industrial-farming, urban-rural decision. The issue was family pressure to run the family farm instead of going off to work in the information sector.

> *My whole family, for generations, were farmers or in work involved with farming. . . I guess there wasn't a lot of pressure on me [to be a farmer]. If I hadn't got a brother -- I have one brother, a younger brother. I'm 31; he's 26 -- there would have been a lot of pressure if my brother hadn't been around. The idea of farming runs very strong in the farming community. The thought of the farm coming to an end or*

*being sold outside the family doesn't go down too well.
They're pleased if anybody stays around. Me being the eldest
son, there's some pressure, but it was obvious early on that I
wasn't the least bit interested in it. I like the open spaces, all
right, but as for agricultural work, no, I don't like to farm at
all. I was fairly academic in engineering. My brother, on the
other hand, was not academic, and probably hasn't gotten a
greater life as my father would have liked, but he wasn't
academic; he didn't really make a great effort to get into
anything else, so he kind of ended up working the farm by
default. [Gerry]*

While explicit pressure on the oldest son to take over the farm may have been
diminishing, the expectation that *someone* would do so seemed to be alive and
well.

The third way that family exerted an influence on the information sector
was more specific to one's behavior at work. American managers explained
that a "family problem" was an almost unquestionable reason for granting a
request. If a worker declined his or her manager's request to do a task and
explained:

Look, there's family reasons,

that would be the end of the discussion. If a man said that his wife was
pregnant and due to give birth the following week or she wasn't well, it would
be taken as a legitimate -- not excuse, but -- explanation for one's behavior at
work.

Another dimension of this was the choice of where to work. During the
late 1980s and into the early 1990s -- the time of my interviews -- the
downsizing and restructuring of the global information sector were under way.
Several of the respondents had already experienced redundancies as a result of
scale backs or multinationals leaving Ireland. Consequently, financial security
was becoming more of an issue. When discussing decisions about where one
would work, the trade-off between security on the one hand and professional
fulfillment on the other was presented in terms of family. For example, Neil
had a choice upon leaving school to go to work for a multinational or for an
Irish start up company. Although the challenges of the new firm appealed to
him, the fact that he was just getting married and would be having family
responsibilities weighed heavier. And so he chose the multinational firm
because he believed it provided greater job security. There was also the
phenomenon -- particularly in the large multinationals -- of several members
of one family working at the same plant. So if there were a family problem,

then several workers would be affected. This also created kinship groups within the workplace.

The fourth way in which the emphasis on family life influenced the information sector was with respect to work-related mobility both within Ireland and abroad. Several themes emerged from my discussions with respondents about work-related mobility. They centered around the decisions people made, and how they coped with their decisions. It was common to place family above career in decisions regarding where one would work and live. They talked about how they would remain in or take a job in order to live in a certain location in Ireland. People from Dublin talked about turning down job opportunities in Limerick while those from the country wouldn't move to Dublin.

> *To me my social life and my life where I live, married life and stuff like that takes preference over my career. So if a job came up in Dublin or in Germany that was exactly what I'm looking for, I wouldn't take that job. [Paul]*

Other times it meant incurring a longer commute to work at a new job because the home and family were settled in some place.

> *My wife and myself are involved in both sporting and other activities in the locality and have passed that down to our kids. Happily, we live in a community that was built in the last 20 years and I would guess five thousand families who were almost a stereotype copy of our family unit. They all have kids around the same age. They all have houses in approximately the same thing. They all have the same worries about mortgages and different things. Now I was living there at the time I was working in [another firm] and it was very inconvenient in terms of getting to [my current job], coming across the city. But the quality of life is such in that particular local area that the kids are involved in between girl guides and running club and sailing club and everything else, that I prefer to live there and work here, than to move simply because of the work. [Francis]*

Nevertheless, many individuals, especially those just starting out in their careers or who were from the rural parts of Ireland found it necessary to move to another part of Ireland in order to find work. But their affinity to place and family was apparent in the pattern of weekend travel "down home."

> *ET: How important is family in your life?*

*I see my parents about ten times a year. They live a two-hour
drive away, so they are not part of my regular life. But I
would say I'm a bit more isolated than the average person.
Adults who live in Dublin will talk about "going home for the
weekend." Most people go "home" on weekends. [Tom]*

In spite of the appeal of home and family, leaving Ireland in search of
work has been ingrained in Ireland's history and culture. The emigration rate
that slowed in the 1970s during the first wave of inward investment by IT
firms picked up again in the 1980s. Some of these young people left not
because they wanted to but because there were no jobs available in their
fields. Others left in order to gain some exposure to other cultures. This desire
typically took them to England or the US and, increasingly, to the rest of
Europe. But the related theme that emerged during these discussions was
about Irish people returning to Ireland in order to raise their families. A view
that was often expressed was that graduates wanted to go abroad for a few
years to get both work and life experience but then wanted to return when they
were ready to marry and raise a family. They wanted to put down roots in
Ireland.

Aside from getting the initial job, the emigration decision arose once again
for more senior people who worked in multinational firms. George told me
that he would not be progressing further up the corporate ladder beyond his
senior management position at his multinational firm because it would require
moving to the American headquarters. He mentioned peers who when faced
with a similar dilemma at other firms choose to move, instead, into consulting
or starting their own companies in order to remain in Ireland. An alternative
meant remaining on a career plateau in order to maintain the primary
commitment to family.

While the themes just discussed show the influence that family life in
Ireland was having on the information sector, I also found evidence that the
economic changes in the country -- brought about by the information sector
and other new industries -- were having an impact on the institution of family.
One of these changes was work-related mobility. In Ireland's rural times,
people tended to marry those within their locale and set up families within a
reasonably short distance from their birthplace. That situation has changed.
Not only are people moving away but also the migration is generally in the
direction of rural to urban.

A second impact on family has been the demand of the information sector
on a worker's time. This theme came up in nearly every discussion about
work and family. I was curious about whether working at an Irish or an
American firm was any different in this regard. There were fewer comments

about this topic from men[xii] working at Irish firms. When comments were made, they were not consistent. Cahal, for example, noted that some software houses expect employees to work very long hours, something that went against the family, he said.

> *You're supposed to enjoy working hard and playing hard and drinking hard. [Cahal]*

However, Colm explained that, to him, family was the all-important thing to the extent that in looking for a job he sought a position that would facilitate time with his children. He said that in his set of priorities family was 95%; work was 5%. For this reason he was not interested in a job that would involve a lot of foreign travel. Martin took the long view saying it all depended upon the economic cycles.

> *During a recession there's no point in working on Saturday mornings because everything's flat. But if they're on a high, the company's doing well, they think their fortune's with it. Then they will sacrifice their leisure time and their family time very, very easily, so I think [the sector] will mature more and there will be less of a distinction of what I see as the newer industries become more established. I think that's already happening in the electric and technical service. It's more mature and people have come to terms with the fact that they need to stabilize people. I'd say Ireland is going through a phase where not just Irish companies but probably even more so, the mobile multinationals do actually experience a tremendous input in time that you wouldn't see elsewhere. [Martin]*

The responses of those working in multinational firms were larger in volume and more consistent. Men working at the multinational firms were acutely aware of the impact, particularly the time demands, of the information sector on families. Work demands took time away from family on evenings, weekends and during holiday periods. Donal, who spoke from experience, explained that the nature of work at a multinational firm sometimes required off-peak working hours. As a manager of a warehouse he had to adjust to the fact of life that flights carrying materials from the US arrived on Thursdays. Consequently, he had to work most weekends. Quality of life to Paul meant working efficiently at his job and then being able to go home and forget about it at the end of the day. When I asked about his ability to achieve that objective while working at his current job, his response revealed the difference between his own priorities and those of his employer.

> *It's work, here, that's kind of high pressure. You're "all systems go" kind of thing. We were just after moving a warehouse and I was getting phone calls at home all the time. And that disturbed me a lot. And you don't get much recognition from that. In fact, I don't think I got any. Not that I wanted recognition; I just wanted to be left alone. So, of late, now I definitely try to get out of here at half four, and make a point of it. I don't think it's good for you and you don't get much recognition for it. I do know people who do spend a lot of time, they stay way past half four and weekends and stuff. [Paul]*

4.   CONCLUSION

The topics of gender and family in Ireland are inseparable in discussions of the Irish workplace. Both the men and the women who spoke in 1990 felt that women bore the primary responsibility for parenthood. While women found it easier to *get into* the information sector than they did other sectors, they still found it difficult to *get on* in their careers in IT. Some women felt they had to choose between career and family. Others expected to maintain two full time jobs if they worked outside the home. In doing so, they knew they would not be able to achieve or earn as much in the information workplace as their male counterparts.[xiii]

When these attitudes were combined with cultural norms that situated a woman primarily in the home, the result was societal barriers to full participation in the information economy. My interpretation of the position of women in the information sector is consistent with Wickham's (1989) study of women in the electronics sector conducted in the early to mid 1980s. He found fewer women working outside the home in Ireland than in other countries, a pattern of moving girls away from technologically-oriented courses, and job demands which made it impossible for a woman to reconcile her professional commitment with her desire to have children. My interpretation is also consistent with more recent studies of women in other sectors. For example, Monks and Barker's (1995)[xiv] study of chartered accountants in Ireland found that those women who did make it into the ranks of top management did so at substantial personal cost. They may have had to decide between career, on the one hand, and marriage and possibly children, on the other.

Nevertheless, the decade of the 1990s has seen a continuation of the trend toward greater involvement of women in spheres outside the home. This decade has seen high profile women in politics with the election of Mary Robinson as the first female President of Ireland followed by Mary McAleese in 1997. In 1984 female labor force participation in Ireland was 36.9% in contrast to rates of over 50% in other developed countries. But by 1994 the participation rate had climbed to 47%, an increase of nearly 28% (Callan et al., 1998). In 1997 with female participation at 49.7%, Ireland was 9% lower than the OECD average and 8% below the EU average. However, with a 1% per annum rate of increase compared to the EU average of 0.5% the gap appears to be closing. Sixty-six percent of women age 25 to 45 are working followed by 46% of those age 15 to 24. The smallest group (24%) is in the 55 to 64 age category (IDA Ireland, 1999). The increased participation of women has been a key factor in the growth of the labor force in the last decade. Women's participation is directly related to levels of educational attainment: while participation by women with minimal education has been low, from 1988 to 1994 participation rates for women with the Leaving Certificate has been on the rise (Fitz Gerald, 1995). Sixty per cent of new jobs since 1992 have been taken up by women (The Economist Intelligence Unit, 1998).

In addition to changes in the participation rate of women, there is also evidence of attitudinal changes in the society. The active involvement of women was one of the themes of *Partnership 2000, for Inclusion, Employment and Competitiveness* (Department of the Taoiseach, 1996). The issue addressed in Chapter 5, Action towards a New Focus on Equality, was the development of a framework to pursue full integration of women and minorities into Irish society. Enhancing equality is seen as part of macroeconomic competitiveness. Some of the specific agenda items include: increasing gender equity in access to vocational education, training and employment programs; promoting childcare to promote equality for women in employment; and supporting family friendly policies in employment.

In this vein, the *Employment Equality Act* was passed in 1998. This law extends the grounds for discrimination from the existing sex and marital status categories contained in the *Anti-discrimination (Pay) Act, 1974* and the *Employment Equality Act, 1977* to include race, religious belief, disability, age, membership of the travelling community, family status and sexual orientation. It also establishes an Employment Equality Authority and a new office of the Director of Equality Investigations. Further, maternity, paternity, adoptive leave and childcare legislation have recently been passed.[xv] In addition, the Government has provided £1 million in public funds for the establishment of new crèches to provide full day and after-school care for the children of working parents.

But recognizing that a family-friendly workplace will not materialize through legislation, alone, the emphasis has been on encouraging industry to work with childcare providers to address the shortage of day care (Houston, 1999, p. 232). In a July 1999 speech to an Oireachtas (Parliament) committee, a senior official in the Equality and Law Reform division of the Department of Justice argued that the vision of equality needed to be expanded to include changes in both men's domestic roles and workplace attitudes. Whereas the societal view in 1979 was that in order to have children women had to leave the labor force, she said, in 1999 that is unacceptable. In order to bring about both changed attitudes and policies, the Department of Justice announced its intention to assist companies in developing programs to take into account gender and family issues (Pollak, 1999, p. 10).

These attitudinal, legislative and administrative changes, if not a direct impact of the information economy, are certainly consistent with the human resource demands of this growing sector. It is no longer the case that a woman working outside the home would be taking a job away from a needy family. Indeed, Ireland's labor shortage in the information sector, suggested a recent OECD (1999) report, could be addressed by facilitating greater female participation. The report suggested, however, that achieving a faster increase in participation rate would require more active government involvement by way of providing childcare and pre-school facilities. Firms, as well, would have to participate by implementing more family-friendly policies (McCarthy, 1995). With an expected 17,500 new jobs being created in the information sector into the early years of the twenty-first century, companies are co-funding training programs for women who want to return to work.

One example is the EU-funded NOW (New Opportunities for Women) employment initiative. Companies such as Intel, Hewlett-Packard and NEC work with the Tallaght Institute of Technology to develop training programs to promote the participation of females in the workforce. Seventy such projects have been undertaken since 1992. Another initiative is the Women in Electronics (WIE) training project designed to provide unemployed women with access to training and education, and to provide a vehicle for women already employed to progress in their careers (Houston, 1999, p. 33). An initiative that addresses both the work-family life and the rural-urban dichotomies is one undertaken by Telework Ireland. Established in 1993 to serve as a voice for those engaged in teleworking,[xvi] this organization is engaged in a project to conduct Internet-based training for people to become software localization specialists to work from home or at a local facility (McCormack, 1998). Perhaps some indication of the impact of the information economy on the opportunities for women in the Irish workplace can be seen in the fact that Irish University-educated women earn more compared to those who complete second-level schooling than in any other OECD country apart from the UK (Pollak, 1998).

As the status of women is changing, so too, are attitudes about sexuality, marriage and child bearing.[xvii] The female marriage pattern has historically been linked to levels of education. Women with third level education were less likely to be married than women with other educational levels. They also tended to marry at a later age. This trend has continued into the present. The increase in the number of women attaining third level education has accompanied a decline in the marriage rate (Fitz Gerald, 1995, p. 4). There was a drop of 18% in the marriage rate between 1987 and 1997. Women who do get married are doing so at an older age (Houston, 1999, p. 235).

---

[i] 30% of the respondents were women.

[ii] Earlier versions of these results are presented in Trauth (1993b, 1994, 1995a and 1995b).

[iii] This positive attitude about multinationals concurs with a similar study of women in County Mayo by Harris (1989) and conflicts with the findings of Jackson and Barry (1989) about women in multinationals in Ireland.

[iv] This view is consistent with Mahon's (1991) analysis of women and equality in the Irish civil service.

[v] Childcare center.

[vi] The writing of Irish novelist Edna O'Brien echoes this theme. In a 1988 interview in the *Boston Globe* she discussed her portrayal of women in her stories: " . . . women strive vainly for freedom in a male-dominated society, and they pay a price, usually ostracism and loneliness. . ." (Claffey, 1988).

[vii] A technical response given "on the fly" even if the person isn't certain that it is correct.

[viii] Clancy, et al., (1988), p. 301.

[ix] Commission on the Status of Women (1972), p. 252.

[x] Nuala, for example, enrolled in a computer applications program as a "mature student." Because these older students had different entrance requirements, she gained admission despite not having taken honors maths.

[xi] In 1990 married couples could legally obtain contraceptives. However, it was still illegal for unmarried people to acquire contraceptives. In a well-publicized incident that year, the manager of a large record store in Dublin was arrested for selling condoms to unmarried individuals.

[xii] Because the topic of time demands of information sector work and its impact on family was considered for women in the discussion of gender, the comments analyzed here were only those of men.

[xiii] Average female earnings are 67% of average male earnings (McEvoy, 1998, p. 64).

[xiv] Data for their study was collected in 1994.

[xv] These are: *Maternity Protection Act, 1994, Adoptive Leave Act, 1995, Parental Leave Act, 1998* and *1996 Child Care Regulations* (of *1991 Child Care Act*).

[xvi] Also referred to as telecommuting.

[xvii] In her analysis of the divorce referendum, Coulter (1997) identifies the development of Ireland's export-oriented computer industry as one of the key factors influencing societal changes, in general, and the roles of men and women, in particular.

Part III
The Workplaces

CHAPTER 5. INTERPERSONAL

1.   INTRODUCTION

Much about quality of life in Ireland and the expectations of the information-sector workplace can be explained by considering the pivotal role of interpersonal relations in Irish culture. The term *interpersonal* embodies several cultural traits. It refers to the easygoing air exhibited by workers, a strong emphasis placed on communication skills, and a genuine interest in and concern for others. If you add to this mix the small size of the society and landmass, a sense of comfortable intimacy results. I wanted to learn more about this dimension of Irish society: the desire to interact with others, to be helpful and friendly, the need to get on with people. I wanted to learn how important it was in Irish society and how it influenced the workplace. What I found was that the focus on interpersonal relations explained much of what I found to be distinctive about the information-sector workplace in Ireland.

2.   SOCIAL

Well, I mean, when you interview somebody [for a job], you try to interview somebody who is obviously sociable. You're not going to interview somebody who you can see is very anti-social because they won't fit in with the environment. We all have a lot of interaction with everybody else. It's obviously very important that we at least get on. It's very important in a company like this that you think that people will get on well with others. [Aine]

One noticeable feature of Irish sociability was that it occurred both inside and outside the workplace. A very large emphasis was placed on sociability in the workplace, meaning that both the environment and the people should be conducive to social interaction. The ability to get on with one's workers entered into the hiring process as part of the criteria used in judging applicants even for the most technical of jobs. Irish workers who had been to American sites of their firms noticed that whereas American workers might be friendly at work, there was much less socializing with co-workers after work, something that was not the case in Ireland. Whereas Americans were seen as having a social life only on the weekends, the Irish, saw themselves as having social life during the week as well. Thus, the information-sector workers thought they had a more integrated life than Americans, one in which relationships at work carried over into social relationships.[i]

The forms of social interaction associated with the workplace included going to the pub together after work, congregating in a central location for tea breaks (as opposed to the American habit of having coffee at one's desk), playing on company-sponsored sports teams, engaging in sporting activities with co-workers, and having parties at work. Activities such as golf outings, they said, helped to strengthen relationships. Having social interaction with people made it easier to interact with them or their areas in a business setting. More than once in the course of my visits to the companies, I directly experienced the social side. At the end of one Friday afternoon spent at an indigenous firm I was invited to the barbecue and softball game that was to be held that weekend. Another time, while I was sitting in the reception area of a multinational firm waiting for my corporate escort, I looked up to see two men in elaborate Native American dress calmly walk through the front door of the building! It was July 4 and these individuals were part of the American Independence Day festivities that would be taking place that day.

Perhaps because the population of the entire country -- roughly three and a half million people -- was the same as a medium size American city there was both the feeling and the reality that everybody knew everybody. Perhaps because Irish people possessed considerable curiosity and seemed to take an interest in strangers and newcomers, the anonymity that existed in larger countries did not exist in Ireland. This was particularly the case in the smaller cities outside Dublin. People would typically encounter co-workers outside of work: at the pub, walking about town or in the shops. There was consensus that people who saw each other outside of work were brought closer together inside work. Consequently, it was easier for people to talk to each other inside of work, to go to another person when they needed something. Information-sector workers in Ireland also stayed in their jobs longer than they typically did in the US. If they planned to be around their co-workers for a long while they might be more motivated to get on with them.

Mark concurred that Irish workers were more sociable than their American counterparts. He believed that because the population was more homogeneous, the workers had more in common and had similar interests. In the Irish site of his firm there would be more conversation throughout the day about shared interests such as the local football match or perhaps about current events. Conversation was also facilitated by shared activities outside work. All these things contributed to team building in the workplace.

While I certainly found the work environment to be quite social, I sometimes wondered if what I was experiencing was limited to the firms I happened to be visiting. I wondered if, perhaps, information-sector workers in America were just as social. For this reason, the strongest validation of my interpretations came from American managers in Ireland, all of whose perceptions were the same as mine. They contrasted the Irish with American sites of their firms and concurred that the Irish sites were indeed more social. In fact, some managers cited this as the *major difference* between the Irish and the American sites of a plant. The social orientation is evident in an easygoing attitude that allowed time for the important things in life: craic[ii], slagging[iii], visiting the pub, engaging in sports[iv] and taking trips down country.

2.1   Easygoing

> ET: *The laid back, easygoing lifestyle, is that connected to farming?*
>
> *It's Irish. Absolutely. I mean you see all those coming here on holidays and say it's so easygoing, so laid back. That's why I think a lot of foreigners find it hard to relate to that. Especially socially. In the work world the ethic is to be there on time and at least to make a very good effort nine times out of ten to be on time. But certainly in the social [side] you can be an hour late. [Margie]*

My exploration into this easygoing nature, informed by my own observations and experiences, combined with the thoughts and reflections of my respondents to form two different interpretations of the term easygoing. One interpretation of easygoing was the vestige of the old Ireland, a post-colonial, agrarian society with little materialism and the accompanying rat race.[v] What mattered more than money was contact with people. Easygoing, in this interpretation, meant not working terribly hard. For example, Paul pointed out that the high tech firm where he worked was not a typical Irish company because a typical Irish company did not have a reputation for being hardworking. He went on to talk about his German father who came to Ireland in his youth to be an apprentice in a jewelry shop. At three o'clock one afternoon not long after he had arrived his boss came up to him saying he could go home since there wasn't much happening. Paul said his father could not understand this at all because in Germany being on time and being well organized had been heavily emphasized. In contrast, the Irish were more lackadaisical and seemed to have more time to chat with each other. And so, he said, a big Irish company would come from that orientation: not very efficient and maybe not very well structured. In contrast, he said, the multinational firm where he worked was different. Things were more structured and more planned and everybody was working efficiently.

In sharp contrast to this interpretation of easygoing was a second one, which was definitely in evidence in the information-sector firms I visited. This interpretation spoke to a new kind of Irish workplace, which was relaxed but also productive. This would include the attitude toward deadlines, starting and finishing times at work, and how to spend one's break time at work. It also included an overall view of the role of work in one's life as David pointed out. David was a British manager who had just arrived at a multinational firm in the West of Ireland to assume the position of human resources manager. Throughout the length of my stay in his firm, he would drop in to ask how it was going. He used these visits as an opportunity to share his own experiences and interpretations. It was clear to me that he was still getting adjusted to this new culture.

> *People are slower, more deliberate. That's why they enjoy*
> *[their work]. Whereas, I guess I'm still reasonably*
> *programmed to do things. I wish I was able to take it a bit*
> *slower. Maybe that's a personal thing. But I look around; it's*
> *a societal thing. [David]*

The overall impression held by both Irish and American respondents was that people in the Irish information-sector workplace talked more to one another and were less formal than people in other countries.

This easygoing approach to life -- whether in the productive or the unproductive sense -- has been linked to the Irish attitude toward time, Irish colonialism and Ireland's rural roots.[vi] Over lunch during a day of interviews at his firm, Charles explained the easygoing attitude through an example: washing up the cups after tea. His wife, he said, cannot do a thing fast enough. He, on the other hand, just wipes the cups with no hurry in the world. It could take him half an hour to do what she could do in two minutes. To him time was of no importance in doing something like that. And that's why the Irish were such an easygoing race, he said, compared to the Americans who he believed were always chasing the clock.

Others attributed this easygoing attitude to Ireland's colonial and rural influences. The colonial explanation was that Ireland was kept under British dominion for many years during which time people had little hope of succeeding. Hence, they had little motivation to work hard. Closely related to this theme was the view that an easier rural setting helped to account for an easy and possibly less ambitious nature. In rural Ireland there was never a need to rush very much except, perhaps, if there was a shower of rain on its way, said Charles. And as for coming in from work and having cups of tea, people would talk for hours until finally somebody would say, "Better get back out to work."

2.2 Craic

> *The Irish are basically friendly. From the rural background, taking the time to talk. Craic is still vibrant. The view is that having fun only occurs if it is shared. Therefore, people also share in the workplace. A happy company is a productive company. Having fun at work is a legitimate expectation of workers even if it is not explicitly said by management. [Matthew]*

The importance placed upon the art of conversation is signified by a specific word, *craic,* which is used to describe the atmosphere of a social setting.[vii] In discussing quality of life most people viewed the financial aspect -- having a job, being able to pay your mortgage and putting food on the table -- as a very high priority. But they wouldn't stop there. The second answer would be that they have some form of social life. There must be some element of enjoyment. The Irish respondents claimed that when they went abroad they found that people did not appear to have the same capacity to just relax and enjoy themselves, and enjoy each other's company. People told me they missed that terribly when they went to other countries. Deirdre commented at length about this. She believed it had to do with Irish history and traditions, such as story telling, and so on. In response to my experience of dinner parties that could go on until dawn[viii] she laughed and observed that to use the phrase art of conversation with respect to Irish people was no exaggeration. It truly was an art in Ireland. She used the example of her parents to depict a culture in which good conversation and good atmosphere were important ingredients in having a good time, what the Irish would characterize as good craic.

> *. . . I can remember having the most stimulating discussions going on at Sunday dinner. Or at a party. Or at a dinner*

party. Or just a family gathering. Anything would be discussed, right? And then the second half of the night would always be, you know, either singing, story telling, reciting poems, or whatever. And it wasn't a proper night, it wasn't a good night, unless it finished that way. I can still remember going to sleep with the sounds of singing from the living room. [Deirdre]

2.3   Slagging

Having and displaying a sense of humor was a noteworthy dimension of having a good time. The Irish viewed themselves as having a good sense of humor.[ix] In the workplace this meant playing tricks and joking around at work, or the use of nicknames and teasing people. Irish people are known for their quick-witted one-liners. Rather than interpreting it as an attempt to put someone down, it is a case of sending each other up.[x]

You find that you can probably slag your boss to their face over here whereas you can't do it most other places. But that's a trait that Irish people tend to slag each other a lot. And it's only if you like somebody that you slag them. [Cahal]

In contrast, Dan, who worked as a programmer in the US in the 1980s, noted that he got reprimanded once for signing a Fax: "George Bush."

I put a little craic into it.

Besides a sense of humor, slagging also suggested a certain informality as well. In noting that in Ireland one can slag the boss, the respondents were suggesting a more informal relationship than might exist elsewhere.

There was a consciously held feeling that if you worked with certain people eight hours a day, it was important to enjoy that interaction. This was something that Irish people consciously managed. Some Irish respondents, however, were more critical of this trait, saying that about 50% of Irish workers placed an emphasis on getting the job done and 50% on having a good time.

As I listened to the respondents talk about having fun at work, I thought about my experience of working and observing others at work in the States. In my experience of work,[xi] if it were seen to be too enjoyable it might be a bit suspect. It seemed to me that the American value was that if one were having too much fun then that individual must not be working hard enough. What motivated this line of thinking was my own reaction to the fun I was having in conducting my research. I noted numerous times in my research journal that I had never enjoyed a research project as much as I was enjoying this one. But in the back of my mind I also felt self-censorship about telling my colleagues back home how much fun I was having doing the research. David understood this feeling and went on to contrast his work life in the UK before coming to Ireland.

> *ET: Based on your experience, say in the UK, the sense you got there was that work isn't essentially pleasurable, that it's more a duty?*
>
> *Yes. It was more than labor. A notion of somebody saying you can have fun at work, you had to be smoking something [if] you think like that. [David]*

The fun that was characteristic of the Irish information sector first emerged in general descriptions of the workplace. When I began to explore the reasons why this might be the case I was told that people *expected* their job to enable them to have fun at work. They expected a considerable level of social interaction. They expected to have social interaction throughout the course of their day, to meet after work in the pub, and to have a sports and social club. "Is the job fun?" they asked. Sometimes, having fun was interpreted to also include stimulating work and being able to make a contribution to the company.

It is important to remember that workers in the information sector made these comments. Older respondents who had worked in other sectors drew a contrast between the information sector and other environments. They said that the work ethic in which they grew up was one of "Be seen to be there, stay late, generate work in a smiling way, but don't enjoy it." Those who had experienced other sectors said it was totally different from the work ethic in the information sector which was "achievement but with a sense of informality." Once again, I had the feeling that the information-sector workplace was unleashing traits that had long been waiting to be expressed.

2.4   Pub

> *One thing you obviously have enjoyed, in your time in Ireland, is that the social center of Ireland is the pub. So a lot of things revolve around that. . . Because of that, and because of the positive approach that [this firm] and other companies would have, the social aspects of the business, that's a fairly*

> *major difference. I think coming back to my point on loyalty,*
> *things like [the pub] drive the feeling of belonging in that*
> *there's also a social aspect to the company as well as just the*
> *business side. . . [John]*

When asked what sorts of things were important to Irish people, they replied with the following list: sport, social life, pubs, family. This response expressed the central role of the pub in both work and social life in Ireland. The pub was the symbol of social interaction in the Irish culture. For example, when Eileen was explaining the closeness that existed among workers in the information-sector firms in Ireland, she expressed it in terms of everyone going our for a pint after work. And Ed, a young American manager recently arrived in Ireland, used interaction in the pub to express the interest that people took in each other and in strangers. With this general attitude toward the pub in Irish life, it was certainly no surprise that the pub would play a key role in work life as well.

Respondents said there was a friendlier atmosphere and closer interaction at work because of time spent together in pubs.

> *Well, I mean we finish here normally on Friday at three or*
> *four -- depending on what schedule you are on, Schedule A*
> *or B -- if we work on schedule. So normally in the wintertime*
> *you might go to the pub for a drink or something after work.*
> *But normally in the wintertime you would go for a drink. Now*
> *we don't do it so much in the summer time. We tend to go our*
> *own ways, you know. That's just purely weather related, I*
> *think, as well. If it's raining one tends to stay around and go*
> *for a drink about three o'clock. [Margie]*

Sue, an American expatriate, indicated that learning about the essential role of pubs was an important component of her adjustment to Irish work life. Early on she noted that everybody went together to a pub on a Friday night. Whereas her initial reaction was, "I've had enough of these people at the end of the week and I sure didn't want to drink with them," she soon figured out that that was part of the scene. You were part of the team if you went to the pub. And you were sort of saying that you were different or better than the rest if you didn't. As these anecdotes point out, going to the pub was not only part of the social sphere it was also part of the work sphere.

Part of the answer to why workers would want to meet after work in the pub is answered by the central role of pubs in Irish society. Further explanation can be found in workers' attitudes toward their co-workers: people needed to know and like their co-workers in order to get on with them at work. And meeting in the pub outside work afforded that opportunity. Taking the time to be with people helped to forge strong relationships in the workplace. People began to develop a connection with their counterparts at work, which they could then reinforce in the social setting of the pub.

> *The Irish are a pretty communicative people. Not a "yes-no" people in the workplace. Friday evening in the pub with workers. You learn more about your friends. And if there is an argument at work, you can clear it up in the pub.* [Kathleen]

The significance of pubs in Irish culture (and, hence, the importance of this dimension of Irish culture to my research) came home to me in a personal way in my interview with Nuala. At our initial meeting to negotiate a time and place for the interview, she indicated a preference for meeting outside of workday hours and away from her workplace. When I agreed and asked for a recommendation I expected Nuala to suggest a meeting over a meal or tea. Instead, she suggested a pub in the Temple Bar section of Dublin. Nuala also brought along her sister and two colleagues who continued to replenish my glass of Guinness throughout the evening. When I sought to understand the significance of the venue, I came up with two possible interpretations, both of which spoke to the central role of the pub in Irish culture. One interpretation was that I was being tested. Proposing that the interview be held in a pub was a test of my willingness to accommodate to this Irish setting. The second interpretation was that being asked to meet in a pub was actually an acknowledgement of my acceptance. When I related this story to other respondents they weren't all that surprised at the interview-in-a-pub. They commented that, in Ireland, business either gets transacted in the pub or finished in the pub. The stamp of approval was a drink, clear evidence that Ireland was, indeed, a pub culture.

2.5 Sport

One of the most dramatic ways in which I experienced the importance of sport in Irish society was through the country's response in the 1990 World Cup Soccer competition. When Ireland participated in the quarterfinals of the tournament virtually all business in the country shut down. Even the multinational firms changed working hours so that all shifts could watch the event.

> *The Irish mix work and sport. The emphasis is on a good sport and social club, organized games. Team sports are*

generally male. Men play soccer then talk about it the next day at work. GAA, soccer, rugby, golf, hurling -- these are the big sports in Ireland. [Patricia]

As with the pub in Ireland, sport was also a symbol of free time and social interaction. When I asked what Irish people liked to do with their free time, sport was among the items consistently given. People wanted to be able to go the match or the pub. When individuals were attempting to explain the importance of social interaction in Ireland, the typical examples used were going to the pub after work or engaging in sports activities such as golf outings. Respondents working at multinational plants observed that one unique aspect of Irish plants that one would not see in sites of multinational firms in the States was the social aspect: their very active sports and social club.

The importance of sport in getting on at work had particular implications for women. Patricia told me that if she had it to do over, one of the things she would do differently at school would be to spend more time on sports. Girls' schools, she said, did not emphasize games and sport like boys' schools did. Consequently, she found it harder in the workplace to fit in because she had fewer things to contribute to conversations about sports. Her comments pointed out that participating in both the *doing of* and *talking about* sport was part of getting on in the workplace.

2.6   Country

The first time I went into [our office in Scotland], the first impression I got straightaway walking into this massive big office area, everybody was sitting there, eyes down, looking really dedicated. As I talked to the people and met them I didn't get any sort of smiles. They were really sort of rigid, I thought. If somebody wandered in here, and said "Hello," to somebody, they'd certainly get a "Hello," back. You can break into conversation a lot more easily. But now within Ireland the scene is, in the country, everybody says "Hello," to everybody. When somebody passes by in a car, you wave to them even if you never saw them before. . . Again, it was, I suppose, the rural influence . . . In the country people just tend to be friendly and give each other the time of day. [Jim]

In abundant ways the rural dimension of Ireland's culture expressed itself as a significant part of the collective psyche of the people. The terms country or down country frequently entered my conversations with respondents. When they used these terms they tended to have one of two meanings. Country in the sense of enjoying the outdoor life was consistently given along with socializing, going to the pub, and sports as the key ways in which Irish people enjoyed their free time. In this sense, then, country referred to enjoying outdoor life and sports such as angling and golf. But in the way Jim spoke of country, it also referred to a state of mind associated with the values and behaviors of small town, rural life. The rural setting was seen as more friendly than its urban counterpart. It was also seen as nonindustrial and, therefore, less regimented. The country values, in contrast with those of the fast life city, were also associated with a greater honesty. I was told about a factory which would only hire workers from Galway County not Galway City because of the belief that rural people worked harder and didn't get into fights the way city people did. The emphasis on friendliness grew as the size of the town diminished. In the small towns people tended to be friendlier. The larger cities, especially Dublin, were perceived to be more impersonal.

The respondents expressed ambivalent feelings about the country. They attributed many of the positive traits in Irish culture to the rural influence. Yet they acknowledged the economic reality that information-sector jobs tended to be in Dublin or the other parts of urban Ireland. Consequently, young people did not intend to remain in the country. However, the fact that Ireland was small enough to enable easy access to the country was a compelling reason to remain in Ireland rather than move abroad. Dermot was an older gentleman whose current position was with an American firm. He observed that even though the information-sector workforce was highly educated and, therefore, potentially quite mobile, Irish workers preferred to stay in Ireland because of the "spirit of life" which included ease of access to people and to family down county.

For most of the twentieth century there had been a migration from the country to the cities for work. But in the 1970s this trend began to subside as government decentralization efforts were undertaken and lucrative financial packages were offered to multinational firms willing to locate at greenfield sites established throughout Ireland. Thus, one impact of the growing information sector has been its role in keeping jobs in the rural parts of Ireland. Despite these efforts, the vast majority of jobs, especially in software, have been located in Dublin. And there was still status associated with young people leaving the country towns in search of opportunities in the city. In the 1980s and 1990s it was just as likely that one would be leaving the country for a high tech job as it would have been for the coveted, "permanent and pensionable" civil service jobs of the past.

The employment landscape since the 1960s has been a steady decline of agricultural work accompanying the increased number of jobs in the information sector. Perhaps this rapid change, sometimes in the span of a single generation, helped to account for the somewhat nostalgic way in which values and attitudes associated with Ireland's rural history were used to help explain or interpret behaviors and attitudes. Throughout my discussions about socio-cultural characteristics, the rural influence in Ireland was a constant.

One of the overriding impressions that I obtained from my time spent observing and interviewing people in the companies of Ireland's information economy was the value placed on the social dimension of work and the expectation that time at work should be enjoyable. People expected the workplace to make workers happy. They wanted to enjoy themselves while they were at work. Ronald talked about how seriously he took his mandate to create a fun environment.

> *We try to preach . . . that if it's not fun in the business, you ought to find a business where it is fun. Work should be fun. By the way, one has to say we had a very tough year last year. . . we didn't show the growth in revenue, practically no growth. Our profit margins were insignificant. Expense constraint was very tight. We are reducing head count. Workload's increasing. We have been going through this tremendous change and some restructuring as we move. I think I mentioned to you that we've moved a lot of people out of the back rooms into front rooms, so to speak, and there's quite significant pressures. [Therefore,] one of the things we're saying [is] we've got to find ways to inject increments of fun. It can be stupid things. They can be things like, if I said "daffodil" today, you might remember daffodils. So we brought in guys, some actors, like Groucho Marx and I forget the others, to each building. Batman. All terribly stupid. But it was a little bit of a frolic, for a bit of fun, and they distributed daffodils to everyone in the company. [Ronald]*

If there were no enjoyment of work, people said, then it would be hard to get cooperation. This atmosphere also helped in the resolution of conflicts arising in the workplace. If a confrontation arose but there was also a good social side to work, then the two people could go have a drink afterwards.

3. INTERCONNECTED

[I was talking to two co-workers. One] had grown up in Cobh. He said it's a small Irish town. You can't spit without everybody knowing about it. Everybody wants to pry into your business, and everything else. It's why he moved up to Cork. "When I go in my front door in the evening," he said, "nobody will know where I'm going or what I'm doing, and that's fine. I can mind my own business." The other guy said he'd grown up in Cork City, which he felt was large and impersonal and you could have fallen down the stairs in your home for a week and nobody would know about it. He moved down to Cobh, where people are always dropping in and out and are friendly. I think it comes down to if you feel threatened by people knowing about you, then Irish society is a problem. [Francis]

Whether through the practice of publishing birth announcements in newspapers throughout the country or in the closeness of a community, the tight knit nature of Irish society came across. People tended to strike up conversations easily at the bus stop or in a supermarket queue. Francis showed the two sides of this closeness. Those who would feel threatened by a lack of anonymity would find Irish society to be a problem. On the other hand, those who felt comfortable that people cared would respond favorably. This feeling of interconnection extended into the information-sector workplace in some interesting ways.

3.1 Everybody Knows Everybody

Ireland is a small country, and the electronics industry probably makes it even smaller, once you're in that circle. Every day you meet somebody in the corridors, from another company. You know them, you know somebody you worked with. People tend, in the industry -- as far as I can see -- to move every three or four years. And given that we've been at it for whatever many years, relatively so few companies, or was, a lot of people have got around to other companies these days, so that you can know a lot of people in the industry, or know of them. [Gerry]

Ireland is a small country in both land mass and population. The country is
275 kilometers at its widest and 486 kilometers at its longest. The population
at the time of this study was 3.5 million people. If the population of the entire
nation is small, the population of the information sector is even smaller. It is
not surprising, therefore, that this sector like this country had a small town
feeling about it. No matter where you might go in the country, you would
always know someone or someone who knew someone who knew you. In the
IT workplace it was the same. You would always know someone no matter
where you worked. In fact, about a quarter of the people obtained their jobs
through contacts.

An important aspect of the small size of the population was that one could
not be different outside of work than inside. "You are not anonymous in
Ireland," summed up one respondent. If in Dublin with its population of one
million, everyone seemed to know everyone, it was even more the case in
other cities and towns. Kathleen was originally from Limerick but she
preferred living in a larger city such as Dublin because in Limerick people
lived more "in each other's pockets."

> *No matter where you go, no matter who you talk to, you're*
> *going to have a connection, whether it be through friends or*
> *family, it's very, very tight knit, not even just the community,*
> *the whole island's very, very tight knit. Which is kinda nice,*
> *you feel kinda nicely locked in and closeted by the whole*
> *thing. But it can be a bit claustrophobic. I don't mind it, but*
> *[coming from America] if you're here for very long you'd*
> *probably find it very claustrophobic. [Cahal]*

There was both a positive and a negative side to this lack of anonymity. On
the positive side friendliness was reinforced because everybody knew
everybody. When walking down a street, it was likely that you would bump
into somebody you knew. I wondered if this helped to account for the
inclination of apparent strangers to strike up a conversation in a public forum
such as a bus or train. On the negative side, however, this closeness could be
stifling. The Irish inquisitiveness enabled people to know each other better.
However, as suggested in the discussion of social class in Chapter 3, this also
meant that it was harder for one to make a change or break out of a mold.
People had predefined roles to play and were assigned characteristics related
to where they came from and who they were known to be. Sue commented on
the difficulty of workers in Ireland moving into the ranks of management.
They would find it much harder than people in the States, she said, to make
that transition because everybody knew where they came from and everybody

knew who they were supposed to be and how they were supposed to behave. Bridie, working for an American firm in Limerick, said that she consciously chose to work in Limerick because she had no relatives there. She said people tended to stay in the same social class if they stayed in their home environments. There was an unwillingness to let people progress, she said. You were more limited because of everyone watching you. It would be hard to be accepted if you were moving above your class.

I knew his father. He had patches in his britches.

The small size and lack of anonymity also led to greater inhibitions. People were more careful in what they did and what they said because they knew somewhere down the line it would get back to them. At the same time it was repeatedly noted that these oppressive and conformist attitudes were less prevalent among the younger generation where there was less concern about what others thought or did. "Live and let live," they said.

3.2 Communicating

We get a number of people visiting -- more experienced people visiting -- in the software center [of our firm] who have commented regularly on the expertise and the skills of the people. Not just in terms of what they do, in terms of their technical knowledge, [but] their ability to communicate what they're doing. [Ronald]

Communication played a distinctive role in the Irish information-sector workplace. Perhaps it was the easygoing attitude that gave people the psychic space to devote to personal relationships. In contrast, they said Americans were too stressed about deadlines to take as much time to interact with other people. Both respondent comments on the topic and direct participant observation confirmed the emphasis placed on verbal skills, and discourse. Irish and American respondents, alike, agreed with this interpretation.

There is a natural gregariousness at the core of Irish people; an American manager described it as a greater need to talk. Eric told a story about a two-day cultural training workshop that was conducted upon his firm's arrival in Ireland. He noted the conversation differential between the Irish and American groups. Each group was charged with listing stereotypes about the other as well as their own values. Whereas the American group took 45 minutes to do this exercise, the Irish group took two and a half hours! This emphasis on discussion and verbal expression could be partly attributed to the country's roots in an oral tradition. Communication for its own sake is highly

valued. Storytelling is a respected skill. Ireland had bards[xii] as recently as 100
years ago. Indeed, one book on cross-cultural issues in business used the
"Irish conversation" as the essential metaphor for depicting the Irish culture.[xiii]

The role of language in Irish culture entered into our discussions through
two avenues. One was discussion of the implications of supplanting the native
Irish language with English. The other was discussion about the cultural value
placed on verbal acuity in both written and oral forms.

> *There was a breakdown in the language after the famine and*
> *language is an indicator of the sophistication you have in*
> *being Irish. The famine broke people down. People began to*
> *ditch culture. Parents and grandparents spoke Irish, but the*
> *children spoke English so they could emigrate and also so*
> *they could work in the civil service. [Nuala]*
>
> **********************
>
> *We speak English. That's the biggest influence of*
> *colonialism. I have contacts, of course, with our*
> *Scandinavian colleagues in other businesses. They have to*
> *speak English as well as their native language. They have to*
> *learn it as a foreign language, and they have to brush up [on*
> *it]. If they don't speak English, they just don't get to work in*
> *the export department, say. We have that advantage from*
> *birth. [Declan]*

These two comments, both by young Irish workers in Irish IT firms, show
the power of language to convey history and culture, and to enable
employment, advancement, and emigration. Indeed, the fact that virtually all
Irish people now speak English is one of the prime attractions for
multinational firms. However, a number of Irish respondents also believed a
significant cultural price was paid for this economic benefit. Those in this
group tended to support the Irish language revival taking place in Ireland. The
importance of language in Ireland was evident both in viewpoints on the status
of the Irish language and in commentary on the level of language skills among
the Irish.

> *About the language, the mother tongue was largely*
> *disregarded. [Aiden]*

A significant legacy of British colonization of Ireland was the impact on
the Irish language. Two opposing viewpoints about the Irish language
emerged from my discussions. One point of view noted the strong link
between language and culture. These people argued that the systematic

destruction of the language by the British overlords not only attempted to destroy the language, but the culture as well.[xiv] Nuala believed Ireland had an identity crisis that could be traced back to the role played by language in breaking down the culture. The combined effects of British colonization, the famine and subsequent emigration resulted in the diminution of the Irish language.[xv]

To rectify this situation, the new Irish Free State put in place structures and requirements intended to make the Irish language a meaningful part of the emerging, independent Irish nation. Certain regions in the West of Ireland called the Gaeltacht were designated as Irish speaking.[xvi] The study of Irish became a compulsory subject. Throughout the land, knowledge of Irish was made a requirement for employment in any branch of the civil service and in education.

In the 1990s, the attitude toward the Irish language seemed to be going in opposite directions. On the one hand the Irish government lessened the language requirement, thereby making it easier to function in Irish society without knowledge of the Irish language. For example, employment in the civil service no longer requires that an individual have a spoken understanding of Irish. But an almost simultaneous trend was a movement in the opposite direction: a Celtic revival, which included the Irish language as a source of national pride. Evidence of this revival was the growing number of people studying Irish. In addition, new programs of study in university using the Irish language were also established.[xvii]

The other viewpoint was that the linguistic legacy of colonialism in modern day Ireland had actually been to Ireland's benefit. Knowledge of English helped Irish information-sector workers find work more easily both at home and abroad. Those who held this view about the Irish language ranged from having active resentment about the money and energy spent on the effort to maintain Irish, to benign acceptance of a somewhat useless skill. Phillip, who was of Anglo-Irish heritage, expressed a representative viewpoint:

> *This obsession with the Irish language is incredibly damaging. People are focused on learning Irish when they should be learning German or learning technology and they get into the civil service because they speak Irish not because they necessarily know how to do calculus. I mean a talented, continental EU member right now who can't come to Ireland to teach is ludicrous. I mean these people having to go out and learn Irish. [My wife] thinks it's sweet, I think it's dangerous! Learning Irish as a cultural subject is one thing*

but having grades associated with Irish compulsorily is screwy.

ET: What about the role of language in preserving culture?

Well as far as I'm concerned culture comes a long way down the list. I mean I don't know exactly what you mean -- world culture, European culture, or whatever -- that's fine. But narrowly Irish culture I do not rate that highly. I like Irish music and so on. But I just don't think it's this. . . I think it [the Irish language] is a sacred cow. [Phillip]

A more tempered view was that while the language ought not be forced upon people and interjected as a condition of employment, there was a role in Irish society for the teaching and the learning of Irish.

Niall explained that the requirement for Irish people to operate in two languages -- Irish and English -- explained the emphasis on language skills within the Irish culture. His comments suggest some possible reasons for the highly developed language arts in Ireland. He went on to explain that Irish is a literary language based on storytelling. The reason that the art forms of fiction, poetry, and theatre were emphasized is that the deprivation of the Irish people precluded the availability of elaborate materials needed for the visual arts. The tradition of being literary continues. Writers are known figures in Ireland the way sports stars would be in another country. People are aware of writers like James Joyce even if they haven't read his works. I experienced this one Sunday during a walking tour of Dublin, something I've done in many cities in several countries. However, unlike any other tour I had been on, as our tour guide brought us to the house of an Irish poet, he proceeded to stand on the front steps of this townhouse and recite some of the poet's works. It was not uncommon to find someone reciting poetry at a party.[xviii]

In the course of my interviews I came across several examples of the emphasis on language and literature in everyday life. Eamon, who came from the rural West, talked about the connection between the agricultural life and storytelling when he was growing up. When the hay needed to be saved[xix] all the neighbors came together and helped. There would be good chat when the ladies brought the tea, and good storytelling. In my own participant observation I was particularly struck by the story telling. Once the stories started the party could go on until daybreak. I had never been to such long dinner parties. I attended social gatherings that went on for six, seven or ten hours, and spanned several meals.

An example of a poetic bent that made its way into the most unlikely of situations was provided in Charles' story about his educational background.

He explained how an interest in poetry led to his career in the information sector.

> *After primary school I went to technical school for a year. More emphasis on the technical side [but] there were some academic subjects: the Irish language, English and math. While I was there I got a love for English poetry. There were guys on the same bus going to the secondary school and I was asking them what it was like. So I said I'd give it a try anyhow. I took the plunge. Something inside me was yearning for knowledge. The definition of a philosopher. A lover of philosophy. A lover of knowledge.*
>
> *ET: And this was all, this all started out with your interest in poetry?*
>
> *Something like that, yes*
>
> *ET: You stayed with it? Do you still read poetry?*
>
> *I still like poetry a lot. I don't read it much, but I do often quote it, even Geoffrey Chaucer. Old English. There's a guy at the moment doing his BA [degree] part-time here. He said he had a problem with some of that stuff --* The Canterbury Tales. *I was actually quoting it to him. He says, "I'm having trouble understanding it." I was very quick to learn poetry in school. In technical school they give a small token prize to the first to memorize lines of poetry. I usually won that prize. [Charles]*

Whatever the reasons, it was taken for granted that the Irish have particularly developed language skills. The highly literate Irish workforce was consistently given as one of the main reasons that IT firms came to Ireland. It was assumed that the workers possessed mental alertness and had well developed language facility.

> *When I lived in New York I met for lunch with some advertising people who immediately talked business over a three-martini lunch . . . I tried to find a common ground for conversation. I asked what they thought about the new movie version of Joyce's* Ulysses. *They said they didn't go to movies. They told me their wives were responsible for culture and children's education. In Ireland a value is placed upon knowing about writing and theatre. Also music. There is a*

> *revival of Irish language through music going on currently.*
> *The largest Irish-speaking group in Ireland after the*
> *Gaeltacht is in Dublin. [Niall]*

The cultural emphasis on verbal exchange translated into predictable behavior in the workplace. People needed to establish a sense of context before getting down to business. They want to know who your people are, where you were coming from and what you wanted from them. They wanted an understanding of where an individual was situated. They wanted to know the big picture. The notion of "just get down to business" was too cold for them. It was hard to force them to get down to business without this background. There was a whole ritual of getting coffee and slowly working into the topic at hand. One had to break the ice first. When I asked Irish people whether this would continue in light of cultural influences from the multinationals and other sources, it was very clear to them that this ritual would prevail.

While I encountered several instances of this need for context during my interviews, one experience, which quite specifically brought this point home to me, occurred outside of my corporate interviews. I was helping to plan an academic conference that was to be held in Dublin. In the course of negotiating one particular gentleman's participation on a panel we agreed to meet for lunch to discuss the matter in greater detail. Or so I thought. Instead, we spent three and a half hours having lunch so that he could get to know me! At the end of it all he said, "Now that I know you, we can get together to talk about the panel." Sue's reaction to this story was that it was a very common experience. One cannot just go into a situation with an agenda and expect the Irish to stick to it, because they have a lot of hidden agendas. In this case the hidden agenda was that he wanted to get to know who I was and what I was about, before he would commit to a particular role on the panel. In thinking about the whole experience later, I understood why he expressed mild surprise that I intended to bring my briefcase containing conference materials along to the luncheon.

A value was placed on the art of conversation, both in and out of the workplace. American respondents as well as Irish people who had been to America noticed the increased amount of verbal interaction in Ireland. They observed more laughing and talking with other people during coffee breaks. It was commonplace for people to talk the next morning about the past night's social events. As an example, Leo told me he just had to accept the fact that after a recent company-wide outing to see the musical *CATS* there would be half an hour of chat the next day before work began. The art of conversation was just that: a valued and practiced ability. Friendly interaction, telling a good story and keeping up one's end of the conversation were not considered optional behaviors; they were expectations.

There were several noticeable effects in the information-sector workplace of this heightened emphasis on interpersonal communication. One was that technical people were expected to be able to communicate with each other, with customers, and with management. Human resources managers explained that the ability to get on with co-workers was an important hiring criterion. Prospective employers also wanted to feel assured that an individual would be successful in day-to-day relationships.

> *Typically, when we're interviewing people . . . someone that won't be looking at them technically . . . will talk to them as well to check to see if they have quote two heads unquote. You have to be reasonably smooth too. So a company like ours wouldn't take on somebody who seems very technically competent but who isn't a good communicator. They'll be a friendly enough person but just they won't be good at explaining what they're doing so they wouldn't be any good for marketing and that's a bit of a downer because all the engineers, may have to give papers here and there, talk to customers, you know, that sort of stuff. [Connor]*

Valuing human interaction also had an effect on management-worker relations. Several Irish respondents expressed this idea by drawing a distinction with England. In Ireland where there was a desire to get on socially with people, managers were less authoritarian. This was helpful in ironing out the wrinkles in personnel issues. When Aine was a manager in London her style had been quite different from what it was in Dublin. In London she was more inclined to get an office, to stay in it and -- she said, laughing -- be very *official*. Whereas in Dublin if there were a personnel issue she would just walk down the street with someone at lunchtime and have a little chat and sort out the issues that way. While the problem might eventually warrant going the official route, people started with the informal approach. To her, the Irish way was much easier. You could start off nicely and hopefully sort it out. That way managers didn't end up with a wall sitting between them and the workers.

The British approach created more of a distance Aine said. There was a bigger distinction between the boss and the workers in London than in Ireland. Whereas she kept to her natural approach of "roll the sleeves up and work," most managers in London did not do that. They would cut themselves off. They would not go and drink with the staff unless it was their duty to take the staff out for a drink. On a social level they would feel they should keep this distance. In fact, Aine was criticized once for socializing with the lower staff. She learned you were not supposed to unless it was a company event and then it was your duty to be there.

A noticeable effect of interpersonal interactions in Ireland was that IT workers had a good overall understanding of the firm. At the end of the day the venue for work conversation switched to the pub. This helped to keep lines of communication open with the consequence of fewer formal meetings. In other cultures such meetings were needed in order to keep people abreast of what everyone was doing. Their Irish counterparts, however, would tend to know already because they took a natural interest in each other and would have spent time during and after work learning what the others were doing.

> *When we went to [the American headquarters] I was talking to a particular guy in manufacturing, and I says to him,*
> *"Who's working in this office here?" I sat across the corridor from him. He looked up at the name on the door and he actually had to read the name off the door.*
> *I said, "What's he do?"*
> *"Oh he works in such and such."*
> *I said, "Don't you ever sit down and talk?"*
> *"No, no. He works in [a different manufacturing area]. Two different things altogether."*
> *No communication, no interest whatsoever, even though [they are] across the corridor from each other. In an Irish scene that couldn't happen. You'd be in chatting. You'd know each other's [jobs]. As I say, proximity in regard to offices. The walls being in between wouldn't stop you. But the only thing that would keep us apart would be [being] away in separate areas. [Charles]*

In the workplace, people tended to be very aware of each other's private and personal progress and were more open about asking and talking about it. It was not considered an invasion of privacy. This type of social interaction helped to strengthen relationships. Interacting with people socially made you more disposed towards them when you interacted with in a business setting. The cost of such an emphasis on conversation might be short-term loss but long-term gain. One man commented that social interaction could sometimes be a detriment to productivity because having conversation at any opportunity takes up time. But, then, he observed that the time spent would be worthwhile down the road when it came to solving problems.

3.3   Connections

"The stroke" does exist in politics, yes. In the workplace, the term grapevine is the more appropriate descriptor. Personal contacts are more important than a CV or academic achievements. The grapevine is helpful. If you do well by someone, they'll tell others and take an interest in your success. "Pulling a stroke" means to snatch a happy resolution from a difficult situation. You "pull a stroke" and things fall into place in your favor. It also means a business opportunity grasped and executed thoroughly, of the moment. Personal introductions are crucial to success, not "the stroke." Personal introductions are based on performance not class or social standing or things like family connections.
[Stephen]

Stephen's comments wove together the various threads of the elusive fabric called connections. My first exposure to this trait in Irish society was in the political arena. Repeated references to clientelism, "stroking" and "old school tie" led me to explore this facet of Irish culture and its possible influence on Ireland's information economy. Part of the reason I found this notion so compelling to explore was its elusive nature. I was also drawn to evocative phrases which embodied it such as "who your people are" and "a nod and a wink." As I soon learned, this cultural trait was both extensive and complex. Several understandings could be applied to this concept. A variety of terms were used and were applied differently depending upon the setting.

On the simplest level connections were about placing people in some context. An Irish woman in the States introduced me to the concept of, "who your people are." She explained that when people were going to do business they wanted to know to whom you were connected. She said that people would do business with people based, in part, on who they were, who their people were, and what their connections were. She contrasted this with her experience in America where such objective factors as the quality of the product and its price would be the determining factors in doing business.

"The stroke," on the other hand, extended the notion of connections to include collaborating to beat the system to the mutual benefit of all concerned.

[("The stroke")] is widespread in all walks of life. In the pubs, publicans [pub owners] and the police are in cahoots. For example, when the inspector comes in, giving him free pints while on duty in exchange for getting a good review. You see

it in the courts, with politics. Employment is also that way. A person with connections with a desirable product, for example stereos, would always be doing a deal. And this is considered legitimate from a company's point of view. Another example is splitting the VAT [value added tax]: just paying for something with cash – and, therefore, [having] no invoice and no VAT -- versus paying by check, having an invoice and having to pay the VAT. Take my mother, for example, who is really holy. She would get £50 for selling something when the VAT is included and £60 when it is in cash, and therefore no VAT. [Aidan]

Closely related to the notion of collaboration found in "the stroke" was the use of influence and favors in order to accomplish something in politics or business as expressed in the phrase "a nod and a wink." In the political arena this might be seen in the influence wielded by lobbying groups who also had financial clout. In the business arena it could range from influencing the hiring process to vendors influencing customers through favors. While "a nod and a wink" is certainly present in other countries what I found interesting was the openness about it in Ireland.[xx]

A quite prevalent interpretation of connections was the use of contacts for personal intervention. Personal intervention was the norm in Irish politics. The TD's (representatives) held regular clinics in their constituencies to hear citizens' requests for intercession with the government. This tradition is a byproduct of the highly competitive election process of proportional representation. Consequently representatives garner favor with their constituents by promising to intervene on their behalf to the government.[xxi]

The use of contacts also extended to securing employment. Friends of applicants, even politicians or the parish priest might ring up personnel managers to ask for a job on behalf of someone else. Quite often employees are interviewing relations. Some people complained about favoritism and this kind of promotion.

He got three people in!

Nevertheless, personal intervention remains a strong part of the culture. Within the information sector I detected a resistance toward this approach, the "who you know not what you know" mentality. Like several other topics we discussed, some thought that things were changing, that while connections used to be *the* way to get jobs, its influence was diminishing overall and was much less prevalent in the IT industry.

This practice had traditionally been commonplace within other sectors. Stephanie talked about her job in one of the large semi-state agencies saying that job applicants were asked to give the names of relatives already working there. If there were two equal candidates, the one who would get the job would be the one who knew the recruiter's father, for example. Because of connections in Irish society it was also commonplace to be required to have someone vouch for you in order to obtain services. Eric told me about his experiences in moving to Ireland to assume the managing director position of his firm. He had direct experience with the legal and social practices built up around the expectation of people knowing and vouching for you. When he moved to Ireland he was required to have someone vouch for him in order to be able to bring his family's silver service into the country. Although he and his wife had filled out the proper declaration forms, he learned that the silver would remain in Customs until he got his Customs form signed. Doing this required that someone at the local Garda[xxii] station vouch for him. When he went to the Garda station the sergeant there wanted to know who knew him.

> *So the law must be that the sergeant can only vouch for me if someone whom the sergeant knows can vouch for me. [Eric]*

Upon further exploration I learned that there were several bases for this trait. It was an artifact of the value placed on social interaction. There was a natural progression from an emphasis on conversation and placing an individual in context to an emphasis on contacts and having connections. Another source was the small town atmosphere of the country, the fact that everyone knew everyone. Closely related was the effect of strong family ties. Remaining connected to extended family in a small society would naturally lead to developing and reinforcing connections. Still others said the class system was responsible for this cultural trait. They said a tradition of personal intervention had developed in order to meet the needs of people who could not break out of roles to which they were confined. Those without power relied on others to speak for them.

When I inquired about the presence of connections in information-sector workplaces I received conflicting viewpoints. While everyone acknowledged that connections existed in Irish culture, there were differing views about the extent to which they existed in the information sector. While some thought the IT sector helped to diminish this cultural trait in the workplace, others thought otherwise. The stories people shared with me showed how integral *connection* was to the culture. But I could also discern two kinds of connection: one, more benign, another potentially sinister. The former type is what I observed in the information-sector workplaces.

The benign forms of connection had to do with hiring and promotion, business and industry relations, and entrepreneurship. The most common way in which connections were played out in the information sector was in hiring and promotion activities. But this was more the case in the early years than in the 1990s. When it came to getting jobs in the newly developing information sector, family connections initially helped considerably. As a result, it was quite common to see several members of a family working at the same multinational firm. In high tech companies connections may have helped people get a foot in the door but then they needed to prove their qualifications. As the skill requirements grew, the role of family connections as a hiring factor diminished in importance. Nevertheless, a typical way of obtaining a job was to send your CV to someone you knew at the firm.

> *If one comes through a contact or a personal reference --
> "the devil you know over the devil you don't know" -- may
> help to get one of the individuals through. But I wouldn't say
> it would be a deciding factor. Everything would have to be
> equal before it would become a deciding factor. But if one
> guy was clearly better than another I think generally he
> would be selected. Now I know that's not always the case.
> And I know that within some cliques they do tend to pull their
> own strings. Some people have talked about, you know, the
> "Irish mafia" or the "Irish Masonic orders" in different
> parts of the country. And I've seen evidence of that, but I
> wouldn't see it as a dominating factor so much. [Liam]*

Eric noted that when a position popped up someone would bring forth a name, not necessarily from the previous job they'd had but maybe from the company before that. Or someone would give the name of a neighbor. While it also happened in the States, he noticed it happening more often in Ireland. An advantage, he noted, was that his firm was able to obtain excellent references. Whereas in the States the usefulness of references diminished when it was not possible to check with the current employer, in Ireland he could obtain references through the network. If he could not contact the current employer then he could turn to an employee who knew someone who either used to work at the applicant's firm or knew someone else who did. Sometimes the role of connections was as simple as identifying people you knew in common at the beginning of the interview process, which made the candidate more relaxed, and the overall recruitment process easier. But there could also be negative consequences of this approach to hiring. Gerry explained that if he sought to recruit new employees from his former place of employment, current co-workers might accuse him of using connections rather than qualifications. These people would say, for example, they had a cousin who could have done the job.

From Mary I learned that both personal intervention and "the stroke" came into play with respect to career advancement:

> *Right, let's say if you go into your supervisor, he may "pull a stroke" for you. D'you know what I mean? If you wanted to get further, he might "pull that stroke" for you, right.*

> *ET: And what would this be like, "pulling the stroke?"*

> *Let's say if you wanted a different job, right, and he knew the person and could set you on him as a great worker, right, and he could "pull that stroke" for you, without even through an interview, like. Mightn't always happen that way but it can be done, like. It seems to be said over and over again in here like, "Such a one 'pulled the stroke' for someone and that's how they got there," like, you know?*

> *ET: Is that accepted? Does everybody just accept that that's the way it gets done?*

> *That's the way it gets done. [Mary]*

Another respondent who read upside down quite well commented on my notation "always through friends" as we discussed career mobility. He laughed but agreed:

> *That's the way things are.*

A second benign use of connections was in business and industry relations. The small size of the population in general, and of the information sector in particular, meant that personal contacts were both more available and expected. In addition, there was ongoing migration from one firm to another. Consequently, in Ireland it was possible, in fact typical, to know everyone in the entire sector. Certainly, a managing director would know all other firms in the industry. Leo observed that people tended to know their counterparts in other companies better than they would in the US. Some of it was formal -- from going to meetings -- but much of it was informal: from networking and talking to people. As a result of this close knit community a rapport was both needed and possible to establish before business deals were done. People were very aware of their reputations.

Connections also helped when one was starting a company because you could get contact chains going more easily. You could ring people up because you were friendly with them, something that would enable you to get assistance. This smaller and more personalized industry could be a definite benefit for start up firms said Liam. Knowing six people in Ireland could lead to opening any door, a great help in seeking people to listen to your proposals.

> *Within our own company would be one or two individuals here who seem to know everybody, everywhere. And so that if we want to do business with a particular company, we may not know who to go to, but we will know somebody there who will tell us who the right person is. And they will effect an introduction for us. To be introduced would be so much better than going in cold turkey. To go in there having been referenced by somebody who's a common denominator in the situation, would be a big help. [Liam]*

The close-knit nature of the industry, however, also meant that reputation played a significant role as well. On the one hand, the small size made it easier to establish a reputation and get to know people. The chances were good that you were "known." Your reputation preceded you. On the other hand, knowing everyone could have its disadvantages. If you failed at your venture everyone would know.

The potentially sinister examples of using connections in the information sector were associated with emphasizing quid pro quo over qualifications. One woman said no one did something for nothing; you always expected to get something in return. Again, there were conflicting views about the extent of such an attitude in the information-sector workplace. One view was that this back scratching or "fix it" behavior was big in Irish politics, Irish society and small Irish industries but not in the multinationals. Another view was that this quid pro quo attitude was indeed carried into the IT firms. On the one hand, respondents talked about the importance of reputation and actual accomplishment because people in IT were so highly visible. Yet they provided numerous instances of accomplishment through influence and "a nod and a wink" rather than through actual achievement.

A dramatic example of clientelism in the information-sector workplace came from the stories I heard from people in several different firms about the first managing director of one particular multinational firm. This firm hired an Irish managing director who, in turn, hired his staff. But the hiring process was more about "the stroke" than about qualifications, and this individual perceived his job as more about external relations than managing the operational aspects of a start-up manufacturing plant. Joseph, who worked at another American firm, shared his version of the story that was making the rounds of the information sector.

> *He was busy being a [public relations] man and -- this is all from what I hear from the guys at work who had worked there and who experienced it first hand -- he was more a politician, not in the inside sense, not in business politics, but vis a vis a community politician, versus running a manufacturing operation. He hired his good old boys. I guess the place started falling apart. What was amazing was what -- people were telling me what this guy was doing -- he was doing, not only did it have nothing to do with manufacturing, it had nothing to do with computers and nothing to do with high tech! It was truly like a politician, like an alderman in the town or something! I couldn't even imagine someone doing something like that! [Joseph]*

If there was a consistent view across respondents it was that while instances of connections were commonplace in the high tech field, instances of "the stroke" such as the one given above were not. Martin, an Irish entrepreneur, acknowledged that upper management in large companies "did deals" off the record. But what was more typical was that there was more "front end" work done in Ireland than might be done in other countries. To him, people in these countries seemed to have forced social interaction because they knew they needed personal working relations. Whereas in Ireland it was more natural, more normal, he said. The interaction already existed. Martin had been embarrassed in his one distinct experience with "the stroke." In his view, such things were normally found only in the political and religious realms.

Despite evidence of the significant role of connections in the Irish information sector, connections played a less significant role in this sector than in others. As noted in Chapter 3, it was easier for a working class person to obtain work in a high tech company than in some other sectors. This was because one did not need contacts as much as one would, say, to be a physician or solicitor, professions in which family links were a crucial factor.

3.4   Personal

The people with whom I spoke made a link between being a small, caring society and having a more caring workforce. A significant number of respondents credited Ireland's small population for the friendliness for which the country is well known.[xxiii] In the minds of both American and Irish managers there were definite benefits accruing from this personalized workplace. As a manager, John saw a contribution to productivity.

> *People know each other better, there's a better chance they understand each other. I think this understanding leads to one's energies going in a more productive way in the work environment, as opposed to the other aspects. Work is like anything else. If you don't understand people, you don't know what they're about. At least if there aren't severely negative things, there's at least going to be a portion of time wasted on not being on the same wave length. I think the [Irish] plant [of our firm] is in a better position in that area than a larger organization where people are more anonymous. [John]*

Workers also commented on the personalized atmosphere in the workplace. People were quite willing to help when they knew people; friendliness was due to people knowing people. The size of the country made it easier to meet friends and to see them quite frequently. As a result of the small population several relatives typically worked for the same company. Because people knew each other better, there was more communication. For all of these reasons the personalized workplace resulted in more of a collaborative effort at work. You may not know people directly but you've seen them in town. Therefore, you could quickly get on more friendly terms with them.

Workers at the multinational plants believed they had a better idea of how the company was doing than counterparts in America because of the smaller scale and more personal orientation. Because Ireland was small, companies were small and people were known personally. There was a greater sense of loyalty to a group, to a company. What started off as loyalty to the group was then extended to the manager, which, by default, became loyalty to the company.

Just as an individual workplace had a personalized atmosphere, so too did the information technology industry itself. Given the small size of the society and the information sector, people knew their counterparts in other companies better than they might in a larger society. One was expected to keep contact with others in the industry; one needed to keep in touch with the right people. You never knew who your boss might be tomorrow.

This closeness left its imprint on hiring practices. Gerry commented that a considerable amount of hiring was based on contacts or friends. If he were in a position to hire he would look to the multinational firm where he previously worked as a source of employees. He would look there for people he knew and with whom he could work. Cahal qualified this viewpoint in commenting that people would not be inclined to "rob" each other's employees. There was not much of the predator-type instinct in the Irish IT sector; rather, firms tended to grow their own employees. He contrasted this with his perception of the American west coast where it seemed "you rob your pal's staff when you needed workers."

In a smaller, more personal company clients knew that they could rely on you to deliver on your promises. A person in the information sector usually had a personal contact in every other IT firm in Ireland. So he could ring up any company and would know somebody and therefore would get an appointment for a visit. Ed gave an example. His firm wanted to observe a company that was using just-in-time manufacturing practices. They identified a firm in Limerick, which had the type of process they wanted to observe. Because of his personal contact, Ed was able to arrange for a site visit. Without a personal contact, he noted, it would have been difficult to achieve.

An implication of such a high degree of personalism was a heightened emphasis placed upon reputation. Reputation was everything. You certainly did not burn bridges in Ireland. You would always know some people when you started a new job. The smallness of society kept people on their good behavior. In Ireland, it was difficult to recover from a mistake because it was so easy to check up on somebody -- through church, sports, social events and business contacts.

It was also easier to ring up friends to get references, something that gave a manager greater confidence about whom he or she was hiring. Fiona noted that people really lived on their reputations. It was good for her firm, she said, because they hadn't messed up. Because the IT industry in Ireland was so small -- there was as much industry in the whole of Ireland as there was in greater Manchester -- it was not the name of the company that mattered; it was the individual's reputation. First impressions mattered. Every businessperson in the IT field knew every other: what they were doing, had done, their track record. People who had gotten it wrong the first time didn't get another chance to do it right, she said.

Another way in which the personalism of Irish culture played out in both society and the workplace was that people truly cared about one another. While this might seem trite, it was, nevertheless, apparent that a significant contribution to quality of life in Ireland came from the enjoyment of others.

> *Dublin is hectic, true, but the rest of the country isn't like that. [There] they hardly have time to stand out anymore*

> *unless they're waiting for a train or a bus. Whereas here, the*
> *train the bus driver will probably wait while you're having a*
> *chat with the neighbors before you board. [Sheelagh]*

Sheelagh, who was from a rural background, worked at a multinational plant
in the West. While she considered Dublin to be hectic, I found the pace quite
slow compared to a typical American city. I found that Irish people took a
genuine interest in others. I was initially amazed at how well people
remembered my name at the firms I visited. Typically, on the second or third
visit to a firm -- which might be spread out over several months -- the firm's
receptionist would remember who I was. The IT firms were not the only place
where this occurred; the same thing would happen at the University. I found
my Irish colleagues wanting to know about me as a person. Since I am an
American, I could partially explain this as a cultural curiosity factor. So, one
thing I wanted to know was whether this trait was also in evidence on the shop
floor. What I learned was that some multinational firms understood better than
others this deeply felt need to interact at work. Una told me about a
multinational firm that was very strict about communication to the point that
the firm would no longer hire people from her company. She said the reason
was that her co-workers were viewed as "spoiled" because they had parties
and expected to have a good time at work and enjoy themselves.

There were several visible results of this friendliness in the workplace. It
was easier to talk to people and to get to know them.[xxiv] Managers at the
multinational firms, especially, observed that the degree of friendliness in the
Irish plants led to easier communication. Michael had just returned to Ireland
after working for a number of years at the American headquarters of his firm.
On several occasions throughout my time at his firm, he registered his cultural
acclimation.

> *I found it difficult, not difficult, strange, initially, when I*
> *came back [to Ireland]. Everybody says, "Hello" to you even*
> *if you don't know their name or you never sat with them.*
> *Everyone says "Hello" . . . In the USA . . . even inside [this*
> *firm] in an elevator or the people who worked with you on*
> *the same floor, they just wouldn't acknowledge you. They*
> *walk by you, and you try and have a conversation with*
> *someone in an elevator and they tend to take a step away*
> *from you. That's strange, whereas there's a bonding in*
> *working in the workforce here. People bound together. We're*
> *all in the same boat. People just say "Hello" to you.*
> *[Michael]*

A second implication of this friendliness was that even technical people were expected to have well-developed interpersonal skills. As Tom pointed out, if you failed to get the job it was not likely to be for technical reasons. The employer would assume you learned the technical material in school. Not being hired would typically be because you were perceived as being unable to get on with others. The requirement that technical personnel also possess interpersonal skills came not just from the friendliness of the culture; it also derived from the structure of the IT firms in Ireland. Whereas a large multinational firm might be able to afford to have computer "nerds" with few social interaction skills, smaller multinational sites and Irish firms needed workers to be more well rounded. Everyone needed to be able to deal with the public. In this way the cultural trait of friendliness, flexibility, an "all hands on deck" attitude that the Irish seemed to possess naturally helped firms adapt to the special circumstances of the Irish information sector. The flexibility and willingness to help others also gave workers a better overall understanding of the whole company and its operations. Farrell, a middle aged man who worked for a Dublin multinational firm, contrasted this deeply ingrained facet of Irish culture with what he knew of America from his brother's experience.

> . . . *[M]y own personal observation [of] Irish versus the US is that relationships are very important in Ireland, in your family, and in society in groups all over, right? And you try to . . . spend the time to establish relationships with people. And you keep in touch with people even after they've moved on type of thing, you know? But my impression of the US is that it's more difficult -- again, I'm taking some of this from my brother and his family over in the US -- especially in California. That it's almost impossible to keep sort of a lasting relationships going with a group. And that is one of the biggest turnoffs, I suppose, for all of them [his brother's family] is not having this comradeship and trust relationship where you can depend on them when you need them and so on. Whereas Americans are going after their own careers or going in their own direction and you get this impression -- I don't know whether it's true or not but -- out of sight out of mind. If you're there, fine, it's grand. But once you're gone there's no hard feelings. And that's one thing that I would find difficult, I'd say, if I was to move to the US. Here, you can drop in on a friend for tea unannounced. I would be trying to make deeper relationships. [Farrell]*

Dermot pointed out that personalism carried over into relationships with clients: they expected considerable interaction. He was not sure that those in the home office in America sufficiently understood this, however. He complained that they told him to lower the head count but if he did, he wouldn't have enough customer coverage. In contrast with the objectivity in the selling process that he ascribed to Americans, Irish clients required personal selling.

The small size of the information sector reinforced personalism. It was relatively easy to make a reputation and get to know people. Because of the importance of reputation and the more personal relationships clients could more easily rely on a vendor to deliver what it promised. In Julie's case this personal relationship went to the extent of clients' recognizing her voice! She said that when she got on the phone, sometimes she only had to say hello, and people would say, "Oh, it's Julie." To her, it was crucial to get to know these people and build up a rapport with them, and keep contact because they would then let her know what projects were coming on. A person needed to keep in touch with the right people.

Personalism was also apparent in the management style. Upon his arrival in Ireland, David immediately noticed how differently his position was interpreted.

> *The guy who was my country boss when I came along here for the interview process, [when] it was lunch time [said], "Let's go have a drink." So we went up to [a nearby town], had a few pints of Guinness, and we didn't talk very much about work. What I'm relating is a comment of his that particularly personalizes the personnel manager's job. "One of the things you manage, expect to manage is employee relations. So social skills, in the context of the environment you work in, are considered to be very important." I wouldn't find that in the UK. Social skills in the sense of being socially nice in your behavior, but not to be able to manage a party and have a 15 year "do." The personal manager is in there organizing. That's great; actually I enjoyed that because it's a fantastic joy. It's part of the job. The external social interaction. [David]*

Deirdre noted a difference in the job descriptions of managers at her site compared to those in other countries. She said that at many of the other locations managers were individual contributors or project leaders as well. In Ireland, managers were full time managers. Their job was about getting the most out of the people, keeping morale up, realizing everybody's potential. It was up to the managers -- not the human resources department -- to develop people: to hire, reward and motivate them.

Ed, who described his preferred management style as "management by wandering," found the Irish approach a refreshing change from America. While he had been criticized in the US for taking a personal interest in his workers, in Ireland, his style fit in naturally. As a result of taking a personal interest in employees and co-workers, he believed people knew each other better. Even though he had worked with some close-knit departments in the US, he believed the in-work relationships were much stronger in Irish firms, because it was not just a working relationship. It was a working relationship, but the core of the relationship was knowing a little bit about the person, having an understanding of him or her. He noticed that difference in workplace interactions.

Personalism, which resulted from an increased understanding of the individual, led, in turn, to a greater understanding of the whole. One man saw a clear application of this more caring attitude. In contrasting the workplace in Ireland with other sites of the firm, he noted that concern about others translated into concern for the whole company. Elsewhere, he said, people just had their own little piece of turf that they controlled and couldn't care less about anything that was outside. The people at the Irish site actually had more concern for the whole group, he thought, than was actually visible in other countries.

Brian noted that the American plant of his company was much more impersonal than its Irish equivalent. One particular experience drove this point home to him. On several occasions he had made phone calls looking for a certain individual. In response to his queries he was told, "Oh, he's not here," or "He doesn't work here. He's in a different area." Then, when he actually visited this American site he realized that the person he had sought was only a few offices away from the people giving those answers! In Brian's view, the person with whom he spoke couldn't be bothered to go three offices away to get the guy for him.

Because people knew each other better, there was a better chance they would understand each other. Such understanding, in turn, led to people's energies being channeled in the same direction in the work environment. By knowing people, there was less time wasted "getting on the same wave length." For these reasons, American and Irish respondents alike believed the Irish plants were in a better position than a larger organization where people were more anonymous.

One symbol of the differences in personalism and anonymity among cultures was the Irish reaction to name tags. Charles was quite articulate in his disdain for them as culturally offensive. It went against the grain, he said, because people were expected to know those with whom they worked.

> *Most people don't wear their badges -- too big and cumbersome. Personally, I would feel like a prize bull at the fair with a rosette in his ear! A new security guard can know people in about a week. Most people say good morning to them or good evening or whatever. [Charles]*

The effect of a culture which places a value on personalism, connection and social interaction came through in an experience that I had about three months into my year in Ireland. It is still so vivid I need no notes to aid my memory in order to describe it. I was returning home from City Centre one evening in December. It was a dark, cold and rainy rush hour. The chill seemed to go right through my coat and woolen clothes. All I could think of was getting back to my apartment and getting warm. As I sat on the crowded bus and looked about me it seemed as though the other passengers -- tired from the day's work or Christmas shopping -- felt the same. The bus had crossed the Liffy River and was winding its way slowly through the North Side of Dublin. In Phibsborough in front of a grocery store, the bus stopped and a blind man and his dog got on the bus. Then for the next ten minutes in the rainy Dublin rush hour, a line of stopped traffic accumulated and stretched two miles back, all the way to the river. Not a single auto horn sounded. Meanwhile, inside the bus, there was considerable negotiation to get this man seated.

The first individual to react was a sullen looking teenager who at first glance seemed like the kind of person one might cross to the other side of a dark street to avoid. I watched him bolt out of his seat to offer it to the man. Then several ladies helped maneuver the dog through the crowded bus to get it settled next to the man. With standing room only in this bus, the whole process was rather complicated. No one raised a voice in protest at the time being taken. Everyone reacted as though on cue. During the ten minutes that people within view got up from their seats to help the man and the dog get adjusted -- which happened to be the front of the bus -- nobody else could get on or off the bus. Everyone waited patiently in the bus and outside in the rain.

When I told this story to Margie, she was quite blasé about it. Whereas I was shocked at the instantaneous and pervasive demonstration of caring and patience, she took it in stride as a rather commonplace event. "He's probably a regular traveler," was all she said. I saw a definite connection between this experience of kindness, caring and patience and what I was hearing and witnessing in the information-sector workplaces I was visiting.

> *If you grow up in a small and more caring society, I suppose*
> *you tend sometimes to be more caring of your workforce.*
> *[Margie]*

The heightened emphasis placed upon conversation skills, connection and interpersonal interaction made for a more personal workplace in relationships with clients, between manager and worker, or among workers. Consequently, whether you were looking for a job or trying to effect a change at work, you would tend to do it through informal means, through someone you knew.

4. CONCLUSION

Quality of life has always been listed among the attractive features of Ireland. Both the pace of life and the interpersonal way in which it is conducted continue to be attractive to natives and visitors alike. A survey of 2,515 business executives in 46 countries ranked Ireland in 1997 above Germany, France, Spain, the US and the UK on quality of life (IDA Ireland, 1998, p. 67). Annual holiday leave was increased from three to four weeks in April 1999 (Houston, 1999, p. 113) and the work week has been limited to 48 hours, including overtime (125).

Ireland has been characterized as a "being" rather than a "doing" society in which the quality of life is valued more than the pursuit of monetary gain.[xxv] A balanced approach to life (including work life) has long been an essential aspect of quality of life in Ireland. But one wonders if an ever higher standard of living,[xxvi] and its accompanying stresses, will result in a degradation of quality of life. Heavy traffic, for example, can seriously erode quality of life even as it increases the commute, thereby lengthening the part of the day devoted to work. On a stroll around Howth harbor on a Sunday in the summer of 1999, I watched the couples and families enjoy the sunshine and the seaside. The scene was reminiscent of my visits to Howth in 1989 until the ring from someone's mobile phone pierced this tranquil scene. Then it seemed as if every person in sight reached into a pocket or handbag to see if it was his or her phone ringing.

Good craic and good humor whether experienced in the pub or elsewhere remain essential features of the Irish social scene. However, some of the pubs have a different face these days. Ireland's booming and open economy, fueled largely by the information sector, is reflecting societal changes in the way people enjoy each other's company. British influence is increasingly being replaced by Continental influences that are producing an Irish society that represents an amalgamation of Celtic and European cultures. Nowhere is this more apparent than in the changes in the essential social institution in Ireland: the pub. The dark, crowded but cozy pub is supplanted here and there by the airy, Euro cafes with plate glass windows, lots of chrome and -- challenging Mother Nature -- outdoor seating.[xxvii]

The culture of connecting the pub to the workplace was adopted by the information sector from existing work sectors. But the existence of this sector which has brought with it greater opportunities for women will no doubt have some impact on the role of the pub. When the man is the sole wage earner he can more easily go out for drinks after work because his wife is at home with the children. But with the growth of two income families in Ireland comes the dilemma of who will go home after work to be with the children.

While the trend of migration from the country to the city that has characterized most of the twentieth century continued to its end, some interesting possibilities are suggesting abatement from the total demise of rural Ireland. One is related to housing. Ireland's fierce attachment to the land is expressed in modern times in the desire for home ownership. Today, there are more than one million homeowners; 45% of homes in Ireland are owned outright with no loans outstanding. However, the recent sharp rise in housing prices is proving to be quite challenging for the youngest group of adults wishing to purchase a home. This is especially the case in Dublin where the cost of housing is getting beyond the reach of first time buyers.[xxviii] Consequently, people are moving to the satellite towns and commuting to Dublin. In doing so, they are breathing new life into some of these rural towns. The other possibility for rural Ireland comes from the decentralization of industry. Begun by the civil service in the 1980s the IDA has strived to attract foreign investment to the rural parts of Ireland. One promising type of work is the teleservices sector.

The population in 1999 has grown to 3.7 million[xxix] but it is still a small society. A recently published book that provides advice for expatriates and returning émigrés contains the following admonition in a chapter on job seeking:

> . . . Ireland is a very small marketplace and you will
> constantly encounter people with whom you find you have
> acquaintances in common. It is useful to bear this in mind in
> all your professional dealings (Houston, 1999, p. 143).

At the same time there are changes afoot. While Ireland is currently one of the most religiously, racially and ethnically homogeneous countries in Europe, its status as one of the world's fastest growing economies is resulting in a trend toward inbound immigration. While most of the immigrants are Irish people returning from the US and the UK[xxx] there is also an unprecedented influx of ethnically distinct immigrants arriving in Ireland. Dell's decision to recruit workers from countries such as Russia and India to work at its Limerick plant illustrates the impact of the information economy on Irish demographics.[xxxi] In the future, this trend may pose a challenge to the ethnic homogeneity that has long made Ireland unique within Europe (Breathnach, 1998).

The focus upon language, communication and interpersonal interaction remains strong. Even as Ireland becomes more integrated into the new Europe and growing numbers of multilingual Irish call centre personnel provide technical support throughout the world, loyalty to the Irish language remains strong.[xxxii] It is flourishing as the cultural repository through the works of Irish language artists. For example, the poet Nuala Ni Dhomhnaill, who writes only in Irish, has just published the first book in Irish ever to be launched by an American University.[xxxiii]

The welcoming atmosphere continues to be attractive to the foreign visitor and returning emigrant alike. Irish agencies currently emphasize this cultural factor in marketing the country abroad:

> For the Irish, the personal element is an integral part of any business relationship. (Enterprise Ireland, 1999, p. 3).

---

[i] Integrating business and private life is a characteristic of collective cultures according to Hofstede (1984a,b). The topic of collectivism is considered in greater detail in Chapter 6.

[ii] Pronounced and sometimes spelled as "crack."

[iii] Slagging means to tease or play a joke on.

[iv] A recently published book for returning émigrés and non-Irish people who would be coming to Ireland to live for awhile (Houston, 1999), offers societal description and advice about current Irish society. In a chapter about Irish culture craic, humor, the pub and sport are highlighted as significant aspects of Irish culture.

[v] Kluckholn and Strodtbeck's (1961) framework for considering a culture include the primary mode of activity in the society as either *being* or *doing*. The people in Ireland, a *being* culture, tend to accept the status quo, enjoy the current situation and go with the flow of things. In contrast, people in a *doing* society change things to make them better, and set specific goals to be achieved within specific schedules.

ⁱ Each of these traits is discussed in greater depth elsewhere in this book. But they are mentioned here because of their connection to this easygoing attitude.

ⁱⁱ This term describes the quality of the camaraderie and atmosphere at a social gathering. It means good time, good company and good conversation. I have been told: "It was good craic last night at the pub." Or after a weekend students have told me: "At the party Saturday night the craic was 90!"

ⁱⁱⁱ Gannon (1994) correctly observes that the focus is much more on the conversation than the food: "Meal time is an event in the Irish household that should not be missed by a family member, not so much because of the food but the conversation. . . the food is really secondary to the conversation, and sometimes the Irish can forget to eat or delay doing so until the food is cold." (190)

ⁱˣ This self-perception is reinforced in the exported image of Ireland. For example, an advertisement in an American travel magazine portrayed Ireland as ". . . a land of music and easy laughter." (O'Connor, 1993, p. 72).

ˣ See Houston (1999) Chapter 17 for a discussion of Irish humor.

ˣⁱ Two points are worth noting here. First, there is considerable variation across regions of the country. The workplaces to which I was referring were in the New England region of the country. Second, there has been considerable change in the 1990s. The last decade of the twentieth century saw a move to greater workplace informality in the US -- particularly in the IT sector -- as witnessed in changes in the dress code for work.

ˣⁱⁱ Bards roamed the countryside keeping the history and culture of Ireland alive through their poetry. See, for example, Carr-Gomm (1991) and Foster (1988).

ˣⁱⁱⁱ See Gannon (1994), pp. 179-194.

ˣⁱᵛ Brian Friel's play *Translations* is an excellent exploration of such issues.

ˣᵛ For further discussion of the factors influencing the diminution of the Irish language, see Foster (1988), Gannon (1994) and Harris (1994).

ˣᵛⁱ For further discussion of the economic development of the Gaeltacht see O'Gadhra (1973).

ˣᵛⁱⁱ For example, one of the universities developed a finance degree whose courses are taught in Irish.

ˣᵛⁱⁱⁱ Testimony to the importance of literature in Irish society can be seen in the annual Bloomsday celebration in Dublin. On June 15 Joycean pilgrims can reenact Leopold Bloom's day, which is recounted in *Ulysses*. See, for example, Behr (1994).

ˣⁱˣ Harvested.

xx See, for example, Clancy et al. (1988) and Schmitt (1973) for a discussion of clientelism in Irish society.

xxi The Oireachtas (Irish National Parliament) consists of the President and two houses. There are 166 members of Dail Eireann, the lower house. These representatives are the TD's (Teachtai Dala). The members of the upper house, the Seanad Eireann, represent societal sectors: education, language and culture, agriculture, labor, industry and commerce, and public administration.

xxii Garda Siochana is the Irish police force.

xxiii O'Connor (1993, p. 74) notes that "Hospitable, friendly, welcoming are three recurring and related epithets of tourist publicity" about Ireland.

xxiv I can certainly testify to the ease with which I was able to engage my respondents in discussion about my research topics in comparison with similar types of research conducted in other countries.

xxv See Gannon (1994) for a characterization of Ireland as a *being* society.

xxvi Breathnach (1998, p. 305) cites forecasts that will put the Irish economy and living standards well above the EU norm by 2010.

xxvii See Cullen (1999c) for a good description of these changes.

xxviii Average house prices increased by 20% in 1996, by 17.5% in 1997 and by 10.9% in the first half of 1998 (Houston, 1999, pp. 204-205).

xxix Central Statistics Office, November 1998 cited in IDA Ireland (1999), p. 3.

xxx See, The Economist Intelligence Unit (1998), p. 14.

xxxi See "Dell Recruits Abroad" (1999).

xxxii Over 73% of second level graduates in 1995 studied a European language and 25% of third level students study a foreign language. These language skills are utilized in the large software localization industry and the number of multilingual call centres and technical support operations that are located in Ireland (National Software Directorate, 1998b, p. 9).

xxxiii Ni Dhomhnaill was the 1998-1999 Boston College Burns Library Visiting Scholar where her book *Cead Aighnis* made its debut in October 1998 (Dunsford, 1999, p. 38).

CHAPTER 6. IRISH

1.   INTRODUCTION

. . . [C]ulture is the collective programming of the mind which distinguishes the members of one group or society from those of another. Culture consists of the patterns of thinking that parents transfer to their children, teachers to their students, friends to their friends, leaders to their followers, and followers to their leaders. Culture is reflected in the meanings people attach to various aspects of life: their way of looking at the world and their role in it; in their values, that is, in what they consider as "good" and as "evil"; in their collective beliefs, what they consider as "true" and as "false"; in their artistic expression, what they consider as "beautiful" and as "ugly." Culture although basically resident in people's minds, becomes crystallized in the institutions and tangible products of a society, which reinforce the mental programmes in their turn. Management within a society is very much constrained by its cultural context, because it is impossible to coordinate the actions of people without a deep understanding of their values, beliefs, and expressions. . . [T]he collective programming which I call culture should be seen as a collective component shared in the minds of otherwise different individuals and absent in the minds of individuals belonging to a different society. (Hofstede, 1984b, p. 82)

2.   BOUND TO THE PAST

There is enormous influence on Irish ways of behavior from our occupied past. You see it in state structures -- the courts

> *borrowed British law -- in language, in attitudes. About the*
> *language, the mother tongue was largely disregarded. In*
> *terms of attitudes and ways of behavior, there are similarities*
> *that are hard to ignore. As a result, there are deliberate*
> *attempts to prove our individualism like taking the opposite*
> *point of view from Britain on any issue. So much here is done*
> *in reaction to the British. [Aidan]*

A defining characteristic of the information-sector workers in Ireland is that they are situated in a post-colonial culture. While significant changes in attitudes and behaviors have occurred over the past 50 years, the legacy of the colonial centuries is unmistakable. The influences I noted were sometimes overt, sometimes subtle, but always present. In my earliest interviews I set about identifying the salient cultural themes to explore in the IT workplace. The consistent message from cultural commentators was that in Ireland there is an emphasis on the past, on living in history. Sometimes this was used as an excuse not to change things, they said. I was warned that I would need to understand Irish history in order to understand the Irish person. In my work I did, indeed, find this to be the case. The legacy of the past is felt not only in the behavior of Irish workers but also in the environment of the Irish workplace. There are four themes, in particular, that reflect the presence of the past in Ireland's adaptation to information-sector work: colonialism, the famine, independence and the Troubles.[i]

Ireland's entire history has been one of coping with outside intrusion. First the Vikings came, and then the Normans. In the sixteenth century, the English began to influence Irish culture, polity, and society,[ii] but it was in the seventeenth century that English influence began to impose itself in earnest. Ireland was on the losing side in the battle for succession between the Catholic James II and the Protestant William of Orange. Consequently, at the close of the war in 1691 penal law went into effect. Catholics were excluded from Parliament, public office, practicing law, teaching, bearing arms and free worship. As a result, the eighteenth century in Ireland was one of stark contrasts. It was a dark century in which and the "traitorous" Celtic Irish Catholics were stripped of their property, and their priests were banished from the land. Unless they converted, Catholics were forbidden to buy or inherit real estate. For the "loyal" Anglo-Irish, however, it was the golden age of the Protestant Ascendancy. The Protestant-run Irish Parliament was in its heyday. The architecture of Dublin is full of the fine Georgian homes that were built during this period. Irish respondents expressed many cultural characteristics in terms of the wealthy Anglo-Irish living in the "big house"[iii] and the poor Celtic Irish who served them.

The period of penal law and the ways in which people adapted have left their mark on the culture in noticeable ways. One was a tendency to be careful around strangers, harkening back to wariness about possible informers to the landlord and the British Crown. The imposition of these repressive laws left an attitude of distrust toward authority and its rules. The landlord and his laws were meant to be circumvented. A history of British oppression in which Irish-Catholic subjects were kept economically suppressed with little opportunity to succeed was often given during interviews to explain Irish people who had a less ambitious nature.

An effect, which was manifested in the information sector in a variety of ways, was ambivalence about making public displays of material wealth. Charles, who was of Norman heritage, likened the plight of the Irish Catholics in the Republic before independence to the plight of Catholics in Northern Ireland in the twentieth century.

> *[When] the Irish Republic was formed we could do our own thing. We could go ahead and succeed and be what we want to be. But all that time in Northern Ireland [before the civil rights movement there] the Catholics were suppressed. If you were Catholic, you had to push hard to get a job. [For] Protestants or any other non-Catholic denomination it was much easier. And it was similar down here back in those days [before independence]. [Charles]*

The nineteenth century brought the repeal of penal law, but one blight upon the culture was replaced by another. The famine decade of 1845-1855 had wide ranging and deep effects that left scars still visible in Irish culture. The population, language, culture and a host of attitudes were forever changed by this event. When the potato crops began to fail in September 1845 much more than the food supply was being lost. While there is imprecise data on the number of people who died in the famine -- the general estimates range around one million -- there is no dispute that significant population decline resulted from the famine. Through a combination of death and emigration the Irish population declined from 8.2 million in the 1840s to 4.4 million by the turn of the century.[iv]

As the population in Ireland plummeted the Irish spirit suffered a deep blow. While Ireland's colonial status engendered low self-esteem and diminished pride in being Irish, the famine exacerbated the situation. In Nuala's view, the famine produced a national identity crisis as it broke people down. Abandonment of the culture was evident in the breakdown of the language. While parents and grandparents spoke Irish, children migrated toward English so they could emigrate or work in the British civil service. To the extent that language is the vehicle for conveying culture, the demise of the Irish language exacted a heavy toll on Irish culture.

Indeed, following the struggle for independence the new Irish nation made a concerted effort to bring back the Irish language as part of an effort to reestablish cultural sovereignty.

> *The other colonial heritage thing is we fought very long and hard against staggering odds. I don't mean in a military sense. The British, who were absolute masters at that -- colony suppression if you like -- came up against probably their biggest challenge, in other words, in Ireland. The Irish resisted them and as a result we're very political animals. The Irish person is very politically aware. He is very much aware of securing independence. He's very much aware of the battle it took to get the English, to* invite *the English, to leave. The steps necessary, the rebel songs, the whole thing is very much part of our everyday life. As opposed to other countries whose independence was more automatic, or who never were, if you like, occupied. [Declan]*

For Irish people the struggle for national independence was something that existed within living history. I spoke with individuals who lived through the War of Independence and the Civil War and talked with middle-aged respondents whose parents had lived through these times. For these people the struggle for independence was very real, very tangible and very personal. It was tied to real people and real places and real events. It was only with the youngest generation of adults that the situation was different. For them the memory was fading. Their grandparents who may or may not have been alive were the closest direct link to the cultural impact of Ireland's struggle for independence.

The wars -- particularly the Civil War over accepting partition of Ireland and whom one supported in it -- was a large backdrop against which much of Irish political life was played out.[v] While party affiliation for the older generations was certainly based upon the past, those in the youngest generation of workers looked more to the present and future in making their political decisions. This youngest generation of workers -- those born after 1960 -- did not relate in the same way to events in Ireland's history as those who directly experienced them or heard first-hand accounts from those who had. For these people who were two generations removed, the effect was much diminished. Gerry expressed a representative view of the youngest generation of IT workers.

> *I think it's diminished an awful lot. It doesn't really matter much to me. I can't relate to it at all. Stories like that don't really ring true to me. I can appreciate they're true, but they don't strike a chord with me. There are undoubtedly people who are staunchly political, staunchly republican, say, who would view the Northern Ireland situation as a lingering [issue]. It's very much diminished. It doesn't have an effect, certainly on my generation at all, but there are a minority of people who are politically, nationally aware. Who see the Northern Ireland situation as an aftermath of that situation. They would say we have three quarters of our independence. [Gerry]*

In contrast, Julie, whose parents were born in the 1920s, talked about growing up in the shadow of the Empire.

> *Daddy would still say, "The Queen's on TV." I mean there's lots of Queens. . . [Julie]*

This was troubling to her. For this reason, it was not surprising to learn she was an active participant in the Celtic cultural revival sweeping through Dublin in the early 1990s.

While the political realm was perhaps the most noticeable legacy of the struggle for independence, other societal effects appeared in daily life, albeit more subtly. References to the War of Independence, the Civil War and Northern Ireland would creep into our conversations at quite unexpected times. In discussing his family's employment history one man mentioned that his family tripled their land holdings because of a grant from the Land Commission for reasons that were unclear to him. He thought some big estate was divided up, but he was not sure because people didn't talk about such things.

> *I had a hunch that it might have been to do with people who served back in the time of the Civil War. Something like that. I'm not sure. I never got the real answer. There were a lot of things pushed under the carpet. We were never told. [Charles]*

During the centuries of British dominion and continuing through the independence movement there was a legitimate safety need to keep certain activities from view, from being overheard by others. In the case of Charles, it was children; in other cases it would be possible informers. I saw a continuation of the posture of not talking about something in the treatment of strangers and newcomers. Charles talked about a co-worker who had come over from Scotland and had bought a house in the country near the multinational plant where they worked. There were many things going on in the community this man would never hear about. They would talk among themselves, Charles said, but not to him, not to any strangers who had not been around when the events occurred. The people were very much keeping to themselves.

While the struggle for independence and its aftermath -- the Civil War -- were defining moments in Irish history, they were not particularly unifying moments. What some viewed as the first significant unifying event for the country was its participation in the final rounds of the World Cup Soccer competition. When Ireland won that match the entire country celebrated. Though they lost the subsequent match the celebrations continued. When the players returned to Ireland on the following Sunday I watched the country welcome the team. People lined the ten kilometers of road from the Dublin airport to the City Centre where throngs had been waiting all day for them. People said there had never been a turnout like this in the history of the country. Everybody was unified. To the young people of Ireland, especially, it was even more significant than the visit by the Pope in 1979, which was viewed as more of an event for their parents' generation.

> *They were just freaked out by it. My generation wasn't so in*
> *awe of the Pope. [Deirdre]*

As if to underscore Ireland's new direction and basis for identity and unification, during the same period as the World Cup matches Ireland also held the Presidency of the European Union. During this time there was a strong atmosphere in the country of unity, renewal, optimism and excitement about Ireland's future.

At the same time, those supporting the nationalist cause believed the struggle for national unity was still going on in the form of the Northern Ireland conflict. This sentiment was rarely expressed to me directly in interviews. It was more often the interpretation I drew from the national media and from participant observation and conversations with Irish people. Those whom I interviewed expressed considerable disinterest in Northern Ireland.

Despite the apparent reluctance to consider the North in any depth, nevertheless, comments about people's connections to and experiences of the North made their way into our conversations in offhand ways. For example, in inquiring into one respondent's background I learned about his connection to and views of Northern Ireland.

> *My father was born in Scotland and lived in Northern Ireland, in County Down. And they were a loyalist bunch. And my experience on religion is that they disowned him when he married my mother and changed religions. I don't understand why it's so important to everybody. I don't really have a problem with it one way or the other. I mean, I've been up to Belfast; I've been up with my uncles and aunts up there. I know they don't like that I'm Catholic from the Republic, but still they're my family and they're nice enough to me. [Farrell]*

Economic cooperation between the North and the South is evident in several ways. For example, the trade union movement in Ireland is still fully affiliated and associated with its English counterpart: all trade unions in Ireland are 32 counties. In addition, the tourist boards of both Northern Ireland and the Republic do joint marketing of the island. A few people spoke of the great difficulty of finding a final solution to this centuries old conflict. Because the scope of my study was limited to the Republic of Ireland I did not intend to include Northern Ireland and the Troubles in my research. I soon learned, however, that that was impossible. The partition of the island and its historical, political, economic and religious dimensions is a significant thread in the cultural fabric.

3. RELIGIOUS

> *Just go back to Church influence. There is a major Church influence that has changed. Some would say it's weakened. But nevertheless is considerably stronger in Ireland than in most countries in Europe and certainly than the States. I think that irrespective of which source it comes from -- whether it's Protestant or Catholic -- it's actually there. I think it will be eroded but it'll erode very slowly. It won't disappear and I think some of the old family virtues would be fairly strongly held. People would put up with a difficult marriage in Ireland a) because there is no divorce, but b) they would actually put up with it. They would suffer it much more than somebody from the UK or Scandinavia or*

> *Germany or in the States. The fact that it's not easy to be*
> *divorced might well be a major help, but I think the Church*
> *influence -- "Stick together for the sake of the children," --*
> *much more strongly applies than in other societies. Lots of*
> *people would argue that a miserable marriage is not actually*
> *benefiting children. I think in Ireland people would say, "Yes,*
> *but they will still be much better for it." I think things like*
> *abortion, I don't think there is any Church dominance here. I*
> *think universally most people are against abortion other than*
> *direct victims or the direct people who are involved. The*
> *general sentiment would be anti-abortion. So I think there*
> *are strong family culture pressures that keep families*
> *together. Poverty, itself, if you want to be crude can actually*
> *keep families together, too. The closer one is to the roots of*
> *poverty the tighter you find the family circle and members*
> *assisting each other generously. The more independently*
> *wealthy each member becomes in any society the less likely*
> *they are to help. [Martin]*

Religion, in any society, plays several roles; religion in Ireland is no different. If family is one essential ingredient of societal cohesion in Ireland, then religion is another. Unlike countries such as the United States, which have a clear constitutional separation between church and state, Ireland has the opposite. Religion is infused in the culture. It is taught in the public schools, many of which are operated by nuns, brothers and priests. Religion and family are intertwined from a person's earliest years.

At the outset of this discussion it is important to point out that my focus is not religion in the sectarian sense but, rather, the role of religion as a societal artifact. Early on I discovered I had to clarify the reason for my interest in religion. As a dimension of society, religion is important to include in any in-depth study of a culture. However, for the case of Ireland, there was another reason to include this societal institution in my research: active participation in religion was unusually high. Published studies indicate that in the 1980s 93% of Irish people were Catholics and 91% were *practicing* Catholics (Nic Ghiolla Phadraig, 1988, p. 140-141).[vi] Of the remaining non-Catholics, the majority was Protestant, mainly Church of Ireland (Anglican).

Two things are noteworthy about these observations. First, the majority of Irish people belonged to the same religion and the minority belong to another Christian religion whose values are not all that different. This religious homogeneity, it seemed to me, ought to have some observable effect on the culture. The other noteworthy point is that Ireland is different from other predominately Catholic countries -- Spain, Portugal and Italy, for example -- in that they were Catholics *in practice* not just in name. This, then, led me to wonder about the extent to which the beliefs and values of the Catholic religion might have entered the information-sector workplace via the predominantly Catholic workers.

The existence of political strife on the island and the association between the opposing forces and their religious affiliation was distinctly in the background of my thoughts about religion in Ireland because Northern Ireland was not part of this study. But the initial reactions to my questions about religion made me very careful in subsequent interviews to precisely explain my interest. In this way, my introduction to religion was different from other topics. Whereas in other cases I simply introduced the item and asked for thoughts or examples, with religion I felt the need to provide a more detailed explanation about the direction of my research interest. This might have contributed to the challenge I experienced in eliciting reflective comments from people.

The topic of religion was one of the most difficult ones to broach with the respondents. Not only did respondents seem reluctant to make reflective comments, but our discussions were often fraught with contradictions. For a long time I was perplexed by this. However, over the course of the interviews I began to gain some insights into why. Then, after conducting an analysis of the responses, another surprise awaited me. What was initially perplexing was that despite the large number of practicing Catholics in my study I seemed to be obtaining little information of the sort and depth acquired in discussing other topics. When I raised the topic of religion the vast majority of respondents seemed to either have nothing to say or else responded only in terms of the institutional Church -- the practices in which a Catholic is expected to engage (or not engage). They would typically end by saying that there wasn't any influence in the workplace. At least that was my perception upon completion of the interviews. For this reason, it was a bit of a surprise when, upon systematic analysis of respondent transcripts, I discovered that the reality was a little different from my initial perception! What became clear during analysis of the data was that while they may have said there was no influence of the Catholic religion on behavior, their stories showed otherwise. Throughout the interviews I found numerous examples of situations and values from which I could infer the influence of religion.

There are a few dimensions of religion in Ireland that can serve to illustrate its significance. These warrant explanation before proceeding to consider respondents' comments. First, Ireland is a fiercely religious country. Since the belief systems and moral codes of both the Catholic and the Anglican religions are quite similar, I was interested in exploring with respondents any possible influence that being such a religiously homogeneous group would have on behavior. Given the large number of practicing Catholics it would be reasonable to expect some evidence of this cultural characteristic in the workplace. Being a Catholic myself (and a product of Catholic education), I am conversant with both the moral tenants of the religion, and the institutional structure and rules.

Second, while Catholicism is a universal religion, it is also culturally expressed. Consequently, Catholicism in Ireland is heavily influenced by almost contradictory traditions (something which, no doubt, contributed to the contradictory I responses I received). One influence is a very conservative interpretation of Catholicism. The other influence on Irish Catholicism has been the beliefs, traditions and rituals of its nonchristian precursor: Celtic paganism.[vii] When Christianity was introduced into Ireland it was overlain on the existing Druidic system and produced a brand of Catholicism with some distinctive features. I saw evidence in the West of Ireland of the continuing influence of this religious system that is intimately tied to nature and place. Throughout the countryside one comes across holy wells offering blessed water. Bushes that adorn these holy wells hold bits of clothing, a photograph or some other personal item left by individuals who have been healed or who want to be remembered. Matthew worked in a small Irish IT firm. He commented that Celtic people are ambivalent about religion. One aspect of the Druidic influence is a certain resentment of authority figures including priests. He said priests can go only so far in terms of the influence they can exert over people.

Finally, religion has also played a significant role in Ireland's history. The imposition of penal law during the seventeenth and eighteenth centuries was aimed at repressing Catholicism in Ireland.[viii] For reasons such as this, the Catholic religion and the right to practice it became intimately linked with patriotism and later republicanism. Formal evidence is the unique status afforded to the Catholic religion in the Irish Constitution. Informal evidence of the links between Church and State can be seen in the educational system. Until quite recently, public schools in Ireland were in effect Catholic schools run by men and women in religious orders who taught religion along with reading and writing and mathematics.

With these insights into religion in the Irish context as the backdrop, we can now turn to the influence of religion on the information sector. The question of religion was raised in two ways. I asked about the influence of the *institutional Church* on people's lives. That is, the influence of Church rules regarding life style and behavior such as birth control, abortion, divorce, education and church attendance. I also asked about the influence of the Christian *value system* on the society and the workplace. A third theme, which emerged from analysis of responses, was the role of religion as a vehicle for *societal cohesion*. Thus, the Catholic Church in Ireland fulfills three distinct roles: social, political and spiritual.

3.1   Societal Cohesion

> *[Religion] is the basis of society. In the country Mass used to be a social thing; you would visit with people after church. And remember, education is under the control of religion.*
>
> *ET: Do you think the Church has significant influence on the people in term of culture?*
>
> *Oh yes. It's the Christian ethic. Taking time for people, showing love, do unto others, being more open, being comfortable in one's surroundings, being less materially sophisticated. [Theresa]*

Religion is woven into the fabric of Irish culture. It is part of the social glue that has held the culture together in the face of extreme adversity. While colonial-era oppression no longer exists in the Republic, its legacy has accounted for much of the power wielded by religion and the reluctance to challenge it.[ix] Deirdre was particularly articulate about the role of religion in Irish culture. When I observed that religious homogeneity is a noteworthy cultural artifact, she responded that religion in Ireland was more social than spiritual and went on to give examples of common rituals that bound the society together.

> *Well, this year was a very interesting year for me because my daughter had her First Communion. We're not very strict observers. I go to Mass occasionally, but I felt very guilty about this and I started to take her to Mass. I must say I got something out of it myself. And it reawakened something that had been dead for a long time. The First Communion ceremony itself was absolutely . . . I couldn't describe it! It was just so beautiful, it was really wonderful. And all the families are there and the teachers are so sincere, the kids responded to it; it was fantastic. And then they had this Corpus Christi[x] procession which very few young people ever go to any more. Every year they ask the First Communicants*

to go and walk in the procession. So of course, she wanted to go. I haven't been to one since I was a kid. We walked from one church in the parish to the other. It was a big procession, there were prayers. And we got into the second church and there was this lovely singing. Just like that they say this Benediction, which I haven't been to in 25 years. And we had a lot of this "Tantum Ergo," a lot of Latin songs and the [Latin] words were coming out of . . . I don't know where they were coming from. Because, again, in Ireland there is this common base. So, it was a very communal thing, I think that was the key. It was tremendous. I got an awful lot out of it [Deirdre]

Her second example was directly tied into the workplace.

I think people observe a lot of the religious rituals without having any consciousness of their own spirituality or life. So I just say that first. Having said that, I think that . . . I'll tell you a little story, right? We had a very unfortunate accident here last year. One of our employees was killed in the plant, which was highly traumatic, obviously. He was very well liked and it was just something that people didn't think could happen. This kind of event. Not in an industry like this. It was awful. It was just terrible. This year when the anniversary came, we decided that we would have a Mass at eight o'clock in the morning, which was a totally Irish thing to do. We went over to the local church and we got some singers to do some of the music. It was really moving. You know, it was very nice. And a lot of people came up to me and said afterwards, that it really meant something to them. And one person said that he thought it was really nice, irrespective of the occasion. That the people who worked together, sort of worshipped together, that he found it from that angle not so much of the anniversary of the accident, that he just found that very moving. Which I had never thought about before. But I think it did get to the root of why people were somehow extremely satisfied when it was over. [Deirdre]

My own experience with the communal role of religion occurred in one of the firms. I was scheduled to conduct interviews at Wang Laboratories in Limerick the day after An Wang, its founder, died. My afternoon interviews had to be rescheduled because the facility was closed early so that all the employees could attend a Mass in his memory.

I think partly because the Catholic religion is so firmly embedded in the culture, it was difficult for some respondents to acknowledge let alone explain the influence of religion in Ireland. Indeed, Sheelagh made two important observations about religion in Ireland. First, she said that she did not believe religion carried over into people's work lives at all. Second she asserted that she would never say that the Catholic is a Christian religion. In my observation, the former comment was consistently made though contravened by other comments, and the latter was a distinctly minority view.

3.2   Institutional Power

> . . . [T]he Church had a very strong influence on the Irish government from the start. It's still there. We've had referendums for divorce, for contraception. The Church ends up influencing, you still have that among the older half of the population, like, you know. If the Church says it, they just do it whether it's right or wrong. They will obey, right. Which is a contradiction, yeah. They mightn't like authority as such, but somehow the Church seems to be accepted as God almost. You don't challenge that, you know. [Jim]

When I inquired about the Church as an institution I was interested in knowing about the influence of the Catholic Church on behavior in general, and in the workplace in particular. The influence of the institutional Church has, in Ireland, extended into secular behavior as well. I noted how the Catholic Church in Ireland was heavily involved in such family-oriented decisions as divorce, contraception and abortion. This led me to explore whether the acquiescence to Church control exerted over peoples' personal lives was carried over into the information-sector workplace.

In my interviews there was passing acknowledgement of the Catholic Church's considerable influence on the personal lives of Irish people. Most of these comments reflected an attitude of, "Well, that's the way it is. You can't do anything about it." The institutional Church's involvement in abortion, divorce and birth control legislation has led some to put the role of religion into a narrow category of influence on sexuality. Indeed, in the early 1980s Ireland's referendum on divorce was defeated, in large part, because of Church activism. I observed two controversies that spoke to the control exerted by the institutional Church. In the fall of 1989 members of a student organization were arrested for providing information in a student orientation publication about obtaining abortions in other countries. What I found particularly noteworthy was not so much that abortion, itself, was illegal but that *information* about obtaining one was.[xi] This particular controversy ended up in the European Court. The other controversy was over the sale of condoms. The manager of a Dublin record store was arrested for selling condoms. At that time contraceptives could only legally be sold to married people and, even then, at the chemist's discretion. This policy was a relaxation of the prior law that made the sale of contraceptives to *anyone* illegal.

The influential role of the Church in these matters came across in people's comments about the divorce referendum.[xii] Respondents said that representatives of the Church openly attempted to influence the outcome of the vote. Nuns and priests instructed school children to go home and tell their parents how to vote. There were stories about clerics preaching from the pulpit at Mass:

> *This is how you're going to vote*

and nuns telling school children:

> *You go home and tell your mommy and daddy that divorce is*
> *bad otherwise they'll be separated and you won't be able to*
> *see either your mommy or your daddy.*

Despite the fact that the Church had it's way in the divorce referendum, respondents generally commented that the Church did not have the kind of influence that outsiders might have thought.

Speaking from the vantage point of early middle age, Deirdre commented on the influence of the Church from a generational perspective. In the older generation priests "got away with" telling people what to do. In the younger generation, they didn't. This view was illustrative of what appeared to be a general recognition that the younger generation had a different relationship with religion. When one remembers that the *younger generation* about which they spoke made up half of the population of Ireland, this observation takes on added import. The young people may have been technically Catholic but they didn't let the Church influence their lives. They showed this in their behavior: come late to Mass, leave early, and stand in the back of church. In some quarters there was even peer pressure *not* to be an observant Catholic. There were two comments frequently given about the role of religion in Irish society. One was that people went to church because it was too much trouble not to but that they did not let the Church get in the way of how they lived their lives.

They will comply with some of the regulations that suit them. The easiest regulation to comply with is attendance at ceremonies. That's what I mean by their compliance. I think that in other European countries people are more direct. They're inclined to say, "Well, I don't agree with this, this and this and therefore I'm not going to go to Mass."

ET: And why will the Irish go to Mass?

Because of a number of reasons. Because they probably will have less family pressure. The Church is a fairly strong influence on the community. It's the sort of thing if the family were going to ceremonies and then suddenly one didn't go, very quickly the religious people would ask why not, what the reasons were, and so forth. Rather than actually have a discussion about why they disagree with the whole thing, they'd probably end up just complying. It's quite a complicated situation. There's a number of aspects. It's easier to do it than argue why you shouldn't. Family has a significant influence. Bringing up children, even though a father may not agree with some of the aspects of the Catholic religion or Christianity, generally speaking, he would like to see his kids brought up in it. [Brian]

The other comment was that young people were not as likely to go to church or be as influenced by the institution as the older generations. I got greater clarity when it was explained to me that the Irish rebel against authority in all areas except the Church.

Theresa, who worked at a government agency involved with the information economy, identified her own religious journey as typical. People stopped going to church at about age 15 or 16 but then went back again when they began to have children. She said they did this partly because they wanted their children to go to Catholic schools and to fit in. In some respects, religion in Ireland functioned as a form of social cement that was invoked at significant life transitions such as birth, marriage, having a family and death. One motivation for regular participation in religious rituals, then, was peer pressure connected back to the societal cohesion role that religion played in Ireland. This seemed to be the case especially in rural towns. Someone characterized it as compliance without necessarily "buying in." There was an ambivalent feeling about the Church's power: resentment against its authority mixed with fear of its power. While the grip of the institutional Church on the younger generation appeared to be loosening, nevertheless, in family matters such as divorce, contraception and abortion, the Church controlled people's lives.

Based on the evidence of the Church's considerable influence on the lives of Irish people, I was interested in knowing the nature of any carryover into the information-sector workplace. Respondents consistently stated that there was no transference from the Church's influence into the workplace. However, when I conducted a detailed examination and classification of responses I found that a third of the respondents offered some commentary about the influence of religion on the workplace. Mary spoke about turning to God if things went against her at work; several employees made reference to Christmas week as being a traditional time off work. There was also the tradition of the local parish priest interceding on behalf of a job applicant in order to influence hiring decisions. Finally, I noted numerous people wearing ashes on their foreheads on Ash Wednesday, marking the beginning of the pre-Easter Lenten season. I also heard people unself-consciously talking in the workplace about what they would be giving up for their Lenten sacrifices.

Probably the most noteworthy link between the institutional Church and workplace behavior was the theme of acquiescence. Bridie commented that the tradition of acquiescing to the priest was part of a larger mindset of being acquiescent in general. But then she added that current workers were different; they questioned decisions. Tom complained about the Church trying to "call the shots," something that he said has led to emigration and diminished church attendance. He contrasted his attitude towards religion with that of his girl friend: if she had a problem with her job she would pray whereas he would do something about it.

3.3   A Value System

The social and political functions served by religion in Ireland speak to its external dimension; the spiritual function served by religion speaks to its internal dimension. With respect to the latter, I was interested in exploring the influence that might derive from the set of values inherent in a religious tradition openly professed by nearly the entire population. One man stands out in my memory of discussions about religion. Unlike the vast majority of respondents who appeared to have little to say about religion, Martin offered several insightful comments about religion and the workplace.

His first comments were about Protestant-Catholic differences. Because he himself was the product of religious diversity and had personally experienced the divisiveness of Northern Ireland, he made a conscious decision to keep his company religiously neutral. I then asked for examples of the way in which the strong religious presence affected people, at work, in life, and in society. He explained that he was brought up in the minority (Protestant) religion and was educated in what he called a very bigoted environment in Northern Ireland. As a result, he rejected just about everything he saw there. He then went to Trinity College, which had moved from being a bastion of Irish Protestantism to being a multi-denominational university.[xiii] He had experienced the spectrum of religions influence, ranging from the totally absorbed society found in Northern Ireland, to a totally nonreligious environment in the UK. Consequently, when he set up his own company, he wanted to set up a very neutral environment.

His other area of commentary was both political and spiritual. He talked about the basis for the Irish ambivalence about wealth. He said that as recently as 50 to 70 years ago wealth was in the hands of the Anglo-Irish, which also reflected religious differences. As a result wealth was a sign of Protestant Ascendancy. The carryover to the present was that one could progress financially but shouldn't be too boastful about it. While he recognized this as a potentially constraining influence with respect to entrepreneurship, others described it as part of the Christian ethic. His daughter, for example, thought it would be ethically wrong for their family to move to a larger yet affordable house when there were people in Dublin who were starving.[xiv] Martin's earlier comment about the constraining influence, notwithstanding, he partially agreed with her position. He said there was a bit of embarrassment about wealth. The direct influence on work was the potential impediment to people's ambition. He contrasted the Irish view with what he saw as the American belief in material success as the root to self-fulfillment.

> *But there's been a big change in Ireland in 20 years. I think it's Southern Ireland is actually a very healthy sort of culture and religious environment. There's enough Christianity to take the sharp edge off of naked materialism, and yet it doesn't have so much that it's confining, as it would have been in the 1930s and 1940s. Maybe even the 1950s. There's still too much religion and too little Christianity, but on balance, people come back to Ireland from America, California, in large numbers because they find it more hospitable to bringing up their families. They're sheltered from the more materialistic environment. They're looking for something else. Maybe it goes a little too much the other way.*
> *[Martin]*

He attributed this diminished emphasis on materialism to Ireland being a Christian society.

> *ET: You would say that the main emphasis or main impact of*
> *the 95% Catholic population . . .*
>
> *Would be on the emphasis on materialism. I think the*
> *combined effect is a lesser emphasis on the worst aspects of*
> *materialism. There is a growing materialism but it's a long*
> *way off [from] unbridled materialism. I think it makes for a*
> *much more Christian society, a much more just society. I find*
> *it intolerable -- I don't mind saying it, I don't wish to offend*
> *an American, I find it intolerable -- that one of the richest*
> *nations on Earth that you have some of the most abject*
> *poverty that matches Calcutta. That's not right. [Martin]*

What was perplexing about these discussions of religion was that I came away with the impression that the respondents acknowledged very little influence on work. It was a surprise, therefore, when my analysis of these comments revealed a different pattern. When all comments (social, political, spiritual) were interpreted and classified, it turned out that there were slightly more comments acknowledging an influence of religion than there were those denying any! Perhaps the reason this was not my initial impression was that the contradictory nature to the remarks clouded my perception. This was partly due to ambivalence about acknowledging the influence of the institutional Church and the unwillingness of young workers to acknowledge the religious dimension of their lives. However, I think it was also due to the difficulty individuals had in commenting objectively about something that was so essential to their culture. For example, Deirdre paused for reflection when I asked her about possible influences resulting from such a religious society. She said she had never really thought about it. She then said that obviously if you're a Catholic it should carry over into everything you do, and concluded that that was the case to some extent.

As to what sort of influence the value system might be having on work, several themes emerged. One that has already been introduced was ambivalence about material wealth. There was a tendency to "knock" Irish achievers. The noncompetitive ethic held that achieving something meant taking it away from somebody else.

> *Well, there's an element of what do you die with a £100 in*
> *your pocket or a hundred million? Who gives a damn?*
> *There's an element of the important things in life. What's the*

important things in life? Some people would say, good family life, just enough money to get by, and good social standing. Whereas the basic American might want to become a millionaire before they die or would not be satisfied. There's an element of that. There's an element of quality of life rather than quantity of the reward. [Michael]

What might have been viewed as a lack of an entrepreneurial spirit in Ireland was the result of a conflict between this world and the next. Since the pursuit of material gain was not seen in a positive light, one needed to balance one's values against one's ambitions. Caring values were emphasized; success was frowned upon.

A second theme, closely related to de-emphasizing materialism, was the message of compliance with one's lot in life. I wondered if an attitude that it's easier to go along with the status quo than to challenge the system carried into the workplace. When I posed this question several respondents helped me sort it out. Whereas in the workplace there was some chance of being heard and effecting change, in the Catholic religion people knew they hadn't any hope of doing so. With the Catholic religion people just saw a hierarchy, which they knew they could not influence, or change, so why bother?

A third theme running through the comments was paternalism in business. Rather than an impersonal "bottom line" perspective on economic decisions, other considerations entered into the equation in Ireland. Religious beliefs had an influence on entrepreneurs. People who started businesses felt responsible for those they employed. The ideal was the Catholic employer who looked after the employees.

The next theme derived from having a single, dominant religion. At work there was an assumption that everyone who didn't have a foreign-sounding name -- a signal of another nationality -- was a Catholic. This theme was about the link between religious homogeneity and cultural homogeneity. Workers believed this homogeneity resulted in fewer tensions in the workplace than in a country like the US which has much more cultural diversity. Respondents claimed that in Irish society there was a sense of oneness, of standardization because everyone had the same moral make up.

The fifth theme was about a caring workforce situated in a caring society. Even respondents who didn't at first see any influence of religion in the workplace went on to acknowledge that people in Ireland were more charitable than people in other countries. So perhaps some of the basis for friendliness in the Irish culture is found in the Christian ethic.

The final theme was about spiritual reward coming from using your God-given talents to the fullest extent.

> *Part of the quality of life in Ireland you would have to tie in
> with the religion where people just get a return from work.
> Spiritual return from working hard, I suppose, in Ireland. . .
> There's a spiritual return in working hard and bettering
> yourselves and improving your standard of living and
> providing for your children and your family. That's a big
> tradition in Ireland. . . You've got your talents, and you're
> using your talents to the best of your ability, I suppose.*
> *[Michael]*

The process of examining this topic turned out to be as perplexing as the
process of collecting the initial data. If I had a hypothesis about the influence
of religion on behavior in the information-sector workplace going into this
research, it would have been that there was a link between the acquiescence of
Irish people to Church dictates and meekness with respect to employers. I
learned, however, that that supposition was wrong. While it was true that the
Irish people granted the Catholic Church considerable power it was not
because of a cultural trait of meekness. Rather, it was the result of a complex
mixture of historical, political and cultural loyalties. But, the claim by the vast
majority of respondents that there was no influence of religion on the IT
workplace was also subverted. The influence of this societal institution was
not to be found in the overt power wielded by the Church. Instead, the
evidence was located in the common values that bound a population together
and were reinforced in the workplace.

4.   PRODUCTIVE

> *I think maybe something has to do with the position that work
> holds in people's lives. In the States people want to "get on,"
> progress and go up the ladder. Earn more money etcetera,
> etcetera. When I first came here an Irish person said to me,
> "In America you live to work. In Ireland you work to live."*
> *[Sue]*

There was a range of work ethics in evidence in Ireland. At one extreme
was the "relaxed" attitude of workers who were quite easygoing about their
jobs, did not feel the pressure of time, and did not display much enthusiasm
about their jobs. At the opposite extreme was the highly motivated,
enthusiastic worker typical of those I saw in the information-sector firms. I
explored the topic of work ethic in order to understand the role and meaning

of work in the lives of the information-sector workers and what motivated them to perform as they did.

The work ethic in Ireland's information sector reflected a balance between one's work life and one's personal life. In contrast to the perception that Americans[xv] were driven to progress up the career ladder, doing whatever it took to get there was an attitude represented in Paul's priorities. He aspired to attain a level, which would enable him to provide adequately for his family, and then wanted to remain there. He had achieved that level when we spoke and, instead of being driven to go further, wanted to enjoy the fruits of his labor. Someone else expressed the difference in the importance of work in one's life in terms of how people used their spare time. He stereotyped Americans as having more than one job in order to pay off luxury items such as the extra car, the boat, the motorbike, all of which are bought on credit. In Ireland, people tended to have one job, fewer luxury items and make the most of their spare time.

4.1 Motivation

Those who commented about work life outside the information sector raised the issue of motivation. They said Irish people would be good workers if they were properly motivated, but that a built-in laziness meant workers needed a good, strong company and supervisor. They said in the state bodies -- the big bureaucracies -- people just went through the motions; the volumes of red tape kept workers from achieving. This stereotype of workers in the traditional sectors was the cultural backdrop against which I asked respondents in the information sector to describe what motivated them, what kept them working at their particular jobs, and what they looked for in a job. Their responses were sometimes about themselves, sometimes about the information sector and sometimes about the change from the old days and the old ways.

4.1.1 Money

> *I notice when I'm in the US, that money and incentives and financial rewards for doing things seem to play a bigger part than they would here, if you understand what I mean. It's not that money isn't important. People are very concerned about what they earn. Typically, if you are in a workshop or something like that in the US, it will always be a US person who will say, "There should be an incentive. We should*

advocate [some reward] for this." There's an immediate relationship with some form of incentive. Extra incentive to do something extra. I find that people here -- possibly because employment opportunities are so limited -- invest a little bit more in the company. They want to be associated with the company. They want to find a lot of things in employment that possibly in other countries they wouldn't. [Deirdre]

The general view among workers was that the information sector paid well compared with other sectors and that the multinational firms paid even better. But money, alone, was not a sufficient incentive. Because Irish workers were generally not as materialistic as Americans, noted an American manager, it was not as easy to motivate them with financial rewards. Instead, recognition of one's expertise and achievement, complementing workers on a job well done, and being treated fairly were also needed. Young workers in the information sector were introducing into the culture both new energy and new notions about the meaning of work in one's life.

One reason that money was less of an incentive than in some other cultures was discussed in the previous section: capitalism and materialism were de-emphasized in Ireland. There seemed to be a cultural bias against material wealth and the methods for acquiring it. People in Ireland were less inclined to declare their wealth for fear of becoming the target of jealousy. Another explanation for a diminished emphasis on financial incentives was the tax structure. Because of the high tax rate, there was a general feeling that earning more money simply meant paying more taxes. Therefore, having achieved the necessary middle class income, other things came into play as sufficient factors. And if a person were going to leave a firm, it would generally be issues other than money, which caused him or her to do so.

The attitude toward materialism, notwithstanding, the trend toward married women working was attributed in large part to the requirement of two incomes in order for the family to have the lifestyle it wanted. The desire to have a higher standard of living, therefore, was motivating women to stay in the workforce after marriage and child bearing. In considering the priorities placed upon the different types of motivation, it must be noted that these respondents worked in a sector that paid, on average, the same or better than comparable jobs in other sectors. So their comments about the significance of money as an incentive at work must be understood as coming from people who had sufficient money for a decent standard of living in Ireland.

4.1.2 Challenge and Reward

After satisfying the basic financial threshold, motivation came from fulfillment found in work. Information-sector workers wanted intellectual challenge, prospects for promotion and status rather than incrementally more money. They placed a strong emphasis on getting on and being challenged. One manager noted that if an engineer were in a position that was not sufficiently stimulating or challenging this individual could and would go somewhere else. To both the workers and those charged with motivating them, intellectual challenge meant accepting responsibility for some task and then doing what it took to accomplish it. This included the autonomy to be able to run with a given job. What motivated them was the challenge in the task followed by the reward for doing it well. They needed to have enough to do, to be learning something new and to be recognized for what they were accomplishing. This recognition of achievement appeared to be especially important to older workers. Whereas younger workers were driven by opportunities for creativity, challenge, independence, advancement and responsibility, older persons valued security, comfort, relationships, recognition, self worth, dignity and benefits.

Despite the importance of recognition -- or perhaps because of it -- Irish respondents criticized their culture for its failure to recognize achievement and its tendency to "knock" people.

> *I think one of the things the Irish culture is inclined to [do is] undermine itself. We always seem to be looking for faults and giving each other a hard time, right? Whereas in America there's an awful lot of encouragement, a lot of positive reinforcement. There's a lot of hoopla and all that type of thing, excitement, recognition of achievements, major awards and stuff. . . [W]hen it comes to awards like, you know, somebody gets the award, and people feel compelled to criticize that person. It seems to be in the nature of the Irish to try and give each other a hard time. . . I think you got to change that. We seem to underrate ourselves for no apparent reason. . . [In Ireland when someone else wins an award] it's a "downer" for somebody else. . . You'd like to think that if somebody got an award and is recognized [others would be happy for him or her]. . . [Whereas in the US] what I saw was that everybody seemed to go forward, and the fact that people got the award, everybody else was quite willing to give them every clap on the back and say, "Well done, let's*

*go forward." And I think this is a slight drawback in the
Irish. Maybe it's in the Irish mentality, in the Irish culture. I
can't understand it, you know. My own personal view is to
encourage people, to give them rewards. [Farrell]*

The youth of the information-sector workforce brought with it a certain
impatience to get on with their careers. Whereas the old way was to patiently
move up through the ranks according to the dictates of senior management,
young recruits were anxious to move and grow at a quicker pace.
Consequently, firms experienced the need to push down responsibility at a
faster rate. In the old days career advancement and pay were more related to
seniority than performance. But in the information sector with its American
influence, advancement and salary were based upon merit. And this attitude
directly influenced people's willingness to work hard and put in overtime
when necessary. Nevertheless, given the context -- the size of the country, the
information sector and the Irish economy -- there were practical limits to how
far one could progress in the IT field in Ireland.

*The reason I am here in Ireland working for [this firm] is
firstly because it's in Ireland and if I was interested in my
career I wouldn't be here. I'd be in the States or in Germany
or some place where I could advance my career a lot quicker.
[Paul]*

Within the information sector, itself, I witnessed a contradiction. On the
one hand there was an impatience to get on and the willingness to move on in
search of greater challenges. But at the same time there was also a different
expectation about progression along a career trajectory. Sue compared her
own career experiences and expectations in the US with what she had
observed and experienced in Ireland. People didn't expect to follow a distinct
career path. They might expect to do approximately the same job for the rest
of their lives. They seemed to have less expectation that they must progress in
a career. People she had encountered did not really expect their profile or the
nature of their work to change as dramatically as one might in the US where
there were more options.

But, if money wasn't the prime motivator and there were limits to career
advancement what was left?

*We used to have a managing director here in the very early
days who was Irish, but worked quite extensively in Europe
and, in fact, was hired from Europe to start up the facility
[here]. He used to get a bit frustrated and he used to say,*

> *"People here have to love each other to work with each other." I think that possibly it has something to do with the culture. We do want to get more from work than just money and security. [Deirdre]*

If a person's current job were simply one step along a career path containing many different places of employment there might be a disincentive to invest much time and energy in establishing connections with one's co-workers. On the other hand, if an individual did not intend to move on to other positions along a career path, if he or she were there to stay, then that person might have much more motivation to make the work environment a pleasant one. A person might have the incentive to invest energy and emotion in the job.

As I reflected on what the respondents said about motivation I could see that the type of motivation had changed over time. The earliest information-sector workers brought with them the rural work ethic with a commitment to hard work because that was what they were used to.

> *. . . [T]he workforce, the business demands in [19]71 [workers] were essentially school Leavers: bright young school Leavers who were involved in assembly work. Some people brought in experienced technicians, but in the main, a young, very young workforce. [They] predominantly came from the rural part of the country with very much an existing work ethic. [David]*

In time, information-sector specialists developed and were motivated by achievement within their profession. These workers, in turn, had begun to see beyond mere career considerations to finding enjoyment inside the workplace as well as outside it. David talked about the progression of these attitudes.

> *When I think back into my past, the work ethic that I was most easily associated with was . . . the traditional notion of work ethic: volume. You had to be seen to be there, apparently, stay late and generate in almost a smiling way. You can't enjoy it. I say that smiling now because when I look back I laugh at myself. I now see a different sort of work ethic. It comes from, yes, still working long hours, but I still think that it comes from, there's still fun. And there's still diversion during the day. There's still laugh about it. But the work ethic we have, there's still a significant sense of achievement. Achievement orientation. Also, there's a sense of family around here. My secretary's been here ten years.*

[Another person] 15 or 16. Joanie will be [here] 20 years next year. [David]

4.1.3   Loyalty and Security

I do think that people look for different things. Slightly different things. Security and employment would be number one, I think, here. The very notion of getting a job itself is very important and then maintaining a job is very important. That's pretty obvious why that would be. In [this city], in particular, it's a very high unemployment. [Deirdre]

Because of an historically high unemployment rate in Ireland and, because of redundancies that entered the information-sector, job security was an important motivator for these workers, much as it has been for workers in other sectors. In the information sector, however, the importance placed upon security varied depending on age, job level, education, and subsector. Those working in the hardware manufacturing part of the information technology industry, especially those working in lower levels of the multinational firms, placed more emphasis on security. Many of the respondents had been at their firms upwards of ten years, often from the time the firm first came to Ireland. It was typical for someone to have come straight from school to the firm when it started in the 1970s or early 1980s and to have remained there.

As the global computer industry's growth curve began to level off in the 1990s security began to become more important to younger workers as well. Ed was involved in the startup of his firm in Ireland during the year prior to our discussions. He commented about the low level of job hopping. In the American information sector with its low unemployment rate that was common practice.

If security motivated people to stay at a firm, then loyalty enabled them to feel good about it. Older workers, in particular, those who had been at a firm 30 or 40 years were very loyal to their employers, were proud of those for whom they worked and had significant identification with the company. This was the case not just in the information sector. Information-sector workers maintained a high level of loyalty toward their employers, despite erosion from redundancies. One worker, in comparing the Irish and American sites of two different IT firms, said that at the Irish sites people were happy to work there, were proud of it. Because it was a high tech industry, workers had a certain mystique among friends and relations. In America, he said, the people who were working for these firms did not seem to derive much status from a very similar environment and were not as loyal. Loyalty was still touted by

Irish industrial policy agencies as one of the reasons that multinational firms should come to Ireland. It was a good place to set up a plant, they said, because there was worker continuity.

In addition to status, another source of company loyalty was loyalty to fellow workers. A woman working at a multinational firm explained that when she worked late it was not done out of loyalty to the firm. Rather, it stemmed from a desire to help out co-workers. This created a synergy, she said. People were friends. In general, loyalty along with the desire for security, benefits and recognition of achievement were greater among older workers. Younger workers were more interested in gaining valuable experience and in intellectual challenge and were willing to change jobs to have these. Consequently, it was the minority of workers -- those who were older -- who were most concerned about the changing fortunes of the multinationals and the impact on Ireland. Nevertheless, younger workers were still affected by the economy of the information sector and security concerns did influence their decisions.

> *People stay at jobs for money and security now. It's not loyalty any more. I have been made redundant three times. And this is typical of workers here. [Patrick]*

4.2 Productivity Challenges

In the course of exploring the work ethic in the information sector I encountered some intriguing discrepancies. There was a day-night difference between what I was told about the work ethic in Irish society in general -- and what I sometimes experienced -- on the one hand, and the prevailing work ethic among members of the IT workforce on the other.

4.2.1 Ambition

Along side the dominant image emerging from my research of the intellectually challenged, highly motivated information-sector worker appeared a contrasting one. This was the depiction of a relaxed and not very ambitious worker. I never directly encountered this type of worker in the information sector; it was only in discussions with managers during my firm visits that this type of worker presented itself. As a manager, Mark found it harder to motivate the software developers; he had to make objectives clearer in order to get them accomplished. He found that there was a decreased sense of urgency about meeting deadlines. An Irish manager at an American firm made reference to a nine to five or "civil service" mentality, citing a worker who returned to the civil service because the hours in the information sector were too long and did not provide enough tea breaks.

> *I've seen too much of people who become millionaires [and] flaunt it. That's totally accepted in California. In Ireland it's not. There's enough poverty, enough deprivation, in my view, to have that be very insensitive behavior. The down side of that is people aren't as openly ambitious as perhaps they are in the States. I think it's less acceptable [to appear to be very ambitious]. Certainly, less acceptable to seem to be very wealthy. [Martin]*

There was a certain ambivalence about ambition and success. As pointed out earlier, religious influences pervading the culture produced a conflict between this world and the next. The resulting embarrassment about wealth, then, became an impediment to one's ambition. Another factor that diminished ambition was related to the desire not to stick out from the crowd at work, as might happen if one were highly ambitious and productive. Martin said that in the workplace the inclination was to be rather formalistic, somewhat nonadventurous, somewhat unambitious and somewhat nonentrepreneurial. This attitude was not what I gleaned from my direct experience with information-sector workers and workplaces, however.

Suspicion of ambition and success harkens back to Ireland's colonial history when virtually all of the nation's wealth was held by the ruling class of Anglo-Irish. Consequently, while it had become acceptable to progress, it was still not acceptable to be too boastful about it.

4.2.2   'twill do

> *ET: Where did this 'twill do attitude come from?*
>
> *If you really want to go into it, it's really more like a public health discussion on the evolution of the Irish character over the last 300 years. Go back to the penal times where if you were Catholic and Irish you were denied an education, denied property, denied any sort of status in life other than being a peasant, and you get 300 years of that you come out quite lackadaisical on the other side. Lacking confidence. 'twill do will also come from the fact that you're working for the local landlord. Probably the conditions weren't as good. The pay is atrocious. And the hours were atrocious. You had no say. You were told, "You take that and you put it on that,"*

*and that's what you do for the rest of your life. You never get
promoted. [Michael]*

Swimming in the same stream as reluctant ambition was a relaxed attitude
toward work which ran the gamut from simply acknowledging a plateau in
one's career, to having a relaxed and easygoing approach to work, to
displaying a complete lack of concern about one's job. David saw a challenge
for Ireland in making the transition from being a slow, easygoing culture to a
highly rationalized high tech society.

For some, the relaxed approach was a response to the career plateau. These
workers had made the decision that for personal and family reasons they
would not progress any further in their careers, because it would involve
moving abroad. Therefore, once they moved past the early years in a job
where they had to prove themselves, they slowed down a bit and focused
attention on other aspects of their lives like leisure time.

At the other extreme existed what has been characterized as a lazy attitude
toward work. Respondents pointed out that this was the case not so much in
the information sector as it was in state and semi-state agencies, banks and
insurance companies. The attitude towards work in Irish information-sector
firms was presented as the exception. Respondents with work experience in
state and semi-state agencies described the workers there as very easygoing
about their work and having lots of tea breaks. This other end of the work
environment spectrum was a laissez-faire approach that reflected a narrow
definition of one's job. Liam shared an anecdote about a young worker who
displayed too much enthusiasm and was consequently told by his managers to
slow down because he was getting the job done too fast and making the others
look bad. Barbara, shared her experience of paying a television rental bill.

> *. . . I went down to pay the TV rental bill today. Now we just
> received a notice that said, "You're in arrears so much
> money." Well, I never got a bill to say that I owed this much
> money! So I went down and the computer system was down
> on Monday. And I went in Tuesday and the computer system
> was still down, so I went in tonight.*
> *"Oh, yes, Barbara, we've taken care of it."*
> *And I thought I owed £45.*
> *"You owe £90."*
> *I said, "Well could someone please explain this to me? I
> thought I only owed 45." I said, "I haven't received any bills
> but maybe that's because I moved."*

"Oh, no, we don't send bills out. That would cost too much money." They don't send bills out, they expect people to come in and pay their bills!

ET: *And that's why you were in arrears, because you didn't . . .*

Because I didn't come in on a monthly basis to pay my bill. Just because what I'm used to in the States, I get my bill in the mail and I write my check and I pay it. And three months had gone by and we hadn't paid anything. And I said, "Well when do I owe my next . . . when is the payment due?"
"Well, you know, you can come in when you want. You know, just stop by some time when you're down in town."
I mean, I'd think [they'd] keep [their] books a little better than that! [So I asked] "Could I please have a receipt that I just paid £90?" [Barbara]

Some Irish respondents said this 'twill do attitude was inherited, that it was part of their culture. Compared to the UK, for example, they said Ireland had always been a sloppy nation. In thinking about why this casual attitude toward work might be part of the culture, I wondered about the rural background of most workers. So I asked if this attitude could be related to rural work values. Jim clearly saw such a linkage.

We're not very regimental so if you go into an industrial-type country or something where there's big assembly lines, everybody has to do something on time, a conveyor belt type business, right? Irish people wouldn't like that, I think, really. You probably have witnessed it at this stage: "Tomorrow will do." Like we're conscious of deadlines, and we'll deliver on time and all that, but within any day or within a week, right, we like to have the flexibility that if you don't feel like working this morning, well, then you'll just take it easy and then work late tonight, or something. For an industrial-type society or company you couldn't have that, you have to be very disciplined. So I wouldn't suggest we're very disciplined, but I don't mean that we're not controlled but the general reaction is: "Don't impose rigid discipline on me. I want to do my own thing." Is that coming from agricultural background? I think it is, actually, you know? OK, you have to milk the cows every day but whether you paint the house this week or next week or things like that, it doesn't really matter, you know? An Irish person always has time to talk to you. It's definitely a cultural thing, I suppose. This pressurized, industrial society type thing has never really impacted us. [Jim]

I was told often and early on in my discussions of the work ethic that Irish workers did better abroad. I came to understand that this statement had several meanings. One was that Irish workers found it easier to succeed abroad where they were also much bigger risk takers and were much more entrepreneurial. Another meaning was that Irish people would work extremely hard when abroad but were sloppy and lazy at home: "Ah, sure, 'twill do." A third meaning was that when people worked abroad they were not burdened by high taxes. A final meaning went back to begrudging success: Irish workers felt freer to be seen as succeeding in another country than at home. Free from the shackles of their family history, they could reinvent themselves.

Part of the discussion about doing better abroad included differences in the work ethics when one went abroad, especially to America. In a society with a prevailing work culture that rewarded seniority over merit, those with ambition would need to go abroad to be satisfied. Americans were perceived as more serious about their work. Nuala worked for a time in New York. She experienced pressure to come in on weekends, something she never felt at the firm's Dublin office. In addition, there was much less social interaction. While the vast majority of those with whom I spoke -- American as well as Irish -- believed that social interaction made a positive contribution to the workplace, on occasion I heard the minority viewpoint. It was that social interaction in Ireland was a detriment to productivity because having so many conversations took up too much time during the work day.

Some respondents considered the behavior of workers to be a function of culture. To others, however, workers' behavior was directly attributable to the way Irish companies have been historically managed: there was no incentive to work. In the industrial and service sectors a complacency and lack of initiative that was mentioned in interviews seemed to have derived from a management style that rewarded following orders and putting in time more than enthusiasm, energy and commitment. One did not have to perform better than another and would be paid the same regardless of productivity. So it did not matter.

I observed four factors that impinged upon work-related incentive. First, until quite recently the management structure of Irish firms provided little opportunity for one to succeed. Another disincentive to working hard was the tax structure. The high tax rate meant that it often was not worth the effort to work overtime because all of the extra income would go to taxes. Third, the ease of being on the dole[xvi] further reduced incentive. The final disincentive was the post-colonial legacy that everyone in the workplace must be seen to be equal.

4.2.3   Working to Live

> *I would be inclined to think of Americans as more workaholics to some degree than the Irish. I think the Irish will work, but we work to enjoy ourselves. We're not workaholics. That's not our problem, is it? I think that the Irish would like to spend more time out enjoying themselves, right. So they work to play, whereas the Americans live to work. [Farrell]*

Another productivity challenge came from the cultural inclination to balance work and personal life. Irish respondents said that Americans *live to work*. In contrast, the Irish described themselves as people who *work to live*. While Irish people took their work very seriously, they also took their social life seriously. Work did not come first. This theme of quality of life surfaced quite frequently during my interviews. In fact, quality of life was one of the first aspects of Irish culture to which I was introduced. Before embarking upon this research project I met with representatives of the Irish government and various Irish people in order to collect background information and to focus my research. One consistent feature of Irish culture that inevitably entered our conversations was quality of life. It was given as a key reason American multinationals would want to set up operations in Ireland. In exploring this notion, I learned that quality of life in Ireland meant maintaining a proper balance between one's work and personal lives.

To some extent the comments of Irish respondents needs to be filtered through the lens of age. Younger workers had more freedom and less responsibility, and were more willing to put in the long, extra hours. In telling about his own work ethic, Paul talked about how when he was younger he was more invested in the company whereas of late he had begun questioning where all the hard work was getting him. He wanted to do less work and spend more time with his family. As information-sector workers got older and had children, there were other, stronger demands on their time.

The range and oftentimes contradictory nature of comments about the Irish work ethic required considerable sorting out. My interpretation is that both a worker's age and work sector were the significant factors in accounting for differences in attitude toward work and level of effort put into it. The characteristics of work in the information sector were attractive to young people: volatility, considerable amount of change, the requirement of a strong commitment to work, unpredictable hours, and the need for worker flexibility. Irish information-sector workers preferred work with considerable variety so that they could avoid boredom. They also preferred work settings that required flexibility and enabled them to take pride in what they did. Running throughout was a strong emphasis on social interaction and having a good time in a relaxed atmosphere at work. Along with this came a strong desire for autonomy and personal control. Older workers, on the other hand, because they had more commitments outside of work, had less energy to commit to work.

As I conducted this research project I was witnessing the radical transformation that was occurring both on and beneath the surface. The emerging information-sector work ethic was attempting to draw the best from its predecessors. It endeavored to be a humane ethic in which productivity, motivation, enthusiasm and flexibility merged with a relaxed, social and caring demeanor. But I also witnessed remnants of earlier work ethics. While the dominant ethic in the information-sector workplace was not the relaxed 'twill do attitude, the comments I have shared suggest that vestiges of the old ways still existed, especially in the life experiences of some older workers.

Interestingly, though, there was one factor consistent in all work ethics. Whether the work ethic was hard driving or easygoing, the exteriors of the workers were very similar. The hard driving workers were as friendly and social as those who were more relaxed. I found this surprising. It was one thing to see nonproductive people being easygoing but it was surprising and refreshing to see highly productive workers behave in this manner as well. I came away thinking that if the Irish information sector could be successful yet have such a human face, this should give mangers from other nations pause to consider how humane our own workplaces were and whether we could achieve similar results with such behavior.

5.   LATE

The Irish are not good time keepers. And they tend not to see time keeping as something that's important. I think they see time keeping [as] more of a flexi-system, and I think flexible systems of time management suit them very well. The Germans tend to be very prompt. That is, "I must take personal insult if someone is late for a meeting." Whereas, if they're in the country for a few years, they ease up on it.

They're not as particular, as insulted if somebody turns up
five or ten minutes late. In fact, they may themselves slip a
little bit on time as well. So that would be one aspect of it.
The other thing would be that they would tend to give orders
and expect orders to be carried out. If one German tells
another German what to do, he tends to go on and do it. If
one Japanese man tells another Japanese man what to do, he
tends to go and do it. If you tell an Irish man to go and do it,
he tends to find some ways to do it differently or not to do it
at all. [Liam]

One does not need to be in Ireland very long in order to grasp the cultural significance of the attitude toward time.[xvii] I experienced it in the time that shops opened, in the time that shopkeepers were willing to take to chat with customers. I observed it in the leisurely Sunday strolls that were so popular. I learned that I if I came on time to a meeting or social gathering I would be early.

From these sources came my curiosity about the cultural exchange in the information-sector workplace. I wanted to know what happened when the Irish desire to take time or a comfort level with being late came up against American attitudes about punctuality. The question on my mind was that if the American work ethic was more structured and time-oriented and the Irish ethic was less so, who changed when an American firm came to Ireland? And if Irish workers in multinational plants did, indeed, change, did this mean that a more pervasive change would spread out into the Irish culture as a whole? As I explored these questions what I found was evidence of mutual adaptation.

5.1   Taking Time

Life in Ireland did not feel hectic; it felt as though there were all the time in the world to accomplish a task. There was the feeling that time was an unlimited quantity. What one could not do today would be done tomorrow. Taking whatever time they had, Irish people stood in stark contrast to Americans who always seemed to be chasing the clock. The Irish were more flexible about time both at work and in their personal lives. While they might not achieve as much in a given day they were more willing to work late or on weekends. People worked an eight-hour day, but not necessarily nine to five. They were also less deadline driven. When I inquired about how the Irish came to have these attitudes towards time I learned that the reasons were bound to Ireland's value system, economy, and geography.

Taking time was part of the Christian value system which permeated Irish society along with such other values as "do unto others," "be comfortable in your surroundings" and "be less materialistic." At a meeting with some representatives of a government agency responsible for promoting inward investment in Ireland we discussed some of the reasons that multinational companies would want to come to Ireland. Theresa, who worked for an economic development agency, made a link between time and values about quality of life. She said there was a value placed on taking the time to talk with someone. And if it made you five minutes late, then that was OK; you'd make it up later.

Quite often the Irish attitude towards time was explained in terms of Ireland's rural culture in which there was not much need to rush. One woman from a rural background who worked at a multinational plant commented about Americans having to adjust to people showing up an hour late for a dinner party or other engagement. Her explanation?

> *Well, in farming you don't do things by the minute.*
> *[Sheelagh]*

Mary talked about her experience of adjusting to the meaning of "on time" as part of her adjustment from agrarian work on a family farm to information-sector work at a multinational firm. They were only allowed to be three minutes late; in contrast:

> *. . . with farming, they kind of seem to put things off, d'you know what I mean? Like as you said, the dinner. Like, I mean, that could be in a few minutes, it could be in an hour, that sort of thing, right? . . . I suppose they know that the wife would wait or the mother would wait for whenever. Like, I mean, it's something that I suppose was just always done.*
> *[Mary]*

Mary was quite clear about her preference for the rural life. She would have returned to farming if it were possible. At the high tech firm there was always pressure to "beat the clock," although it was less than at firms in other sectors. Farming was still an easier work environment in her view.

The willingness to slow down and take time with people led quite naturally to a comfort level with being late. This was the case in both the personal and professional spheres. In the personal realm, I found that social events tended to start much later than they would in America. I was invited to a summer barbecue that didn't get under way until after ten PM! More than once I returned home from an evening's dinner party in time to eat breakfast. David provided contrasts with his experience of living in the UK. He found that he would be on time if he arrived at a pub at nine or nine thirty but that things did not really start to happen until midnight. He thought there was a different sort of pace outside of work. People were slower, more deliberate, which was why he said he enjoyed life in Ireland compared to the UK. At the time we spoke he was still feeling a bit programmed, though, and wished he could take it a bit slower. He still reacted when people talked about going out to a party at ten thirty or eleven o'clock and then didn't return until three in the morning.

Another interpretation of being late was being less deadline-driven. On this topic there were different perceptions, which generally fell along nationality lines. Richard, for instance, who was an Irish manager working outside the information sector, said the notion of deadlines was a relatively new thing to him.

> *Before I met [my American wife] I'd never really heard of,*
> *sort of, deadlines and really working to deadlines. [Richard]*

Sue, on the other hand, initially found it extraordinary in her work environment that project deadlines were not taken seriously. In her experience, when a deadline was set you expected to meet it. But in Ireland she encountered a different attitude.

> *Here it was like, "Ah sure, but you know we'll get it a week*
> *later but what's the big story? Relax, we'll get there." [Sue]*

Jim responded to this type of comment. While acknowledging that Irish people did not like to have deadlines, he said it was also true that people who didn't know what was involved in software development often set unrealistic deadlines. At his firm very high level managers in Europe were setting deadlines for various stages of their project. These people did not have a clue about what was really involved, he said. Software development deadlines should be a goal, not something firmly set. Mark's interpretation was somewhat different as he reflected on his experiences in managing both Irish and Americans. Irish workers just seemed to be less sensitive to time pressure. Whereas Americans lived by the clock, the Irish sense of urgency to meet dates was simply not as strong.

5.2   Mutual Adaptation

> *ET: Did you notice differences in the work culture between*
> *the Irish firms and the American firms?*

I think it's very difficult to try and see it. It's more the culture of the industry rather than the culture of the complement of the Irish. I noticed that the Norwegian culture was very, very lax and trusting, goal-oriented rather than time-oriented. You had to make so many shipments in a quarter and it was up to you to do it, now. Your boss wasn't particularly interested in whether it meant you worked Sundays, or whether you worked two days a week, whatever it meant to do to reach that goal, that was the key, not the fact that you were on the premises at eight in the morning to at night. You weren't measured on that basis. In the Irish company I worked for in the beginning, which was very old fashioned, performance was really measured by how long you were there, how much time you put in, not what you actually did. Around that time I also had some dealings with American companies, and I noticed the change in the American companies now, from being very control-oriented, very strict about when you are clocking out, strict on control of employees, to a much more lax goal-oriented thrust. [Kevin]

Having encountered this more relaxed attitude toward time in the Irish culture, I wanted to know how this relaxed attitude was carried into the workplace in general and the information-sector workplace in particular. I also wanted to know how firms coped with the different attitudes about time in the rural and industrial sectors. Finally, I wanted to know how people who were used to working in more traditional sectors coped with the high tech environment. As suggested in the comments above, the attitude toward time was related both to national culture and industry sector. The adaptation that had occurred, therefore, reflected this complexity.

5.2.1   Relaxed Attitude about Time in the Information Sector

There were several different interpretations of the relationship between a relaxed attitude about time and the influence on the workplace. One group of people thought there was little carryover. They said Irish people were relaxed about time in the social context but not in the work context. According to this view the norms of a global information sector dominated: this was a professional sector and people in it behaved accordingly. About this point, Ed observed that the relaxed attitude toward time did not translate into missed deadlines. He observed that while he, personally, might do a task a little faster than his Irish employees, it didn't mean the deadline was missed.

A second set of answers acknowledged the presence of the Irish relaxed attitude about time in the workplace but focused on its benign (at worst) or positive (at best) effects. For example, when I inquired about the influence of the late hours and weeknight socializing on the workplace I was told that there was no drop in productivity.

> *[This plant] has done a fine job by all the range of metrics you want to put in place in terms of performance. Yes, still folks will be late turning up some mornings because they've been partying the night before. And yes it is casual, but still, somehow, the thing is translated into . . . We don't lose our shape, you know. [David]*

Continuing in this vein is a positive impact from being less conscious of time. The other side of the coin was the willingness to stay late if need be.

It must be added, however, that the whole topic of working overtime was rife with contradictions. At one extreme were the younger people in the information sector who were more willing to work on a weekend because they had fewer family obligations and wanted to get on in life and in the job. At the other extreme were workers in the civil service and semi-state agencies where there was a more relaxed, 'twill do attitude. People there were at the job fewer hours and it seemed -- from my respondents -- they did not work as hard when they were there. They wouldn't work overtime.

> *It'll wait till tomorrow.*

In between these extremes were a myriad of variations. A typical viewpoint of the information-sector workers was that if something had to get done outside business hours they would come in, though they did not believe in working until ten o'clock every night. When necessary, they would do whatever it took, but they wanted that to be the exception rather than the norm.

> *In the recent times the amount of overtime that has been worked in this plant is extremely high. The need is there. The business need is there to be met. People respond very well to the business need. . . There is a commitment to the business. [John]*

The attitude toward working overtime was also related to the seasons. It was fine to work overtime in the short days of winter. In fact, it was a way to get extra cash for summer holidays. But in the summer, it was a different story. People were more reluctant because they wanted their long evenings to themselves in order to engage in sports. But, in general, the attitude was, "If the need is there I will do it."

In Sue's experience of working in both Ireland and America there was more flexibility in Ireland. In Ireland, people might not achieve as much during the day as Americans but they were willing to work beyond six or on a weekend. To her, it was not so much that they were willing to work overtime as much as it was being more flexible about their hours.

A third group comprised of both Irish and American respondents did not approve of the Irish relaxed attitude about time carrying over into the workplace. When I asked Sheelagh about the Irish attitude toward time she first chided me for being late for the interview! Then she went on to tell me she found it a bit aggravating that the Irish were loose about time.

> *ET: Why is that, do you think, that the Irish seem to be loose about time?*
>
> *Because there's no hurry in us.*
>
> *ET: Does that come from the agricultural background?*
>
> *Well I suppose since we were all in agriculture years ago, it must, yeah. "Do it in God's time."*
> *"Go by the moon and the sun."*
> *"If the sun is at a certain height well then we'll call in to see you." [Sheelagh]*

Others observed that all this chatting can lead to wasted time. On the positive side, this usually resulted in people picking up information since the talk often turned to work. If there was any coherence to the seemingly disparate viewpoints on this topic it was that people took the time that they had.

5.2.2   Transition to Post-industrial Perception of Time

> *This is traditionally an agricultural country and so it is taking time for people to adapt. For people from rural backgrounds, it is a hard transition. At [a non IT firm where he had worked] the workers were from rural backgrounds. They had some land and a few cows. They had a dual source of income. They did shift work to allow time for the land. Therefore, there is a conflict of interest regarding their level of commitment. There was this Dutch company that is now closed. They made steel chord for tires. They recruited 1500 people in one year, mostly rural. The people couldn't do shift work, looking after a machine. The issue was mainly discipline regarding time: taken for lunch, start and stop*

times. They had a bad recruitment policy. They should have
had structures to train them. [Brendan]

Firms have had to cope with the transition from work patterns suitable for the farm to work patterns appropriate for the information-sector factory or office. One particular issue with which firms have had to cope was getting workers to come to work on time and to stay there once they had done so. Mary had been working at the same multinational firm since it first came to Ireland. She commented that in the early days you could find scores of factory workers in City Centre at midday. Workers were simply not used to staying indoors all day. Further, people would be wandering in at ten in the morning. Consequently tighter controls were put in place: people could be, at most, five minutes late. The workers accepted these constraints and responded to them because they had no other option. One of the first multinational IT firms to come to Ireland experienced an increased absenteeism and punctuality problem during "the season." Since many of the workers were also small farmers they simply took time off from the company in order to do their planting and harvesting.

Firms approached this transition in several ways. A more control-oriented response to punctuality was to employ time cards and to enforce strict adherence to corporate rules. This approach was not generally used in high tech but it had been in other sectors. Some of the IT firms I visited responded in a more creative way. Rather than attempt to change the workers by fiat -- forcing them to show up for work at a certain time -- they introduced new management approaches. One was flex time. The other was worker evaluation based not upon time spent at work but upon tangible output measures of productivity. The flex time allowed workers to arrive at work any time between 7:30 and 9:30 AM and leave at the end of an eight-hour day, sometime between four and six in the afternoon. To the skeptics' surprise this new management approach was enthusiastically embraced.

People over 40 have this old way of thinking. They are into
the old traditions. They said that flex time wouldn't work.
They said the Irish like to come to work late and would never
come in early under a flex time plan. I said, "Well, let's just
try it." Well, you should have seen the number of workers
who came in at 7:30 AM, especially on Fridays when they
wanted to get an early start to the family farm for the
weekend! [Leo]

While there was some need to cope with attitudes about time that came from the agrarian culture, there was another issue for those workers coming from other sectors. People used to strict adherence to time would show up on time, but they also expected to leave on time. In this case, the information sector needed to overcome the mores of an industrial work ethic suitable for rote assembly work, which emphasized the hours spent on the job. In the post-industrial, information economy, however, the focus is on the quality of the output that is produced not time input. In this regard I could see how Ireland might benefit from not having had a strong industrial background. Without two centuries of industrialism and its entrenched work patterns, there was no regimented time clock mentality to overcome. Declan noted that younger workers with no traditional industrial experience were more flexible than their older counterparts about coming to work but also about leaving. The information-sector work environment required the greater flexibility that was part of the work ethic of these young workers.

The interaction of different cultures was definitely represented in the information-sector workplace with respect to time. A comfort level with taking time even if it meant being late for something else came into conflict with other national cultures' or work sectors' attitudes toward punctuality. The question I wanted to answer was the following. If the corporate cultures of the multinational firms were more time-oriented and structured and the Irish ethic was less so, who changed? Likewise, I wanted to know how the flexibility that is inherent in the high tech culture related to workers from the rural and the traditional industrial sectors. I wondered whether the Irish people working for the multinationals would be able to maintain the values about taking time or whether there would be changes in people's attitudes towards time. What I found was that there was indeed an influence of the Irish attitude toward time on the information-sector workplace. But the different attitudes held by the IT multinationals were also having an impact. It was clear that all parties were changing as an American manager observed:

> *I haven't seen it come down to a conflict. I think both sides give a little. I know I've mellowed out to a degree and likewise when I clearly express a deadline they'll concentrate on it. [We] find a happy medium. [Ed]*

6.   REMOTE

> *I remember talking to some of our personnel people in the States. They flew us over here to see if we'd like to live here and then they were going to show us some videos [about the country]. Well, starting off, I didn't want to believe the*

*cultural differences [were that great] partly because the
people in personnel were telling you this, and it seemed like
at the time too soft and fuzzy for me. And I said, well there
can't be that big of a difference. And then when I came over
here I don't know how many times I heard in the first ten staff
meetings: "Well, this is Ireland; things are different in
Ireland.". . . And I heard so many times: "You don't do that.
This is Ireland." . . . So, I used to keep track in my mind of all
the "You don't do that, this is Ireland. That won't work here,
this is Ireland." [Joseph]*

Despite the government's desire to attract multinational firms to Ireland and the workers' desire to work at them, what was clear from our conversations was that Irish information-sector workers did not want their country to become indistinguishable from America. The phrase "This is Ireland" or "Welcome to Ireland" continuously entered my interviews and my own work environment at the University. Joseph spoke about two aspects of the many-sided "This is Ireland" coin. On the one hand, he knew he had to cope with the difference between American and Irish workplaces. Yet he sometimes found those working for him feeling hidebound by what the phrase implied and appreciative of his different perspectives. In my experience, the phrase was used to excuse what were perceived to be inefficient work practices. This interpretation of the phrase seemed to stem from insecurity. To some extent, this expression also represented a lack of exposure to other workplace settings where similar types of problems and issues also existed.

The phrase "This is Ireland" whether used in defense of or as an excuse for Irish practices suggested a dimension of Irish culture and the Irish information-sector workplace that needed to be included in this picture that I am painting. This other side that sometimes presented itself -- while definitely not the predominant view -- was, nevertheless, intriguing. It was sometimes expressed as insecurity. Other times it emerged as a viewpoint about the lack of anonymity being stifling or even repressive. A few of the Irish respondents acknowledged the personal and professional benefits that derived from a society in which everybody knew everybody and in which sociability was valued. Yet they also noted that these attitudes could hold them back. In these conversations people talked about feeling stifled or needing to emigrate in order to move beyond their roots. A connected undercurrent I sometimes detected in respondents' comments about Irish culture was a sense of fatalism.

As a result of stories I heard and experiences I had early on, I began to explore the phrase "This is Ireland." It emerged as an expression of a cultural clash being brought about by Ireland's rapid shift from an isolated, agrarian society to an information society. In this new world cultural boundaries were becoming highly permeable through exposure to outside influences. The themes that emerged from my investigation began with Ireland being a traditional, conservative and isolated culture that until quite recently had been rather impervious to outside influences. They then moved on to include the tensions resulting from Ireland's reaction and sometimes resistance to the imported culture accompanying inward investment. The exploration of these themes provided a good opportunity to consider how the Irish culture had influenced the shape that the information industry had taken in Ireland. It also revealed the impact of outside influences -- coming from multinational IT companies -- on Irish culture.

6.1   Island Mentality

When discussing aspects of Irish culture, the respondents often drew upon the physical characteristics of the country's landmass -- an island nation on the periphery of Europe -- to explain aspects of Irish culture. They described Irish culture, historically, as inward-focused.

There is an island mentality. [Des]

Indeed, contemporary scholarly writing presented a portrait of Ireland as a peripheral world in every sense: geographic, cultural and economic.[xviii]

Until the 1980s, which brought more affordable and available transportation, being an island nation made Ireland remote in a physical sense. I was interested in probing more deeply the mindset that moved from the physical isolation of the country to the isolation of the culture. In response to questions I was presented with the image of a nation cut off from other cultures.[xix] It occurred first during Ireland's colonial period when the only outside influences were British. Then, following independence, the effort to reestablish Irish cultural identity was pursued through isolationist policies. Consequently, people had little interaction with other cultures.[xx] Louise described Ireland as sleepy repository for second-hand English items -- people, ideas and products -- that was just awakening.

> *You know, we've had the kind of trends arriving here ten years later and legislation arriving ten years later until recently when we have suddenly realized we speak the English language and an awful lot of the exciting things in the world are being reported in English, so we can read American and English books, but until quite recently we were de facto cut off from events on the continent and we were a*

> *fringe and we were cut off, we had a filter of England.*
> *[Louise]*

However, another group of respondents assigned to the Irish culture a decidedly opposite interpretation of its status as an island nation. While agreeing that Irish people felt peripheral to Europe and the rest of the world, they went on to claim that Irish people were not isolated. Rather, because it was a small country and could not survive on its own, Ireland looked outward and was exposed to outside influences. In fact, several respondents believed the Irish had a more international outlook than Americans, many of whom they said had little knowledge of world geography.

As with so many aspects of Irish culture that I examined, age seemed to be the key variable here, as well. In this case, while there was complete agreement across respondents that Ireland was geographically peripheral to Europe, what was different was the response to this condition. Older Irish people's experience of being geographically peripheral led to isolation and resistance to new ways. But to younger people, being on the periphery had increased their desire to travel and their willingness to absorb new cultures.

To some extent the limited exposure to outside influences had reinforced conservatism in Ireland and kept the country from becoming as modern as other European countries. This sense of being old fashioned and less willing to change was usually raised by older respondents or those who had an American connection: Americans working at multinational firms or their spouses, or Irish workers at the multinational firms. The de-emphasis on materialism was also linked to Ireland being less modern. On occasion, American respondents made statements to the effect that Ireland was "20 to 30 years *behind* America." This was their way of saying Ireland was not modern.

Ireland was described as conservative or not modern across a range of factors. Some people used this term with respect to management. It was traditional management that placed high emphasis on status and where standards of quality were not high enough for a high tech society. Others said this about gender and sexuality issues. The conservative nature of society was reflected in convent schools where girls were traditionally taught to be homemakers but not to have careers.

Some workplace implications of this conservatism were offered:

> *They excel, but they don't want change. I don't think anybody*
> *votes for change at all. [But] if you force them to do*
> *something . . . Say, for a moment going out of the computer*
> *business and into the agriculture business, a farmer. They*
> *will work hard at their present method even though they*

know it's inefficient. [But] if you somehow inspired that person to come up-to-date and do something about it, he would likely be more efficient than an English person, the English farmer with the same equipment. If you understand what I'm saying. [Albert]

Two important points lingered after his comments ended. On the one hand, it was perhaps difficult to make the Irish person change. But *if* the Irish person could be motivated to try a new technique, he or she was likely to be more efficient than others who had previously adopted it. I also found it significant that Albert believed this to be as much the case in industry as it was in agriculture.

But people are being forced to be more flexible. Over the past few years, there has been a vast change in Ireland. It has to come whether people want it or not. [Elizabeth]

Offering a different viewpoint on conservatism was a view that the real conservatism came from the British influence, not the isolated Celtic people.

. . . I would think on the side where businesses have been set up on the British or colonial style, you might get difficulty and a conservativeness there when you're trying to change. Whereas if you go to the west coast and you try to change something, you change quite easily. I certainly found when working in Dublin, here, that people are a more conservative type and didn't like change, and you had to be very able as a manager or as an administrator. [Liam]

Over the past 30 years Ireland has had significant exposure to outside influences. These outside influences have come about in several ways. One vehicle was television. Ireland did not have television until the 1960s; many parts of the country did not receive it until the 1970s. A second avenue was travel. A third source of outside influences was Ireland's membership in the European Union. When it joined the European Common Market in 1973, Ireland began the process of opening its doors to the influence of other European countries besides Britain. Ireland, subsequently, became heavily involved in the affairs of the European Union. In my interviews the EU was cited as being a major factor in opening up Irish society to outside influences. The final vehicle for the introduction of outside influences was the arrival of the multinational companies.

I discussed with the respondents how this newer, more open Irish culture was influencing the information-sector workplace. I learned that the Irish people felt the exposure to other cultures wasn't as reciprocal as they would like it to be. In recent years through access to American television Irish people had become better able to understand Americans, their language and their behavior. Consequently, the Irish workers had no difficulty interpreting the language and behavior of their American managers and co-workers when they came to Ireland. However, they felt that the reverse was *not* true. They felt that their American counterparts knew much less about the Irish culture than they did about the American culture.

I observed -- and others concurred -- that the effects of television were also felt in changed attitudes toward competition and material possessions. Television had increased the competitive drive to have material possessions like a car, a house and generally keeping up with the neighbors. George noted that the younger generation -- the first one to grow up with access to television -- had a different sense of Irish culture. It was a lot different from what the pre-TV generations would have said. And those individuals moving into dominant positions in the information sector belonged to the TV generation. He wondered whether they reflected the *Irish* culture at all.

Travel has played a definite role in enhancing exposure to outside influences as well. An ironic twist was the comment from several people about the role of returning emigrants in Ireland's increased exposure to outside influences. The consensus seemed to be that there were no longer any boundaries because people traveled freely since travel had become relatively inexpensive.

Those who worked in the information sector were indeed a new breed. Being younger, they had grown up with the outside influences to which Ireland was becoming exposed. In the 1970s Irish business people would have looked only to England and perhaps America; they would have had problems with the idea of going to France, Germany, Italy or Spain. However, it had become easier for software firms, for example, to make the leap beyond the domestic market. Compared to England, said one respondent working at an Irish firm, Ireland had a *more* dynamic IT culture. This was partly due to the ages of the respective populations. But also because Ireland was on the edge of Europe, everyone wanted to travel and see things. In contrast, because England was so big, people were less inclined to go abroad. Hence, Ireland had more openness to different cultures. Younger workers were quite willing to go abroad for a stint. Because of their exposure to foreign cultures from the television and media, other countries were no longer so foreign to them.

In the past there were three mechanisms for the conveyance of culture: the family, the Church and the school. While these societal institutions have continued to play an important role in Ireland, there have emerged three additional vehicles for cultural conveyance: travel, the mass media and the workplace.

6.2   Circumspect

> *If you had a situation, if you're in a meeting, for example, and people in the room didn't know each other very well in the work scene, they'd be quite shy and, as we say in Ireland, "backward" about coming forward. [Jim]*

Before coming to Ireland I was told that Irish people were circumspect.

> *Don't behave like that, it's too pushy. [Joseph]*

Once I got to Ireland I observed Irish people -- particularly women -- speaking in low tones in public. I often found myself straining my ears to hear what was being said in a pub. The quiet tone of voice seemed to symbolize a desire to keep others at arm's length. There was a clear paradox of a people at the same time open and communicative and yet restricted in their self-expression. There was a reserve that manifested itself in several ways. Sometimes, it was simply "things you don't talk about." Other times it drifted into a fatalistic or pessimistic outlook, feeling stunted or appearing passive and complacent.

6.2.1   Reticent

> *Well, in fact, the Irish are quite friendly to strangers. At one level, yes. At another level, not at all. What I mean by that is that they would be superficially quite chatty and friendly but they really wouldn't tell you a thing about what they really thought. [Sue]*

I found it interesting that despite all the emphasis on social interaction and conversation, there was reserve when it came to sharing information about oneself. People liked to keep others from knowing about them. They liked to spend more time learning about others than having others learn about them. While this cultural trait had been described with the term backward, I think the label secretive is more apt. Interestingly, respondents didn't feel this secretive trait was carried into the information-sector workplace. While this may or may not have been the case, it was the case that there was an atmosphere that was suggestive of secrecy. What was considered normal behavior in America was considered to be pushy in Ireland. Irish workers were inclined to use an indirect way to express their desires so as not to be confrontational. Joseph found this particularly intriguing.

> *One of the phrases in the language that amazed me [is that] . . . [w]hen someone doesn't want you to do something over here they say, "You wouldn't want to be doing that, would you?" "You wouldn't wanna be, would you?" Like an open ended question. What a phrase to have instead of saying, "Don't do that." "I don't want you to do that." "I don't think that's the right thing to do." "I don't like that." They dance around it. That's like as strong as they ever get. They don't like confrontation. [Joseph]*

Irish people described themselves as introverted, understating themselves, not opening up. People were very friendly to strangers in rural Ireland, less so in the cities. When Charles talked about a stranger coming to a small town and said the person would not be fully accepted, he ended with a comment that was made about so many of the topics that were discussed in this research: the old ways were fading; things were changing.

> *He wasn't going to be told too much. It wasn't deliberate. It was just the way things were. Maybe a certain kind of shyness, maybe a rather deliberate hiding or something. . . Still, there's a lot more talking than in the old days. Take the example of sex scandals and marital breakup and all that. The thing of it is you didn't talk about it. You certainly didn't let the priest get to know about it. The parents get to know, but if something happened, you sort of sneaked off and hid somewhere. If it was known in some of those circles it was kept very tight. It wasn't bandied about. [Charles]*

Before coming to Ireland I interviewed some Americans who had been to Ireland and Irish people living in the States. It was here that I first heard about this trait of being friendly of on the surface yet reticent underneath. But in this research I found this a challenging topic to broach with respondents. People often appeared not to know what I was talking about when I raised the topic of reticence. Stephanie's response made me wonder if what had been described as reticence was actually defensiveness.

> *We have this perception that, you know, if I visited your home you're going to have a big home. You're going to be able to accommodate me. You're going to be able to do all these things. So, therefore, if you return the visit I might feel, "Oh,*

where is she going to sleep. What am I going to do? Where will I bring her?" all the problems that I wouldn't perceive you to have because you live in America. Therefore, you had all the answers and all the supplies and whatever. So, I suppose that's an insecurity. [Stephanie]

Eric commented on the workplace implications of this reticence. When he first got to Ireland he attended a cultural orientation in which he learned some things about Irish workers. They were said to be shy, less open, not inclined to be risk takers, took things personally, and were not in possession of much trust.[xxi] He observed that such traits flew in the face of the work culture at his firm where the opposite traits such as directness and risk taking were valued.

6.2.2   Fatalistic

There are few entrepreneurs in Ireland, few millionaires. There is a tremendous fear of failure. I'm not sure whether it is due to worrying about other people knowing about it or whether it's due to the fatalistic attitude: "I know it will fail." The Irish like to go on a sure thing. However, with a tighter job market, people started to feel they had nothing to loose and started taking risks. You see that in music, fashion, film. [Elizabeth]

A sense of fatalism has long been a part of Ireland's history: don't try to control what's beyond your influence. An extreme example is the fishermen on the Aran Islands. Despite living on an island and working on the sea, it is said they never learned how to swim. Respondents related stories about a fisherman falling into the water 30 meters from land and not being able to save himself. If it is your time to die there is nothing to be done about it; if you're going to fall in the water then you're going to die.

This fatalistic trait also expressed itself in a paradoxical form of pessimism. On the one hand, people displayed a relaxed, easygoing attitude. On the other hand, they revealed this pessimism. I struggled to reconcile these opposites. Margaret, who was from the Gaeltacht, helped me sort it all out. In her perception, it is a matter of layers. She explained that the music and the laughter was not so much a reflection of a jovial outlook as it was a means of forgetting, for awhile, the pain. Perhaps an outgrowth of the fatalism that told one to accept what one could not alter was a passivity or complacency that was also evident in the culture. This tendency to be complacent was explained to me -- as were many things -- in terms of Ireland's colonial history: no matter how far back you went, there was some degree of domination. Consequently, people became disinclined to stand up.

> *I think there's a little more respect for authority over here. [Another American manager] and I sometimes comment to each other that they seem more subservial (sic). It's kind of a bad term. It almost implies that we tell them to wash our car and they will. But like as I mentioned earlier, there's some menial aspects of the job, it might not even be their job but you need someone to do it and you tell them to do it and "bang they're off." [Ed]*

The workplace manifestation was accepting the organization structure and assuming the individuals in authority ought to be listened to or followed as being the experts. This would also come across as reluctance to second guess or rock the boat or question the correct course of action. It meant accepting directives because of the position of the person giving them. This occurred both at work and in social settings as a reluctance to complain if an item was not satisfactory.

> *There's an awful lot of acquiescencing folks among the Irish. [Farrell]*

These observations stood in direct contrast to other information I gleaned about the Irish being a questioning people. In attempting to resolve this apparent contradiction I wondered if a questioning stance was what they *wanted* but didn't always achieve. I also reminded myself that oftentimes people were telling me about workplace behavior *before* the information sector came to Ireland, in which case the acquiescing behavior might have been more about prior work settings than their current one. In this sense the information sector has left its mark by empowering workers to question and challenge decisions.[xxii]

Mark experienced one implication for the information-sector workplace. Software groups in the States were more pragmatic about what was realistically doable. In Ireland, software developers were less prone to raise concerns, they didn't want to be the bearer of bad news and be perceived as being negative. Mark complained that he was forever being told what people thought he wanted to hear, what they hoped would happen. "It'll be OK," they assured him, and then some project would get dumped in the end. He found he had to press them to tell him the truth. He had to probe more because if a person raised concerns it might be viewed as being wrong and negative. American workers, in contrast, were more direct and straightforward.

6.3   Confident

I think when it comes to hospitality we're probably intimidated a bit by Americans and that would probably cease to be with our young people going to America as much as they do and discovering that Americans are just like everybody else. I mean when I was growing up America was bigger and better and, you know, they had everything, did everything, knew everything. And we would tend to be intimidated by them. But obviously that has changed. I mean we are an island people and we didn't have much interaction with anyone! I mean travel was restricted, travel was expensive and there wasn't an awful lot of money for extras like travel. And I would say we were quite an insular people and probably very easily intimidated. But, you know, the last 20 years travel has been available to everybody and most people have been away if only on a package holiday to Spain. They have been away and discovered that it's not so great at all and what we have is just as good. I remember bringing my son, we were going through Barcelona. One year we were on a sightseeing tour or something like that. And he brought himself up -- he was all of about eight -- straightened himself up on the seat and said, "Well the next time the Spanish students come to our country," he said, "I won't be afraid of them!" because he discovered that Barcelona wasn't really any better than Dublin. And, you know, I remember it struck me quite, kind of quite forcibly at the time that when he met Spanish students maybe he thought, he looked at them as though they kind of had two heads and now he was here and, sure, things weren't any different than they were at home. And you could see the confidence sort of build. But, ach no, I don't think in Ireland people are as intimidated. As I said, times have totally changed. [Stephanie]

Stephanie's poignant story about her son illustrates the new confidence felt by this younger generation and was clearly in evidence in the information-sector workforce. It represented a dramatic change from a feeling of inferiority, which had pervaded the culture. In fact, an Irish manager mentioned a negative aspect of this newfound confidence. Most of his company's customers came from traditional, civil service and manufacturing type companies whose employees were typically older than those working in the information sector. Some of these customers had a negative reaction and some resistance to what they perceived as these young upstarts telling them what do to about their computing.

This newly confident attitude stood in stark contrast to the inferiority that had seemed to be endemic in the culture. Being a poor, island nation, the Irish had been exposed to fewer outside influences than those living on the European continent. This isolation served to reinforce the collective insecurity of the culture and had concrete manifestation in the workplace. Both the reluctance to be the bearer of bad news and the reluctance to bring up new ideas stemmed from an insecurity about appearing ignorant or appearing to fail at some venture. Whereas in America, probably everyone fails at something, Mark noted, and the reaction to failure was, "The thing didn't work out," the reaction in Ireland would be, "I screwed up." Others expressed it as fear of ridicule. This fear of ridicule was lodged deep in the psyche of rural people.

In a similar vein, concern about appearing ignorant led to workers' reluctance to acknowledge to a superior that they didn't understand something. Part of the explanation, like so many facets of Irish culture, reached back to colonial history. The Irish were held down in the past by the British who called them ignorant. As a consequence they were afraid to acknowledge when they didn't know something. Even though the source of this feeling no longer existed in Irish society, memories of the past lingered. It was taking a long time for people's mindset to catch up with the present reality. People still thought they were being looked at, even if nothing were ever said, because of the way it had been so many years back. In the mind of at least one American manager, this was an instance of the Irish culture prevailing over the corporate culture.

> *This is a thing I will have to work on; you can't change them.*
> *[Leo]*

There were also feelings of inferiority with respect to strangers in general and Americans in particular. Irish people knew much more about America and its people than the typical American knew about them. A tinge of resentment came through in comments about American top management of the multinationals. Irish workers noted that American management didn't often take the time to visit the Irish plants. But, they said, *when* these managers did take the time to visit, Irish friendliness, openness and hospitality impressed them. But only a small number ever came over. As an American I not only listened to comments about this phenomenon, I also experienced it. As I began my interviews my students warned me that, being an American, I would be treated differently. I was told that if a person had an American accent she or he would be treated better. There was an attitude that anyone who was American must have something positive to offer. One of my respondents concurred.

> *We're kind of supposed to treat the Americans better. I mean, I get that impression myself, like. I don't know why. [Mary]*

Another measure of insecurity was an inability or unwillingness to deal with criticism, either about others or about oneself. And yet people were critical of others' successes. This is what made them the self-described "nation of begrudgers." In the end, I found a tapestry of contradictory perspectives on the topic of criticism. On the one hand, they were not positive enough, they didn't give enough praise. On the other hand, they didn't complain about unsatisfactory products or services. There was a tendency not to "rock the boat" in both work and in social settings.

> *The one thing I think the Irish are very poor at I think is, we're very poor at criticizing ourselves. You know, the classic example is you go for a meal with a few people, and one lad says, "Gee, that's a terrible meal," and yet no one will call over to the owner and say, "I'm sorry, but I really think that was a lousy meal." But instead, the Irish will say, "No, no, no, let me pay them." And then you go to the pub and tell everyone you meet in the pub, and tell them how lousy it was. We've got to get much more positive about our own inefficiencies, about our own shortcomings and realize that it's from getting feedback and using it positively, that we can get better. And, you know, no matter what industry you are in, I'll always reckon it's never good enough. There's always room for growth, getting things done better, room for change. Room for development. And the day you stop developing, stop growing. You've got to be constantly checking from the guy coming in and buying my product: "Is he getting the best product? Is he getting good value for the money? Is he getting the best service?" [Robert]*

Some of this anxiety about criticism came from low self-confidence. An Irish woman working at an American plant said that as recently as the early 1970s schools didn't boost one as an individual. Consequently people developed without confidence. People reared in these times did not talk about accolades. But she did concur that some of this seemed to be changing; young people seemed to be oozing with confidence. My most notable direct encounter with insecurity was my experience interviewing women working in the information-sector firms. In reflecting upon these experiences and discussing them with my colleagues at the university I saw their behavior within the context of insecurity: these women were insecure members of an insecure population.

As with many of the cultural traits that were discussed in this study, running through the discussions about self-confidence was the theme that times were changing. People of every age conveyed the sense that it was time to leave the insecure past behind and focus on the future. It was time to let go of bad habits like self-condemnation. The younger people were, indeed, exhibiting this forward-looking attitude. Middle-aged respondents commented with pride about the young folks who refused to see any big obstacles in their way. They had a good education and were ready to take on the world.

7.   COLLECTIVE

> *We don't like to stand out, yet we don't want to be told everything to do. Won't put the spotlight on ourselves. At [this firm] there was a grading structure that kept people from rising up the ranks too quickly. Promotions occurred through filling an open position, not as a reward for doing a good job. The theory of merit pay and reward for performance is hard to implement here. [Patricia]*

The communal feeling reinforced by religious homogeneity was played out in the collective psyche of the workplace. Tension between individualism and collectivism appeared in my interviews, observations and experiences. The attitudes expressed about this topic represented a duality about the role of the individual in Irish society. In his seminal work on cultural differences in the workplace, Hofstede (1984a) included Ireland among the 50 countries that were studied. One of the dimensions of culture that he studied was individualism. This cultural trait expresses the relationship between the individual and the degree and type of collectivity that exists in the society. In some cultures individualism is seen as a positive trait; in others it is something to be repressed. I was interested in understanding how this cultural trait was manifested in Ireland, what influence it was having on the information-sector workplace and any impact of the IT culture on individualism in Ireland.

According to Hofstede, Ireland lay in the middle of the continuum from individualistic to collectivistic. However, my participant observation suggested otherwise. It seemed that people were, at times, either one extreme or the other. As I probed this aspect of Irish culture, it was clear that I had to go deeper in order to understand the circumstances in which the various dimensions of this trait manifested themselves. I also found that people assigned different meanings to these words when I asked them to place the Irish along the continuum from individualistic to collectivistic.

7.1   The Individual versus the Group

The Irish are strongly individualistic. You will rarely find two people agreeing on anything. There is an unwillingness to have a group view. The Irish are shy and don't like to broadcast what they feel. This is part of the rural background. They don't want to impose views on someone else. They are scared of being ridiculed. In a rural setting, ridicule was death because you're stuck with these people. This is why people whisper and make bad public speakers, politicians being the exceptions. [Matthew]

Three distinct views about individualism were evidenced in the workplace. One was that Irish people were individualistic at work. Another asserted that they were individualistic at home but not at work. A third view was that a group mentality dominated at all times. With respect to the view that Irish people were individualistic at work, the responses were highly nuanced. They spoke to the value placed upon personal autonomy: Irish workers wanted to behave and be treated as individuals. One man drew upon the literary tradition in Ireland to link the Irish antipathy toward boredom with workplace behavior. He said they were individualistic workers, disdaining the nine to five work mentality and, therefore, were not good at assembly line jobs. He cautioned multinational managers to find a path that worked for *Irish* people.

A reluctance to adopt or demand a group view in the workplace was expressed in several ways. One line of thinking was that Irish people were not inclined toward teamwork because being individualistic was more natural. According to this view, Irish people needed training in order to be able to think in terms of teams. There was a "live and let live" attitude at work. No one cared what you thought or did. People liked to do their own thing; they didn't like to work on teams. The desire for personal autonomy outweighed even the Irish interest in sociability. One manager explained that an emphasis on social interaction should not be construed to mean team behavior. He said Irish sociability meant you could talk easily to somebody for an hour at a time but that did not necessarily mean that you identified yourself as part of a certain group of people.

There seemed to be both positive and negative effects for the information-sector workplace, as Mark explained. To the extent that workers were disinclined to work on teams they would be less suited to standard software development work that occurred in teams. On the other hand, he acknowledged that this attitude probably made workers more suited to innovative work. This notion was reinforced by another Irish man's comment that Irish were individualistic, creative and intelligent; they had traits that suited them to R&D work.

The second view of individualism contradicted the previous one. This group of respondents claimed that Irish individualism exerted itself not in the workplace but on the home front. In this view, Irish people were more individualistic at a personal level, after work where eccentricity was more the norm. It was in the personal realm that this "live and let live" mentality prevailed. While at the personal level Irish people liked to be highly individualistic, in a business setting they were collectivists. There was the feeling that one must be "one of the herd" in their employment. They did not want to be singled out or to single themselves out in their work. In some sense this dichotomy expressed an inner conflict between competing desires to be treated equal and yet be regarded as an individual.

The assessment of this perspective was that people were much freer to express themselves in the personal realm than in the workplace where there was a reluctance to take risks and stand up as an individual. Two dimensions of this came out in my interviews. One was the presumption that all Irish workers must be seen to be equal. They did not like any sense that someone else doing the same job was being treated differently. Leo told a story about punctuality at work, which reflected this sense. When some people at his firm seemed to be abusing the honor system for hourly workers, company management considered implementing time clocks. However, Seamus, the Irish human resource manager, pointed out to the American management team that if time cards were to be used for the workers they would have to be used for management as well. As the managing director, Leo, reacted strongly to this, noting that he hadn't punched a time clock in 15 years and didn't intend to start then! Such across-the-board behavior was an affront to him. Punching a time card signified an attack on his status as managing director; to the Irish it signified equality.

Another theme embedded in this viewpoint was peer pressure to conform, not to stand out or not to stick one's neck out. At one multinational firm I was told that workers did not avail themselves of the open door policy and the ability to skip over levels of management in order to file a complaint. To go over the head of someone was interpreted as "informing" and was anathema in Irish culture. There was also fear of retribution if one's manager found out. In discussing this point, people emphasized that this Irish trait, would prevail over outside influences.

A final viewpoint was that the Irish were always more oriented toward the group than the individual. They made connections between a sense of community derived from the focus on family and the desire for a similar feeling in the workplace. Jim contrasted the atmosphere at the Irish site compared to other sites of his firm.

> *But, you go to any other site and I think -- I don't know whether it's the size or not -- everybody just has their own little piece, and they control that and -- very often what disgusts me was that -- they actually would give the impression that they couldn't care less about anything that's outside. That's their little patch and there's a fence around it. And once you cross over that, they don't care what happens, you know. The place could be on fire on just the other side of the fence and it doesn't seem to worry them. Whereas we actually have more concern for the whole group, I think, than is actually visible in other countries. [Jim]*

This group also believed that the Irish were collectivistic outside of work as well. Joseph compared Irish and Americans in both work and social settings. He did not see as many "loud mouths" or attention getters at parties in Ireland. At work he didn't see people trying to steal the spotlight or take credit for things.[xxiii]

One measure of individuality within a culture is the level of cooperation and competition that exists. Ed told one of the most compelling stories about the cooperative spirit that existed among the Irish IT workers. He had this experience soon after arriving in Ireland.

> *We ran out of some component parts and the people here said, "Let's go across the street and ask some of the other companies." That would be unheard of in the States! But we actually did it a couple of times when we needed some fuses. Went over and they gave it to us. We said we'd get even when [they] need a part. And no one really knew anyone over there. In one case I knew someone who knew someone and in the other case it was "Well they must have a photocopier over there, let's just go and ask someone." Part of it could be*

the quality of life because people are friendlier, part of it could be that it's manufacturing and not marketing or hard core engineering so all manufacturing plants are in the same boat. It's not that they're really a competitor. They have shortages just like we do. So let's go over and ask them. [Ed]

As with so many aspects of Irish culture, the younger generation seemed to be different. They had a more open, aggressive attitude. The world was much different when the generation before them was young. There were fewer options; people were less mobile. This young generation also expected to be continuously learning in order to be competitive in the labor force and to distinguish themselves from the pack. To some, however, this change was not a welcome occurrence, as Patrick pointed out.

The Irish used to be more collectivistic. They were into the group, what was for the good of the company. That was then. Now, people are individualistic, stepping on people to get ahead. Yuppies are people who have everything but got it too quickly and too easily. They are the epitome of the individual. Workers are more collective at [this multinational firm]. As a society, we still are collective in that we emphasize social welfare laws. [Patrick]

7.2   Recognition

In America the demonstration of ability is rewarded but not in Ireland. Irish people are shackled by their history and background. You can't make inroads into new areas of work once you are pegged. There is not as much fluidity. . . Part of it is the rigid educational system. . . Also, it is not [typical] to stand up as an individual. If you are in America and you made it big, people in the old neighborhood would stand up and cheer. Whereas in Ireland, they would slit your tires. The Irish culture is begrudging, negative, not a supportive culture. In contrast, I received a lot of encouragement in the US. [Nuala]

The group mentality could also be observed in the attitude toward reward and recognition at work. Irish people didn't want to stand out from the crowd and be recognized. Information-sector workers, when reflecting upon their behavior at work, said they did not want to "rock the boat" in a group situation; they would rather go with the group. The best worker crumbled in a formal presentation, someone told me. They would be embarrassed to be given an award. Lack of self-confidence contributed to the avoidance of recognition.

Oh, I couldn't do that.

Or self praise. They saw themselves a quiet about their work and less inclined to bring up their new, good ideas. In contrast, Americans were more confident and seemed quite happy to promote themselves. When I sought reasons, one direction in which I was pointed was the educational system. Schools in the early 1970s (when many of the respondents were students) didn't boost one as an individual. As a consequence, people developed without confidence. Despite the occasions of sociability, people in Ireland were introverted, did not open up and did not give accolades.

Distaste for recognizing the achievements of others reflected a zero-sum attitude: if one person won an award that meant the others had lost. This attitude might have resulted from the fact that Ireland was not a land of plenty. "If you get something it means I get less," was an attitude of begrudging the benefits to another person, which derived from a communal view of society. If one town got a factory, another one wouldn't. This begrudging attitude was manifested in the habit of "knocking" the person who did well. However, there was also evidence of change. Older respondents noted that school Leavers entering the information sector recently had much more confidence.

An impact of the information sector on this cultural trait could be seen in career development practices at a multinational firm in Ireland. Past practice was to send all the up-and-coming managers to the European headquarters to develop their managerial skills. Everyone moved along the same path. But things had changed. Whereas workers used to be happy to have their career planned for them, workers now wanted to develop themselves. They wanted time out to get an MBA. And management was recognizing that if they wanted to retain these young workers they had to accommodate to their desire for personal, professional growth. As a result, firms were making a greater effort to push down responsibility and to recognize and reward achievement.

As I analyzed responses about collectivism and individualism and reflected upon them, I came to two conclusions. The first was about Hofstede's work. Whereas he determined that Irish workers were "average" on the individualistic-collectivistic scale, I found that not to be the case. Instead I found them to be bimodal. That is, I found the Irish to be at both ends of the continuum. Sometimes they were distinctly individualistic; in some other situations they were distinctly collectivistic. There was evidence of both extreme individualism and extreme collectivism in the workplace; there was evidence of a similar contradiction in personal life.

But this conclusion, alone, did not resolve the conflicting perceptions I had obtained. I also received completely contradictory claims about the nature of Irish individualism. Irish workers were at the same time described as more knowledgeable about the company than their American counterparts, yet some claimed that they were less team-oriented. After considerable reflection I determined that resolution of the conflict could be found in an understanding of the concept of group. While the term group in American firms relates to organizing at the team level, I was beginning to believe that in Irish firms the group was the entire firm. The term that came to mind was *tribe*. Americans organize at the nuclear family level and the Irish at the extended family level. In thinking this way I was able to make sense of both the individualistic and the collective orientations ascribed to the Irish: they wanted to act as individuals yet have a sense of belonging to the larger unit -- the firm, extended family, community. Perhaps teams were too small for them, perhaps too confining.

8.   CONCLUSION

> . . . [Ireland] is a new country. Many returning emigrants will
> find enormous changes, even if they have only been away for
> a couple of years (Houston, 1999, p. 167).

Ireland's past is too intimately woven into the fabric of Irish culture to ever disappear. However, with each new generation comes further remove from the direct experience of colonialism and the struggle for independence. The demographic weight on the side of youth reinforces this trend. For the majority of Irish people, today, the struggle for independence exists more in the history books than in the direct experience of someone they know. As Ireland's past loosens its grip on the cultural psyche, new images come to the foreground. Until quite recently, the UK had been Ireland's economic reference point. Europe and the US are now filling that space. Evidence of this can be seen in recent changes in the destination of Irish exports in 1997 and 1998.[xxiv] Whereas exports to the UK declined from 24% to 22%, exports to the US and the EU increased from 11% to 14%, and from 42% to 45%, respectively.

While the Catholic religion is still a large and visible presence in Ireland, it appears that its role is diminishing. As new immigrants and returning emigrants come to Ireland along with the globally mobile workers of the multinational information economy, the cohesive force of the Catholic Church is lessening. Recent European studies on values show that Irish attitudes to the Catholic Church have changed considerably. Increasingly, individual Catholics make their own decisions on moral issues and feel less obliged to follow the Church's teaching (Houston, 1999, p. 279). Further, the 1990s have provided evidence of a loosening of the hold of the institutional Church on Irish society. While the Church was successful in its 1980s attempt to block the legalization of divorce, a subsequent divorce referendum, the *Family Law Act 1996* was passed on February 27, 1997. With respect to abortion, the right of a woman to receive information about abortions was also granted. Nevertheless, the importance of religion remains strong in Ireland as evidenced by debates about values that remain common fare in the daily newspapers.[xxv]

There is also clear evidence of growing materialism in Ireland. It is accompanying the wealth that has poured into Ireland in the decade of the 1990s. This was immediately noticeable to me in the growth of the food service industry. More and more varied restaurants exist, not just in Dublin, but also in smaller cities and towns throughout the country. The growth of restaurants is fueled by higher disposable incomes -- resulting from lower unemployment, higher incomes and more two-income households – as well as more work/leisure-related travel. Other evidence of new wealth comes in the form of the large second homes that dot the landscape of Sligo, Galway and other once remotely rural areas. They are replacing the thatched roofed stone cottages that used to own that land. Symbolic of the role of information technology in promoting Ireland's wealth was the considerable attention given to the buying and selling of Telecom Eireann shares in July 1999 when the state body became privatized.[xxvi]

Commitment and loyalty to the workplace which has produced a tendency for workers to stay at their IT jobs longer than those in other countries, is now being touted as a source of comparative advantage for Ireland. In its promotional literature The National Software Directorate (1998b, p. 7) emphasizes the strong work ethic of Irish workers reflected in a rate of employee turnover well below the European average. The advantage claimed for firms in Ireland is greater commitment from their staff, a higher proportion of experienced personnel and lower annual training costs.

If Ireland's economic health is burning bright, its historic feeling of remoteness is fading fast. This is due to several factors, some of which were in a nascent state ten years ago. These factors are: the media, travel, returning emigrants, other forms of immigration and the presence of (primarily information-sector) multinational firms. In addition to the radio and television stations operated by the national broadcasting authority, Radio Telefis Eireann (RTE), independent television and radio stations have recently been launched. Further, Ireland has embraced the World Wide Web as a communications medium for both domestic and international communication.[xxvii] In the Internet age Ireland is not an island. In stark contrast with the island mentality that was referenced in discussions during the early 1990s, the Irish labor force at the end of that decade is touted as both comfortable and experienced in cross-cultural relations,[xxviii] something upon which Ireland's marketers have capitalized:

> A distinguishing feature of the Irish population is that a very high proportion have at some time lived and worked abroad. Irish people generally have an ease in working and interacting with other cultures. . . (Enterprise Ireland, 1999, p. 3).

While the increase in travel within Ireland is providing greater exposure to outside influences and cross-fertilization of ideas and perspectives, it is also accompanied by an increase in traffic congestion. About 150,000 new cars were purchased in 1998, almost three times the number purchased in the mid-1980s (Houston, 1999, p. 271). Since Ireland currently has a low rate of car ownership relative to other EU countries, continued prosperity in the country means increased traffic on the roads. The blessing of a new economy may become a curse in this regard.

The effect of all these outside influences is exacerbated by the age demographics in Ireland. The bulk of the population belongs to the group that is being most heavily affected by these influences. Significant changes can be expected as this large cohort of young people absorbs the attitudes and values from a variety of external sources, removing forever the image of Ireland as a remote and peripheral society.

The collective-individualist continuum continues to challenge one's understanding of cultural attitudes toward group behavior. For example, despite evidence of the collectivist perspective in the information-sector workplace, which emerged from this study, another more recent study of the software industry in Ireland suggests a low level of appreciation for the role of teams in software development. Finnegan and Murray (1999) found that human resource practices focus on managing software engineers as individuals and neglect the fact that software development takes place in a team environment.

[i] The intent of this discussion is not to explain Irish history. Rather, my intent is to show how Irish history as a component of socio-cultural context has an influence in information-sector workers and workplaces.

[ii] For example, in 1541 King Henry VIII assumed the title "King of Ireland" replacing Ireland's status as a "lordship" of the English Crown since the twelfth century, and Plantations were established in various parts of the island. (See, for example, Foster, 1988, Prologue.)

[iii] The manor house, typically owned by the Anglo-Irish overlords, on whose land the peasant Irish worked.

[iv] See Harris and O'Keeffe (1993), Woodham-Smith (1962, p. 411), Boyle and O'Grada (1986), Mokyr (1980), and Foster (1988, p. 323).

[v] For example, the various political parties in Ireland -- what they stood for and the one to which a person would belong -- have historically had everything to do with the past and little to do with the present or future. Whereas political parties in other countries would be connected to social and economic viewpoints, Ireland's political parties have historically derived from positions taken in the Civil War.

[vi] During my interviews, respondents regularly used the number 95%.

[vii] For a further discussion see, Delaney (1989), pp. 77-105.

[viii] For example, in 1697 Catholic bishops and clergy were formally banished from Ireland. See Foster (1988, p. 154). Invoking their Celtic past, Irish Catholics resorted to engaging in religious rituals at secret outdoor locations that came to be known as "Mass rocks."

[ix] As Breen, et al. (1990) point out, " . . . the Catholic Church emerged from the nationalist struggle with enhanced authority and prestige . . . the Church had served as a counterweight to the power of London for generations. . ."(2)

[x] A minor religious holy day occurring in late Spring.

[xi] What interested me was how this censorship could be realistically implemented in an information society with its myriad options for electronic communication.

[xii] Respondent comments were consistent with contemporary writing on this topic. See, for example, Prendiville (1988).

[xiii] Prior to 1972 Catholics were forbidden by Church edict from attending Trinity College.

[xiv] I found this viewpoint both echoed and criticized in contemporary writing about religion and modern Ireland. See, for example, McDonagh (1989) and Garvin (1989).

[xv] While this research project was not a comparative study of Ireland and the United States, both Irish and American respondents often found it easier to reflect on the Irish culture by drawing contrasts between it and another culture such as the US or the UK.

[xvi] Receiving unemployment compensation.

[xvii] In writing about Ireland as a tourist destination, Cronin (1993, p. 61) asserts that, "The edge of Europe is seen as a refuge from the tyranny of timepieces . . ."

[xviii] See, for example, Cuddy and Keane (1990), Grimes (1992, 1995), Grimes and Lyons (1994), and Jacobson and Mack (1995).

[xix] This feeling of remoteness is reflected McBride and Flynn's (1996) compilation of reflections on the role of the cinema in people's lives in mid twentieth-century Ireland: "During the 50s in the Irish countryside, there were no televisions, telephones or indoor toilets. The only people who had cars were priests, doctors and rich farmers. Radios were only beginning to appear in most people's homes." (45)

[xx] Where interaction with other cultures did occur, as in the case of tourism, the identity that was portrayed, and which O'Connor (1993) argues was internalized by Irish people, was of ". . . a place of picturesque scenery and unspoiled beauty, of friendly and quaint people, a place which is steeped in the past traditions and ways of life. In short, it is represented as a pre-modern society." (70)

[xxi] Houston (1999, p. 174) advises the newcomer to Ireland not to confuse Irish people's informal friendliness with directness. I observed that whereas Irish people felt comfortable criticizing aspects of American society and culture, direct criticism of Ireland by nonIrish people was not well received.

[xxii] This topic is taken up again in Chapter 7 in the discussion of Authority.

[xxiii] Contemporary writing argues for caring values as an antidote ". . . to counteract the corrosive 'ism' of individualism." (McCann, 1995, p. 9)

[xxiv] These data are for the whole of 1997 and the first nine months of 1998 (Central Statistics Office, 1999, cited in IDA Ireland, 1999, p. 3).

[xxv] Examination of a typical Sunday newspaper, the July 18, 1999 *Irish Independent,* for example, yielded two Letters to the Editor devoted to an ongoing debate about a cleric's stance on Catholic Church teaching and an article about the demise of moral codes among teenagers (Redlich, 1999).

[xxvi] A humorous depiction of the societal engagement with owning and trading shares is given in Glacken (1999).

[xxvii] An example of the former is TechCentral (www.techcentral.ie) that was created to serve as Ireland's comprehensive online information technology resource, providing access to

everything from IT suppliers to software to download to web addresses. An example of the latter are the sites established by government agencies such as Enterprise Ireland (http://194.106.146.103) and the IDA (www.ida.ie).

xxviii Writing in 1995, Fitz Gerald points out that in the early 1990s more than a quarter of third level graduates had lived abroad for at least a year.

CHAPTER 7. EGALITARIAN

1. INTRODUCTION

I think it may go back to the time, as well, when we literally had to look after ourselves and we had to find ways around existing structures. We had to be more manipulative, if you like. For instance, there was a time when we weren't allowed to own things or we couldn't be elected to government or we couldn't take office of any kind. So we weren't rulers of our own destiny. So the official structure wasn't available to us, so we had to find unofficial structures. And the unofficial structures were almost cell-type structures. And the cell-type structures interlaced with each other. So that there was no center on it. . . [I]t was pretty much an open structure where people could enter it and be accepted within it, at different levels. Depending upon how much influence they could bring to bear on it. How much influence they could bring to bear very often depended on who they knew or how many they knew. Where their connections were. [Liam]

The information-sector workplace was different from other workplaces I had observed and Irish people had described. I was interested in understanding the reasons for this difference. In seeking an answer, I explored two lines of investigation: the nature of information-sector work and the influence of American culture introduced through the corporate cultures of the multinational firms. What I found was that both factors have contributed to the IT workplace that has evolved in Ireland. But the most significant finding was that it occurred because these two factors appeared to have fallen upon very fertile ground. This type of work, with its multinational influences, released the Irish workers from the constraints of a different and foreign workplace and ethic. The information sector enabled them to be the kinds of workers who were much more consistent with their cultural heritage.

2.   ANTI-AUTHORITARIAN

*[The Irish attitude toward authority] is that laws are
optional, unlike the US and UK. This is due to our
occupation by the British. Then, it was right to go against
them. It's totally pervasive. . .*

ET: Does this attitude enter the workplace?

*Yes. I'll tell you a story. Recently some men from the US
[headquarters of our firm] came here and were appalled at
the lack of security. No one was wearing their ID badges
because we were told we had to and besides, we all know
each other, unlike in the US. There is an attitude of flaunting
authority. So headquarters gave us the pronouncement, "You
have to wear an ID badge." After vetting[i] it here, there was
passive resistance to it. Management insisted that we wear an
ID badge, so we did. We wore each other's but each of us
wore an ID badge! [Aidan]*

Through their words and their actions Irish people exhibited a
contradictory attitude toward authority. There was evidence of an
unquestioning acceptance of the control exerted by individuals whose
authority was derived from position power. Yet, there was also resentment of
formal authority. Irish respondents admitted to having a bad attitude toward
authority. When I asked respondents about the Irish attitude toward authority
they consistently answered that Irish people resent authority and do not like
being told what to do. Yet in looking at behavior or attitudes toward certain
institutions, an opposite image arose. What was consistent across my
interviews and observations was evidence of this tension. I began to get
greater clarity about the dimensions of this contradiction by probing more
deeply into the different attitudes about authority and circumstances under
which they were held.

2.1   Accepting Authority

*I would think that the Irish to some degree would accept the
organization structure and would assume because the
structure exists the individuals in authority ought to be
listened to or followed as being the experts. And they're less
reluctant to try and second-guess or rock the boat or question
as to whether what's been said is really the correct course of*

action. So, from that point of view, we've got to learn to ask questions and understand. And not just understand but also put forward our own point of view more strongly. I think there's an awful lot of acquiescencing folks among the Irish. Maybe it's because of the years of domination. Going back in history and so on, we've always been dominated by British or Vikings, no matter how far back you might go, there's some degree of domination involved and therefore we're not inclined to stand up. [Farrell]

One response to authority under British dominion was active resistance. Another response that was part of the colonial legacy was passivity and unquestioning acceptance of authority structures. The unquestioning accedence to authority could be seen in the power of the Church in Ireland.[ii]

See, there's "no go" areas in Ireland, as well. There's areas you just don't discuss, you don't challenge. The Church was set up in Ireland as a cultural thing. The Church is in everything. If they say "yes" it's yes. If they say, "It's black," it's black even though it's obviously white, you know? You just steer clear of it. [Jim]

Despite such comments by Irish respondents, it was the Americans who offered most of the responses about Irish acquiescence to authority. It must be remembered, however, that the majority of American respondents were managers. Thus, their viewpoints might naturally differ from the majority of Irish respondents who were not managers. They offered examples of authoritarianism from diverse sectors of society: from interactions with the government, to relations with the health care sector, to authoritarianism in education and religion.

Jean was an American of Irish decent and married to Andrew, the managing director of one of the multinational plants. She characterized the Irish as nonconfrontational and accepting of the circumstances that they had been dealt. From her observation, they were willing to accept other people telling them what to do. She shared a story about her dealings with local government. One afternoon she saw a man in her neighborhood in a white outfit resembling a space suit. He was spraying herbicide on some foliage along the road. Her children would soon be passing by the area on their way home from school. She was concerned that this herbicide would be harmful to her children or others who might play in the shrubs. So she phoned the local County Council to see if the chemicals were harmful. Neither the sprayer nor the County Council could say what the chemical was; it took them 45 minutes to find the name of the person who made the chemical. They finally had to contact the researcher at home. No one had ever questioned this before.

Joseph told a story in some detail about his experience with the Irish medical establishment. He had been in Ireland working for a multinational firm less than a year when we talked. His story echoes Jean's perception of unquestioning acceptance of authority. Joseph went to his physician about a preexisting medical condition. The physician told Joseph he would go to hospital for some exploratory surgery.

> *And I said, "Wait a minute!" Like it was no questions asked or anything. So, you just go in. And I was like shuffled out of his office pretty quickly.*
> *And he said, "Ah it's no problem, just a small surgical procedure," and just blew it off. It was obvious that there was no room to question the guy.*
> *So I went to the hospital but they wanted to do a minor surgical procedure before they did this X-Ray where they inject dye in and all this stuff.*
> *And I said, "Well, no, I don't want it done that way. I want to find out if I have something wrong with me first before we do this."*
> *And they said, "Well that's not what the doctor recommended." [Joseph]*

He found that his attempts to consider options were met with resistance by a medical establishment that was unaccustomed to providing explanations.

> *. . . they injected dye into me and did all these X-Rays and they bring me back down, and this nurse comes in and they wanted me to put a johnny*[iii] *on when they were just going to do X-Rays and -- I'm sure to them it's their every day job so I was being a pain in the ass -- I said, "Well, can't I just like take my suit coat off and my shoes and just leave my tee shirt on?"*
> *"Oh, I guess so."*
> *So they did the X-Ray and injected dye and brought me back down and this nurse came up to me and said, "OK put a johnny on now,"*
> *and I said, "Why, where are we going?"*
> *"You're going to surgery."*
> *And like, I had a test done and they weren't going to give me any information, and I was going to go into surgery not*

knowing why, what the results were of the procedure, what
they were going to look for, and what they were going to do.
And I said, "Well, I don't think so." I said, "I want to talk to
the doctor."
. . . And I waited another hour. . . I saw her and this older
nun talking -- and I surmised later that that was her boss --
they're gabbing about it and they just left me there for an
hour and nobody said anything to me. Then the boss nun
comes in and she throws me the johnny and she says,
"OK, here, put this on."
She ignored my whole conversation, like the boss is now
going to come and tell me what to do! [Joseph]

After considerable delays and persistence, Joseph eventually got to speak with the doctor who confirmed Joseph's understanding that surgery wasn't absolutely necessary.

. . . as I walked out I was amazed at the whole episode and I
thought about it later, then. Like the lack of information that
was available to me, that it was so outrageous that someone
questioned the guy. [Joseph]

Irish respondents talked about educational institutions reinforcing an authoritarian value system and perpetuating traditional authoritarian values in young people. While respondents acknowledged that they received a good education, they said the discipline was excessive and unnecessary, and not the way to get the best out of people. Margaret, who was raised in County Limerick, described her boarding school experience as one that placed considerable emphasis on discipline and authority. She felt scarred for life by the experience. Another respondent characterized it as acting through fear. He said students were terrorized at school.[iv]

Others said simply that teachers were held in high regard in Irish society, that there was a tradition of respect, that Irish students respected authority and viewed professors as authority figures. In listening to people's comments about their educational backgrounds I could see that authoritarianism had contributed to the dichotomous attitudes that existed in Ireland. On the one hand, schools taught that one should accept authority. On the other hand, it was individuals' experiences with this authoritarianism that made them reject it as adults.

My attitude toward authority, I don't know, I think it possibly
stems almost from school. I spent five years in a boarding

school, for example, that was run by clergy. It was originally
a seminary. But it was authority and discipline for the sake of
it and just, you know, power. And I think that has switched
me off for life. There's no way I'd send one of my own kids to
a boarding school. [Jim]

With respect to religion one could clearly see the unquestioning acceptance of authority. As I investigated the power wielded by the Catholic Church I found the reasons in Ireland's history. It was the Catholic Church that united the people, gave them hope. This was translated into unquestioning loyalty. To the extent that religion was suppressed by the British in the past, the late twentieth century's practice of religion could be seen as evening the score. In a sense, the widespread practice of Catholicism has been an expression of national identity.

. . . even though I don't want to I'm going to go because I
couldn't before. I'm going to go because that's what's
making me Irish. That's what says I belong in my own nation.
It's a form of nationalism. [Sue]

Besides acquiescence out of respect for its link to Irish nationalism, the Catholic Church in Ireland appeared to engender passive acceptance simply on the basis of the power it had over people. One Irish woman ventured that there might still be a deep rooted fear of speaking out against the Church. She also thought there was a sense of hopelessness; it would not matter what people said. The Church would just go ahead and do what it wanted anyway. On balance, she thought people's acquiescence was due more to perceived impotence than anything else. People did not feel they could do anything about it, so why bother?

Yet compliance with religion was different from what it was at the early part of the twentieth century or before, when people internalized the strictures of religion. What I perceived from watching and listening to people was that compliance was a matter of adhering to observable behaviors.

I think that part of the whole discussion around religion goes
back to the family situation as well. Generally speaking, the
mother of an Irish family usually is quite religious. This is
also, I think, true in Spain and Italy as well. And probably in
other Catholic, Christian areas. That has a strong effect on
the kids. And so as well as complying to the religion's
requirements, they're also kind of inadvertently complying
with family pressures. I think that if you talk to individuals,

what I would call the group who comply, there are a lot of things that people perhaps disagree with as part of the Catholic religion. Like birth control, etc. etc. But they will still comply. "Aye yes. We'll keep these guys happy and show up on Sunday." But at the end of the day if they were really asked, are they really committed to the beliefs and values of that tradition, I don't think they are. [Brian]

Acquiescence to authority in the workplace was quite evident to Americans. They noted more respect for authority in Ireland than in the US. If the workers were told to do something, they would do it. Joseph offered a positive take on this trait. His firm was implementing a quality program that involved inputting quality control data from the factory floor. Whereas there had been resistance among the technicians at the American site to the chore of "data entry" -- a task perceived to be menial and beneath them -- their Irish counterparts were quite willing to do it.

Linking acquiescence toward authority to Ireland's colonial history allowed for insights into the contradictory nature of this cultural trait. There was great respect for authority and people in authority. Irish people had been oriented toward accepting authority figures, accepting directives because of the position of the person giving them. However, while they may have *accepted* being told what to do they did not necessarily *like* it. Union strikes, I was told, were a vehicle for expressing this resentment.

2.2 Resisting Authority

ET: Why don't the Irish like to be told what to do?

I'm not sure why. But I think it may be something to do with they didn't like who was telling them to do it for so long.

ET: That suggests. . .

A colonial thing, yeah. If you go back to a pre-colonial time here, I believe -- from readings of the older texts -- that the Irish tended to elect their chiefs. And that if a chief wasn't a good chief, then he got pushed, and that the son may become the chief after his father. But if he wasn't up to the job that he was replaced again. So they tended to have that approach to having elected leaders or chosen leaders that were able to do the job rather than people who had it by any right of birth. It was something that was there before the colonial thing came

in. It was maybe turned into very negative effects through the
colonial system. Before that they had that in a positive way,
they reacted to each other, to change things in response to,
you know, pressures on a given situation. If the leader wasn't
good he was replaced. Whereas when the colonial influence
came in, regardless of whether he was good or not [he
stayed]. He was a man appointed by the British to look after
the situation over here and he wasn't replaceable. And they
tended to react to having somebody that they couldn't change
and who was giving them orders and telling them what to do.
[Liam]

Despite all the evidence of authoritarianism in Irish culture there was simultaneously evidence of an opposite reaction toward authority as well. This attitude was expressed in rejection of laws, resentment at being told what to do, an unwillingness to accept regimentation and a disinclination to tolerate rigorous discipline.

This is a stupid rule; let's see how we can bugger it up! [Sue]

The Irish people seemed to delight in opportunities to undermine authority. One man described his fellow Irish as "cute" meaning sly or crafty. He said they liked to twist a situation to suit themselves, to feel they could influence the situation to get what they wanted out of it.

Older people have more respect for law and order than
young people. Except when it comes to taxes and the dole.
Then it's OK to go outside authority, to fiddle as much tax as
you can. [Rosemary]

An example of this is "pulling a stroke," a topic discussed in Chapter 5. The stroke illustrates this delight in getting the upper hand from those in authority. Examples were getting away with not paying one's car, television or income tax.[v] Some of this behavior came from the perception of an authority figure as the distant "other" whether it was the government or the large corporation. The attitude was that paying taxes was for other people to do, that government was far away and uncontrollable.

An Irish person wouldn't dream of stealing, say, a garden
spade from a next-door neighbor, right. But if that spade
belonged to the government or the Electricity Supply Board
or something, right, that's common property, and they don't
see anything immoral or wrong with taking it if it belongs to

a company, right, a corporation. So we've funny ideas on things like that. [Jim]

I was provided with several examples of the strong reaction to being told what to do and how people might respond when this occurred. One story, filled with irony, was about the workers' reaction to being *required* to socialize!

In fact, in the company I worked at before with Irish people and an American manager -- a multinational -- and he sort of made it a command performance that you had to appear at the Christmas party. Jeez, people went bezerk. They had always come before because they wanted to, but if somebody told them they had to, they weren't going.

ET: Did that happen?

Yeah. Now, they didn't say, "I'm not going because you told me I had to." Suddenly granny was ill, "Oh, I have another engagement that night," "My wife's social do is that night," "My son is sick." But you get what I'm saying? They didn't tell him why they weren't coming but if he was going to insist that they do something for fun because they had to they weren't going to do it. [Sue]

My personal favorite was the story told at the beginning of this Chapter about the visit from headquarters during which the American staff were very disturbed to find that people were not wearing their badges. From the Irish workers' point of view, since they all knew everyone who worked at this smaller plant in a smaller country in which everyone knew everyone, and were quite often related, what was the point? (I can certainly verify this by my own experience. On my second visit at this particular firm, the receptionist knew my name.) The decision to wear each other's badges, like the excuses not to attend the Christmas party, were signature forms of passive resistance to perceived authoritarian behavior.

What I found particularly interesting about these two examples was that they embodied both dimensions of the attitude toward authority: respect for it and resentment against it. No one complained openly to the visiting executives; it was just their own private joke and a statement to each other that they were not going to be cowed by these people in authority. Similarly, no one told the American manager that they resented being required to attend a party, but neither did they acquiesce. They would go out of their way to undermine authority but they would not openly flaunt it. They would flaunt it in their own ways.

A similar incident occurred during the startup of another American firm. During initial planning meetings American managers told Irish managers that workers would have to *adopt* certain features of the American work style, such as being more direct. The Irish managers responded that the Americans had to *adapt* to the Irish culture. One issue that arose was about meetings starting on time. Eric told the Irish managers they had to come to meetings on time, to which they replied, "We don't *have* to do anything." But having said that, they conceded to the American position on time and altered their behavior.

These anecdotes revealed an ambivalent attitude toward authority. Passive acceptance sat along side an attitude that to subvert authority was to show loyalty to Ireland. To be seen as subverting the formal structures and organizations was to be seen as being supportive of "Mother Ireland."

You hook the system as much as possible. [Neil]

Another colonial legacy was an attitude that obeying laws was optional. This was a carryover from when it was respectable to go against laws during the British occupation of Ireland. Finally, some of this resentment against authority came from the class system that was also related to colonialism. They said that if you approached people with an "us-them" attitude you would get them undermining you whenever they could; it raised their hackles.

Resentment of authority was expressed in the workplace through unions. Their strength had historically derived from a view that people in authority were under suspicion and could not be trusted. Management did not have workers' best interests at heart. Besides the impact on union participation, other management implications of this attitude toward authority were that workers stuck up for each other and against the company (authority). Some people viewed management and government in the same light. These people felt that if given the means, management would and did abuse workers. Therefore, unions were needed to keep them in line and to make sure workers interests were looked after. It could not be left to ad hoc reliance upon management's good will.

If part of the reason for the negative attitude toward authority was the reaction to centuries of mandatory respect derived from position power, another part of the reason lay in the cultural characteristic that is described as undisciplined. At first, I was surprised to hear Irish people describe themselves as undisciplined. I have always assigned a negative connotation to the word. It brought to mind memories of school report cards and punishment for misbehavior. So people describing their own culture in what I perceived as a negative light initially confused me. However, I came to understand that this was not the sense in which the term was being used. Rather, the term was used in reference to attempts by those in authority to cramp one's flexible and easygoing style.

There were several management implications of this manifestation of the Irish attitude toward authority. It meant an affinity for an informal and flexible work environment. For example, people might come late for work but would be willing to work holidays. Undisciplined also meant a dislike for strict, operational supervision. Another implication -- that was noted several times by Irish respondents -- was that Irish workers required a sufficient level of motivation and leadership. They rejected regimentation and hated to be bored. This was the explanation for why they considered themselves to be unsuited to assembly line jobs: they didn't want to be told what to do. They did not like "nine to five" jobs. Consequently, multinational managers observed, management needed to find a path that worked for Irish people.

Leo recognized this early on in his tenure as a managing director in Ireland. You couldn't tell an Irishman anything, he said. Don't try to impose your will on an Irish person. To be successful, firms like his have had to adjust to the Irish culture. He emphasized the importance of learning about the Irish culture before coming to Ireland to work. In his experience, the best way to deal with the Irish workers was to give them a considerable amount of flexibility. He didn't tell workers what to do. At monthly meetings they decided together how many units to produce. And when the workers had accomplished the agreed upon daily amount, they could go home.

2.3 Questioning Authority

> *[I was] working with the Irish where they came straight off the farm. In the West of Ireland where they weren't as influenced by the British presence.*
>
> ET: *All right, now tell me about the people right off the farms who are not influenced by the British. What are the characteristics of their work that struck you?*
>
> *Intelligent. Interested.*
>
> ET: *Well, do you think genetically the Irish are more intelligent than other people?*

Intelligent, more intelligent? I'd be biased, and I would say yes.

ET: How did they get to be more intelligent? I mean how do you define intelligence? Is that raw brainpower or is it developed?

It's a curiosity, and they're curious and they want to know about things. They really are interested in what they are doing. [Liam]

Theresa commented on the flexibility of Irish workers and their willingness to work at any task. If they were needed to work a 24-hour stretch for a rush job they would do it, she said. She went on to say that their frame of mind -- being eager to learn -- and their training suited them for a range of jobs at the multinational IT firms. The more variety the job contained the more interest they had in it.

We don't stand on formality, and that helps a lot too, and that's probably why the high tech industry is very informal. Say, when [our firm] would try to introduce a rather formalized structure. Irish would have great difficulty with it. I know a friend of mine, a college mate of mine, works at [a] Japanese company. They had great teething problems as well because the Japanese couldn't really cope with the Irish people, and the way they were so undisciplined and so unstructured. They weren't predictable.

ET: What do you mean the Irish were undisciplined?

They would question, actually, if some supervisor told her to do something. That person would be quite justified [in asking] why he was doing it. Should he do it now? Would it not be better to do it tomorrow, or was it really the best thing to do, at all? He would feel quite justified in doing that, whereas I gathered, if he was back home in Japan, the person would just take that as dogma and do it. He would presume that the person telling him knew better. The Irish wouldn't make that presumption. [Gerry]

One end of the questioning spectrum is genuine curiosity; the other is a challenging stance. The inclination to discuss what needed to be done and why fit well with the American style in which goals were discussed in advance of commencing the work. Workers responded very favorably when they discovered that people in management were prepared to listen to reasonable objections and showed that they were prepared to change the way they were doing things. But this approach was a radical change from what workers experienced in other sectors. In some interviews I was told that Irish people did not do well in the traditional industrial workforce. The reason was that Irish workers liked to question things and would want too much autonomy. This tendency to question things expressed itself in the lengthy discussions that would take place before a decision was made. In the home, if something needed fixing, you could have the family sitting down and discussing it for days, weeks, months, and never get anything done about it, I was told.

Deirdre drew a comparison between the Irish and Asian sites of her firm to illustrate the distinctiveness of this cultural trait in the workplace.

> *People do tend to question more [in Ireland]. For example, we make some comparisons between us and [the Asian site]. And we do think that their workforce is more submissive. That they are more inclined to do what they are told to do and do it very well and would not question in the same way that people would question here. I have been in the [Asian] plant, and at the risk of drawing stereotypes; you can sense that to an extent. If you walk around the floor here, people will look at you, first of all. And if you catch their eye, they'll smile at you or "Hello" or whatever. In [the Asian plant], one thing that struck me walking around the plant, people will not catch your eye. They're very intent on what they're doing. I don't know if they don't necessarily see themselves as it's their place to do it. I think more so here. We find that when we've done some things this year regarding participatory management and we've taken people out and trained them and we've done some kind of labor groups. And the overriding impression of the people in manufacturing is they are just dying to contribute. They are just, you know, straining at the leash to get to it. [Deirdre]*

In a similar vein, Jim drew a comparison between the German and the Irish work setting. In Germany, where he had worked for a time, standard practices within industry were quite different from Ireland. It was not just a matter of employment law; it was the thought process. Everything came from their attitude. The thought process in Germany was very much about a procedure to be followed, which one never questioned. The same applied to the way they organized for work. As a result, a German plant with the same sort of production that existed in the Irish plant would be organized quite differently.

The questioning attitude, however, sometimes went beyond discussion and bordered on resistance.

> *I think there's an Irishism [that] we tend to challenge much more. [T]he historical thing, decisions were made for us by our masters. I'm talking about historical masters. We always challenged their decisions and their ability to make any intelligent decisions, and their right to live [off of us] and that flows over. I know that once decisions are made in your German company, I would have the view that they're made, they're carried on. In Ireland we still argue and debate that decision. We won't accept it readily. We never readily accept it. But I suppose that's part of the culture. We're never ready to accept authority. [Jim]*

The potential for resentment at being told what to do had clear implications for management. Deirdre explained that the authoritarian approach didn't work in Ireland, that Irish workers resisted authority and were given to questioning management. She told applicants for managerial positions that job titles didn't mean anything. Managers must earn respect or people would bypass them.

Considerable contradiction came through our discussions about this topic. On the one hand there was evidence of questioning behavior at work. At the same time, there was evidence that Irish workers didn't question enough. I was told about an authoritarian environment at traditional Irish firms yet I never observed this in Irish information-sector firms. I learned about it secondhand, from respondents' comments about the contrast: the refreshing and open atmosphere of the information-sector workplace. While Irish respondents acknowledged the passive acceptance of authority as a norm, they also suggested changes were in the air. Things that had previously gone unchallenged were being questioned. Procedures for complaints were being put in place. Respect that had been obtained from position was having to be earned. It almost seemed as though this questioning attitude was just there below the surface of the culture, waiting to be brought out. The information sector appears to have provided the outlet.

Respondents said people needed to learn how to use authority properly; some managers confused discipline and authority, shouting and threatening instead of using motivation and leadership. Irish people responded to leadership, not to an authoritarian attitude. People in authority who were energetic, fair, set clear goals, and communicated what, why, and how things were going received support. Brendan worked at a multinational computer manufacturer in the West. He described the Irish attitude toward authority quite simply: if the person in authority was fair there was a positive attitude. However, if the person was arrogant, there was a negative attitude. Respect had to be earned.

> *In general, the Irish people resent authority. But it depends on how it's handled. But the Irish respect ability and leadership based on performance and ability. This goes way back [in our history]. Both at [two multinational IT firms], the one who "knows his stuff" is respected. [Eamon]*

An implication for information-sector managers was that they needed to get to know people. Another was that the Irish workers at multinational firms wanted and expected autonomy. At one American firm there was a bit of a problem as the firm was becoming more and more centrally managed. Headquarters in the US viewed the plant in Ireland as just another location of the firm, much as they would a plant in any American city. The Irish workers, however, thought of it as an Irish company.

> *I have no problem with being given a high level kind of statement, "This is what I want you to do. This is what you should achieve." And then I go off, thank you very much, and I want to do it my own way. That is not to say that I won't listen to somebody. I'll take advice from anybody that I think can contribute to me. And I can change my views. But I definitely want my autonomy to do things as I feel they should be done. I don't dictate to other people. There's a joint type of thing. [Jim]*

Jim recommended that instead of ordering people to do something, a supervisor should make workers understand why they're engaging in or being asked to do a certain task. When this occurred, the workers would get all fired up about it. While some people called this approach manipulation, he called it effective management. Eric concurred in this view about an appropriate management approach for Irish workers.

> *ET: Well, if Irish people can't be told what to do, then how will you cope at [your firm?]*
>
> *Well, first, the caveat is that we have to build a product to succeed, and the workers know that. Then, we don't say, "We need the product in 20 minutes. " We say, "We'll give you a*

job, nice computers and let you think. All we ask in return is that you produce so many today," and they respond OK. At other factories [in Ireland] workers are told what to do. The workers [here] are given lots of flexibility. So when the 72 -- or however many the number of -- units are done, people go home. Workers know they have to do 72 a day. We then have a management meeting each month to decide how many units to produce a month. In the States if workers are told to think and improve, they would run out of steam. They don't have the" stick-to-it-iveness" to work until ten PM to get the job done. [Eric]

The independent-minded and autonomous inclinations of the Irish were well suited to the information-sector workplace. This management style was very attractive because reasons and goals were discussed. People were thrilled that management would actually listen to workers and perhaps even alter procedures. Additionally, the youth of the information sector has had an impact. Young people in Ireland, who have had exposure to new cultures and ideas in a way unparalleled in previous generations, were no longer blindly accepting the unquestioned authority of the old, established institutions.

I mean compared to our UK counterparts in the late 1800s we were a far poorer nation. We had to make do with a lot less. Again, I mean, we came from a very subservient type of society. We looked up to the English. Whatever they told us to do, we did it. I think, you know, that prevailed very much down to my parent's attitudes in that when my parents went to school if the teacher told them to do something, they never questioned it. And I don't mean to be "cheeky" here but I think our generation is going to question a lot more. If someone tells us to do something we might say, "Hey, maybe there's no need to do it that way. Maybe there's a better way or a different way." But, you know, it's taking time to change our attitude of subservience to "We're all equal." The one thing I feel is good insofar as if something is good with emigration, is that it has given the Irish people who've had the experience of going abroad and coming back a far greater recognition of their own capabilities. Because people have taken on responsibilities abroad that they never had the opportunity to take on here. And also when they come back

they realize the talents they have and the abilities they have.
[Robert]

The consequences of this change in attitude about authority have implications for management styles beyond the information sector. As workers question more, management is called upon to take their views into account when making decisions. A viewpoint that was often shared with me was that managers should seek consensus about tasks to be done. In this regard there seemed to be a fit between what could be considered an essential characteristic of Irish people and the American approach to management. Irish people got the job done, but differently, perhaps, than the UK model, which they described as following the paper rules. But as Liam pointed out, this *new* style of management was fitting in perfectly with *old* traditions about authority in Ireland.

From the words of Irish respondents and the experiences of Americans it was clear that the attitude toward authority was at the same time respectful and rebellious. In the workplace it meant that managers would be most effective when they were clear about expectations and reasons why something needed to be done and the benefits to be derived from doing it. This, in turn, placed more pressure on management to develop relationships with the employees, ones that defined rules and constraints.

No matter what the topic it always seemed that when we delved into some aspect of Ireland's past as an explanation for present behavior, some portion of the respondents would be sure to note that things were changing. When discussing this topic, one young Irish man noted the big turnaround both in the economy and in ways of thinking. The blind acquiescence to authority was a way of thinking based on the old philosophy. But the kinds of people who mistrusted authority were gradually dying out. The younger people coming up were getting away from it. They did not see England as an enemy. Past history was not as solid with them.

3. NON-HIERARCHICAL

Maybe in the farm situation, they're working in an area where they have room for more initiative. They're told to go and look after a field or it's their own farm and it's up to them to go and look after it. And if they don't plow the field it doesn't get plowed. So they're used to getting up early to get on with their work to make the farm a success. They're used to applying themselves to the task without somebody having

*to tell them to do it. Especially those coming from small
farms, those growing up as farmers, those who have grown
up with the idea from the time they were small that the work
is there to be done year after year. And if you don't do it, it
doesn't get done. So they're in the habit of getting off to do it.
[Liam]*

Some very different images of the Irish information-sector workplace
emerged during discussions of management style. However, one factor
remained consistent throughout: the influence of one's previous employment
sector. Those from an agrarian background were used to working
independently and with little supervision; they seemed to have internalized a
sense of personal responsibility. In contrast, those coming from traditional
Irish industries were used to a much more controlling and restricted work
environment. These two sets of experiences, then, converged in the
information-sector workplace.

Unlike the indigenous firms in traditional industry, the civil service, or the
financial sector an informal, egalitarian atmosphere characterized the firms in
the information sector. When I encountered this atmosphere in the IT firms, I
was initially confused. What perplexed me was that everything that I had been
hearing and experiencing to that point had led me to expect that this kind of
informal management style would not sit well with the Irish people. When I
heard descriptions of traditional industry and the civil service, I was presented
with a totally different model. If the Irish culture took naturally to an open
kind of management style, then why, I wondered, were most of the Irish firms
using a management style that was the exact opposite?

In my exploration of the management style in Ireland and in the
information-sector firms, in particular, I found a dichotomous picture of
management style in Ireland. When I first inquired about the work culture of
the information economy, respondents described the environment in this
sector -- in both the indigenous and the multinational firms -- in terms of how
it contrasted with firms in other sectors. Respondents used the term "British
management style" to describe the restrictive and hierarchical atmosphere at
these firms. They contrasted this atmosphere with what they considered to be
the more open management approach in the information-sector firms.
Therefore, to better understand the management style and work culture of the
information economy in Ireland, I begin by examining the management styles
of firms from which information-sector workers had come.

3.1   Post-Colonial Management

> *I mean, in [this non IT firm] the whole right hand side of the*
> *car park was graded. You know, first row for the directors*
> *and then you have the grade 36 and then the grade 34s, you*
> *know? And outside contractors couldn't park in there at all!*
> *So we had to park beside the street. [Aine]*

Respondents used the term "British management style" when characterizing an autocratic management approach that seemed to incorporate a hierarchy reminiscent of the rigid social class structure within which it developed. When Aine worked for a time as a software development manager in London, she said it was all about having separate car parks and canteens and rest rooms. Such markers of status were used to reinforce a social distance. Whereas in Ireland Aine said she could casually stop by someone's office, in London she was *the boss*. In addition to social distance, respondents repeatedly mentioned the company car as a marker of status. Albert related a conversation with a friend working at a UK firm. This man viewed his career progression through the lens of company cars.

> *"Oh I can only own half [a liter engine car] in my [current]*
> *position, I can only own a 1.6 [liter engine car]. Whereas if I*
> *moved up another grade I could get a 2 [liter engine car]."*

This hierarchical management style found its way into the Irish workplace for several reasons. The legacy of Ireland's colonial status was not only political. The development of industrialism in Ireland and, consequently, the development of management practice were also intimately tied to Britain.[vi] During Ireland's colonial period, the Anglo-Irish power structure with its close ties to Britain dominated the management ranks of Irish firms. In addition, until the establishment of the outward-looking industrial policy, which began in the 1960s, the majority of foreign investment in Ireland came from Britain.[vii] In this way, the British management approach diffused into Irish society through the subsidiaries of British-owned companies that brought their management style to Ireland along with their corporate cultures. Finally, after its independence Ireland made a conscious decision to inherit both the British banking system and the existing British civil service structure,[viii] a decision that served to further reinforce this management style.[ix] People were in awe of the Anglo-Irish, Bridie told me. Thus, the large number of British-owned and controlled firms in Ireland, coupled with Irish managers learning from and adopting the British style resulted in a hierarchical and authoritarian "us-them" atmosphere in traditional industrial sectors and in the civil service.

There was a subtle and complex relationship between worker behaviors and this traditional Irish management style, a style that stood in stark contrast to the management style found in both the indigenous and the multinational firms of the information sector. In some respects it could be seen as resulting from worker behaviors; in other respects it could be viewed as contributing to them.[x] Traditional Irish management was viewed by those who had observed and experienced it as stern and autocratic. Charlene and her husband Eric had recently arrived in Ireland where he was setting up one of Ireland's newest multinational IT plants. They were an older couple with grown children. She was quite observant about the cultural acclimation she was experiencing. My conversations with her always covered a wide range of cultural experiences and observations, including her critical views on Irish management. She spoke of Irish supervisors with an autocratic manner who kept workers under their thumbs, treating them as though they were unable to think for themselves. Her initial impression of Irish management and workers was reminiscent of the American workplace of the 1950s. She observed a heavy emphasis on status and symbols such as office size. She thought some Irish managers in multinational firms while saying they believed in democracy, reverted back to traditional ways when the pressure was on.

What brought credence to the sentiments of someone who had only recently arrived in Ireland was that they were repeated in the comments of Irish respondents. Michael characterized the management style in terms of language. When he went to work in a large Irish-owned factory he was required to address his boss as "Mister." This felt, to him, like a natural extension of the feudal system.

> *. . . back in the last century, who would have the factories would be the landed gentry, or the aristocracy or the Anglo Saxons, who would again have to be treated in that fashion, along with the manor type of stuff. "Yes, my lord," and all that shit. "Yes, Sir" also grew up, I suppose, with Irish industry. [Michael]*

Julie contributed another dimension to this theme about language when we discussed evidence of Ireland's colonial past in business operations of the present. She commented about the surnames of mangers.

> *I find myself when information comes into the company, looking at the directors to see what the [sur] names are. We've got an awful lot of people, say [the name of an individual at an Irish government agency]. [His name] isn't an Irish name. So I look and think, "They were the sons and*

*daughters of whoever, the crowd who was in control over
here, who got the opportunity to get an education and get
into these nice, easy jobs." They would be in the . . . banks
and they're the solicitors and the lawyers and they're
stockbrokers, etc. [Julie]*

It is ironic that even as Ireland rejected British *political control* of the country, in some quarters it willingly adopted the British style of *management control* of its companies. Perhaps one of the more enduring legacies of British colonialism was its manifestation in social and management structures. In these Irish firms perhaps both management and workers were reenacting hierarchical behaviors because these were most familiar to them.

Those Irish workers who came to the information sector with previous work experience in other industries or the civil service tended to expect strict supervision. On the other hand, younger workers who came from rural backgrounds did not have this orientation toward supervision nor did they expect it. In this respect, the agrarian sector seemed to be more consistent with the needs of the information sector than the traditional industries were. As respondents pointed out, it was difficult to have a productive work environment with an "us-them" attitude because of the communication barriers that resulted.

Liam offered an explanation for why Irish workers would prefer the management style found in the American IT firms over that found in the traditional Irish firms.

*I think the American work ethic, in many ways, would be a
reflection of what the Irish work ethic would have been if the
country hadn't grown in a colonial way. For instance, I
worked with people in the West of Ireland. Some of them
were directly from farms. Directly into new technology. And
they were fantastic. There was no stopping them and they
weren't anxious to go home at night, they contributed to the
full, they were communicative, they were intelligent. They
really took a great interest in what they were doing. But then
when they were in the situation for a period of time and the
[hierarchical] influence came more to bear on them they then
reverted to type and adopted a lot of the attitudes I would
have considered normal in the British [setting]. [Liam]*

3.2   World Class Management

> *I think the Irish, by their nature, find being told what to do
> absolutely contradictory to their wishes and would far rather
> have at least three reasons before they'll do anything which
> involves work. The American style, where goals are
> discussed, is therefore very attractive. When you discover
> after a year or two that the management are prepared to
> actually listen to what you consider reasoned objection and
> actually change the way they're doing things, this is like
> manna from heaven. This is a radical change from where we
> were before. [Declan]*

Both multinational and indigenous firms in the information sector
evidenced this same management style. This observation suggests that the
management style found in the information-sector workplace was the product
of several influences. One was the American culture present in the corporate
cultures of the multinational firms. This cultural influence, in turn, diffused
into the general IT culture and permeated the indigenous workplaces as well.
Other influences were the nature of information-sector work and the newness
of the IT industry. As a new industry it did not carry the baggage of older
industries. Consequently, it was easier to incorporate leading edge
organization designs and management approaches. What respondents
characterized as the "American management style" is in reality the
management approach associated with world class manufacturing (WCM).

WCM represents new ways of thinking about how firms are organized and
managed, and relate to their trading partners. It subsumes such concepts as
just-in-time (JIT) and total quality management (TQM). The essence of this
management approach is to develop flexibility within the organization, to
develop the ability to switch focus and rapidly adjust to new environmental
demands.[xi] Compatible management structures are less hierarchical than those
attributed to the "British management style." World class manufacturing was
introduced into Ireland in the late 1980s and early 1990s -- just as this
research was commencing -- primarily by American multinational
companies.[xii] Some of the firms included in this study were at the leading edge
of this movement.

Colm explained this phenomenon as an example of the "spillover effect."
Since many of those who were working at Irish firms had their earliest work
experiences in American multinational firms, they adopted that management
approach when they went on to start or manage people in Irish firms. The
adoption of WCM by indigenous firms suggests that the nature of work in the

information sector is more suited to this flexible organization design and management approach.

The respondents clearly preferred this open management style. Helen worked in the factory of an American electronics firm. In the Irish company where she had previously worked people were afraid of management, she said. The boss was very authoritarian towards the workers. At the American firm it was totally different.

> *[T]here was this manager. She had this way about her; like that she was the boss. And, like, she had been in her office all day long, and she came down on the floor, and she saw a group of people around talking she'd just scream her head off. And everybody would run. But here it is totally different. [Helen]*

The IT firms' management style that was so attractive to the respondents had two components. It was open and it was egalitarian.

Openness referred to both an open door policy and the open exchange of information. Managers, Irish and American, as well as workers commented on the revolutionary effect of an open door policy. The workers were truly surprised, if not a little suspicious, at being told that they could actually speak to someone in the corporate hierarchy above the level of their immediate superior. This had not been part of their work experience to date. At first, some were fearful of interrupting the chain of command. I was told about workers wanting to see a senior manager outside the workplace in order to speak in private and avoid notice by fellow workers. The American managers believed that workers feared later recriminations for going over their boss's head. Workers connected such behavior with the Irish cultural disdain for the informer.

But in more instances than not I was told that workers took quickly to this style with its open door policy. Andrew had been in Ireland as managing director just over a year when we spoke. In his view, the workers were quite happy because he brought not only discipline but also an open door policy. And opening the door was like opening a floodgate, he said. Irish workers felt that this approach brought with it much fairer treatment. They believed this American, high tech style of management encouraged people to talk to their bosses, something that worked well at the Irish sites of multinational firms. At another multinational firm, Ronald noted that some of the new management approaches such as the open door policy worked especially well in Ireland. While it was the official company policy to have this in every country, the actual implementation of it was another matter.

Another aspect of openness was communication. In general, American managers found that Irish workers responded quite favorably to open communication even if they were a little uncomfortable in the beginning. Ed noticed initial awkwardness on the part of his employees when he went along to the pub after work. But this tension dissipated over time. In fact, he found that his personal management style, which placed an emphasis on interpersonal interaction and communicating, did not have to be adapted at all when he came to Ireland; it fit right in.

> *My style [is] "management by wandering." I always try to take a kind of personal interest in my employees. It always means a lot if -- I found when I was working in the [American] plant, for example -- you would walk around in the morning with the coffee cup and say "Hey, so how did putting a new roof on your house go last night?" And you could tell that it meant a lot to them that someone took an interest in them. So it worked perfectly here, I personally really didn't have to adjust. [Ed]*

David shared with me what he learned early on at the Irish site of his multinational firm: *influence* not *status* was the way to accomplish things in Ireland. The use of influence over status, he believed, was something that was part of the corporate culture of his American firm that fit in especially well with Irish culture. Managers consistently noted the Irish preference for flexibility and autonomy: give them a goal and then let them go off and find their own way of achieving it. Instead of ordering people to do something, make them understand why they're doing it. Connor, who worked at an Irish IT firm in Dublin, illustrated the effectiveness of this approach.

> *If [the managing director] comes in and says, "Look, I want you to drive to Cork tomorrow morning and spend three days down there, and I want you to go to London. I wouldn't ask you to do this, but I feel you're the only person to do it," and I go. Whereas, if he come in and he says, "You're to go down to Cork and I'm not interested in any objections. If you have any objections you can go somewhere else for a job." These are two different things. One, I go, and I go willingly. And if my wife says, "Why are you going off like that and spend a weekend?" I say, "[my boss] asked me to." It's because I know that he's putting in extra hours and different things. The authority is matched with his own personal input, and he is providing the leadership. In the same way, if authority is*

*put more in the form of threatening behavior, and people
simply asking people to do things because that seems to be
the role, then you don't get the same response. [Connor]*

In some respects this "American management style" seemed to work better
in Ireland than in America! Deirdre commented on the more personal
management style employed at the Irish site. In her view, it included much
more individual empowerment and personalism than existed at American sites
of her US firm.

*I suppose that the identity that the people have with the
company is probably a little bit stronger here. Another major
element of our culture was formed by the people put in
charge and I think we probably entertain that a little bit
more. I think we've kept the openness a bit more. There
seems to be, at least in some parts of the [firm around the]
world, there are more sanctions now than there were in the
past about speaking your mind. Although again, that's
beginning to change a little bit better. But certainly for a
period of time that was true. I think that there's other things
that play here, right? For example, generally speaking,
Ireland, when you employ somebody you have to work with
them, right? You can't fire them very easily. Legislation is
fairly restrictive. You can do it, but you've got to work very
hard at it. As a result of that, people are inclined to take the
approach that this person is going to be with me for a while,
so I've got to do my best to manage that person in such a way
that they contribute. I think in other parts of [the firm],
people are probably written off a little bit more quickly. Now
there's pluses and minuses obviously with that. What it has
done is put more onuses on managers here. I think managers
here are better at managing their people. And there is more
value put on it at this site than I see at other sites. [Deirdre]*

My efforts to understand the different management styles in Ireland and
reactions to them brought me back to the revolutionary changes in the
workplace that were being ushered in along with the information economy.[xiii]
Those working in the information sector were the new breed of workers who
wouldn't stand for position-based authority. They were the ones who might
have emigrated in another decade. They had had a taste of a more egalitarian
management style and wouldn't return to the old ways. This attitude, in turn,

played well in the multinational world-class manufacturing firms that stressed flexibility, empowerment and personal autonomy.

4.   NONUNION

> We've inherited a lot of this stuff from the UK . . . because of occupation and so forth. Most of the big unions in Ireland are subsidiaries of big English unions. The biggest Irish union I think is the ITGWU, the Irish Transport General Workers Union. That's actually a subsidiary of the equivalent in England. So a lot of the practices and a lot of the attitudes came to Ireland in the late 1800s. There were basically care practices. In the UK they tended to have much more of a hierarchical structure within industry: four levels of canteen, etc. etc. We don't have that in Ireland. Today Ireland is getting industrialized. There isn't that much indigenous industry in Ireland like there would be in England. Whether it's called mining, or whether it's shipbuilding or whether it's steelworks or whatever. So there isn't that much history around ingrained thoughts and practices and so forth like they have in the UK. So a lot of the issues that the English unions used to fight against weren't present in Ireland. So if you extend that a bit further, I think the industrialization of Ireland has happened in probably the last 20 to 30 years, and you've companies like Apple, Stratus, IBM, Digital, Wang, etc. etc. who are the people who are industrializing Ireland. They're doing it on a much different type of labor relations concept or mindset than the UK approach, which is very much hierarchical. So I think that all contributes to the minimal influence that the unions have. [Brian]

One of the more notable societal changes accompanying the evolution of Ireland's information economy has been the diminished role of unions. While viewpoints differed as to whether this was a positive or negative effect, or whether this was a matter of correlation or causation,[xiv] there was agreement that unions did not possess the power in Ireland's information sector that they had wielded in the civil service and traditional industrial sectors. In spite of what I had read and heard about the importance of unions in Irish society, when it came to the high tech companies -- both the Irish and the multinational -- unions were either absent or had only a nominal presence.

Therefore, in my exploration of the role of unions in the information-sector workplace, I was interested in learning from respondents what aspects of the work and the workplace accounted for this change.

The management dichotomy discussed earlier in this chapter was reflected in respondents' perceptions about the role of unions in the Irish workplace as well. My background research before coming to Ireland suggested that I would encounter a society in which unions had a strong presence.[xv] I had heard the stories and read the statistics about strike actions in Ireland.[xvi] But the viewpoints I heard in the information-sector workplace once I got to Ireland presented another side altogether. It would not be correct to say that all IT firms or even all American IT firms were nonunion.[xvii] However, it would be accurate to observe that unions were not a significant force in the information sector. Where they existed, I was told they were not really needed, existed in name only, or did not function as a vehicle for collective bargaining.[xviii] On this basis one might be inclined to conclude that all was well and that the choice to be nonunion was a free one. A more sinister interpretation provided by cultural commentators suggested that the multinationals were consciously breaking up the unions, that being nonunion was a condition of setting up a subsidiary in Ireland, and that this wasn't necessarily what the Irish populace desired.

When I began to inquire about the role of unions in IT firms I received conflicting information. Despite an employee's right to join a union[xix] some respondents said that job applicants were often required to decline union membership as a condition of employment. Several respondents (both hiring managers and workers) mentioned that the "union question" was brought up in job interviews.

Because of the conflicting responses to my questions about the role of unions in the IT work environment, I decided to conduct a quantitative analysis of the respondents' comments to inform my interpretation. The results of this analysis are shown in Tables 7.1 and 7.2. Table 7.1 shows the characteristics of those who discussed the topic of unions.

Table 7.1
Respondents Commenting about Unions (n=42)
Total Number of Comments about Unions (n=70)

	% Total Respondents about Unions	Nationality & Gender of Responding Group	Responses by Nationality & Gender of Group Members
American	33.33% (5/15)[xx]	11.90% (5/42)	11.42% (8/70)
Irish	42.25% (30/71)	71.42% (30/42)	88.57% (62/70)
Male	46.66% (28/60)	66.66% (28/42)	58.57% (48/70)
Female	53.84% (14/26)	33.33% (14/42)	31.42% (22/70)

Six distinct themes emerged from their comments. As indicated by frequency of response, three of these were major themes and three were minor ones. A seventh category of miscellaneous comments contained those that did not fit in the above six categories. These themes are shown in Table 7.2 and discussed in the following sections.

Table 7.2
Themes about Union Presence in the Information Sector
Total Number of Responses about Unions (n=70)

Theme	% Total Responses
Good working conditions diminish need for unions	31.42% (22)
Nature of information-sector work not suited to unions	25.71% (18)
American firms do not want unions; make non-union participation a condition of employment or coming to Ireland	24.28% (17)
The British management influence on Irish work made unions popular	7.14% (5)
Hiring workers with no union experience; screening for possible union agitators	5.71% (4)
High unemployment rate diminished union influence	4.28% (3)
Impact of the information sector on unions	1.42% (1)

4.1   Work Environment

The unions seem to play a big part of, say, the older industries and the post office where you probably have this environment where people are really not being motivated and stuff and therefore the union probably has to fight for the wages and they probably all get the same wages and they all get the same increases. Whereas here I think the tradition has been that people here [in information-sector firms] probably do get paid more than their equivalent job outside and therefore there has been no great need for unions to intervene. In other words they're kept at bay by keeping

people happy first, therefore there's no need for them to go to
unions. [Paul]

The explanation most frequently given for the lack of union presence in the information sector was that good management practices and good working conditions obviated the need for them. Unions were not needed in high tech because the atmosphere was more laid back and permitted bright people to contribute. In recalling her hiring process, Margie said the multinational firm had made it quite clear that "no union" was a condition of employment. Since these firms did not have deep roots and could leave Ireland at any point, this condition was taken seriously. However, she also observed that since multinationals could give a better wage package than indigenous firms, why should one want to join the union anyway? The multinationals' approach was to provide an environment so attractive that the union would not have had any base. Ethna linked environmental factors to the information sector. She said there was no need for unions in the information sector because management had already made provisions for treating people like people. She cited the open door policy as an example.

My own conclusion was that attachment to unions was not inherently very strong. Therefore, if the benefits that unions provided could be obtained by other means then workers appeared quite willing to opt for alternative mechanisms. One respondent offered evidence to support this view. A large number of working people in Ireland being members of trade unions did not translate into votes for the Labor Party. He said there was as much fear of socialism (embodied in organized labor) as there was of capitalism (embodied in nonunion, American-style firms). An active union seemed to be more a reflection of the Irish rejection of authority than any inherent loyalty to the union concept. A few other respondents added an interesting viewpoint. They believed unions, themselves, were anti-Irish because of their bureaucracy and hierarchy, which ran counter to the egalitarian nature of the essential Irish character. One Irish respondent thought that as a people, the Irish did not like to organize themselves. If union representatives came in from outside to organize, they would receive almost the same response that would be given to an authoritarian manager coming in. He saw unions as just another form of management.

4.2 American Influence

They're a very important piece of the traditional Irish
industries. And in the high tech companies, I think they
weren't allowed in here, to my knowledge. One of the

prerequisites was you're not to be a member of the union. We had to sign something saying you weren't. I can't recall properly. But I don't think there's any requirement here for it. It's not perceived as being a requirement in high tech companies because they pay so well; the conditions are very good. You don't have to fight all the time for your rights. They're more or less given to you, you know? And your reviews and your pay increases. A lot of perks here. So I wouldn't have any desire for a union here, especially looking at the way they're treated at [a particular traditional Irish firm which has a history of labor unrest] and all the other places. [Margie]

The remaining two major themes received roughly equal emphasis and are closely related. A quarter of the responses attributed diminished union presence directly to the desire of American firms not to have unions. During a meeting with American executives from one of the IT firms before coming to Ireland we discussed the union issue. They said that despite Irish advisors' recommendation to introduce a single union so as to preclude the establishment of several at the firm, they were adamant about their position. This firm looked to Digital, the first major firm not to have unions. These executives said Digital being the first and largest nonunion American plant in Ireland, had a major impact. It also brought a different culture, they said. Christopher, a manager at this firm, was familiar with the history of Digital in Ireland. He said the IDA advised Digital to bring in a union from the beginning, since Irish law allowed it, in order to preempt establishment of multiple unions. But Digital was adamant in its nonunion stance. Those telling me this story said the position of Digital and other American firms on the union issue reflected their own "antisocialist" perspective.

At one particular IT firm 60 or 70 people qualified to join a union yet only seven actually did. Unions tended to be strong in the old industries such as clothing, textiles, bread milling, brewing and cigarette manufacture. But the new industries -- pharmaceuticals, high tech and financial services -- were not unionized. The general perception among the Irish respondents was that the American multinational firms did not like unions and did not want organized labor. The American firms believed management could do what was necessary to get the job done. Further, the Americans believed that the Irish workers genuinely *liked* the nonunion IT work environment.

Ed had never worked in a union environment but recalled that during hiring in Ireland his firm asked the "union question." He explained it as: did they work in a union before, which ones, what did they think about it. He told me that all the applicants responded that while at other firms they had a union and workers were expected to join it, it didn't mean anything to them. It is, of course, a matter of interpretation as to whether these job applicants spoke their true beliefs or expressed the viewpoint that they thought would serve them best in getting the job.

The other explanation was that the American multinational firms introduced work practices and management principles that anticipated certain workplace issues. In so doing, these firms precluded the unions.[xxi] George agreed that it was, indeed, unusual for a company the size of his firm in Ireland not to have a union. And people always asked him why it didn't. But, he said, employees chose it that way; no one was barring them.

> *I think that the inflow of multinational companies, the culture shock that they brought was more organized management, the value of which was recognized. More organized, in a sense more autocratic, but at the same time more paternalistic. It was a mixture of autocracy and paternalism. The mixture of the two was designed to remove union influence. Which it largely has done. [Martin]*

Even where a union existed in a firm, its power was diminished. For example, in one American firm that did have unionized employees management did not negotiate with union representatives. Rather, management communicated with workers directly. The result was openness of communication and process, and direct access to management. Part of the reason for direct communication with workers was that they didn't listen to their union leadership anyway. This, in turn, led to the propensity for unofficial strikes. Because management could not count on the union delivering what the negotiators negotiated, they concluded that there was no real reason to work with the union representatives.

As I considered my discussions with respondents about the "union question" I returned to the connections among union presence, work ethic and management style. The traditional industrial and service sectors that had unions also had a hierarchical management style and an "us-them" divide between management and workers. Where union presence was either nominal or nonexistent -- for example, in the information sector -- the work ethic was associated with youth, hustle, greater productivity, high tech and an open management style. When asked, my respondents concurred with the correlations I made. But whether the degree of union presence was a cause or an effect of the work ethics and management style is open to interpretation.

4.3   Nature of Information-sector Work

> *It's funny, my grandfather would probably hit me over the*
> *head with a shovel [if he heard how I'm talking about*
> *unions] because he was an Irish immigrant and he belonged*
> *to a union. And my grandmother was an Irish immigrant. And*
> *my father was a teacher and when he came back from Korea*
> *when he was going to school he worked in construction and*
> *he was in the union. I think originally unions were necessary*
> *and came about because of the conditions in the workplace,*
> *and just the general treatment of the workers. And to look*
> *after his basic needs like safety and health, general working*
> *environment. From school [I learned] that's the reason why*
> *unions were needed and why they got started. [But] as a full*
> *time job I've never worked in a union environment. It's hard*
> *to make a general broad-brush statement because if you're*
> *working in a coal mine in Georgia and someone's kicking*
> *you to go down there you're going to say unions are great.*
> *And if you're sitting in a high tech environment where it's*
> *air-conditioned and you are wearing a tie and you don't have*
> *people dying or anything you're going to say unions are*
> *useless. From my work experience and I would say in high*
> *tech in general, I would say they're counterproductive*
> *because by nature you're delineating workers and*
> *management, which to me seems to be -- although*
> *historically it is there -- seems to be an unnatural delineation*
> *unless they have separate goals and needs. I guess I wouldn't*
> *understand why they would have separate goals and separate*
> *needs. Given that you work in a capitalist society I don't see*
> *why there would be [a difference]. In the US, in high tech in*
> *general, you don't have the issue. [Joseph]*

Joseph expressed a representative view that the nature of work in the
information sector would make a union environment counterproductive. The
clear delineation between worker and manager that is characteristic of a
typical union environment was unnatural, he pointed out. There was greater
similarity between the Irish and American sites of his firm than between the
American site of his firm and other American plants in the traditional
manufacturing sector. Irish workers expressed a similar sentiment.

The IT world seems to attract people; they enjoy their job, probably. They get rewarded for if they do well, right? So there's almost an in-built incentive there. And if you do well, right, you get rewarded, therefore you're not unhappy, therefore, you don't need trade unions. Whereas unions tend to make everybody equal, like. So they tend to take down the top to make everybody equal to the bottom, because they can't take the bottom up, yeah? And I think individual enterprise and innovation, initiative is impeded. Without a union if I do well, the sky's the limit. Whereas if there's a union involved it's only going to hold me back, almost. [Jim]

Such comments suggested that the characteristics of both the people and the work in the information sector were incompatible with a union environment. People who worked in IT enjoyed their jobs, had incentive to perform and were rewarded for it. Because they were not unhappy with their jobs, they did not need trade unions. In this view, unions impeded individual enterprise, innovation and initiative. Unions held back the people who did well. In addition, the argument continued, the professionalism and autonomy associated with high tech work was different from other industrial sectors. The sharp divisions between management and worker that made unions necessary did not exist with IT. Further, the autonomy involved in the work was incompatible with unions. Finally, technologies such as electronic mail facilitated access to information. This, in turn, led to greater openness, which further diminished the need for unions. There was also a sentiment that unions equalized people and that their presence held back the high achievers.

A union mentality at [our firm] would hold people back. Too much equality leads to low productivity. [John]

Some respondents used the evidence from other industries to argue that the absence of union power was not so much due to the American influence as it was the nature of the work. They noted, for example, that American firms in the medical field in Ireland *did* have unions that negotiated binding contracts between management and workers. Whereas in IT, even where there were unions, they didn't have contracts to the same degree that they did in other industries. Others contrasted a traditional manufacturing work setting with modern IT work. In the former there was heavy labor involvement, strict working hours, heavy presence of a foreperson, and someone checking your work. In the latter there might be assembly line work but there was less supervision and workers felt a sense of personal responsibility for their tasks. There was more social contact with managers. The generally held view was that American firms in the IT sector did not want unions because the nature of the work demanded flexibility, which they saw as being anathema to a union mentality. At the same time, they acknowledged that without unions, management had to play a larger role to keep workers happy.

There were a few respondents who did not view the nature of IT work as being significantly different from other industrial work. These individuals did not agree that the nature of IT work precluded the need for unions.

> *I mean, I can't see any reason, if a company is making iron bars as opposed to little bits of plastic put on a board, why is there any difference? [Richard]*

What seemed to influence such views was the scope of the information sector, whether it was limited to hardware manufacture or included information services or software development as well. Another respondent made a distinction within the information sector when talking about why unions weren't needed in it. In the information technology manufacturing plants it was the good work environment that kept unions out. But in software firms it was the nature of the work itself that would make unions counterproductive. Unions did not deal with such educated people as those who worked in IT firms. Engineers would not likely join a union.

Consistent with their multinational counterparts, the Irish firms appeared to have the same view about the need for unions in the information sector. Sean explained that in the smaller IT firms which were also the indigenous ones and tended to be in the software business, there was less cushion. People worked very hard, were highly skilled and highly intelligent. They were in the top 5% to 10% of their age group. As a manager, he was more concerned about the issues of job satisfaction and challenge than about financial elements and "putting in time," things he said one might find in bigger firms and those that were unionized.

Some of the IT workers who came from unionized environments brought those work habits with them. Clashes sometimes resulted. For example, one of the reasons people believed the union mentality was unsuited to IT work was that with IT work the orientation was much more toward getting the job done (the product) than putting in the time (the process). For that reason, the IT firms would be less inclined to be strict about *when* and *how* something got done as long as it *did* get done. The bumps in the road of this transition occurred as workers accommodated to a radically new work environment. An illustration is the multinational firm's experience with the issue of time cards that was discussed in Chapter 6. Because workers who came from union environments were used to punching time cards, there was an initial problem with tardiness when new employees realized that no one was monitoring their arrival. The creative management response was to shift more responsibility to the workers in the form of flex time. Allowing workers to arrive between seven and nine in the morning and leave after and eight-hour shift eliminated the issue of coming late to work altogether. In addition, workers appreciated the flexibility that enabled them to leave work earlier during good weather to allow for a golf game or travel down country on a Friday.

The three minor themes about unions that emerged from my analysis of respondent comments were minor in numerical terms only. While these themes were not discussed as frequently as those just considered, they are, nevertheless, important to discuss. They provide background and context for understanding respondents' comments about the diminished role of unions in Ireland.

4.4   British Influence

> *The larger companies in Ireland were typically branch offices of the UK company until Irish industry gradually grew -- Smurfit 50 years ago was unimaginable. The trade union movement is still fully affiliated and associated with its English counterpart. And so much integrated that in fact all trade unions in Ireland are 32 county.*[xxii] *It's the Irish version of the English version. We therefore inherited this hostile "them and us" situation where management were entitled to go off and play golf in the afternoon. It was their function. It was their function also to decide what was going to happen with the underlings. [Declan]*

The first of these three minor themes is that a strong union presence in Ireland was part of the legacy of the British presence in Ireland. Due to British ownership of firms and British or British-educated managers, a union mentality migrated to Ireland along with the other facets of the British management style discussed earlier. Since this management style was autocratic and hierarchical, the thinking went, unions were needed in order to insure improvements in the workplace. Therefore, even though Ireland did not experience an industrial revolution like Britain, the British legacy was an "us-them" relationship between management and workers, which made firms ripe for unionization. Britain's continued influence was felt in that many of the Irish unions were directly affiliated with British ones. Indeed, along with the banking system and the civil service the structure of Irish trade unionism was the other significant institutional inheritance from Britain (Lee, 1989).

In some quarters of society there continued to be a strong affiliation with unions. As attitudes about unions were changing from one generation to the next, some young workers were having to confront a serious dilemma between family and tradition on the one hand, and employment advancement and the future on the other. Those who were beginning to move up the ranks, to pass through the door into middle management were being forced to make a decision about the union. Sue illustrated this dilemma in a story about a worker who chose to derail his movement along the management track rather than go against a prounion family. Family pressure and tradition were that strong.

> *I'll just give you an example of a chap. His name is John and his father had worked for, I think it was perhaps, the* Irish Times. *Heavily trade unionized environment. And his father had been shop steward in that environment. John came to us from Dublin Gas. And [our company] was only partially unionized. Probably 50% of the staff were unionized. And John joined the company and was very committed and very interested in seeing [himself] succeed and very clear on the fact that management was saying, "Those of you who are not in the union will succeed on your merits and reward, and those of you who are in the union will be treated as part of the mass." John joined the union. And John worked for me and I called him in and I said, "John, why did you join the union?" and he said, "Well, my father was in the union; it would be expected of me." And I said, "John, well do you realize what effect that has on the statement you're making within [the company]?" and he said, "Yeah, but when I get home Dad's gonna want to know why I'm not in the union, so I'm going to join." He was willing to accept the fact that in management's viewpoint that was a statement of, "I want to be one of the mediocre mass rather than one of the people who's willing to be judged on my own achievements," because in his family that's the expected behavior. [Sue]*

There was also an element of patriotism in the attitude that Irish people have historically had towards unions. Because the British controlled big business, there was a feeling that being part of a union was akin to fighting for freedom from the oppressor. Belonging to the union was, thus, an expression of sticking together against the company, the common enemy.

> *Irish and English owned companies are big union*
> *environments. . . I suppose it's patriotic: the Jim Larkins*[xxiii]
> *of the world fighting for the freedom of the country. [Donald]*

It seemed, then, that the British influence on Irish work and the workplace
contributed to the strong presence of unions in Ireland. But it also followed
that as British influence gave way to American influence, the prominence of,
interest in, and perhaps need for unions was diminishing as well.

4.5   Minimizing Union Influence

> *[A firm] closed due to strikes and so [this town] had a bad*
> *name in terms of unions. Fitters and electricians were*
> *considered high risk regarding strikes and so when [this*
> *multinational firm] was starting out, it didn't hire them*
> *directly and instead subcontracted them. [This firm] is*
> *unique in regard to subcontracting out like this. I was told to*
> *make the process work. If there were union troublemakers, I*
> *could get rid of them. My approach was to spend time in*
> *hiring. I wanted to hire at least one mature person and the*
> *rest younger. [Brendan]*

A few respondents went beyond the general comments about the American
preference for a nonunionized work environment to speak more specifically
about the ways in which this objective was being achieved. Some of them
spoke knowledgeably about the active steps taken by some American firms to
keep the unions out completely or to keep union presence ineffectual. Having
such a young workforce certainly assisted in the effort to make the
information sector nonunion. Whether intentional or not, the practice of hiring
young workers with no other industry -- and, therefore, union -- experience
helped to minimize union influence. With a predominance of young,
inexperienced workers a firm could, build up its own culture. Having no union
influence, said some managers, meant having no "bad influences." Young
workers had none of the habits of older employees since they were growing
up in an open management situation. They were allowed to develop where
they could contribute their best. For these young people, there was no
understanding of what was expected, what was the norm in other industries.
The advantage was that a distinct work culture could be created. Sometimes,
however, they appeared a bit ungrateful to older Irish workers. Because they
had no basis of comparison, these workers complained when more
experienced workers thought they should appreciate how good they had it! In

contrast, older workers described working at the American multinationals as coming to a holiday camp![xxiv]

Another way of minimizing union influence, as already discussed, was asking the "union question." During recruitment employers inquired about an applicant's own or parents' union activities. While both American and Irish respondents made reference to the "union question" having been posed to prospective employees, there was a difference in understanding about its impact. Americans characterized the question as an informational exercise; some Irish respondents believed the question was intended to screen out potential union agitators. Other Irish respondents believed that an agreement had been reached between American multinational firms and Irish policy makers to keep unions out.

One American firm chose its location in Ireland, in part, based on the desire to limit union influence. It purposely stayed away from parts of the country that had a strong union presence. In addition, many of its workers had relocated to that area. Hence, there was not the tight knit community in the workplace that would have been the case in Dublin where workers would have known each other better. It was less clannish and clannish people started to talk among themselves and made mountains out of molehills. The firm thought that in such an atmosphere there was more union agitation.[xxv]

4.6   Unemployment

> *I'm pretty light on unions. I belonged to a union for many years but I belonged to it inasmuch as my subscription was deducted from my salary and was about as much interest as I had in the union. In the trades, sections like that, they would have been quite strong. But I think the role of the union is also changing. Again, I suppose, going back to unemployment. People are more reluctant to strike, more conscious of holding on to a job rather than putting it in danger by going on strike. [Stephanie]*

Another factor related to the influence of unions was the unemployment rate. A few people noted that a high unemployment rate made workers feel more vulnerable about factors that might jeopardize their employment. Therefore, they might be reluctant to get very involved in unions for fear of losing a job or not getting hired in the first place. Indeed, the American management of one firm told me it specifically chose a locale in Ireland, which had high unemployment, so it would be easier to keep unions out.

Individuals accepted that if they wanted IT employment in American firms they were agreeing to be in a nonunionized work environment, as well.

4.7   Impact of the Information Sector on Unions in Ireland

The final theme contained a loose collection of thoughts about the general impact of the information sector on the position of unions in Ireland. A few respondents suggested that something was lost by not having a union presence. The trade-offs affected both management and workers. With respect to management, they said things happened that unions would not allow. An example was the amount of time taken to make personnel decisions. Unions would have forced these to be made more quickly. At the same time the absence of a union made management more difficult. More people had to be consulted in making personnel decisions. It was also harder to assess the acceptability of management decisions. Decisions about maintaining comparable pay rates were also made more slowly than in union environments. Without unions there was no pressure to make such decisions, they said. However, a nonunion work environment also made *doing the work* easier as long as there were good conditions. An impact of a nonunionized environment on workers related to working overtime. One worker said that at her American firm people were expected to put in some overtime. If temporary workers refused, then it would be held against them when they wanted to become permanent employees.

Rosemary, who worked in an Irish software firm, discussed the impact on unions, themselves. She thought the American management style and anti-union stance had significantly changed Irish unions -- for the better. She believed people's jobs were genuinely being changed. She described a draft union agreement shown to her by someone in one of the large unions. It was full of notions such as flexibility and having no demarcation between management and workers, and everyone working together with no hierarchies. It had all the trendy things and all the things a worker could possibly want and was totally against what people typically associated with union approaches.[xxvi]

Bridie summed up the general attitude of many of the respondents regarding unions.

> *Traditionally unions were big. It was the only way the worker had a voice. The multinationals are steering clear of unions. [The founder of this firm] was against unions and made it a precondition of coming here. Most strikes in Irish companies are because of technology changes in old companies. Being*

> *nonunion is mostly due to the American attitude, and bad*
> *press in the late 70s in the UK and Ireland about strikes and*
> *time lost due to them. In general, the plant is just like*
> *America. The Irish culture is giving way. [Bridie]*

They seemed to believe that the American influence had been significant in diminishing the power of unions. They also believed the type of industry was a significant factor. At the same time, they appeared to be acquiescing to it. While they all seemed to acknowledge that unions were losing their power, they didn't seem particularly bothered about it. One possible explanation is that they were telling me -- an American who was in their company under the auspices of the management -- what they thought I wanted to hear. But since the viewpoints of workers at Irish firms were similar and because they were at other times critical about their American employers, I believe that the respondents were speaking honestly. My interpretation is that there was no deep loyalty to unions, that they were viewed as a means to an end. If unions were needed in order to obtain a certain work environment, fine, they would have them. If, on the other hand, the type of work and/or management style could produce that same environment without unions, then the IT workers were content to not have unions. However, I also detected wistfulness in their hint of a trade-off of culture for jobs in which Ireland was losing something.

5. CONCLUSION

The evidence I consistently obtained in my interviews pointed to the existence of a rigid, status-oriented, hierarchical work environment in traditional Irish firms. This was in direct contrast to the more open environment of the multinational and indigenous information sector. However, it was not a simple dichotomy. A number of forces were interacting to produce a range of management manifestations, not all of which surfaced in our interviews.[xxvii] The work cultures and management styles experienced by the respondents in the traditional Irish industries and in the information sector were the result of a range of influences. One was national culture. When Ireland opened wide its doors to inward investment, new cultural influences entered the country and the management philosophies of these new firms. Another influence was the work sector. As discussed in Chapter 1 and reinforced throughout this book, the information sector has characteristics that are often quite different from those of other sectors.

Further, the "traditional Irish management style" which respondents used as the backdrop against which they discussed the information economy workplace was much more textured than what emerged from their comments. For example, Monks (1992) conducted research into human resource practices in Ireland contemporary with my study. She found evidence of Irish firms moving beyond traditional personnel approaches to include "innovative/professional" practices that were more collaborative. Perhaps the respondents sought extremes in order to draw comparisons between American and Irish management practices, and between traditional and information economy workplaces.

Leavy (1993) points out that the concept of "Irish management" is a rather recent phenomenon, having been forged through the process of social, economic and cultural development only since the country became independent in 1921. He also notes the other management influences that have contributed to the evolution of Irish management. One was the predominance of state-owned enterprises. These firms and their managers -- who originally came from the ranks of leaders in the War of Independence -- were the first "professional" managers, challenging the management-by-inheritance approach that had governed the predominantly family-owned firms up until that point. The other influence on the evolution of Irish management style was the cooperative movement in Ireland. By the 1920s there were over 400 co-operative creameries established throughout the country. Creamery managers emerged as another important class of managers. Until the 1960s they had high status in the rural communities on a par with the local teachers and the parish priests.

The 1960s ushered in not only a change in economic development strategy for Ireland, but also a significant new influence on management style in Ireland. With the coming of multinational companies came the introduction of new management thinking and practices (Leavy, 1993) due to the sheer size of this sector. In 1996 there were approximately 990 multinational firms in Ireland employing 40% of the industrial workforce and representing 50% of manufactured output. The American segment, in particular, has been at the forefront of introducing innovative management practices in Ireland (Monks, 1996, p. 721-2). But as the respondents pointed out, it was not just the American influence that was driving these innovative approaches to management; it was also the nature of the information sector. In a study of personnel practices in a range of Irish sectors Monks (1992) found that

> . . . those involved in the high tech manufacturing sector . . . utilised complex human resources policies . . . explained by the need to recruit highly qualified knowledge workers, to continually upgrade these workers' technical skills and, from an organisational perspective, to support the conditions

required for innovation, change, and employees' continued
high performance. Non-union companies were also more
likely to employ sophisticated personnel practices. (37)

Such management and human resource innovations have, no doubt,
contributed to the decline of unions, something that continues into the present
(Houston, 1999).

Much more was also going on regarding unions than what surfaced in my
discussions with respondents. What did emerge was a rather static portrayal of
unions. In reality, considerable change was fermenting. As Roche (1982)
points out, there had been a gradual change in the role of unions dating back
to the 1960s and the change in Ireland's industrial policy. The achievement of
this bold new plan to attract inward investment required a high degree of
solidarity and cooperation. It required that employers, unions and the
government become social partners in the process of national economic
development [xxviii]

Through wage agreements and partnerships trade unions were, and
continue to be, gradually changing their role. As unions have become
involved in industrial policy formulation, collective bargaining has become
increasingly influenced by the government in the form of social contracts.
Indeed, the system of moderate national wage agreements has played an
important role in promoting peaceful industrial relations and in holding
inflation to very low levels (Breathnach, 1998). One such wage agreement,
Programme for National Recovery (1987) was in effect at the time of this
research. *Partnership 2000* (1996), a framework for economic policymaking
for 1997-1998 was the fourth national economic programme agreed to by
employers, trade unions and the government. It established a framework for
the conduct of relations between employers and trade unions. It continued
wage moderation in return for cuts in personal taxation.

However, there have been some cracks in the edifice. Employers have
been pushing for more privatization and more tax cuts; trade unions have been
calling for mandatory trade union recognition, a minimum hourly wage, and a
greater role for workers in company decision making. Unions believe such
things will give workers a greater share in the spoils of economic growth.
Unions are also concerned that the tax cuts in the 1998 budget came in the
form of reductions in tax rates benefiting higher earners, rather than increases
in personal allowances and a widening of the standard rate tax band. These
would have been of greater benefit to low- and medium- income earners (The
Economist Intelligence Unit, 1998). Community groups have called for a
widening of the context of social partnership to include not only the sharing of

existing wealth but also exploration of the means by which that wealth is created (Crowley, 1998).

These observations about management and unions suggest that the picture, today, is both different and a bit more complex than that portrayed by the respondents ten years ago. Part of the reason is that the status of both management and unions has evolved since the time of these interviews in the information-sector firms. There has been continued diffusion of world class management concepts throughout Ireland and, in particular, in the information sector. The social partnerships have contributed to the changing role of unions from an adversarial to much more of a human resources approach.

But the other reason that these nuances did not appear in our discussions is perhaps because at that time both management styles and the role of unions were in such a state of flux. As such, it would have been difficult for individuals to have the perspective necessary to see across so many different dimensions of management practice. Respondents could only speak to their specific experiences with the information-economy workplace, experiences that reflected a narrow slice of all that was occurring. One thing, however, is clear. The information economy, brought about through a large multinational sector, has had a significant impact on the workplace in Ireland.

---

[i] That is, to consider and review the procedure for its appropriateness.

[ii] Foster (1988) cites a 1962 survey of Catholic attitudes in Dublin showing wide consensus about the ". . . right of the Church to exert social, economic and political authority -- and an accompanying distrust of politicians. In the event of a Church-State clash, 87% of those questioned said they would support the Church; 88% endorsed the proposition that the Church was the greatest force for good in the country." (573)

[iii] Hospital gown.

[iv] For further discussion see Schmitt (1973), Chapter 4: Irish Authoritarianism.

[v] See also Coogan (1987), Chapter 7 for a discussion of the black economy and attitudes toward taxes.

[vi] Lee's (1989) discussion of Ireland's economic expansion between 1958 and 1969 makes several allusions to this. For example, in discussing a 1958 *Irish Banking Review* article which asserts that in Ireland ". . . Labour relations are reasonably good by modern standards," ("Favorable Aspects of the Irish Economy," 1958, p. 3) he replies, "('Modern standards' meant, of course, British standards.)" (349) Elsewhere, in discussing the rationale for shifting emphasis from agricultural to industrial exports he observes that in 1958 . . . "[t]he hope was that in due course the models of managerial efficiency presumed to be provided by foreign firms would inspire imitation in the protected sectors." (352) Finally, he

notes that ". . . Ireland was so closely locked into the British economy that many international trends affected her only as mediated through Britain." (359)

[vii] O'Malley (1989) notes that: "Industrialisation since the early 1930s had been subject to the *Control of Manufactures Acts of 1932-34*, which required that Irish citizens had to hold a majority of assets, voting shares and votes on the board of directors in new manufacturing companies starting operations. However, this did not prevent the involvement of many foreign companies, especially British ones, in the industrial growth of this time, since joint ownership arrangements and manufacturing under foreign license were common. . . [I]n 1973, two-thirds of Britain's 100 largest industrial companies had one or more subsidiaries in Ireland." (63) See also Daly (1992), Chapter 6: The Political and Social Implications of an Irish Industrial Revolution, and Foster (1988), pp. 570-571.

[viii] Lee (1989), p. 89.

[ix] Leavy (1993) observes that: "Irish public administration was, from the outset, firmly rooted in the traditions of the British civil service." (127-8)

[x] Hofstede (1983) speaks of "self-fulfilling prophecy" in discussing mechanisms by which culturally determined ways of thinking perpetuate themselves.

[xi] For further discussion of these concepts see Hayes and Pisano (1994); and Hodgetts, Lee and Luthans (1994).

[xii] For further discussion of WCM in Ireland at this time see Brennan (1990), Chrystal (1990), Corkery (1990), Jacobson (1996) and Smyth (1990).

[xiii] My interpretation of the role of multinational corporations in introducing innovative management approaches was supported by Monks' (1992) findings in a study of personnel practices in firms in 1989-90. All but one of the firms that manifested "innovative/sophisticated" practices was multinational. In these firms personnel issues were integrated into management practices, management was proactive, companies endeavored to secure the commitment of their employees, they used autonomous work groups and emphasized flexibility.

[xiv] Coogan (1987) notes that the weakening of the trade union movement accompanied the industrial policy change toward inward investment and the national wage agreements that were introduced in the 1960s. (110) As evidence he cites an Irish industrialist's call for an end to "anachronistic processes and practices of industrial relations" so that ". . . labor-price determination should be subjected to the disciplines of a competitive market. He argued that the rights and powers of trade unions can no longer be justified." (113)

[xv] The labor movement has played a significant role in Ireland's history though it has changed over time. There have been some memorable strikes such as the 20,000 strong strike in 1913 by the Irish Transport and General Workers' Union led by republican leaders Jim Larkin and James Connolly. Another was the strike by the national teachers' union in 1946 that lasted for seven months (Lee, 1989, pp. 19-20, 289). During the early 1980s trade union

membership was half a million workers which represented 55% of eligible workers (Roche and Larraghy, 1987 quoted in Breen, et al., 1990, p. 163). The high rate of union membership in Ireland relative to other European countries was partly accounted for by the large number of state-owned enterprises, that existed in Ireland. The public sector, along with Irish-owned enterprises also accounted for most of the strikes (Clancy, et al., 1988, p. 82-3).

[xvi] For example, O'Donnell (1980b, p. 135) provides the following information about the number of working days lost through industrial disputes in the late 1970s when some of the American multinational firms in this study were considering coming to Ireland: 1977: 449,000; 1978: 588,000 and 1979: 1,427,000.

[xvii] Indeed, according to a Price Waterhouse (1989) publication contemporary with this research, approximately 75% of employees in manufacturing firms were members of trade unions. The "manufacturing firm" category would have included the hardware subsector of the information economy but not necessarily the software or services sectors. Breen, et al. (1990) provide other contemporary indication of unionization in the information sector: 20% of US firms in 1990 were non-unionized. (177)

[xviii] This perception of the respondents is supported in Murray and Wickam's (1982) observation that in many instances trade unions set up agreements with firms before the factories opened. Consequently, workers had little active involvement in the union. Further, many of the more recently arrived foreign firms had a company policy to actively oppose trade unions.

[xix] The Irish Constitution guarantees the right of citizens to form associations and unions.

[xx] That is, of the 86 respondents in this study, 15 were American and 5 of these spoke about unions.

[xxi] For further discussion of pre-emptive measures by the multinational firms see Clancy, et al. (1988), p. 83.

[xxii] These unions cut across national boundaries to include members from the 26 counties in the Republic of Ireland as well as the six counties in Northern Ireland. Contemporary literature (Price Waterhouse, 1989) states that 70,000 union members belonged to unions with headquarters in the UK.

[xxiii] Jim Larkin was a prominent labor agitator and leader during the struggle for independence and the early years of the Irish Republic, and served as an Independent Labor TD for a number of years. He founded the Irish Transport and General Workers' Union. (See Foster, 1988; Lee, 1989).

[xxiv] A vacation resort.

[xxv] Clancy, et al. (1988, p. 82) claim that locating foreign-owned industry away from the centers of traditional trade union activity is both a conscious decision and a common practice.

[xxvi] I believe she was referring to documents associated with the national pay agreement achieved in *Programme for National Recovery* (1987) which was in effect at the time of these interviews.

[xxvii] See Jacobson (1996) for a review of a variety of forms of work organization in various sectors contemporary with this study.

[xxviii] For further discussion of social partnerships as they relate to the industrial policy see also: Breen, et al. (1990), Clancy, et al. (1988) and Leavy (1993).

Part IV
Lessons for the Information Age

CHAPTER 8. LESSONS FROM IRELAND

1. INTRODUCTION

And one of the few products, which can be shipped without using the ferry, is information. If it's a small amount, it can be electronically transmitted. If it's a large amount a small tape on tomorrow morning's jumbo out to New York will carry the entire records of an American insurance company for a week. It would fit in a briefcase, without costing a thought. We have several advantages which I've mentioned several times, I think. The main one we have is our education and our ability to speak English. And -- funny -- ex-colonial advantages as well. The reason that the whole information services center, if you like, is viable, is that Dublin's stock exchange always was and still is a branch of the London stock exchange. So that relationship didn't have to be created. It was there. It took 70 years for somebody to think of hanging something onto it, to make it more useful to us than it had been to date. But it's something that has always been. Perhaps, if you like, we're only now getting around to using our talents. [Colm]

This book has been a journey through culture and history as it considered the ways in which the Irish context has influenced the emergence of its information economy. Throughout the journey, impacts were also noted. This Chapter assesses the information economy that has resulted from Ireland's industrial plan. It considers the fit between Ireland's information economy and the country's socio-cultural characteristics. Finally, it considers challenges for Ireland's information economy in the future.

2.   THE INFORMATION ECONOMY AS ENGINE OF INDUSTRIAL DEVELOPMENT

There were six expected outcomes from Ireland's new industrial policy. The first was job creation. This meant not just more jobs but more sustainable jobs in a wider range of new industries to offset the decline in agricultural jobs and reduce unemployment levels. The second was the stimulation of indigenous industry. The multinational companies were expected to offer opportunities for sourcing from indigenous firms. At some point, Irish spin-offs from multinational firms were also anticipated. Further, the multinational firms in Ireland were expected to help the country quickly develop an entrepreneurial capacity and a new business climate. The third expected outcome from the new industrial policy was a change in educational credentials. More people would go to school and stay there longer in order to acquire the skills necessary for employment in these new sectors. Greater employment opportunities, in turn, would lead to the fourth outcome: stemming the tide of emigration. The combination of more jobs, more indigenous industry, higher levels of education and the ability to hold on to the "best and brightest" could not help but enhance the overall economy. Such was the thinking about the fifth intended impact. Finally, it was believed that these economic impacts would, in turn, produce social, psychological and political impacts of their own.

2.1   Employment

The goal of job creation was eventually met in the second half of the 1990s when the effort to refocus the economy was finally bearing fruit. Unemployment in Ireland went from 15.1% to 10.3% in 1997 (The Economist Intelligence Unit, 1998). In 1998 this trend continued with a 9.1% unemployment rate. And in 1999 it was 8.4%, just above the OECD average of 7.3% (IDA Ireland, 1999). Between 1992 and 1998 there was a 17% per cent increase in total employment with 193,000 net new jobs created. Of these 146,000 or 75.6% were in services while 34.7% were in industry. This impressive employment growth helped to offset the decline of 20,000 jobs or 10.3% in agricultural jobs (The Economist Intelligence Unit, 1998).

New jobs have been created in an expanding and entrenched information economy. These new jobs have reduced unemployment as they absorbed the labor force that is moving away from agriculture. In keeping with the kind of industry that Ireland sought, the information sector represents an employment area that is dynamic, leading edge and "clean." In recent years particular emphasis has been placed on the software subsector. In 1998 this sector employed nearly 20,000 people (The Irish Software Association, 1998).

2.2 Indigenous Industry

The goal of the industrial policy with respect to indigenous industry was to create a fertile field that would sprout linkages with the multinational firms and result in a variety of benefits. Through sourcing and the creation of spin-off firms, the indigenous sector would grow. Employment experiences in the multinational sector would help Ireland quickly develop an entrepreneurial capacity. These outside influences would help the culture shift from paternalism to risk taking. Further, foreign firms would bring with them a new business climate that encouraged initiative and private enterprise, and would employ modern management techniques. As the evidence shows, the success of this industrial policy vision is especially apparent in the information economy. Total employment in Irish-owned manufacturing and internationally traded services -- where information-sector work is classified -- increased from 127,428 in 1991 to 148,349 in 1997, an increase of nearly 11% (IDA Ireland, 1998). Employment in indigenous software firms in 1997 more than doubled the 1993 level of 4,495. In that same time period the number of indigenous software firms grew from 336 to 561 (National Software Directorate, 1998a).

2.3 Education

In order to have a qualified labor force for the new jobs that were going to be coming from multinational and indigenous firms, it was important to raise the overall level of education of the potential workforce. It was also necessary to provide educational opportunities that were compatible with employment prospects. In particular, this meant developing a highly skilled workforce in electronics and other information-sector specializations. In this regard, Ireland's success has been mixed.

Completion rates to the end of the secondary school cycle reached 77% in 1996. While this is a significant improvement over the rates of 30 years ago, it is off the 90% target for the year 2000. With respect to vocational education, Ireland's preparation for work in the information economy is markedly different from that in other OECD countries. In contrast with the OECD average of 50% and 75% in some countries, only one-fifth of Irish secondary students enroll in vocational programs. Because of the traditional emphasis on general education up to the age of 18 fewer resources have been devoted to vocational and technical training. Recent initiatives and spending have tended to focus more on third level education. Consequently, Ireland has one of the highest third level attendance rates in the OECD. Education levels among the population aged 25 to 34 are considered high by international standards. Further, Ireland now produces more science and engineering graduates as a proportion of all graduates than any other OECD country except Japan. Despite such efforts the number of technology graduates has failed to keep up with demand to the point that an emerging skills shortage in the electronics and computer sectors threatens to impede future economic growth (The Economist Intelligence Unit, 1998).

2.4   Emigration

One approach to satisfying the demand for information-sector workers is consonant with another goal of the industrial policy: reversing the steady flow of young talent out of the country. As the industrial policy, in general, and the information economy, in particular, have taken hold this goal has been achieved. In 1998 there was a net migration of 22,800 (IDA Ireland, 1999), which shows no sign of abating. For the first time ever, Ireland has recently seen more people returning to work in Ireland than were leaving it to take up positions abroad (National Software Directorate, 1998b).

2.5   Economy

The changed industrial policy was intended to contribute in a significant way to Ireland's economic health. Opening the country up to foreign capital, technology and industry was to be the route to Ireland's increased participation in the world economy. Such participation, in turn, would create an overall competitive advantage for Ireland. Economic indicators of Ireland's success in this regard abound. An obvious one is the growth of the economy. Between 1993 and 1997 the economy expanded by 40%, with an average annual growth rate of 7.7% (The Economist Intelligence Unit, 1998). In 1997 the economy grew by 9.5%, the fastest growth rate in the OECD for the third successive year (Department of Foreign Affairs, 1999). For the four years to 1999 Ireland had the highest economic growth levels in Europe. The 1998 economy grew by over 9.1% and the projected growth for 1999 was 6.7% (IDA Ireland, 1999).

The growth of the economy is largely accounted for by the steep increase in manufacturing output. From 1992 to 1996 output levels increased by 55%, triple that of the mid-1980s. This increase in manufacturing output is the direct result of the information economy: the foreign-dominated, export-oriented, high technology sector has been responsible for most of the growth. By 1997 it produced over half of Ireland's total manufacturing output and over two-thirds of its manufacturing exports (The Economist Intelligence Unit, 1998). Another economic indicator is standard of living. In 1987 the standard of living -- measured in terms of private consumption per capita -- was 65% of the EU average. Ten years later it was 90% and overtook the UK (Department of Foreign Affairs, 1999; The Economist Intelligence Unit, 1998).

The role of the information sector in this economic success story can be seen in the performance of its various subsectors. In 1980 the electronics or hardware subsector accounted for 14% of Irish exports; in 1996 it was 30% (IDA Ireland, 1998). Once it was recognized as such, the software subsector was quickly incorporated into Ireland's industrial planning.[i] Successive Irish governments have recognized the software industry as a key strategic sector because it exploits the highly educated workforce, does not rely on natural resources that Ireland lacks and does not compromise the "green environment" (National Software Directorate, 1998b). Ireland is now the second largest exporter of software in the world after the United States and is the most important center within Europe for software localization (Enterprise Ireland, 1999). In 1997 electronics and software represented 40% of Ireland's exports (IDA Ireland, 1997b). The information services subsector has been the newest subsector of the information economy to be recognized and exploited. Ireland is now the top European location for telemarketing, customer support and technology services call centres (IDA Ireland, 1997a). Ireland has achieved competitive advantage through an industrial policy that increasingly emphasized its information economy. This fact is evident in the *World Competitiveness Report* that ranked Ireland in the top twenty-fifth percentile of industrialized countries (Department of Foreign Affairs, 1999).

2.6 Social Change

As Ireland pursued its economic and employment goals it also experienced a shift in perspective. This change resulted from the recognition that the effort to enact an industrial development policy that focused on new and clean industry was resulting in a diversified information economy. To varying degrees in different sectors of Irish society, there was also a conscious recognition that this change in economic and employment focus would result in social, political and psychological change as Irish people shifted from an inward- to an outward-orientation and from agrarian to information-sector employment. The tensions and contradictions that have been discussed in this book bear witness to these social, political and psychological changes. Coping with these changes is a work in progress. Success requires that Ireland maintain a balance between characteristics of the information economy and the particular characteristics of the Irish culture.

3.   FITTING THE INFORMATION ECONOMY
TO THE CULTURE

There is ample evidence in this book to support the argument that each information economy is distinctive. It is situated within a particular socio-cultural context that interacts with it. Further, the characteristics of this context can be used to support or impede the development of the information economy. In Ireland I found significant areas fit between the characteristics of the socio-cultural context and the characteristics of the information economy.

3.1   Information-sector Work

> *There is a view that people over 40 are too expensive and old fashioned. Therefore, it is hard for them to get employed. One has to get jobs commensurate with one's experience. Forty would be much too old for a financial controller. Too much experience is viewed as negative. You are less marketable with more experience. The attitude of flexibility is valued and older people are seen as resisting change and modern ideas. [Aidan]*

While work in the information sector is different from agricultural work, it is also different from work in the traditional, nonfarming employment sectors such as the civil service, manufacturing, banking and insurance. Information-sector work emphasizes intellectual rather than physical skills. The speed of technological innovation pushes for continuing change and creative responses. The resulting work is, therefore, highly dynamic.

Work in the Irish information sector was perceived as engaging the entire brain. While one might expect to hear information-sector workers and their managers in any part of the world discuss logical and technical skills as being important, it would be less typical to have them include verbal capabilities as well. But it was precisely in such areas that I found Ireland and Irish people particularly suited to information-sector work. Ironically, an unanswered question is what effect Ireland's rapid movement into information-sector employment will have on the traditional emphasis on a well-rounded education in which language arts is prominent. Will the movement to create information-sector employment shift the emphasis too much toward business and technical education and too far away from these subjects? I wondered out loud about all this to Niall with whom I had one of my earliest interviews. In his view, Irish workers and managers had a tremendous asset in their interest in and ability to carry on intelligent conversation about cultural and literary matters; he expected that advantage to continue.

The youth of the Irish population looms large in considerations of fit between socio-cultural characteristics and work in the information economy. Young workers were characterized as more flexible and open to new ideas, something seen as very important in the information technology industry where constant technological changes required quick response in order to keep up. Some respondents also observed that young people at their client sites showed greater willingness to accept new technology. The same thing held for the time needed to train them. Young people were more excited about new technology. Recent university graduates were considered more capable of keeping up with continuous technical demands on their own; you could just give them the manuals and they would figure it out.

As I reflected on Ireland's rapid movement into information-sector work I began to see the benefits of its agrarian starting point. I was reminded of a conversation I once had with an American high school teacher in a Pennsylvania steel town in the late 1970s. She was trying to explain to children whose families had for generations worked in the mills -- from the time that their immigrant ancestors came to America -- that the jobs they had always assumed would be there for them were disappearing. She tried to tell them that their generation should not expect to find employment in the mills. These children and their parents who had had a certain mindset about work, workplaces and "us-them" management, about using their hands not their heads were being told to embrace a type of work that was totally different. They were being told to prepare for work that required flexibility, would probably be nonunion and which would engage their minds more than their bodies.

My thoughts then turned to Ireland which largely skipped this industrial-era influence and went directly from the kind of agricultural work which is flexible, diversified and self-employed to information-sector work. Ireland stands in contrast to the US or the UK, countries in which workers had been doing industrial work for generations before moving on to IT work. In Ireland most people were going from a work situation of personal self-control directly into information-sector work.[ii] At the end of my reflection I saw the benefits of leapfrogging. A tradition of using one's head as well as one's hands, of flexibility, autonomy and independence made one suited for information-sector work. In fact, as they suggested in their comments about the traditional work sectors in Ireland, the Irish workers' frustration grew when they were put into a situation where these factors *did not* come into play.

Irish government officials described the Irish information-sector workers as hungry for intellectual challenge and the opportunity to use their minds. The emphasis on social interaction and having fun in the workplace did not preclude working hard. On the contrary, feeling stimulated was included among the items that contributed to a pleasant work environment. The respondents sought opportunities to use their minds and derived enjoyment from being challenged as well as by having interaction with co-workers. Nuala believed that time for socializing contributed to the workers' productivity. She commented about the need for "down time" in order for creativity and productivity to flourish.

Two characteristics emerged from this study, which, at first glance, might seem negative. Upon further reflection, however, they can be seen as having a positive influence on the information economy. One was a flexible attitude toward deadlines: what wasn't accomplished today would be done tomorrow. The other was the lack of discipline sometimes ascribed to Irish workers. While these could be perceived as negative traits, they can also be viewed as setting an example of appropriate work habits for creative endeavors -- such as information-sector work -- for others to emulate. The negative side to 'twill do and lack of discipline is abnegating responsibility. But the positive side is freedom from rigid procedures whether about the production of a product or the time frame for doing so. This flexibility not only accommodates the unforeseen, it also allows for unplanned but valuable social interaction.

However, creativity, like several other characteristics of information-sector work seemed to be at the same time consistent and in conflict with Irish culture. While examples abound about Irish creativity in the arts, there was also evidence that the education of the Irish workforce did not prepare it for work that required creativity.

> *When I was in school we were not able to be creative. We*
> *had to learn the three R's. [Elizabeth]*

Statements such as this suggest that the culture was stifling rather than supporting creativity. For example, an American expatriate talked about a training session in which workers were surprised to see that he actually listened to and valued their opinions. They were apprehensive at first about telling him their opinions. They didn't seem used to being asked their opinion or being asked to come up with solutions. They weren't used to being asked to be creative. They were still adjusting to the reason they were hired at his firm: not for their hands but for their *heads and* their hands.

After well educated, flexible was the next most frequently given reason that Ireland's exceptionally young labor force was particularly suited to information-sector work. The point was consistently made -- by young and old alike -- that flexibility was bound up with age. Nearly every respondent who commented about age noted the flexibility associated with this young workforce. A considerable degree of insight about the nature of information-sector work was embedded in commentary about age. Flexibility was directly related to being inexperienced in the minds of the people. Because the Irish workers were young, they were less experienced, but they were also more adaptable to change. Therefore, there was little resistance to changing methods, methodologies or technologies. Along with flexibility was the perception that young workers were more easily influenced, less conservative and more willing to embrace new ideas. Older people were more set in their ways and seemed to find it harder to change. Several middle-aged respondents commented on the way they had changed -- for the better -- since coming into contact with so many young people in the workplace.

Paul talked at length about his own life. He seemed to embody the issues and trade-offs associated with fitting information-sector work into the Irish culture. He said social life, life where he lived, married life all took precedence over career. However, he acknowledged that his desire to leave work on time because of family responsibilities separated him a bit from the younger workers without families who might think differently about working longer hours. Conversations with other respondents were consistent with his view that the volatility of the industry and the work seemed more suited to young people.

> *I found when I joined that people were working long hours and sacrificing to get on at [this firm], but now I find that enough is enough. Now I would rather do less amount of work and spend more time outside. I sometimes stand back and I ask myself, "What will I be thinking in ten years?" and looking back and there I was working very hard at this, and where did it get me, exactly? [Paul]*

3.2   Information-sector Workers

> *There was a jump from the eighteenth to the twentieth century. For example, workers were not used to eating together in a canteen. They were used to eating alone. And they would bring their tea in flasks. They would be uncomfortable having a conversation. They were used to working alone. This also showed up in resentment at having a boss and rules and regulations to follow. They also didn't consider it real work. After farming, it seemed too easy. This resulted in very high output. In fact, they were frustrated when there was no work to be done. They also found company meetings strange, when people would be asking for their input about company management. But they got over that quickly enough. Now they're involved a lot. They also want to extend their expertise. [Seamus]*

Seamus' memories about the early days of the information economy illustrate a few of the dimensions of the radical change that occurred in Irish employment when this sector was introduced. Along with industrial work habits, an industrial infrastructure was also underdeveloped. Roads to carry finished goods to ports, cities where industrial work went on, the development of a business mentality needed to run the factories, and a market for the finished goods were all only partially developed when Ireland began to import information-sector work. This led some Irish people to hold a less sanguine view of Ireland's status.

> *There's still a missing chunk to me, there's still a missing chunk of culture here. To me Ireland is still very much a developing country. So the fact that somebody is a computer whiz doesn't mean they're God. If you like, culture in depth, means their son may have it or their daughter may have it . . . but it takes time before you'll get . . .*
>
> *ET: Breadth of knowledge?*
>
> *Umm. Judgment. Perspective. It's a very hard thing to explain. I don't quite know what it is, but I think you're right. I think it's a breadth of knowledge, it's a tradition. What is a tradition? Tradition is inherited values; it's expertise. It's a whole mass of things. It's certain shared values. That, I think, still has to arrive. These are all the things about culture and*

expertise in Europe. And several generations were exposed to it whereas for Ireland it is still first or second generation, mostly. [Phillip]

That people from an agrarian background were not used to working set hours had both positive and negative dimensions. On the one hand, they were used to doing what it took to get the job done. On the other hand, because Anne had been at her firm since the beginning, she had witnessed the adjustment required of the earliest IT workers. Coming from agricultural work, they were not used to an environment that had set times and places for doing the work. On the other hand, they were used to working independently on small farms. She said people would just leave in the middle of the day. It would not be unusual to find workers from the plant milling about in the City Centre at all times of the day!

Among the positive results of an agrarian past were several links I was able to make between the nature of agrarian work in Ireland and information-sector work. Both can be done on a small scale and involve significant personal investment. This fact is especially relevant to indigenous IT firms. In both cases one is working to achieve some tangible goal, not simply putting in time at a large bureaucracy, as is often the case with traditional, industrial-era work. People coming from farming backgrounds seemed to bring a different value system to their work. Gerry talked about farming as a small business. You get quick feedback on your efforts. Within a year, you know whether your crops will fail, and your animals will live or die. That's your motivation. Your fate is in your own hands. In the Irish startup firm where he worked, individual efforts had a similarly direct impact. His contributions would typically be measurable within six months. The company was not big enough for one to blend into the background.

Despite the positive connections that can be made between farmers and information-sector workers, it has not always been easy for Americans to get beyond the observable differences in culture and work history. Early on, some firms had fears about how well Irish workers would make the transition from agrarian to information-sector work. Joseph, whose previous exposure to Irish culture had come from his immigrant grandparents, saw value in attending to both the similarities and the differences in the cultures.

I knew things about Ireland from hearing them from my grandparents. But, when people describe a place they usually only describe the differences between the two places. So that was my view, my whole perspective was this 20% [that was different] and so I had this concern that -- it's funny, it's

> *ridiculous when you look back on it -- I'd be trying to get*
> *people to come to work and they'd be down in the pubs,*
> *saying "Ah, don't worry about it. We'll get there when we*
> *have to." And it's not true at all. I mean, I look at the hours*
> *that people work here -- and this is probably a function of*
> *this being a start up situation -- we probably average ten*
> *hours a day here throughout the quarter. At the end of the*
> *quarter when we ship it's probably up to 13 hours a day. And*
> *in the US at the end of the quarter it would be similar.*
> *[Joseph]*

Some of the firms in my study were able to learn from the experiences of the earliest multinational firms in Ireland. They could capitalize upon the unique characteristics of the Irish work ethic and anticipate adjustment issues. The result was significantly enhanced productivity.

At the inception of the information economy in Ireland those workers with nonfarming experience had acquired the work habits imported from the UK. Workers in traditional sectors such as the civil service, manufacturing, banking and insurance were more rigid, less enthusiastic and required more supervision to be motivated.

> *So you would have the English influence. A lot of our*
> *industry essentially grew up along English lines. We would*
> *have taken our management practices from England. It's*
> *only with the advice of the Americans coming in, the*
> *Japanese coming in, opening up to Europe more, that we*
> *have seen where we actually look beyond England. It's*
> *something which is coming into the country, and you hear*
> *more often -- coming from government, the union people*
> *themselves, and various spokespersons from industry -- not to*
> *look to England any more. England is obviously not going*
> *that well at the moment from an economics point of view.*
> *They would say, why not look to France, look to Germany or*
> *the United States as examples, rather than England. [Neil]*

Ireland had no manufacturing because there were no raw materials. Therefore it was not encumbered with an infrastructure centered on manufacturing. This had positive consequences for rapid development of an IT labor force. Countries such as the UK, in contrast, had to switch from a focus on heavy technology to preparation for the information economy. "It's like turning the Queen Mary around," Seamus told me. They had to stop and evaluate their position, change management structures, and change the universities. Ireland, in contrast, was poised for quick response. It had more of an open mind. For example, his firm successfully implemented creative policies about attendance in response to issues about tardiness, and absenteeism during "the season" (for planting and harvesting). His company implemented flex time and productivity (i.e. output) measures for evaluation rather than time spent at work. This resulted in much greater productivity. Ireland's direct leap into information-sector work was perceived as yielding both benefits and challenges.

The younger workers in the information sector entered without prior work experience and habits. This was to their benefit, it seemed. These new workers had none of the rigid attitudes characteristic of workers used to assembly line work. Quite often during discussions of this topic both Irish and American people said that since there had never been an industrial revolution in Ireland there were not the "bad habits" to overcome.

> *I think the Irish generally have a flexible attitude. I think in all honesty if somebody came in Monday morning, and it was explained to them that from now on we're going to be doing it this way, that is not as much a problem to the Irish as it can be for the more industrial revolution background English person. In other words, from what I've seen particularly of the midlands and the north of England, people like their job to be very stable and very certain. And [trouble at mill] type background where, "I've been using this machine for the last 12 years and nobody's going to make me change this machine unless they give me extra money," and all that [doesn't occur here], I think, because we're glad to get jobs, because we're reasonably well educated. And I make a big distinction here between average education in Ireland, which is now into Leaving Cert and the UK where they stop at the O levels. [Declan]*

For good and for bad, Ireland had less of an industrial base as it forged ahead into its information economy. It didn't have the business and production-oriented workplace habits derived from industrialism. But neither did it have as much baggage such as rigid job definitions, worker-management divisions and resistance to change, dimensions that are challenged by the information economy. As a result, the makeup of the Irish information-sector worker fits with the demands of the information economy. The characteristics that Tapscott (1998) ascribes to the newest generation of information-society workers, the "Net-Generation," are a very close fit with those of information-sector workers in Ireland.[iii]

3.3   Information-sector Workplaces

> *ET: Does this attitude come from agrarian life? Where*
> *you're run by the seasons rather than the clock? I heard*
> *a joke where somebody says, "What time is it?" and the*
> *answer is, "Half past Spring." ...*

> *You could well be right, that's an agrarian thing. You know,*
> *when the cows need milking you decide you're going to do*
> *that, and when that's finished you go off and do the next*
> *thing you're going to do. [Sue]*

Information-sector workers did not have work habits sunk deep in the soil of the industrial era; their work history was intricately entwined with agrarian roots. Some of these workers had only recently left farming; others continued to work a farm even as they came to work at the information technology firms. For many, farming had been the family tradition for generations. There were several connections to the agrarian life represented in the people with whom I spoke. One was that the vast majority of people doing information-sector work -- or their parents -- had worked in farming. They might have been the children who did not inherit the farm or those whose parents had left the farm. But the country was still in their lives, and they talked about going down country for holidays and weekends. Another type of connection was the person who still lived on a farm but who commuted to an IT firm to work because the farm could not support him or her. Despite the fact that their IT job was their primary source of income, some still saw themselves as rural people. These people worked at plants that were primarily in rural areas and the workers still lived on the farm. Some of them commuted as much as 100 kilometers to work. They identified with the farming class.

Information-sector workers with these backgrounds brought an approach to their jobs that reflected the agrarian influences on their lives. Agrarian work is holistic, requiring flexibility and adaptability. Farming in Ireland was at the same time an independent activity and a group endeavor. Farmers were autonomous, independent workers when operating their individual farms. But when in came to harvesting, a team-orientation was required. In this regard, agrarian work is like information-sector work: independent yet collaborative, individual yet holistic, carried out in a balanced and informal way.

Frank, an Irish human resources manager at one of the multinational firms, believed that Irish workers were particularly suited to adopt new work methods such as world class manufacturing. They wanted flexibility and autonomy. They were motivated to be multitrained and to exert self-determination and control over what they did. Irish workers liked to question decisions and procedures. This questioning was closely aligned with the desire for autonomy and some degree of control over their work. Margie commented that her work group didn't really need a supervisor. She believed they could work things out themselves. They didn't need someone standing over them.

At the same time that autonomy and personal control are needed for information-sector work, there is also a need for collaboration. There were contradictory viewpoints on this topic. Respondents discussed a reluctance to adopt or demand a group view in the workplace, which several said, made the Irish not so inclined toward teamwork. In one woman's view the natural individualism of Irish people resulted in some workplace problems she experienced regarding teamwork. She believed that considerable training was needed in order to be able to think in terms of teams. People liked to do their own thing; they didn't like to work on teams. The desire for personal autonomy outweighed even the Irish interest in sociability. One manager explained that an emphasis on social interaction didn't necessarily affect team behavior. He said Irish sociability meant you could talk easily to somebody for an hour at a time but it didn't necessarily mean that you identified yourself as part of a group of people.

Nevertheless, there was ample evidence of a cooperative spirit in carrying out the work. People were described as more willing than their American counterparts to learn about another person's job or to fill in where needed. The story about workers at an American plant going to another plant to borrow a part, illustrates the personal, helpful atmosphere that existed. Some respondents went back to Ireland's agricultural past, noting that working together in information-sector work came naturally to the young, Irish IT workers used to coming together to save the hay. It was the duality of people coming together for a task while remaining fiercely independent. Perhaps the term *cooperative* rather than *team* captures the essence of the group interaction that occurred in the Irish information-sector workplace.

The collaborative aspect of the work that was quite appealing to the Irish workers was tied to its informality. Managers and workers in the IT firms were all on a first name basis, ate in the same canteen, and used the same rest rooms. The markers of status that existed in other sectors were absent from information-sector firms. Several respondents drew upon experiences working in the UK and made comparisons with the British work environment in order to make a point about the Irish information-sector workplace. Nuala spoke of how the absence of an industrial history in Ireland had benefited engineers by according them a higher status than they had in the UK. At the beginning of the industrial revolution, she explained, British engineers emerged from the ranks of craftsmen, and hence were associated with the working class. Britain applied its rigid class structure to this new industrial setting with the result that management was considered part of the upper class and workers (including engineers) constituted the working class. These origins kept engineers in the category of working class. In contrast, because Ireland had no such industrial history engineers had emerged, not from working class origins (the ranks of craftsmen), but from educational origins (universities). Since Ireland had no industrial era attitudes about technical workers and because Ireland was less hierarchical, she said, people who could do the technical job in Ireland were well regarded for it.

When asked to describe the work atmosphere in the information-sector companies, the respondents often drew comparisons with employment in other sectors. The civil service was very status conscious. You only speak to one level of management, your direct manager. It was a very formal management system. In contrast, while one of the long established multinational IT firms did have a formal management system, the management personnel didn't always use it. Even though there was a protocol the managing director would talk to anyone; he knew most of the workers by their first names. Nor would he be called "Mister." The respondent who was making this comment noted that at the firm's UK office, his equivalent would have had to go through seven levels to talk to the managing director! So, obviously, the chances of that happening were very remote, he said. Emphasis on the social element combined with a less hierarchical organization resulted in a more person-oriented work environment than in the IT sectors of some other countries or other work sectors in Ireland. The natural informality of work that could not neatly delineate management and workers sat well with Irish workers who did not stand on formality. Liam mentioned a college friend who worked at a Japanese company. The firm had great problems in the beginning because the Japanese could not cope with the Irish people, and their undisciplined and unstructured behavior, the friend said. Irish people weren't predictable enough.

In order to cope with these competing demands, maintaining a sense of balance was crucial. Not only was balance needed between the collaborative and the individual aspects of the work, it was also needed between the private and the professional spheres of one's life. Therefore, despite the high energy levels required for work in the information sector, both Irish and American respondents were consistent in their depiction of Irish IT workers as placing a priority on maintaining balance in their lives.

> *The Irish work to live, not visa versa like the Germans. Work doesn't come first. We have a balanced way of life. [Matthew]*

****

> *Quality of life is a good salary, life after work, don't bring work home, flexible hours. [Colm]*

Quality of life in Ireland was not primarily defined in terms of material benefit as embodied in the term standard of living. Rather, quality of life in Ireland was about friendliness, acquaintances and contact with people. And in order to achieve these things people needed sufficient time. Therefore, maintaining balance also had implications for material wealth and time.

Against these generally positive views of the information-sector workplace is Finnegan and Murray's (1999) warning to the Irish software sector. Their survey of the top 100 software organizations in Ireland revealed relatively low emphasis on the management of human resources, in general, and teams, in particular. The concept of a team was shallow and did not emphasize what made a true team. The majority of the software organizations in their study had the individual, not the software team, as the basis for operations. However, the need to pay attention to teams in software development work is supported by their finding that those organizations that provided sufficient resources to software teams had lower staff turnover rates than those that didn't.

Hints about one question that looms on the horizon were given in the interviews. While respondents generally praised the workplace atmosphere and management at the multinational information-sector firms, a few made comments about the "old days" in the 1980s when the work environment was even better because the industry was doing better. This gives one pause to consider the depth of management's commitment to workplace "hygiene" factors. If the information-sector firms experience economic downturns, will the commitment to human resource management policies change?

4.   THE CHALLENGES OF THE
INFORMATION ECONOMY

Lingering in the wings of its significant success are challenges that Ireland must address. Some of these challenges come from Ireland's history. Others are embedded in its culture and society. Even as many socio-cultural characteristics serve to further Ireland's progress into the information economy, there are some that could hold it back.[iv] These challenges emerged from the landscape I visited just before the dawn of economic benefits resulting from Ireland's changed industrial policy. Changes and adaptation have occurred in the ensuing years, but challenges remain.

4.1   Supporting Entrepreneurship and Risk

> *ET: What about the lack of anonymity in this country? Again, the small population. Do you think that affects people's risk taking behavior?*
>
> *Definitely. Almost certainly. The Irish who travel abroad are much bigger risk takers. Much more entrepreneurial. [Martin]*

The entrepreneurial nature of information-sector work is both complex and challenging to understand, and appeared to fit uneasily with Irish culture. My respondents offered a range of viewpoints about the Irish attitude toward risk taking. At one end of the continuum was the belief that Irish people were less willing to take risks because if they did and failed everyone would know about it and would hold it against them. At the other extreme was the belief that there was no sanction on failure. The more frequent viewpoint was the former: Irish people were not risk takers because they had the fear of "I told you so." Failure was taken to heart personally. If people failed they felt that others disapproved of them.

> *ET: You mentioned that the Irish didn't have the entrepreneurial instinct. Is that a function of this "everybody's going to know" if you fail?*
>
> *I think so. . . There's an element of scandal there, business failure.*
>
> *ET: In America there's also an attitude about entrepreneurship [and those who fail]. They almost have an elevated status.*

Yes. They've been to the rough edge. At least they tried. But they tried and failed. That would be the opposite in Ireland. I think in Ireland it's a little more begrudging and provincial. People aren't generous to somebody who's failed. There's a distinct fear of failure in Ireland. Certainly, there is a fear of failure. There is no question about that. There's too little entrepreneurship. It's not that it's too easy to live without it, but a lot of people would settle for less rather than stretching and taking that extra risk. And resent those who do. [Martin]

This excerpt from an interview with Martin summed up the basic attitude toward risk that I kept hearing again and again: Irish people who traveled abroad were much bigger risk takers; they were able to spread their entrepreneurial wings whereas in Ireland they felt held back. In the US, for example, no one cared if someone failed; it didn't follow one around in the way it did in Ireland where there would be an element of scandal. Therefore, a high premium was placed on avoiding risk, of not being seen as a failure. This aversion to risk taking that impeded entrepreneurship had a myriad of antecedents: economic, historical, societal, cultural and religious.

It's not to say there isn't venture funding in Ireland for entrepreneurs, but there isn't the same entrepreneurial infrastructure. Maybe it's because the economy [in western Europe] is a bit smaller. It won't have the blazing success story but certainly it's got some. But you haven't had them as obvious as you have them in the States. [Martin]

The economic explanation was that economic conditions within the country inhibited risk taking and entrepreneurial ventures. Ireland did not have a sufficient economic infrastructure including venture funding.[v] Consequently, if an Irish person invented something he or she would be inclined to sell it rather than develop it and bring it to market. In addition, there wasn't sufficient economic payback for taking risks. Irish entrepreneurs expressed a view that government red tape could strangle little companies while the established government agencies weren't as helpful as they could be. Some of these entrepreneurs believed that agencies such as the IDA were too conservative, were not interested in providing funding for new, unproven ventures. This was especially a problem for software firms. Some claimed that Choras Trachtala (the Irish Export Board), for example, did not sufficiently understand the kinds of small Irish firms that *developed* software. It only understood large, multinational firms in Ireland like Microsoft or Lotus that were *publishing* software. CTT only seemed to understand the software subsector in Ireland insofar as it was about taking an essentially American product and internationalizing it. They felt that in order to be able to obtain venture funding, software development firms first had to educate such government agencies. There was a general feeling among these entrepreneurs that the government agencies were too conservative to be of much help and although schemes existed to help new ventures, the help didn't become available until after the need had passed.[vi]

Economic considerations influenced not only the entrepreneurs but also the workers at these start-up firms. Some respondents chose to work at a multinational firm for economic security, whereas if they were young and unencumbered, they said, they would have preferred to work for a start-up firm. With a family and mortgage, these people wanted to reduce the insecurity associated with the IT industry. Older people cared too much about job security whereas young people did not think about disasters and were more willing to take risks. Once again, the youth of the information-sector workers appeared to be a crucial factor.

Other explanations for the diminished entrepreneurial spirit dipped into a complex mixture of historical, sociological and cultural influences.[vii] The typical historical explanation was that in colonial times entrepreneurs would have been those in the power structure. Therefore, the feeling went, others who had initiative were seen to be getting above themselves. Thus, came the malicious satisfaction in seeing people fail. Additional historical explanations are also part of the legacy of colonialism. One was that colonial policies that favored Britain kept Ireland vulnerable to economic forces. Consequently, Irish people adopted cautious economic strategies designed to assure survival and avoid risk. I heard repeated reference to "permanent and pensionable" jobs both inside and outside the information-sector firms. The typical Irish worker's history was more likely that of a worker than a manager or entrepreneur. The Irish adult would likely be working for somebody else and the message that a young person received was to "get the job" and hold onto it. There was little exposure to the option of being an entrepreneur. Since Ireland wasn't an active player in the industrial revolution no entrepreneurship class developed. As a result, there is little entrepreneurship history in Ireland. The paucity of industrial work also meant there didn't develop in people much of a sense of business or of taking control. A final colonial influence was that people developed techniques of guerilla warfare instead of exposing themselves. The carryover was that while the Irish didn't brag neither were they risk takers.

These historical influences were heightened by cultural factors that encouraged Irish people to be cautious.

People are more defensive. I think they're more grudging of success. And I think basically there's an underlying class structure . . . which can be very demotivating and gradually be an impediment to people's ambition which is the base of it. Whereas in the US, it's more open in terms of, they don't really want to know what your dad did or whether you're monied or not before you start. Basically, it's what you can do, or what you've done. That's certainly our perception. [Martin]

An important dimension of the attitude toward entrepreneurship was perceived peer pressure that kept people from moving outside their socio-economic status. People tended to stay in the same social class structure if they stayed in their home environments. There was a cultural unwillingness to let people progress. For all these reasons there was resentment toward entrepreneurs, toward those trying to get ahead.

As far as holding it against you, if there were two guys talking and one had a business that failed, the other would say, "I knew it couldn't be done," and would be glad, or "Arragh, they'll never make it." [William]

Fear of failure was another cultural inhibitor to risk taking that cut like a double-edged sword. Given the entrepreneurial nature of information-sector work, this culturally pervasive fear of failure posed a challenge to those in the Irish information sector. This challenge was exacerbated by the lack of anonymity. Because of Ireland's small population and even smaller IT population, there was little anonymity. In addition, large parts of the information sector such as the software subsector were located in and around Dublin, which further reduced anonymity. And not only would everyone know if you failed but they would also hold it against you.

ET: I have been told that people are not risk-takers.

I would agree with that.

ET: And I have been told, not by everybody, but I have been told by more than one person that if you try something and you fail, everybody's going to know about it for one thing. Plus they might hold it against you.

You yourself would feel you've been a failure; it'll make you not want to get up and go on again. You feel, "I'm a failure." We were talking about something like that the other day. We

were just discussing how they suddenly -- down the street --
[appeared] as a new company. These guys obviously weren't
put off by their failure. Maybe they were responsible, maybe
they actually closed down the business and did willingly, but
by and large, an Irish person who was failing anyway, who
hasn't measured up to what was expected of him, must
certainly feel upset by that he's failed, regardless even if
people say nothing. He'll still feel that they're looking at you,
that they're saying something without talking. [Charles]

They would also remember. Consequently, one whose business failed
would feel he or she had been a failure as a person. One young man
acknowledged that even though he had entrepreneurial tendencies, fear of
failing would make him more cautious. When I asked him about the social
stigma attached to failure, he said unless people were strong willed it would
be difficult to get back on their feet. If he failed at a business, he said he
would definitely hide it on his resume. Another person said failure was taken
to heart personally. If she failed, she would feel that others disapproved of her.
A third respondent talked about people getting great social mileage by giving
interviews about someone they knew well whose business failed and how they
had known that the person would not achieve, that he or she was
overreaching. The overall effect of "everybody knows everybody" was
inhibition among Irish entrepreneurs and the end result was a form of self-
censorship, which held people back.[viii]

Another dimension of fear of failure went to the heart of the Irish value
system. The notion of social conscience came into play when the topic of risk
taking and entrepreneurship was being discussed. People who started a
business were seen as having responsibility for those whom they employed.
Irish entrepreneurs recognized that when a company failed the creditors and
employees also suffered. The influence of religious values was evident in a
view of business responsibility that extended beyond the office doors and into
the community.

I mean, certainly, I think there is an ideal of a Catholic
employer who looks after his employees in a very
paternalistic way. [Gerald]

The influence of religion on entrepreneurship was felt in other ways. Part
of the reason for avoiding risk and the apparent lack of entrepreneurship in
Ireland was that Irish people didn't seem to be all that interested in it. This
connects to the lower level of materialism that I witnessed in the country.
Indeed, one person commented that the reason the Irish were not risk takers

was not because of the absence of anonymity and the fear of everyone knowing, but rather that they were content with the status quo.

However, not all respondents felt that Ireland was stuck in a pattern of low risk taking due to a lack of anonymity, a begrudging attitude and deep-seated fear of failure. A minority of respondents suggested that more important issue was not whether one's business failed but rather how one handled it.

> *In Ireland you're actually allowed to fail and you can try and try and try again. And it doesn't really bother people. There's one guy, he tried supermarkets, he tried pubs and he tried everything. And every time he had a big publicity stunt, you know. Didn't cost him anything, he always went back in for whatever he wanted to do.*

> *ET: No one thinks badly of him for failing?*

> *No. Because it's more how you come across, you know? If you were enthusiastic -- and you will find a lot of Irish people are enthusiastic about everything -- it counts. But if you were a sulking person, needless to say, if you failed, you know, you deserved it, didn't you? [Rosemary]*

According to this view, if you failed nobody really noticed. A person may think others were looking at him or her but, in truth, nobody cared much because Irish people didn't get that excited about such things. The Irish didn't give people swollen heads over achievement and they ignored failure as well. Rebutting the fear of failure argument was the claim that entrepreneurs in Ireland had a fairly "hard neck" and bounced back. These respondents noted several entrepreneurs whose companies went under and a year or two later were back in business with people thinking highly of them. The social stigma tended to be forgotten. These respondents believed that the small population made for higher risks because of the smaller market and, therefore, if people failed for honest reasons, no one held it against them.

Among those with a more positive outlook on risk taking in Ireland was a consistently expressed opinion that the new generation of entrepreneurs represented a distinct departure from the past. While it was true that Ireland had long been a begrudging society, the modern entrepreneurs were operating in a different milieu. While the lack of anonymity may have inhibited people 20 or 30 years before, it was not inhibiting the younger generation. The high premium placed on the avoidance of risk and the perception of being a failure was less prevalent among the younger generation. Cahal thought people his age and younger did not see the stigma of failure. They had more of the "go for it" attitude than the older people who had come of age in a different world. In the old world there were fewer options, people were far less mobile and there were fewer things within one's grasp.

> *It's not the same in America where they say, "Well good luck to you, you tried." What you tend to find here is that if somebody succeeds, you tend begrudge them for it. As a nation, we're slightly begrudging people who do well. We can be. It depends on how it works. And it just may depend on the humor of the day. We can be begrudging people. If you've got the right attitude that's not going to stop you any. And any of the people I've met who refer to themselves as entrepreneurs, here, tend to bounce back. They just don't care. [Cahal]*

Adding to this was the fact that the economic environment was encouraging greater risk taking. Historically, the Irish -- including those in IT -- might have gone with a sure thing. But the job insecurity in established multinational firms during the late 1980s and early 1990s was changing that. People had begun to feel that they didn't have as much to lose.

When probing the undercurrents of entrepreneurship and risk I found myself back in discussions of social class and colonial history which seemed to be the source of societal norms and values that were inclined to hold one back. Ireland's class structure had served to demotivate and impede people's ambition. Looking into Ireland's past, one respondent connected social class and the work ethic. A strict dichotomy in the Irish class system between the "ruling class" and the "ruled class" influenced attitudes into the present toward both authority and initiative: the "ruled class" rejected authority and possessed less initiative. Further, there was peer pressure not to stand out or be seen as too successful. Symbolic of this attitude, the grading structure at one of the information-sector firms kept people from rising through the ranks too quickly. Promotions came from filling an open position, not as a reward for a job well done. The concept of merit pay and reward for performance, they said, would be hard to implement in Ireland.

4.2   Building Wealth

> *You know, as a nation, I don't think we're never proud enough of what we have achieved. But, again, you have to go back to our own culture. Again, the Irish tend to always be very modest about their achievements. Modest, in a way,*

among ourselves and jealous as well . . . You build somebody up when they have nothing. And as soon as you think they have it, out with the hurdles.

ET: Why the jealousy?

I dunno. Maybe it goes back, again, to the old days where you had the British landlord system. And you resented those who had anything to do with the British aristocracy. Again, I think in our generation you see it changing. A bit more sensible. But you see that in my generation, not so much in my parent's generation. With my parents there was more modesty. People didn't openly display any signs of wealth for fear of the "attitude problems."

ET: What is the fear?

It's the fear of what the neighbors would think.

ET: If you display signs of wealth that shows that you're successful?

In my parents' generation -- in the late 50s and 60s -- Ireland had very little industry. It's only in the past ten years that things are changing.

ET: And you don't want to display signs of wealth because people are going to begrudge you your success?

Yes. [Robert]

The good news about working in the information sector was that it was a valued activity within the global economy. However, insofar as Irish people were successfully engaging in information-sector work, there was an interesting challenge at hand. As a nation, Irish people would have to come to terms with the reality of being economically successful, and with ambivalence about the attendant materials signs of wealth. Evidence of a deep inner conflict about success came out in the way people spoke about this topic. People on the verge of "succeeding" in the workplace, of moving into management, felt a sense of betrayal to "their people" if they did. Those who displayed signs of material wealth were looked down upon. Perhaps because Irish people were unable to succeed for so many generations, not being successful became part of the culture.

4.2.1   Begrudging

> *We are called "a nation of begrudgers." That is a typical*
> *description. It means being critical of other people's success.*
> *But I don't really find that to be true. What I think is that*
> *there is no tolerance of posing and posturing. I also think we*
> *are not positive enough. In one sense, we don't complain*
> *enough like in restaurants. On the other hand, we don't give*
> *much praise either. [Eileen]*

Everyone understood what it meant to be called "a nation of begrudgers."
And everyone acknowledged its presence in Irish culture. The only
disagreement was over the extent to which this attitude influenced behavior.
Some characterized it as wishing people bad; others called it just plain
jealousy. A third group described begrudging as doubting the legitimacy of
another's achievement.

> *Where somebody's a success, people always "knock" that in*
> *people and say, "Well, he must've been cheating on his*
> *taxes." [Sue]*

In searching for the origins of this cultural trait, a simplistic explanation came
from the fact that people had tended to live their whole lives in the same
vicinity. As families grew up within sight of each other, everyone came to
know everyone's dark secrets. And scandal made for better stories than
beneficence.

> *"Oh, he's the one who committed suicide back in 1935." You*
> *get all the scandals going back in time. [Michael]*

But generations of people have lived in small villages in other cultures that
do not exhibit such an attitude toward success. So the explanation for the low
tolerance for posturing or displaying signs of wealth must be found elsewhere.
Some reached back to Ireland's colonial past for the explanation.

> *Sure and didn't I know your father!*

> *Didn't your father come into town on a bicycle?*

> *"Who is he, he's only an Irish Catholic? Why should he own*
> *property? Why should he do better? I knew his father." That*
> *was the old expression. "I knew his father. He had patches in*
> *his britches." [Michael]*

That this attitude toward success did not extend into the multinational firms suggested that some of this begrudgery was rooted in a deep-seated insecurity. This double standard was part of the reason why Irish were said to do better abroad than at home.

> *If, for argument's sake, I wanted to set up a factory or do something. There is a begrudging attitude to Irish people who have gotten successful. If a foreign company comes in and sets up and employs people, that's OK. They're foreign. But if a local does it, there is the attitude, "Well, who does he think he is, setting up a factory and thinking he can employ people? He only went to the school down the road. He's no better the rest of us." There's this strange attitude that we have a place and if Digital comes in from the States and sets up a factory and employs 2000 people, well, after all, they're American. It takes a long time to actually believe that anybody anywhere, if they're positively motivated, can achieve. Irish people tend to achieve more when they go abroad. You've got Tony, the head of the Heinz Corporation, Tony O'Reilly. People say, "Well, after all, he left Ireland, and he got into these bigger circles, but if he was here, just working as an Irish entrepreneur, he wouldn't necessarily have got so far." [Francis]*

The most common interpretation of this term was peer pressure not to succeed or resentment toward those attempting to rise above their station. Part of this was a reluctance to stand out in a crowd, part was jealousy of those who attempted to. It was also reflective of a zero-sum mentality: if one person wins it means the others have lost.

Look at yer man; who does he think he is?

Another unanswered question about the inheritance of begrudgery was the implication for management styles. Begrudgery came into play in the workplace when managers behaved as though they had achieved a higher plane altogether and would begin to look down on their colleagues. Then, when such people happened to fall off their pedestals, they got what they deserved. The managerial challenge was determining how much personal credit to take. If you insisted on being individualistic, I learned, and you wanted to do everything yourself, and you wanted to take all the credit for something, then you were left on your own. Whereas if you adopted a management style that recognized and attributed good ideas to others, you would have fewer problems. A potentially more sinister influence of begrudgery on information-sector work was the reluctance to accept an Irish IT entrepreneur.

> *Whereas in the US if there's a 35 year old guy who started his own company, everyone would think, "This guy is great!" He'd be envied, like. He'd be considered successful in the United States. And over here, they'd doubt it, you know? They'd be questioning. It would be just different, they wouldn't recognize it. [Joseph]*

4.2.2   Embarrassment of Riches

> *Built in [are] the ethic and codes of behavior for a long time. The attitude toward authority is one of them. I think the attitude toward success is another. Don't appear to be successful. Because it'll be taken away from you. It'll draw attention to you. [Sue]*

If the begrudging attitude toward those who succeeded wasn't enough of an impediment to the information-sector entrepreneur, an internalized ambivalence toward materialism added to the dilemma of one pursuing a success track by taking advantage of the opportunities found in the information economy. At its most benign, this cultural attitude was expressed as simply a lower level of materialism, less of a "rat race" in Ireland than what existed elsewhere.

> *The Irish are not as materialistic as the Americans. [Sue]*

Patricia was living in Dublin when we talked. She complained that materialism was on the rise and criticized her friends back home in Limerick who seemed to be caught up in "keeping up with the Joneses."

Progressing along the continuum toward more sinister effects I discovered an attitude of low expectations. In discussing this topic with my respondents I pointed out that America was deeply influenced by an immigrant ethic in which people wanted their children to do better than they. So it was almost expected that the next generation was going to be another step up on the economic ladder. That was not the case in Ireland, however.

> *I think in Ireland a lot of people wouldn't necessarily have that expectancy. If they did have, they would expect to have to go abroad more. The self-made man in Ireland, sometimes becomes an item, becomes a target, not least because very*

often he can't hold up his head and let success rest easily on his shoulders. It's not like California where, so you're successful, but then so's everybody else in that pub on a Friday night. They've done well. In Ireland that would be rare. [Martin]

A third attitude was that it was wrong to be materialistic. Stephen argued that the lack of entrepreneurial spirit in Ireland was a failure of education and personal development, not of Irish nature. He pointed to Irish successes abroad as evidence of what could be achieved when Irish people were taken out of this framework.

It is a conflict between this world and the next. The pursuit of material gain is not seen as positive. Therefore people have to balance their own values and the values present in their ambitions.

ET: Does this value conflict come from the Church?

Not consciously. I consider myself a good Catholic. But there is a distribution of caring values passed on from one generation to the next. Also involved in this is frowning on success; having envy of success in the bitter sense. [Stephen]

Finally, if one did manage to become wealthy, it certainly didn't do to display it. Those with whom I discussed this topic said that Americans who did well declared it openly. In Ireland they wouldn't declare it and would become the target of jealousy of they did. This attitude made itself felt in subtle ways. Whereas highly successful people in American society tended to wear their success openly and display it in their dress, automobiles and homes, Sue noticed that it was very common for people who were well paid and were high in their professions to have a very limited wardrobe, and never think much about it.

Lack of anonymity and aversion to risk were not the only challenges to entrepreneurship. As I was conducting this research it was unclear whether a diminished emphasis on wealth and ambition, or at least displays of such, would diminish entrepreneurial instincts among those participating in Ireland's emerging information sector. There are two potential ways in which information-sector work could be influenced by the attitude toward materialism. One would be that a low emphasis on materialism might lead to lower motivation to succeed. If people weren't as interested in becoming personally wealthy, they might not put as much effort into wealth generating activities. The second influence would be that because the Irish were not as materialistic it was more of a challenge to motivate them. Since it was not as easy to motivate them with financial rewards, motivation became subtler. Instead of simply financial reward, the motivation had to come from recognition of skill and achievement. There was a greater unwillingness to display wealth, less of a willingness to accept wealth as a virtue and certainly less acceptance of wealth that was achieved.

4.2.3   Gombeen Man

> *The gombeen man is from the famine times. He was the "cute" man who ran a shop and who abused his position to get people into debt to him. He was therefore discretely doing well. It has carried to this day to refer to someone who has the trappings of wealth. The gombeen man was obviously hated. [Louise]*

At various times during my conversations with Irish people about success, wealth and begrudgery this gombeen man would join us. The context was usually my question about why the Irish culture frowned upon displays of wealth. To be labeled a gombeen man implied that one was making money at the expense of one's own people. Doing so when there was an occupying army meant being disloyal to your own kind. Since those being oppressed should stick together, one who was making money off of other oppressed people was rebuked. The extension of this line of thinking into the present was that making money meant having dealings with the oppressor. At the same time, there was also an element of envy. While the gombeen man was despised he was also envied for feathering his own nest. Thus, the gombeen man became another layer of "the enemy." Some of the antipathy toward the gombeen man of the past had been transferred to the contemporary entrepreneur. This helped to explain the begrudging tendency:

> *If you are successful, you must be doing something underhanded. [Margaret]*

The legacy of the gombeen man was felt in several ways with respect to wealth. One was distaste for people "putting on airs." Charles' story about the treatment of the young man who came back from England with an affected manner emphasized the importance of remembering who you are.

While there was considerable commonality of view about the sanction on displays of wealth, a minority and contrary opinion was represented in the views of Richard, one of the few Protestant Anglo-Irish respondents with whom I spoke. In his view, the trappings of success were *very* noticeable in Ireland. He attributed this to Ireland's relatively recent emancipation.

> *Probably that has something to do with the fact that it's a nouveau riche society, basically. It's really, only two generations, really, of successful Irish people. And I'm sure that right throughout the world nouveau riche people tend to go for the trappings of success. [Richard]*

Eileen, who was Irish Catholic, concurred with this viewpoint. She spoke of people with working class roots who had worked their way into the middle class. She thought their emphasis on possessions was overdone.

> *Like they're trying to prove something. [Eileen]*

Despite these ominous clouds on the horizon, there were definite signs that the impact of the information economy was being felt in attitudes toward materialism. With information-sector work came more money and perhaps more desire for material possessions. Young workers in the information sector -- especially those with two household incomes -- received nice salaries and had more purchasing power than their parents. Joseph used his encounter with an Irish woman, a self-proclaimed "yuppie" to make this point.

> *I remember she said to me after she had been working awhile, "'Yuppie,' they look at as degrading," she says, "I like that, I want to be a 'yuppie'." And she loves America, you know. And I think she resents what she thinks she doesn't have. [Joseph]*

As Irish IT workers have had greater opportunity to travel to the US and other countries they have brought back new and different notions about wealth and material possessions. Further, once a few began to improve their material standing, it was thought, a "snowball effect" might result in others following suit.

> *Irish are not less materialistic than Americans. When everyone is a "have not" then it's OK. But once one person begins to get more, then they become status oriented. They want recognition by way of symbols like the company car to show they have arrived. [Charlene]*

The extent to which materialism would change with changing economic fortunes is an open question. Nevertheless, the deep ambivalence about success and the amount of economic reward one wanted to attain would continue to leave its mark upon those engaged in information-sector work. To a person like myself who comes from a strongly capitalist nation such as the United States, the ambivalence about wealth seemed strange indeed.

> *I think that Ireland and Europe are socialistic in their*
> *outlook whereas the US is capitalistic. You can see this when*
> *you look at the social welfare plans of Ireland and Europe vs.*
> *the US. We are more paternalistic. I have talked to many*
> *people in the US who were surprised to learn that the EU had*
> *a social charter. They thought it was just an economic union.*
> *[Frank]*

But the need to balance materialism and ambition with social values and historic resentment of success was deeply felt among those engaged in information-sector work in Ireland. The cultural value placed upon maintaining this sense of balance came across in a multitude of contexts. For example, in describing one of the political parties in Ireland, Martin, himself an advocate of Irish capitalism, explained:

> *It's a party, I think myself, that has grown with the culture*
> *and the politics, between begrudgery and the charity values*
> *[of its leader]. [Martin]*

4.3   Removing Barriers

> *I would say -- again, I'm talking narrowly, because there are*
> *a lot of young people who aren't so well educated, and our*
> *industry tends not to attract those -- for the group that have*
> *been to third level colleges of one type or another, I'd have to*
> *say I find it very highly [encouraging]. In fact, I'd say they're*
> *exceptionally highly motivated. What they're doing is*
> *actually putting the effort in to live here if they can. That may*
> *sound strange, but I think that's a high motivation. I think*
> *they actually come to a very mature judgment within two to*
> *three years of leaving college. I think they have a darn good*
> *life here in the high tech sector. If things go right for that*
> *particular company, that sector. If things go right for them.*
> *The people I feel sorry for are the less educated younger*
> *people whose opportunity abroad is less obvious. Whose*
> *opportunity here would be below the threshold, below which*
> *things in Ireland are not so good at all. [Martin]*

A third challenge for Ireland was to remove barriers that stood in the way of full participation in the information economy by all members of Irish society. Two groups that emerged from this study as warranting special consideration were women and low skilled workers.

4.3.1 Gender

In the course of my interviews and observations I witnessed the tension between opportunity and restriction with respect to this labor pool. On the one hand, women, especially those working in multinational firms, thought it was easier for women to get on in the information sector than in traditional industries, banking and the civil service. Because information work depends upon intellectual not physical strength, women can theoretically compete equally with men. Skill is what counts. The information sector represents a good work setting for women because, as a new industry, there hasn't been as much time for the old, traditional, patterns to develop. There had been less time for traditions regarding gender-typed work to become established. The final reason for greater opportunity in the information sector was the way in which it was developing in Ireland. Because American multinational firms dominated the sector, the values about gender that existed in America were being transmitted to Ireland through the corporate cultures of these firms.

However, these positive sentiments about gender co-existed with an acknowledged stereotype of high tech work as a male activity.[ix] Both men and women recognized that women were not full participants in the information sector. From there, viewpoints diverged. Men weren't sure why, thinking that women must want it that way or that things were changing in the younger generation. Some women believed women *should* be less involved in work outside the home while others felt that the demands of family made women hold themselves back. The status of women in the information sector emerges from a cultural context of large families and a perception of child rearing as a woman's responsibility. Given that reality, some women simply left the workforce once they began to have children. Others chose not to progress as far in their careers in order to have time for their family responsibilities. Those women with whom I spoke who had both families and demanding jobs acknowledged the inner conflict between career and family.

4.3.2 Poverty and Social Exclusion

Another type of barrier relates to working class and less skilled people entering the information sector. This is a complicated barrier to address, in

part, because of the reluctance of many Irish people to acknowledge the
presence of social class boundaries in Ireland. Part of the country's post-
colonial legacy has been the desire to reject rigid social class categories.
Nevertheless, there was ample evidence of social class boundaries even if they
are more permeable, perhaps, than in other countries. To the extent that
information-sector work is knowledge-based, education is the key. But
attitudes are also intertwined with this issue.

Until secondary education became free in 1968 there was a concrete
barrier to participation in information-sector work. Since a secondary school
education was a requirement for IT employment, there was clear evidence of
social class distinctions among workers who would have been of high school
age or older in the late 1960s. But even after secondary education became
freely available to all, attitudes about education continued to serve as a barrier.
In family settings without a history of or value placed upon education there
was pressure on young people to enter the workforce as soon as possible in
order to add to the family income.

Other types of barriers -- both educational and attitudinal -- came not from
the working class people or their families but from middle class people. These
types of barriers were in evidence primarily in the indigenous firms.
Indigenous firms tended to be smaller and focused on the software and
information services subsectors. These are also the subsectors having higher
educational requirements. Whereas the multinational firms employed workers
at a range of levels from technician -- with perhaps only the Leaving
Certificate -- to graduate engineers, the Irish firms tended to require university
credentials. Thus, to the extent that there was a barrier to university attendance
among working class people, there was a barrier to their employment in
indigenous firms in this sector. In addition, I found evidence of attitudinal
barriers in Irish firms. Informants talked about the importance of one's accent
and address in securing employment. While they acknowledged this to be
much less prevalent in the information sector than in other sectors in Ireland,
it, nevertheless, existed.

Greater opportunity to attend university made it easier for working class
individuals to obtain information-sector employment. But in order to ensure
that this continued to occur, both concrete and attitudinal changes have been
required. Characteristics of secondary schools, which served as a barrier to
university admission, needed to be addressed. Greater availability of third
level courses at night was also needed. But changes in the attitudes of some
parents and employers also needed altering. Working class parents needed to
understand the relationship between post-secondary education and
employment opportunities. The attitudes of some information-sector managers

needed to change. In order to overcome the class-based barriers to IT employment, employers needed to understand that individuals from any social class were capable of being productive workers in this industry. Making the fruits of the transformation to an information economy available to individuals from all social classes was not something that could be achieved overnight. Assumptions about one's life chances, which were fixed for generations, take time and conscious intervention to alter.

To the extent that an information economy is a meritocracy, all workers should have an equal chance of succeeding in it. Data from a variety of sources, however, suggest that members of the middle class have received disproportionate benefits from this societal transformation. In his study of who attends higher education in Ireland, Clancy (1988) observed that in 1986 55% of the entrants to higher education were children of professionals, managers, and salaried employees, yet this group accounted for only 30% of the relevant cohort. In contrast, 24% of new entrants came from working class backgrounds despite the fact that they represented 55% of the target population. This is further reinforced by O'Toole's (1990b) observation that the social class of one's parents is a predictor of one's own social class in Ireland more than in any of the western European societies with which it has been compared.

4.4   Remaining Irish

> *Well, I certainly think [this firm] is adapting to the Irish*
> *culture. For one thing, they never saturated the place with*
> *Americans . . . therefore Americans never had a major*
> *impact. I find the Americans becoming more Irish, socializing*
> *more, drinking Guinness, going fishing, enjoying the outdoor*
> *life. [Brendan]*

In the face of all the changes Ireland experienced in its journey from a traditional agrarian to a modern information economy, a significant challenge has been to maintain the delicate balance between welcoming outside influences and remaining true to its cultural roots.

4.4.1   Imported Culture

From the beginning of the 1970s through the 1990s significant cultural change was being ushered into the country from its exposure to foreign cultures. This foreign exposure came, in part, through the medium of corporate culture. While there is no doubt that the introduction of foreign cultures into Ireland has also been influenced by greater travel and broader exposure to media,[x] what is more germane to this discussion is the introduction of foreign influences via the corporate cultures of the multinational firms.[xi] Of particular relevance to this research were the norms and values of a foreign culture coming up against an existing and different culture. When I raised this point about foreign cultures with American managers, to a one, they were quick to correct me. It wasn't national or American culture that they were bringing with them to Ireland, they all said, but their own, unique corporate cultures. However, if the people who establish the firm shape the corporate culture, then it stands to reason that the corporate culture of an American-based multinational firm would reflect the norms and values of the American culture. This is, in fact, what I found across the American IT firms I visited. There were considerable similarities across the corporate cultures of these American information-sector firms when they were compared with Irish firms in other sectors. The challenge for multinational managers, then, is to determine how to cope with these differences.

> *One of the other companies I was at, was an American multinational. They were talking about pressures from the home office to have equal opportunity numbers etc. When they came over here, they were saying you had to have more women in management and the response was: "But that's in conflict with our culture." [Margie]*

As this example shows, the influence of imported culture takes many forms and is not easily reconciled to the existing culture. One way in which imported culture is manifested is through work techniques and management processes introduced by multinational firms. Where there was resistance to such changes it was typically expressed by the response, "This is Ireland. We do things differently here."

One interesting difference had to do with equal opportunity. The American IT firms had explicit policies about promoting racial and gender representation within the ranks of management. The challenge at the Irish sites was to determine how this would play out there. As Margie's comment indicated, some thought gender equity was a distinctly American issue. But as the discussion of women in the information sector in Chapter 4 points out, Irish women were quite glad that American multinationals had the attitudes about gender that they did.

Sometimes there was friction when an Irish way of doing something clashed with the American norm. One difference between Irish and American sites of the recently established manufacturing firms had to do with work scope. For a variety of reasons, Irish workers had a greater understanding of the overall operations of the firm than workers did in other country sites. They wanted and needed an explanation of how some activity would fit into the big picture. Some of this was a function of plant size. The quality assurance manager at one firm explained that in Ireland three engineers were expected to cover the whole plant whereas in the States the same job was much narrower. As a result of his management experience in Ireland, his interaction with American counterparts frustrated him; they had narrower views and disinterest in understanding how a particular directive would fit in with the total picture.

Critics of Ireland's industrial policy of development through inward investment made a connection to Ireland's colonial past and drew analogies with British imperialism. Some believed that the industrial policy was replacing one form of imperialism with another: substituting British domination with multinational domination. They feared that the wrong message was being sent that Ireland couldn't develop its own industry, that it had to import it by bringing in overlords from the outside. These people wondered whether, given Ireland's history of domination, it was appropriate to once again invite foreigners to come and take over and tell them what to do. After all Ireland had gone through to establish its own cultural identity it was now going to import these people with other national cultures and corporate cultures! The optimistic yet pragmatic response was that there didn't seem to be an alternative.

> *It may not be the best for us as a nation and it also draws into question: do we want to retain some kind of an identity that's different from everybody else? Or do we want to become involved in some kind of an amalgamation of cultures on a world basis? I think there's a happy mix of the two. I wouldn't like to see us lose our identity and lose our sense of place and lose our sense of identity. But I wouldn't like us to become, you know, unconnected with the rest of the world. I think there's a happy mix to be achieved there. But as regards people coming in from abroad and influencing us here, that has good influences and bad influences. Good insofar as we hopefully will learn the best of whatever they have to offer. And hopefully we will reject the worst. That's in the best scenario. In the worst scenario, we would adopt everything, the good and bad, and get lost, ourselves, in the rush. [Liam]*

A good example of the positive outcome of the cross-cultural influences was the experience I had on my final day of interviewing at an Irish software company. I was invited to come to Phoenix Park in Dublin the following week for a softball game and barbecue. I found it particularly interesting that this was an Irish rather than an American firm having this type of social activity. Clearly the manager who was responsible for arranging this event had been to America or had worked with Americans or somehow developed an interest in softball. Aine, who invited me, referred to her experience working in England to make the point that her Irish co-workers were much more sociable after work than her English ones. She explained that this would be a real family event with people bringing their children. What I found noteworthy was that while the softball part was clearly an American influence, the way in which it was taken up and implemented felt characteristically Irish.

At the heart of the reaction to imported culture was the desire to maintain cultural identity. This concern was expressed in terms of nationalism and a desire to maintain a degree of cultural independence from the multinational companies. Despite a welcoming attitude toward the multinationals, the Irish respondents also expressed a parallel desire to maintain Ireland's uniqueness.

> *ET: I have been told in response to several questions, "Well, this is Ireland," or "Welcome to Ireland." What does that mean to you?*
>
> *It means this is how it's done here. It is said in reaction when an American is saying how something would be done in your country. It is said in reaction to perceived criticism. [Ethna]*

This uniqueness was expressed in several ways. A British man who had made Ireland his adopted home expressed his views on the topic of retaining cultural identity. To him it meant retaining an emphasis on the things he loved about the country: the social life and the emphasis on sport.

Others looked to Ireland's historical struggle to maintain its cultural identity in the face of external influences. It was through this lens that they viewed the cultural identity issue with respect to multinational influence. During the penal laws of the eighteenth century, education was seen as a way of maintaining Irish identity. That is, national and religious identity -- the components of Irish cultural identity -- were kept alive through the "hedge schools" maintained by the Catholic Church and through the oral tradition that kept the history and culture of Ireland alive. These people believed that the fierce attachment to independence that kept Ireland's culture alive through the centuries of external domination would keep Ireland on track in the face of outside influence in an increasingly global economy.

I would also accept we are simply minnows compared to the German economy, and the Big Seven, if you like. Mitsubishi could buy Ireland if they felt like it. If it was useful to them to have a very large parking lot in Europe, in essence, they could raise the money on the world market to buy the place. . . . So if the Japanese felt like owning a lot of golf clubs, Ireland would be a good buy. To that extent, we're never going to play with them. It'd be dangerous. At the other end, we are taken, because of our long cultural background of independence, our Celtic identity, which we somehow maintained throughout our colonial occupation, we are taken as a credible paying partner. [Declan]

4.4.2   Who Adapts?

I certainly know most of the Americans who came to visit us ended up being more like us. I mean they adopted our attitudes and they fitted in beautifully. [Stephanie]

The question of who adapts raises the issue of winners and losers in the new cultural milieu. Given the mix that resulted from the foreign influences introduced via the corporate and national cultures of the multinationals, the question was who would accede and who would dominate? For several of the American multinationals Ireland was their first foray into international waters. So their experience with Ireland was more than a single country experience. Ireland was also helping to shape their image of "foreign" or "European" work sites. On the matter of who adapts -- the multinational or the indigenous culture -- the views varied, predictably, by nationality of respondent.

One whole stream of viewpoints on this topic was that the foreigners -- whether American or otherwise -- adopted Irish ways. In her comment above, Stephanie was speaking about her experience at one of the first American computer firms to come to Ireland. An example of this adapting was the Irish emphasis on context. Irish people required a firm grasp of the big picture and needed to know where an individual was situated within it. It was difficult for Irish workers to get on with a task without this background. I asked about foreign influence from the multinationals and other sources, and whether this particular behavior would continue to dominate. There was an unequivocal response that the Irish ritual would prevail; it created a more open, friendly atmosphere. Closely related to context was the emphasis on social interaction. Once again, the viewpoint was that the Irish trait of group rituals definitely had an effect on the workplace and would prevail over outside influences.

Other traits that were expected to prevail were part of Ireland's colonial legacy. American managers recognized the need to be cognizant of Irish resentment toward authority. Over time, suggested Liam, it would be the other who adopted the Irish way.

> *ET: If you tell an Irish man to do it . . .*

> *They tend not to like to do it. They don't like to be told what to do. They like to have it suggested to them or in a less authoritarian [way] with regard to what they're doing. But the Germans and the Japanese who are here for a while, they tend to soften their approach to work and to giving orders [from] what they would have been like when they arrive. [Liam]*

American managers commented on their need to cope with Irish feelings of inferiority that got expressed as fear of failure, reluctance to take risks and willingness to admit when they didn't understand something. Leo understood that he and his management style would have to adjust.

> *This is a thing I will have to work on; you can't change them. [Leo]*

An Irish worker at an American firm offered an interesting perspective on the topic of adjusting to the Irish culture. He strongly disagreed with those who thought there was not much difference across manufacturing sites in different countries: a plant is a plant is a plant. This man began by explaining that his work involved designing computer-based applications that controlled manufacturing. He then pointed out that before one can implement a series of applications to control a manufacturing plant, he or she had to understand the philosophy that the people used to manage the manufacturing process. The computer-based applications were basically an automation of that philosophy. For this reason he always started with developing an understanding of the particular philosophy-in-use. And these philosophies varied across countries.

Two examples of the influence of cultural context that arose numerous times in my interviews were the work ethic and the attitude toward time. Managers at American firms commented on the need to adjust motivators to suit the Irish culture. As discussed in Chapter 6, motivational factors such as job satisfaction, job security, salary, relationships at work and the opportunity to develop had their own particular meaning and priority for Irish workers. I wondered about the juxtaposition of the relaxed attitude toward time in Ireland and inclination toward sociability against the hard-driving work stereotype of the American programmer. I wondered about the long-term prospects for the information technology industry in Ireland. I wondered if this were an example of some fundamental conflict between aspects of Irish culture and what it took to be successful in the information economy. When I asked a manager at an Irish software firm he wondered if, perhaps, it was the work ethic that needed to change. In his view the Irish ethos brought something new to the industry. He suggested that the typical programmer profile ought to be widened. The notion of staying up all night to work on a problem, he said, was not necessarily the most productive way to solve it. Rather, taking it slower in the early stages and doing a better design has been shown to be more beneficial in the long run. In the end, both Irish and American respondents saw the probability and the benefit of the corporate culture of foreign firms adopting aspects of the Irish culture.

ET: Will [your firm] adjust to the Irish culture?

To be successful, we will have to. I suppose one question is: How successful do we want to be? I would recommend an Irish culture training course to Americans coming over here. This will enhance their communication effectiveness with the Irish. The Irish have many good values. The good things about Ireland happen because of the culture. [Eric]

The opposite viewpoint was that Irish culture and people have had to adapt in order to be successful in this new type of economy. Margie reflected on the adaptation process. Some of the workers found it hard to adjust. They found it difficult to remain indoors all day. But they had to adjust not only to working indoors but also to working a set amount of hours and to time pressures. Not surprisingly, there seemed to be a relationship between length of time a foreign manager was in Ireland and the direction of the adapting. Albert explained that one American manager at his firm was only in Ireland one year and ran things his way, keeping himself apart. He wanted to run the factory as an offshoot of a US site. In contrast, the current American managing director would do things in the US but not in Ireland. His conclusion was that there was about a 50-50 adjustment assuming the American manager was there for three to five years. They would change because the culture would be affecting them, they would become more influenced by the culture.

If you are only here a short time you live like a visitor. [Albert]

Eric shared one of the most poignant anecdotes about cross-cultural give and take that I heard during these interviews. His plant was still gearing up for operations at the time of our conversation.

We plan to employ 2600 people. The population of [the town] is 1600. We want to be a good neighbor so I wanted to get in contact with opinion leaders. I thought the teacher, the priest. But no, we got the president and vice-president of the Chamber of Commerce, one head of [a large insurance company], one head of a bank, the head of the Town Council -- who is also the principal of the Irish school -- and two representatives from the Residence Council, a combined residence association. We had a meeting with these people. I said [our firm] would have an impact on the town and the culture. I commented on conflicts that I saw [between the cultures] and said I thought the [firm's] culture would diffuse into [the town's] society. But one man from the Residence Council said, "Vikings and British tried that before you and it didn't work." [Eric]

Perhaps the final word on this topic was given by Eamon. He worked at an American firm that had been in Ireland about ten years when this interview was conducted.

ET: Does this work environment feel Irish or American?

It feels Irish. [Eamon]

5.   CONCLUSION

The findings of this study of Ireland's information economy demonstrate the interaction between the socio-cultural context, and information-sector work, workers and workplaces. There is strong economic evidence of the success of Ireland's policy of conscious, adaptive movement into an information economy. Cultural evidence suggests significant areas of consonance between characteristics of Irish culture and the needs of the information economy.[xii] Nevertheless, there remain challenges to be addressed as Ireland moves further into the information age. These challenges stand out in the form of contradictions that float on the surface of the changing landscape that is Ireland.

Others besides me heard the complaints about the lack of venture funding for Irish start-up companies. During the 1990s several initiatives were undertaken to address these concerns. Initiatives of the National Software Directorate, for example, have provided support to software firms in Ireland's information sector.[xiii] Another initiative enacted in 1998 was the Millennium

Entrepreneur Fund. This fund, which is jointly sponsored by a consortium of private sector and governmental agencies,[xiv] was established to provide early stage risk seed capital funding to Irish entrepreneurs. The fund grants up to £100,000 to individuals or teams which possess international experience and who intend to set up a business that is technology-based and which has high growth potential. In addition to the financial help, the project provides mentoring assistance to the firms (Enterprise Ireland, 1998).

Economic change in the form of increased funding from government agencies, the private sector and the European Union has been accompanied by cultural change in the form of greater experience and comfort with entrepreneurship. The result has been success stories such as the software company Iona Technologies. The lessons from Iona speak to what is and is not changing for start-up firms in Ireland's information sector. What has changed is the method of motivating employees. An impact of the multinationals is the expectation of receiving stock options. What has not changed is the pull of Ireland. Early in its history Iona Technologies rejected US venture capital and a move to Boston in order to remain in Ireland. Quality of life, including time for oneself and one's family remained a top priority even in the throes of entrepreneurship ("From Humble Beginnings", 1997).

Yet for every indicator of progress with respect to entrepreneurship there still remains counter evidence of a culture that continues to be deeply in conflict with the principles guiding entrepreneurship and risk. In a recent book on entrepreneurship in Ireland (Garavan, O' Cinneide and Fleming, 1997) the authors note that:

> Despite some notable exceptions, Ireland does not have an advanced entrepreneurial culture, a fact accounted for by a combination of economic, social and educational factors. It is claimed that the school system tends to laud the professions as the best career for the children. . . Several entrepreneurs [in one study] claimed that parents were totally opposed to the idea of giving up a secure job in favor of a business start-up. The entrepreneurs interviewed believed that an individual aiming to set up their own business in Ireland is treated with some suspicion and the general perception is that they are "rising above their station." (89)[xv]

Cultural contradictions regarding entrepreneurship are matched by similar contradictions regarding wealth. On the one hand, signs of greater wealth abound in Ireland. New cars clog the streets of Dublin and the roads that link the major cities. European-style cafes where people linger over expensive cups of cafe au lait have sprouted on the sidewalks of Dublin. Dramatic evidence of Ireland's economic health can be read in the scholarly and popular publications proclaiming the Celtic Tiger, in the news that computer companies such as Dell Computers in Limerick must go abroad to recruit a sufficient number of IT workers,[xvi] and in the optimistic and affluent attitude of the young.[xvii]

Nevertheless, some authors continue to decry the diminutive enterprise culture in Ireland.

> The Irish economy needs more enterprise. Specifically, it needs more entrepreneurs who will seek out market niches and employ people to exploit them. . . It is often said that the Irish can be very enterprising. Sometimes the enterprise is not commercially motivated, as in the case of the missionaries. Also, much Irish entrepreneurial talent of the economic kind has been deployed to the benefit of countries overseas. . . Ireland is not short of enterprise in a general sense. It is short of the right type of enterprise. It needs much less of the zero-sum enterprise of lawyers, doctors, trade unions and other pressure groups squeezing more out of the taxpayer, and much more positive-sum enterprise directed at market demand, making money for entrepreneurs and their employees, contributing to state revenues and general welfare instead of draining them (Burke, 1995, p. xxi).

Another source of concern is the growing gap between those reaping the benefits of the information economy and those still on the outside looking in. Perched aside the good news of Ireland's economic miracle came the news in summer 1999 that Ireland has the highest levels of poverty in the industrialized world, outside the US. For the second year in a row the United Nations' Human Development Report ranked Ireland sixteenth out of 17 Western countries with 15.3% of the population living in human poverty. Reports such as this point out the socio-economic contradiction of Ireland: it is at the same time one of the most desirable places to live and a place where there are still massive inequalities in the distribution of wealth. Large pockets of poverty co-exist with the Celtic Tiger economy.[xviii]

Government agencies have enacted programs in response to this recognized gap between the "haves" and the "have nots" in the Irish information economy. FAS has created several programs specifically targeted at the unskilled and long-term unemployed. Under the FAS-Jobstart program employers are paid £80 per week for one year to subsidize the cost of employing a person who has been unemployed for three years or longer. The FAS-Whole Time Jobs Option/Jobs Initiatives provides full-time work for three years at the going market rate for jobs with local sponsor companies. It is designed for people aged 35 and older who have been unemployed for more than five years. Coincident with these programs, unemployment rates among people out of work for more than three years have been falling faster than the national average. By September 1998, unemployment was 9%, down from 12% in 1997 and 17% in 1990 (Houston, 1999).

The economic contradictions are also evident in current analyses of the Celtic Tiger phenomenon in Ireland. Two books published in the same year and employing that metaphor offer opposite interpretations of the economic condition of Ireland. Sweeney (1998) digests a vast amount of economic evidence in order to explain Ireland's "economic miracle."[xix] O'Hearn (1998), on the other hand, takes a stance that is critical of the economic model of development through invitation. He challenges the received wisdom of a new "miracle economy" and points to the difficulties of those who are not young and highly educated. His work reminds the reader of the economic vulnerability of a nation heavily dependent upon inward investment.[xx]

There is already evidence of changes in Ireland in response to the challenges and impacts of the information economy. The educational infrastructure has been altered to support the needs of information-sector work, transportation and telecommunications have been upgraded to move information goods and services, and -- criticisms notwithstanding -- Ireland's economic prospects have greatly improved over the time period of this industrial policy. All the while Ireland has been engaged in significant cultural give-and-take as it has invited multinational firms to its shores, sent its young abroad to absorb other cultures and extended a welcoming hand to outside influences.

While the information economy can be viewed, in one sense, as a threat to cultural identity it can also be seen as a means of supporting it. An example is the project on IT for the South West Islands of Ireland (Carey, 1999). The objective of this rural development project is to study the potential of IT for helping islanders to survive and thrive as year-round communities. The transportation challenges posed by islands makes the potential for telecommunications all the greater. The Internet, in particular, can offer ways for people to remain on the islands even as they become more connected to the mainland.

A similar project being carried out in a different fashion in Country Clare is the Ennis Information Age Town project. Ennis became Ireland's "information age town" on September 24, 1997. It was selected from a nationwide competition carried out the previous year to select a small town to become a test bed for technologies to transform people's lives in the twenty-first century.[xxi] It received a £15 million grant from eircom[xxii] to carry out a range of programs for residents, businesses and community groups in the town.[xxiii] Residents who had never owned a telephone began receiving not only telephone service but also voicemail, personal computers and free or discounted Internet service. The business community has begun to think of ways to use information technology to grow existing firms and attract new ones. Schools and community groups have also been equipped with computer labs and training.

As a result of such efforts communities that would have been viewed as remote a decade ago are now "online." While the Internet was barely in use ten years ago, it quickly came into widespread use in Ireland. Today all of the government agencies have web sites. Public policy documents, which a decade ago required a trip to the Government Documents Office on Molesworth St. in Dublin, are now available at the click of the mouse. Universities publicize their programs, share research and engage in distance learning via the World Wide Web. The growth of the Internet reveals the impact of the information economy in Ireland. It is fueled by a growing population of technologically skilled citizens in a society that recognizes the economic significance of information-sector work.

---

[i] National Software Directorate (1992) is such an example. Documents such as this indicate the recognition of a distinct software subsector and its strategic contribution to Ireland's industrial policy.

[ii] Of course not everyone came directly from family-owned farms but its predominance in the economy has resulted in this cultural mindset.

[iii] The "Net-Generation" characteristics that are a close fit with Irish information-sector workers are: curious, self-reliant, contrarian, smart, focused, adaptable, possessing a global orientation, high independence and autonomy, and intellectual openness.

[iv] For example, one of Tapscott's (1998) characteristics of "Net-Generation" workers is high self-esteem. I did not find this characteristic in abundance among Irish IT workers. To the extent that Tapscott is correct, the absence of this characteristic could pose a challenge for the Irish information sector.

[v] For further discussion of this topic see Foley and Griffith (1994).

[vi] While this was the typical sentiment expressed to me it is worth noting that some quarters of the government recognized the need to create the proper climate and infrastructure to support entrepreneurship. See McCall (1989) and Rea (1988) for a description of such efforts that were contemporary with these respondent comments.

vii See Murray (1981) for a contemporary discussion of entrepreneurship in Ireland and O'Farrell (1986) for a discussion of socio-cultural factors that have inhibited entrepreneurship in Ireland.

viii The work of Hogan and Foley supports this interpretation of socio-cultural impediments to entrepreneurship. One earlier study of fast growth firms in Ireland from 1978 to 1992 (Hogan and Foley, 1996) found a failure rate of 54%. Another study of start-ups in manufacturing between 1986 and 1995 (Foley and Hogan, 1998) showed a decline in the number of start-ups during this period.

ix Other countries are not immune to this stereotype either. See Kwan, Trauth and Driehaus (1985) for an expression of societal attitudes in America during this time.

x At the time these interviews were conducted -- before the World Wide Web -- the Internet had very little presence in Ireland. In education, Internet use was limited to electronic mail and that was severely limited.

xi For a more detailed discussion of this theme see, Trauth (1996a, 1999a).

xii Leavy's (1999) discussion of strategy makes the point that innovation in the knowledge economy springs from an organizational culture that nurtures it. Such a culture emphasizes tacit understanding, values and relationships. All these characteristics were in the foreground in my study.

xiii See, for example, National Software Directorate (1992).

xiv Including Enterprise Ireland, L.M. Ericsson Ltd., Bank of Ireland, Neil McCann and the European Union.

xv The study mentioned in this passage is found in O'Connor (1983).

xvi The company revealed that the difficulty of finding Irish people with relevant experience was forcing the firm to look to other countries to find workers ("Dell recruits abroad," 1999).

xvii See Norton (1999) for an example of current articles describing the changes in Irish society at the end of the twentieth century as a consequence of its economic fortunes.

xviii See Cullen (1999a, 1999b) and O'Connor (1999) as representative of the range of commentary on this report.

xix See, in particular, Chapter 4: Keys to Success in which he identifies the external factors -- EU structural funds, the Single Market, foreign direct investment and the communication revolution -- and the internal factors -- a stable economic environment, the new industrial policy, the fall in the dependency ratio, national consensus, an educated labor force and new forms of work organization -- to which he attributes Ireland's economic success.

[xx] This had been a theme of his work long before the Celtic Tiger phenomenon. See, for example, O'Hearn (1989).

[xxi] An example is the "electronic purse" a reusable smart card intended for purchases under £5.

[xxii] Telecom Eireann changed its name to eircom in 1999 when it changed from being a State telephone company to a privatized multimedia business.

[xxiii] For further description of these programs see "Programmes" (1999).

CHAPTER 9. CONCLUSION

1. INTRODUCTION

> The rise of the class succeeding industrial workers is not an
> opportunity for industrial workers. It is a challenge. The
> newly emerging dominant group is "knowledge workers". . .
> The great majority of the new jobs require qualifications the
> industrial worker does not possess and is poorly equipped to
> acquire. They require a good deal of formal education and the
> ability to acquire and to apply theoretical and analytical
> knowledge. They require a different approach to work and a
> different mind-set. Above all, they require a habit of
> continuous learning. Displaced industrial workers thus cannot
> simply move into knowledge work. . . At the very least they
> have to change their basic attitudes, values, and beliefs.
> (Drucker, 1994, p. 62)

Peter Drucker's words apply equally to established and emerging
information economies. They apply to nations moving out of traditional
industrialism as well as to those who are leapfrogging from an agrarian
economy. Though they may have followed different paths, all countries are
finding themselves in the same place: straining to reap more fully the rewards
of the information economy.

There were three goals to be achieved in this research project. The first
was to consider how national, industry and corporate cultures influence the
development of an information economy. This investigation of Ireland has
demonstrated the relationship between factors in the socio-cultural
environment and the form of an emerging information economy. Chapter 8
reviewed the considerable congruence between socio-cultural factors and the
demands of the information-sector workplace. This congruence is a source of
competitive advantage for Ireland relative to other nations. However, I also
found in Ireland's history, culture and society influences that pose important
challenges for the future. That Ireland will change in response to these

opportunities and challenges is evident in the impacts that have already occurred.

The second goal was to investigate this subject by employing interpretive methods. I wanted to understand what was behind the statistics and industrial policy documents about Ireland's information economy as it was emerging. I wanted to get inside the minds of the workers and managers who were bringing this information economy about. I wanted to better understand their work and how they accomplished it in the Irish context. I wanted to explore the information-sector workplace as it unfolded in ordinary ways. To do this I used a range of interpretive methods. I conducted formal and informal interviews, engaged in participant observation in the IT firms and in society in general, conducted document analysis and did member checking to validate my results.[i]

As I come to the end of this story about Ireland's journey into the information economy, it is time to explicitly address the third goal: What are the lessons from this in-depth exploration of an emerging information economy that are applicable to other countries and cultures? The evidence from Ireland suggests that the information economy is played out differently in different settings. There are strengths and weaknesses in every culture. At the same time there are also generalizable themes. The insights gained from this exploration of Ireland have resulted in themes for the attention of a wider audience, whether they are following a similar path of rapid evolution or are assessing their gradual progression toward an information economy.

The lessons from Ireland that are applicable to other contexts are organized around three themes: understanding the characteristics of the information economy, leveraging the socio-cultural characteristics of the context, and adapting the vision along the way. This book began with the promise of the information economy and what Ireland hoped to gain from it. It is ending with a look beyond individual socio-cultural characteristics to the lessons for the global information economy and the future.

2.   UNDERSTANDING THE CHARACTERISTICS OF THE INFORMATION ECONOMY

Behind the facts and figures detailing the emergence of the information economy are the deeper social and cultural changes that are occurring alongside this transformation in employment. This is particularly the case for nations leapfrogging from agrarian to information-sector employment through inward investment by multinational firms. The transition to an information economy is an evolution of both consciousness and employment.

2.1 Facilitating Information-sector Work

The lessons about the transition from both industrial and agrarian economies to an information economy can be highlighted by juxtaposing the characteristics of information-economy work against those of industrial and agrarian work. In some cases, the predecessor economy helps to smooth the transition; other times it makes the journey bumpier. An important caveat to the discussion of information-sector work is that the characteristics vary considerably by subsector: hardware production, software development, and information system services. Nevertheless, some or all of the characteristics described below apply to any given information-sector workplace.[ii] Information-economy work can be characterized as knowledge-intensive, creative and dynamic.

Information-sector work requires that intelligence be incorporated into the tasks being carried out. With the commodification of information and information technology, the service component of information products increasingly becomes the key to competitive advantage. And it is intelligence that provides the value-added features of such service. Information-sector work also requires creativity. Because of the pace of technological change, innovative responses to the marketplace are the hallmark of the information sector. New ways of thinking are needed to fuel the continuous search for new information products and services.

Information technology also relaxes the constraints of time for all types of work, including information-sector work. And the creativity demands of information work reinforce the need for time flexibility. Rigid working hours are not conducive to the generation of creative ideas. But while information-sector work can increasingly be done *any time* there is also the expectation that it will be accomplished *faster*. Just-in-time approaches to the management of manufacturing and other aspects of business are shortening the time lag between demand for and provision of products and services.

Information technology also frees the worker from location constraints.[iii] As is the case with time flexibility, creativity is supported by location flexibility as well. Especially for those engaged in the creative parts of the information sector, being "at work" occurs at home as well as in the office. Even for those not engaged in particularly creative work, telecommuting is breaking down the physical bounds of the workplace. The global economy further extends the bounds of the workplace as job functions are distributed around the globe.

2.2 Ensuring A Supply of Qualified Information-sector Workers

While people in agrarian and industrial economies also process information, it is not the defining characteristic, nor is it the primary objective of their work. Further, in an information economy the processing of information and the production of information tools engages members of the middle and working classes as well as the professional class. This means that new classes of workers must obtain the general and specific skills that are necessary for this work.

2.2.1   Productive

Just as work in the information economy differs from industrial and agrarian work, so too do the workers' needs. What is needed to promote productivity of information-sector workers is different from what is needed in other sectors. In the information economy, the quality of work life is an important component of worker productivity.[iv] A nation's socio-cultural characteristics can serve to enhance or hinder the creation of a supportive work environment.

With information-sector work the focus shifts from physical to intellectual or value-added output. Productivity is measured more by the quality than the quantity of the output. Consequently, personal and environmental factors play a larger role than in the industrial paradigm where productivity is governed by the assembly line. For information-sector workers financial compensation is necessary but not sufficient. Intellectual stimulation needs to be included high on the list of motivational factors. If financial compensation and intellectual stimulation will attract and keep workers in the information economy, what "hygiene" factors will bring out the best they have to offer? The range and priority of factors may depend, in part, upon where one is in life's cycle. Younger workers may be driven more by opportunities for creativity, challenge, independence, advancement and responsibility. Older persons, on the other hand, may place more value on security, comfort, relationships, recognition, self worth, dignity and benefits.

But both sets of factors are expected to produce the same result: satisfaction with work and happiness in the workplace. A simple but often ill-understood management maxim is that happy and satisfied people make productive knowledge workers. The Irish cultural emphasis on enjoying life both inside and outside of work shows the fit between socio-cultural factors and the quality of work life needs of the IT workplace.

Nevertheless, in the global information economy, there is an ongoing tension between the forces that would enhance quality of work life and those that would undermine it. There is much irony that some of the factors that directly contribute to a good work environment are disappearing at the same time that there is increasing demand on a global scale for productive information-sector workers. Key among the factors that are threatened is loyalty. Loyalty is increasingly absent from the new paradigm of employer-employee relationships in the information sector.[v] This changing paradigm in a global employment sector points to the challenge of coping with diverse cultural value systems. Perhaps replacing loyalty with high salaries fits well with the American culture; it may not fit so well with others. To the extent that this paradigm is exported, it may run headlong into what information-sector workers require for a satisfying workplace in another culture. There is already some evidence of these changes in Ireland. Participants talked about how loyalty had diminished as they watched mobile multinationals come and go. A paradigm that contains no commitment to the IT person, just her/his skill set exacerbates this trend.

Another quality of life issue relates to possible discordance between the culture of the information-sector workplace and personal quality of life. In Ireland this was most visible in the effort to balance the importance of family and the demands of the workplace. While the American zeal for achievement has helped foster an entrepreneurial spirit in Ireland, some have wondered about the effect on the quality of life. Quality of life in Ireland means a strong emphasis on family, value placed on social interaction, and sufficient free time to enjoy oneself outside work. While high tech employment brings financial rewards and contributes to quality of life in the form of an improved standard of living, it often takes the worker away from the family more frequently. The desire to maintain a balanced life was emphasized by Irish respondents across all levels in the organizations.

2.2.2   Skilled

Recent labor studies have documented the information technology (IT) workforce crisis that has accompanied the emergence of the global information economy. The result of the information economy growing at an unprecedented speed is a global demand for qualified information-sector workers.[vi] This crisis is also an opportunity, however, as nations and regions recognize the economic benefits of this employment sector. Therefore, a critical consideration for the information age concerns human resources. Appropriately qualified information workers are needed to fuel the information society by producing the computers, developing the software and providing the information content and services that keeps it going. The challenge applies throughout the workforce supply chain from educating through recruiting to motivating and managing these workers. Ensuring a supply of appropriately qualified information-sector workers raises issues of both educational and social policy.

One of the most important dimensions of the human resource issue is having an educational infrastructure that is consistent with the skill needs of the information economy. Such an educational infrastructure encompasses not only what is studied, but also the plan for how it is to be studied and how the subject matter is to be kept compatible with the ever-changing IT sector. The kind of educational infrastructure that is needed to support an information economy has three major requirements.

The first requirement relates to what is learned. In his treatment of knowledge workers, Drucker (1994) discusses the need for both specialized skills and the general skills required for continuous learning. General education is needed for several reasons. First, the demands of information-sector work require not only technical understanding but also skills in human interaction. Thus, communication skills and an understanding of people in context become important. Second, the dynamic nature of the information disciplines requires considerable flexibility. The ability to adapt to continuous change is aided by a broad understanding of one's field, job and industry. Finally, the educational need goes beyond continuous learning as the curve of technological change sweeps steeply upward. In order to remain at the leading edge of technological innovation workers also need the ability to engage in critical thinking and to make the mental leaps into new ways of thinking that accompany these new technologies. It is through a classical education that one hones such skills.

But a general education, no matter how good, does not provide a sufficient educational base for work in the information economy. Information-sector workers also need to acquire the specialized skills and knowledge needed for the specific type of work they will do. Thus, there is a need to develop specialized curricula around: information technology (hardware) design; software development; information system design, implementation and services; and information content creation.[vii] Different educational requirements and educational programs in the fields of engineering, library science, computer science, information systems/science, business, and media studies have grown up to support these subsectors.

The second requirement of the educational infrastructure relates to how the subject matter is learned. The need for adequate university preparation for information-sector work has implications for primary and secondary education as well as for the university. For example, an adequate grounding in mathematics and science is needed in order to have adequately prepared students coming to the university. Prior to the inception of this industrial policy the Irish university system was not oriented toward vocational education much less vocational education of a technical nature. Ireland is not unique in its historic differentiation between those destined for the university and those destined for the trades. Consequently, the challenge for Ireland is also the challenge for other countries: to incorporate some preparation for the workplace into university education.

In addition to the alignment between the university and the knowledge demands of the information economy, two other mechanisms need to be incorporated into the educational delivery system. One is continuing education. University programs for part-time students can meet some of this need. Such programs enable people to develop their skills and employment prospects while retaining their jobs. Training programs in the workplace also meet the need for continuing education. University graduates who lack the proper technical skills as well as workers made redundant in other fields can acquire the requisite information-sector skills through such programs. In Ireland, part of the industrial policy was to offer training grants as an incentive to develop these human resources. This is particularly beneficial when the existing university system is not yet prepared for rapid deployment of information-sector workers. The final aspect of the educational delivery system is to provide alternative third level educational options for those wishing to acquire technical skills. In response to this need, Ireland created a network of regional technical colleges throughout the country. The American managers of the multinational plants that hired them, held these graduates in high esteem.

The third requirement of the educational infrastructure relates to its adaptive capacity. It needs to be adaptive for two reasons. First, the rapid changes in the information disciplines require constant monitoring and adjusting in order to be compatible with the skill sets required of information-sector work. As new technologies become available, new applications become possible. These changes need to be incorporated into the curriculum. The educational system needs to be able to educate its students for the knowledge demands of information-sector work as the technologies, applications and expectations change.[viii]

Another rationale for an adaptive educational infrastructure is coordination of educational and employment policy. The employment objectives of the policy makers and the educational plans of the universities should evolve in concert. In the case of Ireland, there was much irony in the fact that an industrial policy intended to stem the tide of emigration had resulted in some of the best and brightest leaving the country. As Ireland learned, it was not sufficient to reorient a nation's educational system to make it compatible with an industrial policy focused on building up an information economy. It was also necessary to have jobs for the people once they graduated.[ix]

2.2.3   Entrepreneurial

The information economy is also bringing about a change in the relationship between the employer and the employee. Paternalism is being replaced by entrepreneurship. A requirement of the information economy is that workers be flexible and able to adapt with changing technologies, consumer demands and competitors. But part of this flexibility also involves changes in one's career as the information professions, themselves, change. In this new paradigm the employer hires a skill set not a person. According to Thurow (1999) when new technology makes old skills obsolete, firms employ workers who already have the skills rather than invest in training. There is no obligation to a person beyond "fee for service." When an organization's need for skills changes, the employer scans the marketplace of workers to see who provides the best fit (AEA Manpower Committee, 1998). As a consequence, having a single job (or even a single career) throughout one's work life is becoming the exception rather than the rule.[x]

2.3   Managing the Information-sector Workplace

The nature of information-sector work is producing a shift in focus from individual to organizational productivity. Whereas the industrial economy measures productivity in terms of the physical output of an individual worker, the information economy increasingly evaluates productivity in terms of the quality of the good or service produced by a work unit. Workers in the information economy will increasingly be required to work in teams to accomplish their task. Doing so helps workers to carry out specific tasks with a clearer picture of the whole. The ability of information-sector workplaces to accomplish such productivity is related, in part, to the orientation of the workers.

A society that developed its information economy on the back of an industrial economy also developed the concept of a separate *workplace* and all that it entails. Erstwhile farmers learned to leave their homes and travel to a specific location to engage in work. They learned to work within established time and space parameters. They learned to answer to someone other than themselves. They learned to be accountable to narrower and more frequent measures of productivity than the size of the crop at the end of the season. They learned to exchange labor for money.

However, the fruits of the industrial paradigm also produced the seeds of discontent in an information economy. The industrial mentality is rigid, inflexible, not given to creativity and at times hidebound by labor unions. Irish respondents described industrial-sector workers as complacent and lacking initiative. They described industrial-sector managers as more inclined to reward those who followed orders and put in time than those who displayed enthusiasm, energy and commitment.

The second wave of nations to develop information economies has been doing so from a distinctly different base. These traditional agrarian societies did not participate at all or to a great extent in the industrial paradigm. In Ireland these former or part-time farmers experienced both space and time constraints. They had to adjust to working indoors for set periods of time. They had to leave the home to go to work. They had to answer to bosses other than themselves and deadlines other than their own. But as often as I heard about the adjustment that workers from agrarian backgrounds had to make, I also heard about the beneficial effects of having no industrial baggage. These workers were more flexible, holistic in their thinking, less bound by time constraints, and willing to work together with others to do whatever it took to get the job done.

3. LEVERAGING SOCIO-CULTURAL CHARACTERISTICS

At the dawn of the twenty-first century there are important lessons for every nation to learn about the alignment between its socio-cultural characteristics and the dimensions of the information economy. In order to do so, however, it is necessary to recognize the differences among information, industrial and agrarian economies. It is also necessary to develop plans for coping with the differences between the type of economy that currently dominates and the type of economy towards which one is moving. This involves leveraging those national characteristics that are consistent with information-sector work. It also involves developing plans for removing the barriers in the path.

3.1   Recognizing the Influence of Cultural Context

Cultural context has several layers. One is national culture. Because the information economy is global in character, there may be several national cultures to be reconciled in a single company. A second culture exerting an influence is the IT industry culture. My discussions of cultural influences often turned into discussions of a global IT culture. Finally, there is the corporate culture of a particular firm. While these are three distinct levels, they exert their influence in an integrated fashion. Thus, even the workplace of domestic firms in the information sector is cross-cultural in that it incorporates all three layers.

After working for a year in Ireland Joseph had learned that these cultural factors were a significant influence on what and how things got done.[xi] The lesson he learned underlies the challenges associated with managing information-sector workers in a cross-cultural work environment. Coping with different cultures can be made easier by focusing on the common points, the aspects of culture that are shared. For example, Irish workers responded very favorably to the open, nonhierarchical management style of the American firms. They saw this style as more similar to Celtic-Irish culture than those essentially British modes of thought, feeling and behavior that they experienced in Irish firms which reflected Anglo-Irish culture.

Recognizing that there is more than one culture exerting an influence is only part of the challenge, however. The other part is grappling with the direction of cross-cultural influence. I witnessed a tension between American and Irish managers over the direction and extent of cultural influence when they differed. American managers tended to think that American culture should be influencing Irish culture. Some American managers believed that the multinational firms *ought* to have a significant cultural impact on Ireland. This perception, however, may not always sit well with the indigenous people, as was the case in Ireland. The perception held by the Irish workers and managers was that while the multinationals were bringing certain welcomed values and attitudes to the workplace, there was and should be a significant influence of Irish culture on the multinational information-sector workplace as well. This line of thinking argues for tailoring the corporate culture of the multinational firms to the particular national context.

But sitting side by side with any resistance to multinational influences is the recognition that importing another work culture is often part of the plan. Like many newly industrializing countries leaping from an agrarian to an information economy, Ireland wanted to import another work ethic. Therefore, part of the invitation to multinational firms in the information technology industry was the expectation that Ireland would be able to import a well-established work ethic that would have taken considerably longer to develop if done indigenously.

The lessons about managing information-sector workers in a cross-cultural environment derive from a simple but significant premise. It is that more than one distinct culture is involved when a multinational firm sets up operations in a country, all of which have positive contributions to make. Accepting this premise requires some work on the part of both multinational and indigenous workers. First, multinational managers must recognize that the host country culture, however different, can make a positive contribution to the workplace. Second, they must understand that in introducing a corporate culture they are also introducing a different national culture. At the same time, host country managers and policy makers need to recognize that changing the culture is part of the bargain when the intent is to import expertise in order to quickly introduce an information sector. In the cross-cultural information-sector workplace it is necessary to acknowledge that cultural influence goes in both directions. It is natural that the home culture of the multinational firm will influence the society it enters. But it is also natural that the workers will want to tailor the corporate culture to make it compatible with their own culture. By building a permeable wall, with the open exchange of values and norms both cultures can be enriched, something that bodes well for the global information sector.

By recognizing that there is more than one path to excellence, multinational managers can develop procedures and management approaches that exploit the best features of the host country. For example, in resolving human relations issues American managers in Ireland drew upon the role of the pub as the focal point for social interaction. A potentially serious personnel situation could be diffused by having the parties meet in the pub to discuss it. Clearly, this management approach fits well with Irish culture but may not suit another cultural context. Likewise, what works best in Japan or in America may not be suitable in Ireland.

3.2   Exploiting Distinctive Characteristics

Those countries that were the first to establish information economies have their predominant position as a source of competitive advantage; the second wave has had to take another approach, often using different criteria. According to Porter (1990) differences in national values, culture, economic structures, institutions and histories all contribute to competitive success. The Irish case provides a good example of how a country can leverage those socio-cultural characteristics that are consistent with information-sector work.

The Industrial Development Authority touts characteristics of Ireland's labor force along with its attractive financial incentives. The young, well-educated, flexible, English-speaking workers are recognized by Irish policy makers as a source of competitive advantage relative to other countries. But in thinking specifically about information-economy work, some others can be added. The workers bring intelligence to the job through their curiosity that enables them to do their jobs from the perspective of the big picture. The cultural emphasis on sociability enables people to work effectively in groups. The caring values in the society motivate workers to help each other. Workers' fierce resistance to authoritarianism contributes to an egalitarian workplace which emphasizes accomplishment rather than position power.

3.3   Overcoming Barriers

But not all of a nation's socio-cultural features are positively aligned with information-economy work; some features are more problematic. For example, Ireland's information economy faces challenges from a lack of inclusiveness and post-colonial attitudes toward risk taking and success. As the information economy grows, other issues that may arise from having a broader base of workers are related to productivity, ambition, resistance to change and a collective mentality that may hold high achievers back.

3.3.1   Cultural Influences that Could Hold It Back

Because of the specialized skills required for employment in the information sector, education is key. Clearly, the educational infrastructure must provide the requisite skills and knowledge. But in order to ensure that all citizens are able to avail themselves of the *economic opportunities* present in the information sector, it is important that they have equal *employment opportunity*. In Ireland and elsewhere attitudes toward age, race, gender, ethnicity and socio-economic class may inhibit full and equal participation in the emerging information society (Clancy, 1988; Trauth, 1993a; Trauth, 1995b).[xii]

The information technology field is viewed as a young person's field. The respondents in my research considered a person over the age of 35 to be old. This attitude is exacerbated in countries such as Ireland that have particularly young populations. For countries rapidly creating information economies there is an added dimension to the age issue. Those in middle age may not have had access when they were young to the kind of educational resources required for information-sector employment. Consequently, they will be fewer in number and will have come from families affluent enough to have been able to send them away to acquire these skills. In the case of Ireland, "away" meant private boarding schools. In another country it may mean sending the young people abroad. Thus, there can arise in other countries just as there has arisen in Ireland a significant divide between older and younger workers. Looking a few years into the future when the current cohort of young workers will be in middle age and beyond, some challenging future scenarios arise.

The first scenario is that discrimination against these "old" people will persist because of a perception that older people are not capable of the mental alertness needed to cope with technological change. In such a scenario a country will be depriving itself of the wisdom of experience and the talents of part of its population. Another scenario is a tension arising between the personal needs of younger and older adults. For example, young workers with fewer outside obligations -- especially those who are single -- might be expected to be more willing to work overtime in order to get on at the firm. Older workers, on the other hand, who are more settled, have more obligations away from the workplace. Will the information-sector firms be able to accommodate workers with a range of motivations and levels of commitment? The final scenario is about career paths. If an employment mentality that only young people can work in the information sector continues, what will happen when people with the proper credentials have worked in information-sector firms for 20 years and want to move up? Will there be a place for them to go? Will the information sector be diversified enough to accommodate the career needs of experienced workers or will it only be able to accommodate young, entry level workers?

With respect to gender, cultural norms about family and childcare will heavily influence attitudes about a woman's place in the information economy. On the one hand, the information economy can be seen as bringing new opportunities to women because there has been less time to develop entrenched attitudes about gender. On the other hand, there are stereotypes about information-technology work being a male activity and a woman's primary place being in the home.

The final type of barrier relates to race, ethnicity and socio-economic class. How it is enacted varies by country. Given the racial and ethnic homogeneity of Irish society, socio-economic class barriers generally did not include race and ethnicity.[xiii] Instead, there was reluctance to acknowledge the existence of social class boundaries because of the country's post-colonial legacy. Despite the ways it is played out, the universal issue is the barring the entrance to the information sector for the culture's underclass. Because information-sector work is knowledge-based, education is the key. But attitudinal barriers prevent a society from reaping the benefits of full participation in the information economy. In order to ensure a supply of qualified information workers, nations need to address barriers that might be keeping potential talent from making a contribution.

Another aspect of adapting attitudes about socio-economic class is the issue of the "haves" and "have nots" in the information economy. The good news for the information age is that knowledge is portable capital and can be acquired -- in theory -- by anyone. Daniel Bell (1973) describes this economy as a meritocracy. In the agricultural economy, power and status are largely fixed and out of one's control. This is because they are based upon the ownership of land and characteristics such as birth order, gender and social class. In the industrial economy, power is in the hands of those with control over the means of production: the capital and the raw materials. While social mobility is not as fixed as in the agrarian society, a clear division between the managers and the proletariat exists. In contrast to both of these economies, the information economy with its emphasis on meritocracy and credentials should allow for greater social mobility. If one believes that intelligence is not a function of family name, address or income, and if educational opportunity is available to all, then -- theoretically -- everyone has an equal chance of sharing the fruits of the information economy.

The problem is that in all societies there is a gap between the theory and the reality of the meritocracy. It is this gap which widens the division between the information "haves" and "have nots." The case of Ireland is illustrative of this point; it highlights the connections among social class, education and social mobility. When the multinational firms first came to Ireland in the 1970s, the labor force was not adequately prepared for the type of work to be done. Consequently, the firms received grants from the State to provide the necessary technical training. Thus, in the early years of the information economy, workers from diverse social class and educational backgrounds were able to obtain employment in it. But that situation changed. A combination of greater competition for jobs and a change in the nature of the work means that formal credentials are now required for employment. At a minimum, the Leaving Certificate is required; for many forms of employment, post-secondary credentials are required. Therefore, to the extent that there are barriers to advanced education there are also bars on the door to the information economy: members of the underclasses would not have equal opportunity for success in the information sector, despite the apparent permeability of class borders in a meritocracy.

The exercise of recognizing competitive strengths and identifying barriers to be overcome shows that each particular nation has its own unique mix. The lesson here is that the solutions must make sense for the particular context in which they will be implemented. When the electronics sector was emerging as a key target area of Ireland's industrial policy during the 1970s, there was a clear expectation about the payoff for the financial incentives given to the multinational computer companies. It was expected that a spillover effect would result. This spillover would include the creation of new indigenous firms. Some of these firms would be suppliers to the multinational companies; others would be IT companies themselves. This expectation was based upon observation of the high tech region in the Boston area during the 1960s and 1970s where such a phenomenon did, indeed, occur. However, Ireland has learned that the spillover effect is neither automatic nor monolithic. Firms are not inherently motivated to source locally. Further, the placement of a single high tech firm in a particular location is not sufficient to stimulate the development of an industry in that region. There must also be a market, a sufficient number of qualified personal, an infrastructure, and an entrepreneurial presence in order for a high tech region to develop.

Interventions are necessary in order to respond to the socio-cultural forces that work against the information economy. In this research I saw how a nation's history, traditions, institutions and people can be at the same time the basis for its competitive advantage and the source of its undoing. In Ireland, I witnessed an ongoing tension between the forces of change and those of a risk adverse, resistant, traditional and conservative nation. At its best, a nation moves on its way into this new age with an appreciation for its unique position and its past.

3.3.2   Special Needs of Leapfrog Countries

There are two significant differences between the paths which first wave and second wave countries are taking to create their information sectors. Countries such as the United States moved from an agrarian phase through an industrial phase lasting over one hundred years on their way to establishing information economies. Newly industrializing countries, however, are proceeding differently. They are moving directly from traditional, agrarian societies to modern ones with employment in the information sector as a key component of this transition. In so doing, they are bypassing the lengthy period of industrialism that developed countries experienced as they moved toward this new economy. The second difference between these two types of nations is that the latter endeavor to accomplish this rapid economic transition by *importing* both *information sector jobs* and *information sector expertise* through inward investment by multinational firms. This approach to economic development raises a series of societal issues.

Irish society has changed dramatically in a matter of a few decades. Ireland was once a traditional society on the periphery of Europe where people operated within a network of personal relationships based on kinship and the direct face-to-face contact that comes from living in a small village. Here, individuals were bound together in community by mutual interdependence. That depiction of Ireland has been superseded by the image of a quickly modernizing society that is introducing all the benefits and problems accompanying this transition.[xiv] Since Ireland is representative of countries pursuing the alternative route to establishing an information economy and rapidly changing their societies, the lessons learned from the Irish case are especially relevant to other countries that have embarked upon a similar path.

The most immediate and observable economic benefit deriving from multinational information-sector firms is the direct and indirect employment that has resulted. Direct employment is the actual job in the multinational firm. Indirect employment arises from multinational firms that source from indigenous suppliers. Another indirect benefit to employment is the role that multinational firms play in stimulating the growth of the indigenous information sector. There is evidence of that occurring in Ireland.

However, against this benefit must be considered the costs. There are several. First, inward investment is not an economic panacea. Significant trade-offs are implied in the decision to base economic development on outside interests. These trade-offs should be considered as part of the decision making process about pursuing this sort of economic development policy. Ireland has had to come to terms with two significant trade-offs: economic vulnerability and proper allocation of financial resources. In an effort to compete with other locations in Europe, Ireland originally promoted itself as a low wage country. While this may have been true at the time, some unintended negative effects also resulted. Ireland learned that firms whose only commitment is to the location with the cheapest labor and the best incentive program could easily leave in the pursuit of a cheaper workforce. There were some abrupt departures from Ireland as other parts of the world entered the competition for mobile foreign investment. What followed was a sense of vulnerability on the part of the labor force. The most common concern about multinational, information-sector employment was about the vulnerability the workers felt as employees of internationally mobile firms that could abruptly leave Ireland at any time.

Dependence on overseas investment for the development of its information economy makes a country particularly vulnerable to financial fluctuations in the world economy. This economic dependence is felt at both the national and the personal levels. The departure of a multinational firm can devastate an entire region of the country. At the personal level, there is the constant fear of arbitrary redundancy occurring at any moment. An American manager recalling his earliest impressions about Ireland noted the role that employment security played in decisions about job changes or career moves. When doing initial hiring for his firm in Ireland, the number of resumes that reflected recent redundancies gave him pause. This nervousness was demonstrated once when the president of his firm was due to visit the Irish plant. Whereas the real reason was to observe operations because the plant had been so productive, workers were convinced that he was coming to deliver bad news.

Consequently, employees of the multinationals communicated a feeling of powerlessness at not having control over their destinies. They expressed a fear that some faceless manager at corporate headquarters halfway around the world might make a decision that would have grave consequences for them and their families. If the multinational firm is located in a large city then other employment opportunities might exist. But if the firm is in a smaller city or in some village in the country, then one might not have other information-sector options nearby.

Another trade-off involves the allocation of financial resources. To the extent that grants and tax relief are given to foreign firms, there are fewer resources available for indigenous firms in that industry. Thus, the trade-off becomes one of short-term versus long-term gain. The price being paid for jobs in the short term may be investment capital to support indigenous firms and permanent jobs. In the case of Ireland, policy makers have engaged in an ongoing process of policy analysis. In the early 1980s the issue of Ireland's economic vulnerability was first raised (National Economic and Social Council, 1982a). As a result of more extensive assessment that followed (Foley and McAleese, 1991; Industrial Policy Review Group, 1992), a substantial shift occurred. Ireland now places much more emphasis on developing indigenous firms and it is much more selective with regard to the type of multinational firm it wants to attract.

A final consideration relates to the ability of a latecomer to compete in the international information arena, particularly in the face of a general trend toward privatization and unfettered competition.[xv] O'Malley (1989) notes three significant barriers to entry that are experienced by late industrializing countries like Ireland. Early entrants can offer products and services at lower costs because of economies of scale. They have already achieved product differentiation and recognition. Finally, later entrant countries must cope with the capital expenditures necessary to enter an industry. Singer (1970) frames this issue as one of dualism, the growing disparity between the "haves" and the "have nots" in the global arena.

The lesson for Ireland and other later entrants into the information economy is that what worked for the first wave of post-industrial societies like the United States may not be the solution for succeeding waves. Whereas a high level of competition and privatization may have worked for the first entrants, later entrants may require government stimulation programs or other policy interventions.[xvi] To return to the thesis of the information economy in context, it is important to differentiate between the means and the goals. While later entrants may share the same goals as first entrant countries, the means by which they achieve them may be different because of the changed circumstances in which they are operating.

4.   ADAPTING THE VISION ALONG THE WAY

Ireland learned that when constructing a national climate that would support an information economy constant monitoring and adaptation was required. Changes were needed for two reasons: to respond to opportunities as they unfolded[xvii] and to respond to impacts as they were experienced. As Chapter 2 points out, Irish policy makers did not set out to create an information economy. Rather, they wanted to attract multinational firms in modern and "clean" industries to Ireland. For these reasons electronics was a good candidate. It was only through observing and responding to the effects of this strategy that the vision of an information economy unfolded.

In order to attract multinational firms in the electronics and then the software subsectors, aspects of the societal infrastructure needed to be taken into account. These included the educational system, telecommunications, transportation, utilities, physical plants for the firms, and housing for the workers. This need is especially acute when there are significant population shifts accompanying the arrival of this new employment sector. In Ireland, these aspects of the physical infrastructure needed to be upgraded and, in some cases, put in place for the first time. Thanks to funding from the European Union, Ireland was able to greatly improve its transportation infrastructure. The upgrading of the telecommunications infrastructure, especially in the rural West, had the unintended benefit of helping to expand Ireland's information economy. It was the state-of-the-art telecommunications system that encouraged a second wave of multinational firms to look to Ireland not just for hardware manufacture and final assembly but also for software development and offshore data processing.

Having a national climate supportive of information-sector work means more than having the proper physical infrastructure, however. Government policy must be in sync with this endeavor. And a business climate may need to be adjusted, something that requires government, industry and academic collaboration. Finally, in order that all citizens can participate in the information economy, the issue of information "haves" and "have nots" needs to be given serious attention.

4.1   Reconfiguring Industrial and Information Policy

To the extent that public policies are at counter purposes with the business of an information economy, they require adjusting. In the case of Ireland, what was required was a complete reversal of its industrial policy. As it became clear that the policy establishing post-colonial economic sovereignty through protectionist measures was not working, the substitution of a new vision required that public policies be adjusted. Existing policies related to import and export tariffs, tax laws, and protectionism were altered. New policies related to anti-discrimination law, economic incentives for inward investment, and the establishment of educational and training programs were created.

In addition to aligning industrial policy with the goals of the information economy, another type of policy that may need attention is information policy. Privacy, freedom of information, censorship, intellectual property and telecommunications policies may be at cross purposes with the information economy. In Ireland, for example, the absence of a comprehensive privacy policy was a disincentive to European firms wishing to locate back-office data processing in the planned Financial Services Centre. These firms required the same level of privacy that existed in their home countries. Therefore, in order to further the information economy by promoting offshore data processing services, Ireland implemented a privacy law. Another example was the change in telecommunications from a state-controlled monopoly to privatized, competitive firms in order to provide greater economic incentive to upgrade telecommunications facilities.

Policy makers need to be cognizant of the economic trade-offs associated with developing an information sector through inward investment. One way to minimize the economic vulnerability is by developing indigenous firms as well. However, it is important that aspects of the information industry targeted for development be suited to the circumstances of the country. For example, Ireland's industrial policy for indigenous information-sector firms increasingly focused on the software rather than the hardware subsector because fewer capital costs were involved. In addition, Ireland's abundance of well educated, young information professionals meant it had the proper natural resource -- people -- necessary for the software subsector.

The overriding recommendation to policy makers is to acknowledge that both intended and unintended consequences will result from policy decisions. To recognize this is to build into the policy making process mechanisms for ongoing assessment of the steps along the path toward the information economy.[xviii] As the example of Ireland has pointed out, these unintended consequences can be both positive and negative. It is also important to remember that the objective is not to simply emulate what another successful country has done, but to develop strategies and policies that make sense within the context of one's own country.

4.2   Adjusting the Business Climate

Just as public policies need to be aligned with the needs of the information economy, so too must the business climate. A healthy business climate will encourage entrepreneurs to produce ideas and will provide a receptive marketplace in which to reward their efforts. Achieving such a climate requires that the government, industry and academe work together.

An entrepreneurial capacity needs to be part of an infrastructure supportive of an information economy because the flow of innovation is the lifeblood of this sector. Some nations, however, may not have such a tradition for a variety of reasons. Countries with planned economies, or that history, may have populations that lack incentive for and experience with innovation. Other countries with colonial histories might lack incentive because of their aversion to risk taking. Both types of countries tend also to be ones that, like Ireland, are following the alternative path to the information economy.

Ireland's issues with entrepreneurship point to the challenges involved in changing the cultural perspective on risk taking and success. Not only has there not been an entrepreneurship tradition, but part of its post-colonial legacy has been an aversion to risk taking and a begrudging attitude toward success and those who achieve it. Innovation must be included along with the technical infrastructure of the information economy. People must know how to engage in innovative knowledge work and their society must reward them for it.

Another piece of the entrepreneurship pie is providing financial reward for innovative ideas and products. The local economy and domestic market is an important part of this. Once again, we can see that later entrants into the information economy cannot necessarily follow the path taken by the first movers. The American information sector evolved in a domestic market robust enough to fuel it with growing demand for products and services throughout the 1970s and 1980s. Smaller and later entrant countries such as Ireland cannot do it that way. With a population the size of an American city, a country such as Ireland has more limited opportunity for growth domestically.

This is manifested in several ways. For one thing, it's a riskier venture. Stephen told me he had to be more competent in his computer support services business in Ireland than he would have to be in London. The reason was that the larger British economy provided a natural market for computer support. One has to work much harder in Ireland, he said, where there is less of a cushion because of the size of the population and economy.

It is also more difficult for firms in countries with smaller economies to obtain the large capital investment required to manufacture computer products for a global market. Countries like the US and the UK have more risk capital available. In countries like Ireland venture capital firms have fewer investment options, making it a riskier endeavor. As a result, whole subsectors of the information economy may be economically unrealistic to pursue.

In Ireland the recent trend has been to favor the software subsector because of the lower capital costs involved. However, pursuing the software subsector is not unproblematic. The market in a nonindustrial economy is smaller than in industrial countries because of the absence of a market for these products. Consequently, information-sector firms in nations with small domestic economies must look outside the domestic market much sooner than their counterparts with larger populations and markets. And there is always the danger that a start-up firm will go abroad too soon. Nevertheless, a firm eventually needs the bigger, global market.

Finally, what is needed in order to have the proper business climate, especially when the domestic market is small, is to have meaningful collaboration among the government, industry and the educational infrastructure. This collaboration can help to eliminate redundancy and wasted resources.

5.   CONCLUSION

The reason for conducting this research and writing this book was to investigate the influence of socio-cultural context on the evolution of an information sector, its workers and their workplaces. I also wanted to explore the congruence between the characteristics of information-sector work and the features of the socio-cultural context within which it occurs. I chose Ireland as a laboratory for study because of the way in which its information economy is being developed. The combined influence of multinational and indigenous cultures in the information-sector workplace highlights the role of socio-cultural context. In addition, its information economy is emerging from an agrarian rather than an industrial base. Thus, its path is fundamentally different from countries such as the US or the UK whose information economies were layered on top of an industrial infrastructure. At the same time Ireland's path is typical of other nonindustrialized nations. For these reasons, the story of Ireland is one from which other nations can learn lessons.

The results of this research support the argument that information economies are not monolithic. Rather, they are shaped by the demands of the information economy and by the subtle interplay of foreign and domestic cultures as they adapt to one another. This case study of a country also shows how a country's unique socio-cultural factors are a source of both competitive advantage and roadblocks to be overcome.

The purpose in telling Ireland's tale has been to uncover the story behind the statistics about the global information sector. In this way we can begin to understand the subtleties of an environment's culture and history, and how these influence and are affected by the emerging information sector. In this story can be heard the voices of those who are bringing it about. The themes and lessons that have emerged are meant for all ears, multinational and domestic, established and emerging information economies. Ireland is a tangible setting within which to consider important themes about how the information economy is played out in context.

The goal of this research was to achieve a better understanding of the complexity of the interaction between the information sector and the societal environment within which it functions. It has focused on the cultural, economic and policy issues that can arise in the establishment of an information sector. It has identified some of the unintended consequences that can accompany the development of an information sector in a nonindustrialized country. An examination of the impact of the information sector on Irish society yields some general lessons applicable to other nations traveling a similar path. Learning the lessons from the experiences of another country can help policy makers to address societal issues that challenge the successful development of an information sector in their own nations. These lessons can also suggest to multinational managers some ways of working in a cross-cultural context. Finally, these lessons reinforce the perspective that it is the individual people, in all their complexity and diversity, who hold the key that will unlock the promise of the information age.

---

[i] Member checking is a method of establishing the credibility of the findings in which the researcher checks her/his interpretations with representatives of the people being studied. See Appendix for further discussion of member checking.

[ii] See Drucker (1993) and Tapscott (1996) for further discussion of the characteristics of this new workplace.

[iii] This is a good example of the caveat about the information subsectors. Hardware production is much more tied to a particular location than software and systems development might be.

[iv] Bilmes, Wetzker and Xhonneux (1997) found a strong link between investment in "hygiene" factors in the workplace and stock market performance. Some of the relevant practices include: flexible work hours, prevalence of teams, opportunities for workers to learn skills in new areas, and opportunities to share in company performance through profit-sharing and performance pay.

[v] Trauth (1999b) discusses this changing relationship in the United States.

[vi] See, for example, American Engineering Association Manpower Committee (1998), Freeman and Aspray (1999), Information Technology Association of America (1998), and NSF Informatics Task Force (1993), which discuss the dimensions of the IT labor force issue.

[vii] The information content subsector was not within the scope of my research project but has become a significant part of Ireland's information society agenda as witnessed, for example, by the recent expansion of the Irish film industry.

[viii] In the United States, for example, Trauth, Farwell and Lee (1993) and Lee, Trauth and Farwell (1995) found noteworthy discrepancies between the skills/knowledge being taught in the university and the skills/knowledge being expected in the workplace. The objective of such research was to inform curriculum changes.

[ix] As a result of the new wave of emigration in the1980s, industrial policy assessments in Ireland have recommended a closer match between the educational plans of the universities and the employment opportunities available in the country (Industrial Policy Review Group, 1992).

---

[x] For further discussion of this topic see Drucker (1994) and Dyson (1997).

[xi] See Hall (1994) for an account of how he learned this lesson while working with two different groups of Native Americans in the American Southwest.

[xii] See National Telecommunications and Information Administration (1999) for a discussion of the information "haves" and "have nots" in America.

[xiii] However, as Ireland finds it necessary to go abroad to find qualified information-sector workers, this situation may change in the future, particularly as the supply of labor would tend to come from the developing nations (Johnston, 1991).

[xiv] See Fukuyama (1999) for a discussion of some negative societal trends accompanying the transition from the industrial to the information society.

[xv] Several works about Ireland have pointed out the difficulties associated with unrestricted free trade and capitalism. See, for example, Jackson and Barry (1989) and O'Hearn (1989).

[xvi] Sen (1999) argues for well-thought-out economic and social development programs. See also Trauth and Pitt (1992) for an application of this argument to the telecommunications industry and Trauth, Derksen and Mevissen (1998) for a discussion of government stimulation programs in The Netherlands.

[xvii] See Drucker (1999) a for discussion of the information revolution and unexpected opportunities that are arising from it.

[xviii] See Trauth (1979 and 1986) for discussions of adaptive approaches to policy making.

APPENDIX: NOTES ON METHODOLOGY

1. INTRODUCTION

There are two reasons for writing an Appendix that provides additional detail about my research methods. The first is that good science expects it. The reader should be provided with adequate information about the research methods in order to be able to understand how I arrived at my findings. The first two sections of this Appendix provide greater detail about the methods employed for data collection and analysis. The second reason for writing this Appendix is to contribute to our developing understanding about the use of qualitative -- and in particular interpretive -- methods in conducting information systems research. As this research has progressed, issues about methodology gradually shifted from a background to a foreground position. In the process of conducting this research, writing papers, and now completing this book, I have gone through an intense learning process. In the spirit of sharing what I have learned with others who are interested in conducting similar research, I conclude this Appendix with some thoughts about the issues I have encountered and what I have learned from responding to them.

2. DATA COLLECTION[i]

Several options were available for collecting the data I sought. I could have relied solely on secondary sources to analyze socio-cultural factors that were influencing the development of the Irish information economy. Alternatively, I could have explored cultural influences in the information-sector workplace by sending a questionnaire to information technology firms. A third option was to employ ethnographic methods. The use of a questionnaire was ruled out for several reasons. Because I did not know at the outset the relevant aspects of Irish culture to study, I was unable to prespecify them in a questionnaire. In addition, a survey would not have captured such subtleties as the difference between what people say they do and what they actually do. Finally, a survey with its fixed questions and categories would not have given me the flexibility that I believed was needed in such a dynamic research setting. The socio-cultural influences were happening all around me, and their impacts were just bubbling to the surface. For these reasons I determined that the best way to obtain the information I sought about socio-cultural influences and impacts was to immerse myself in the world in which they were occurring. I would observe people and events, read documents and literature, and talk to people both formally and informally. I would spend an extended period of time in Ireland followed by repeat visits to check my interpretations. I would conduct an interpretive investigation of Ireland's information economy by employing ethnographic methods.

2.1   Ethnographic Interviews

Interviews supplemented by participant observation and documentary materials was the means by which I collected both background data about Irish culture and specific data about socio-cultural influences and impacts in relation to the information economy. Interviews can range from the survey interview in which each question is asked of each respondent in the same way and in the same sequence, to an ethnographic interview with a minimum of questioning or directing by the interviewer. In an ethnographic interview the researcher does not usually decide beforehand all the questions to be asked but typically has a list of issues to be to covered. This type of interviewing allows for asking people different kinds of questions based on their cultural knowledge. It also allows for the interviewer to steer and focus the interview on the basis of what the person is saying. It enables the researcher to return on other occasions to pursue further lines of inquiry, and to check hunches and hypotheses.

Beside the unstructured nature of the ethnographic interview, another difference with structured interviews is the type of data that is collected. Since the data collected in the latter type of interview is factual, emphasis is placed upon objectivity and consistency in data collection. The ethnographic interview, on the other hand, is used both as a source of data, and as a topic in itself. The ethnographic interview is used in situations where the researcher needs more than an easily remembered and specific piece of data or a simple "yes" or "no" answer. It is used when in-depth and less easily accessible information is sought. It also enables the researcher to treat the interview accounts as both a source of information and as a source of data or evidence of the perspectives of the people who produce the accounts. In between these two ends of the conversational continuum there are a number of possibilities.

I engaged in a variety of types of ethnographic interviewing in this study. They ranged from the semi-structured interviews with officials at government agencies, to the open ended interviews I conducted in the information-sector firms, to the ad hoc interviews I had with colleagues at the University or friends I had made in Ireland. The structure of the interviews often depended upon the type of information I sought and the degree of control I had over the situation. My most structured interviews occurred with Irish policy makers and cultural commentators. I spoke with them primarily in the beginning of this project as I was doing background research. I was seeking generally factual information regarding public policy. My most unstructured interviews were usually spontaneous ones that I had with friends, students, colleagues and people I would meet in social situations. What would typically begin as a casual conversation at a party would turn into an interview as we delved into some cultural topic. Other times my effort to get clarity about an impression turned into an interview with colleagues at the University as I encountered alternate or confirmatory interpretations. Between these two extremes were the open-ended interviews that I conducted in the information-sector firms.

Over a 16-month period I conducted in-depth interviews with 86 respondents[ii], the majority of whom (80%) worked in information-sector companies. Seven of the interviews were conducted in the US during a five-month period prior to my departure for Ireland (April - August 1989). The interviews conducted in Ireland occurred during an 11-month period (September 1989 - July 1990). The IT workplaces in this study included seven American multinational firms and seven Irish firms. These firms were in the hardware, software and information systems/services subsectors. Respondents who did not work in the information sector included individuals from government agencies charged with promoting aspects of Ireland's economic policy, spouses of American information-sector managers at American firms, or others in a position to comment either about Irish culture or the information sector. Eighty-three percent of the respondents were Irish. Summary data about the respondents and the information-sector firms is shown in Tables 1 and 2 respectively.

Table 1.
Respondent Characteristics (n=86)

Nat.	Gender	Am. Firm	%	Irish Firm	%	No Firm	%	Total	%
Irish	Male	24	28%	15	17%	10	12%	49	57%
	Female	10	12%	9	11%	3	3%	22	26%
Am.	Male	11	12%	0	0%	0	0%	11	12%
	Female	0	0%	0	0%	4	5%	4	5%
Total		45	52%	24	28%	17	20%	86	100%

Table 2.
Firm Characteristics (n=14)

Nationality	Hardware	%	Software	%	Services	%	Total
American	6	43%	1	7%	0	0%	50%
Irish	2	14%	3	22%	2	14%	50%
Total	8	57%	4	29%	2	14%	100%

Once I had decided to conduct interviews in these firms rather than disseminate a survey, the next decision was whether to conduct structured or open-ended interviews. The trade-off is that with structured interviews there would be consistency in responses; each respondent would talk about the same topics. On the other hand, open-ended interviews would give me the opportunity to explore specific aspects of Irish culture according to the inclination of the given respondent and the situation at hand. That is, if a certain topic "struck a chord" with an individual, we could explore it in more depth, placing less emphasis on other topics. Further, open-ended interviews would enable me to incorporate my developing interpretations into my later interviews.

I conducted some interviews with individuals at multinational companies in the US prior to coming to Ireland. At these meetings I explained the project, solicited general information about the company and its site in Ireland, and obtained the name of a contact person. In the case of the remaining multinational and indigenous companies, I made contact after arriving in Ireland. The first meeting at these companies was with its managing director. This interview involved questions of a general nature about the company, and in the case of the multinationals, the reasons for coming to Ireland. The initial interview was followed by one with the human resources manager who served as my primary contact within the companies and with whom I arranged for other interviews. Depending upon the size of the company, between three and eight interviews with personnel from representative levels in the company were conducted.[iii]

During interviews lasting a minimum of one and one half hours, respondents working in the information sector provided information about their family, educational, social class and employment backgrounds in order to provide me with some context for interpreting their comments. In these interviews we discussed employment in the information sector and how it fit with the Irish culture. We also discussed the impact of doing this type of work on their personal and professional lives, and on Irish society in general. Some workers, particularly those who worked at multinational firms, also discussed foreign influences on Irish culture and on their lives. Oftentimes the respondents addressed aspects of the Irish culture by drawing contrasts with the US, the UK or some other country. In order to preserve anonymity, I have given all the respondents pseudonyms and omitted the names of their employers. In excerpts that include my comments or questions I am identified as "ET."

In this research project I came to learn that the identification and selection of respondents would not be straightforward. There were the expected respondents: those who worked at government agencies or IT firms with whom I had scheduled interviews. To this were added the collection of unexpected interviewees. Some of these even occurred in the firms. For example, during one of my days spent interviewing at an American firm, a worker whom I was not scheduled to interview had been designated by management as my luncheon companion. As we ate I told her about my project and she, in turn, told me about her background, her work history and gradually began to offer unsolicited comments on the items I was investigating in my interviews.

In this study, interviews provided three types of data. The first type was about aspects of Irish culture as they applied specifically to the respondent, such as the person's own work ethic. The second type was her or his perceptions about Irish culture, such as the general attitude toward authority. The third type of data was metadata, information that resulted from what was not said, what was conveyed through nonverbal communication or what differed from factual data collected elsewhere. The last two types of data point out the differences between structured and ethnographic interviews. While subjective and perceptual data might be considered suspect in the former type of interview, it is actively sought in the latter.

Ethnographic interviews were used for two purposes in this study. One purpose was to learn more about Irish society during the early stages of my research. In these interviews we discussed socio-cultural influences and impacts with respect to the information sector. The purpose was to help me to identify those factors I wanted to explore in later interviews. In these early interviews I began with a list of classical socio-cultural factors, drawn from the sociological literature, from which I intended to choose a subset to explore. As a result of these interviews I was also able to identify socio-cultural factors that I had not previously considered. These interviews also helped me to interpret my observations about and experiences with Irish culture. Finally, the interviews helped to clarify my understanding of public policy activities. This was done by speaking with persons knowledgeable about Irish industrial policy. I reviewed with them a growing list of industrial development documents until I was satisfied that I understood the history of Ireland's industrial policy and had identified all the relevant policy documents. While many of these discussions, such as those with the Industrial Development Authority, were planned interviews an equal number occurred during chance conversations with people.

The second use of the ethnographic interviewing occurred in the multinational and indigenous information technology firms. The set of socio-cultural factors identified through previous interviews, examination of prior research, and feedback from colleagues formed the basis of these interviews. I asked respondents about aspects of Irish culture that were influencing the structure and operations of information technology work. We also discussed impacts of the IT sector on Irish society. These items are shown in Table 3.

While the interview form was my general guide, I did not strictly adhere to it. I took my cue from the respondents. The approach was to start with the information that I was interested in exploring and let the session be determined by the particular "expertise" or inclination of the respondent. For example, if an individual had experience working in both multinational and indigenous firms, the discussion might focus on comparisons between these two types of firms. On the other hand, if the individual was raised in a rural environment or had worked in agriculture, the discussion might focus on comparisons between farming and information-economy work. Both the order of questioning and the level of detail varied as well. Some respondents needed direct questioning. When that was the case I went through the form asking questions. Others anticipated the items that I wanted to explore and the order was, therefore, determined by them. When they came in with things on their mind to talk about, I let our conversation flow accordingly. Those items that elicited little response from interviewees were explored in less depth than others.

At one extreme was an Irish man who had thought long and hard about our upcoming meeting. Without having seen my interview items he came in with what amounted to a 90-minute prepared speech on capitalism in Ireland, his views, Ireland's past, and it's future directions. At the other extreme would be the occasional reticent respondent, only there because management told her or him to do so, who gave close to yes-no answers. The vast majority of the respondents fell somewhere in the middle.

Table 3. Interview Items

Respondent Background
Job Description
Educational Background
Work History
Family Background

Cultural Factors - Individual
Work Life
    Work ethic
    Work culture
    Management style
    Unions
Personal Life
    Quality of life
    Standard of living
    Family
    Religion

Cultural Factors - Societal
Population
    Age
    Size
    Women
    Education

Cultural Factors Societal (cont.)
Cultural Traits
    Authority
    Personalism
    Individualism
    Ireland's colonial past
    Social interaction
    Time
    Ireland as an island nation

Policy Factors
    Industrial policy
    Multinational firms

Economic Factors
    Irish economy
    Vulnerability
    Societal infrastructures

2.2   Participant Observation

In order to place the information obtained from these interviews into a larger context I also collected information about Irish society by means of participant observation.[iv] While I was carrying out this research I was also living -- and during some of the time teaching -- in Ireland. I initially lived and worked in Ireland from September 1989 to August 1990. I made subsequent trips to Ireland in 1992, 1993, 1995 and 1999. Thus, at the macro level participant observation occurred in the course of every day living, working and communicating with Irish people about every day affairs. I participated fully in the society by teaching at the University, socializing with colleagues, attending staff meetings, making friends outside the University, and joining organizations. In this way I learned about Irish culture both by experiencing it and through my informal conversations with people. Doing this enabled me to observe and directly experience Irish culture and to compare this experiential information with the information I was obtaining from my interviews.

At work I would regularly have conversations in the staff lounge with colleagues at the University about my experiences and interpretations, followed by their views on these topics. I also had conversations with acquaintances and friends that I made while living in Ireland. One particularly good source of data was my membership in the American Women's Club of Dublin. This organization is made up of American women who are living in Ireland. When I was there, the organization was comprised of three types of women: wives of American multinational executives stationed in Ireland for a few years; American wives of Irish men who lived permanently in Ireland; and me. Their own experiences in adapting to the Irish culture provided me with additional data as well as a sounding board for my own experiences.

In addition to learning more about Irish culture, living in Ireland also gave me access to individuals whom I could interview. From colleagues at the University I received suggestions about Irish firms where I might conduct interviews and received introductions to facilitate entry into them. Through social functions of the American Women's Club I met managers at some of the multinational firms I wanted to study. Chance conversations also provided access. One evening while talking with the wife of a colleague, I was referred to a man who had experience working in two of the multinational firms I was studying as well as in indigenous firms. Further, he belonged to a union and therefore had perspectives about unions, which he could share. Through this chance conversation, I was able to gain access to this person. Another time, through a relative of one of my students I was able to gain access to two indigenous companies where I had no contact person.

At the micro level, I engaged in participant observation of the information-sector workplaces where I conducted my interviews. I spent considerable time in the 14 IT firms throughout the 11-month period that I was interviewing information-sector workers and managers. On these site visits I was able to observe the work environment, atmosphere and management style. I would spend whole days at a company, eating lunch with personnel there, and having informal chats with people during coffee breaks. I was able to directly observe features of the work environment, such as management style and level of social interaction, which were also being discussed in my interviews. In this way, I could contrast my own perceptions about the work environment with individuals' comments during interviews. I was able to incorporate these observations into my discussions with the respondents during our interviews. I maintained a research journal during all the times that I lived in Ireland. In this journal I recorded thoughts, observations and questions about experiences at the firms I visited and in the society as a whole.

Upon my return to the US I was able to continue my participant observation and maintain my close contact with Irish culture in two ways. One was through correspondence with several of the people I had come to know in Ireland. The Internet and electronic mail were very helpful in maintaining contact with Irish people. The other means of continuing my participant observation in Irish culture was by participating in the Irish Studies community in America. This community is comprised of both American and Irish scholars of Irish history, literature and culture. I joined two Irish Studies scholarly organizations,[v] presented papers at Irish studies conferences both in America and in Ireland and published in an Irish Studies journal.

The benefit of immersing myself in the culture was that I was able to directly experience many the socio-cultural factors I was studying. This enhanced my ability to perceive cultural nuances. As a result I was able to contrast three sources of information: what I had learned from my background reading and conversations with people in the US prior to coming to Ireland; what I heard from people during interviews; and what I was experiencing myself.

2.3   Documentary Analysis

Written and visual documents and records are an integral aspect of society. These records and documents range from the formal to the informal, from the census records to the novel, from the policy document to the play. While I did not want to base my study exclusively on secondary sources, I did want the results of previous work to inform my own questions and to serve as a source of triangulation for my interpretations.[vi] Documentary data that was used in this research included: public policy studies; documents from government agencies charged with supporting the industrial policy; and published materials about Irish history, culture, society and public policy. This information came from laws, public policy documents, and Irish newspapers, films, plays, magazines and books. As this research progressed, I was also able to turn to websites as a source of documentary information. This documentary information was used in determining which societal factors to explore in my interviews, to refine the coding categories and subcategories and to put into a broader perspective what I learned from my interviews.

One purpose for examining documentary material at the societal level was to help me trace and understand Ireland's economic development plan as it related to information-sector work. These plans are expressed in a series of industrial development documents developed since the 1950s. In addition, several assessment studies have also been conducted. For example, the *Telesis Report* (National Economic and Social Council, 1982a) was an important evaluation of Ireland's industrial policy and contains recommendations that helped to direct Ireland's information economy. These documents were examined for two reasons. One was to use them as evidence that public policy was part of the mix of societal factors having an influence on the development and structure of the information economy in Ireland. The second reason was to consider the influence of specific public policy initiatives on the evolution of this sector. For example, documents relating to industrial development since the 1950s enable one to trace changes in the employment sectors as a way of documenting the impact of information-sector work on employment in Ireland.

Another type of documentary data that was used is literature about social, historical, and political aspects of Irish society. These scholarly sources provided insights into aspects of Irish history and contemporary Irish society, and in some cases specifically addressed issues related to industrial development. Written materials about Irish society in general, and about specific aspects such as Irish culture enabled me to refine my understanding of the factors I was exploring in my interviews. Finally these materials were used to enhance my understanding by helping to clarify issues that arose in the course of conducting my interviews. Documentary data was also collected from the organizations at which I conducted interviews. Corporate data was used to elaborate on items discussed in interviews, to clarify points and to provide another perspective on comments made by respondents.

3.   DATA ANALYSIS

To facilitate my analysis I created a database of respondent comments. The data that populated this database came from transcripts of taped interviews and notes from interviews that were not taped. Each transcript was content analyzed using open coding. This process involved dividing each interview transcript into meaningful content segments, coding each segment according to an evolving set of themes, assigning indexing categories and subcategories, and entering the segments into a database.[vii] The database also contained respondent and firm characteristics. In analyzing the data, two types of interpretations were carried out. The first interpretation was the process of developing the coding categories. The second interpretation was the process of understanding *what* the respondents were saying, *who* was saying what, and *why* certain people held the views that they did. The objective of this interpretation was to understand *how* people made sense of their reality (Feldman, 1995).

3.1   Open Coding

I evolved a set of coding categories to use in retrieving the data through the process of open coding. Once the on-site interviews in Ireland were completed and I returned to the US for the data analysis phase, I was faced with the challenge of how I would carry out the content analysis of the data. In considering my options for data analysis, one was to employ software that would search for certain key words taken from the interview protocol and then retrieve surrounding text. To go that route would have considerably shortened the lengthy process of the alternative: dividing transcripts into meaningful units or content chunks, creating coding schemes, coding each of these content chunks and then loading them into a database for retrieval. There were two problems with this streamlined approach, however.

The first was that identifying a concept was not as easy as locating a specific keyword. For example, one important socio-cultural factor that emerged from my research was social class. Social class was closely related to who went to college to get the credentials to work in the information sector. The problem, however, was that people rarely used the actual words *social class* when speaking about it. In fact, Irish respondents regularly denied any influence of social class in Ireland, and then went on to give examples of it. I learned that people found a myriad of ways to signal social class such as a certain part of town where they lived or would never consider living, or the particular religious order that taught them in school. For these reasons I could not rely on keywords as a way of organizing my data for retrieval.

Once I had determined to divide the transcripts into topical chucks and code them, the next decision was which categories to use. My choice was either to use categories present in the interview protocol or to let the categories evolve from the data. I chose the latter, the open coding approach. I determined that to do otherwise would be to overlook some of the unplanned voices and messages present in my interviews. Maintaining consistency across transcripts when using evolving categories for data analysis, however, was a significant challenge throughout the coding process. But I eventually reached a point where the categories and subcategories were sufficient to capture all the meanings contained in my transcripts.

It is techniques such as open coding which highlight the interpretive nature of this research. My choice of open coding meant that I was approaching the data without an a priori framework to shape the information processing. Instead, I was allowing the interpretive lens to evolve as I interacted with the data. Open coding is part of the grounded theory approach to qualitative analysis developed by Glaser and Strauss.[viii] Using this approach I engaged with the data without a preconceived commitment to a particular line of thinking. The essential features of open coding are: 1) the inductive development of provisional categories; 2) ongoing testing of categories through conceptual analysis and comparison of categories with data that is already coded; and 3) the altering of existing categories as other ones are created or eliminated (Strauss, 1987, pp. 11-13). Open coding required considerable flexibility on my part. I had to let go of initial control over the categories and be willing to adjust them as the analysis progressed.

I began reading the transcripts with my mind a "blank slate" and let the coding categories emerge as my interpretive understanding of the transcripts progressed. In this way I let the data "speak" to me. In applying open coding to the chunks[ix] into which I carved each transcript, I began with inductive development of provisional categories, engaged in ongoing testing of categories and comparison of new categories with data that was already coded, and subsequently altered existing categories as other ones were created or eliminated. As I moved through the coding process some categories expanded, others collapsed. In the end I had a set of categories and subcategories, which went beyond the topics listed in my interview form. Had I not engaged in open coding I would have missed some key socio-cultural factors that emerged from this research.[x] The full set of coding categories and subcategories is shown in Table 4.

Table 4. Coding Categories

Main Categories	Subcategories
Culture: Work Life[xi]	
Work Ethic	Productivity issues
	Type of work suited for
	Motivation for staying at, liking work
	Importance of work in one's life
Work Culture	Work environment
	Atmosphere
	Status
Management Style	British
	American
Unions	In general
Culture: Home Life	
Quality of Life	Sport
	Easygoing
	Income
	Standard of living
	Free time
	Pub
	Good time
	Country
Family	Attitude toward children
	Childcare
	Family life
Religion	Institution
	Values
Women	Discrimination
	Career
	Homemaker

Education	In general
	Third level
	Secondary
	Primary
	Training
	Skills

Culture: National Characteristics

Culture	Gombeen man
	Imported culture
	Circumspect
	Irish language
	Insecurity
	Repressed
	Curiosity

| Age | Young |
| | Large |

Size	Small
	Anonymity
	Risk taking

Network	Personalism
	Connections
	The stroke

| Colonial Past | In general |
| | West Brits |

| Authority | In general |

Class System	Basis for class assignment
	Trappings of social class
	Working class jobs
	Middle class jobs
	Gap between classes

| Individualism | Begrudging other's success |

	Competitive vs. cooperative
	Recognition of accomplishments
	Group vs. individual orientation
Social Interaction	Interaction with foreigners
	Role in culture
	Friendly
Time	Taking time
	Being late
	Punctuality
Island Nation	Physically separated
	Not modern
	Peripheral in Europe
	Television's influence
This is Ireland	National identity
	Resistance to outside influences
	Excuses
	Who adapts

Public Policy

Industrial Policy	Indigenous firms
	Multinational firms
	Industrial Development Authority
	Government agencies
	Spillover effect of multinational firms
Information Policy	Privacy
	Censorship and freedom of information
	Telecommunications
General Policy	Other laws
	Tax laws
	Laws pertaining to women

	Trade protectionism
	Government monopolies
Infrastructure	Transportation
	Telecommunications
	Utilities
	Post
European Union Policy	In general

Economy

Economy	In general
	Vulnerability of current
	industrial policy
	Social welfare
Emigration	In general
	Reasons for
Employment	In general
	Unemployment
	Redundant workers
	Career mobility
Work Sectors	Information economy
	Civil Service
	Industrial
	Agricultural
	Traditional
	Leapfrogging from agricultural
	to information economy

3.2   Interpretation

In carrying out my interpretation I systematically retrieved and analyzed content chunks according to the categories and subcategories shown in Table 4. I was examining the content chunks on three levels. On one level I was interested in the information contained in the comment. An example is what the respondent said about IT skills learned in university. On another level I was interested in those respondent characteristics that might help to account for the particular response that was given. I examined both respondent and firm characteristics in this regard: company nationality, and respondent nationality, gender, and position (i.e. worker vs. manager). For example, I learned that firm nationality helped to account for attitudes about women in the information-sector workforce. Finally, I was interested in exploring both the *influence* of socio-cultural characteristics on the Irish information economy and the *impact* that the information sector was having on Irish society and culture. For this reason, I also coded and analyzed the content chunks according to whether they were expressing an influence of socio-cultural context on the information sector, an impact of the IT sector on socio-cultural context, both, or neither.

As I conducted my interpretation of the respondents' comments I continued the process of breakdown analysis (Agar, 1986). This would occur when I encountered an anomaly in the data. One was the example of social class. I saw that despite uniform claims of Ireland as a classless society, respondents peppered their comments with reference to social class. I responded to this contradiction by referring to additional sources of information to enhance my understanding. In the case of social class I referred to my participant observation data, which was consistent with respondents' emphasis on social class. I also referred to sociological and historical literature, which helped me understand the Irish experience with social class. In the end, this "breakdown" was resolved not by producing a consistent view but by developing a deeper understanding of Irish ambivalence regarding social class. The "resolution" was my new awareness of an inherent contradiction.

The process of interpretation also caused me to revise my initial assessments. This occurred, for example, in analyzing my data about religion. The impression that I had formed at the conclusion of my interviews was that religion was not a significant factor in the information-sector workplace. This was due to the consistency of respondents' comments to the effect that religion was not an influence. It came as a surprise, therefore, when my reading of the transcripts began to undermine that impression. As I encountered more and more comments about religion I began to revise this initial impression. My intrigue led me to the point of counting responses. What I learned was that over half of the respondents actually gave examples of the *influence* of religion in the information-sector workplace.

3.3   Evaluation

A significant concern for those conducting interpretive research is: How can I trust my results? How can I expect others to trust them? The subjective nature of interpretive research requires one to find alternatives to validity and reliability as evaluative measures. Rather than consistency and correctness my goal was to achieve *authenticity* (Golden-Biddle and Locke, 1993). Authenticity is achieved when the account that is rendered makes sense or rings true (Geertz, 1973; Miles and Huberman, 1994; Sanday, 1979). An authentic account comes across to the reader as genuine; it reflects the researcher's connection to the people (Klein and Myers, 1999). It is the product of both the analysis and the narrative style.

An authentic rendering of my interpretations was achieved through the evocative quality of the narrative, the use of quotations, rich description and my "confessional" stance. By inserting myself into the narrative and revealing my connection to the research context I showed how the interpretations developed. I revealed how my gender, age, religion, nationality and work experiences contributed to my interpretations. I revealed the process whereby I worked through anomalies to find resolution. To help me do this, I recorded my own introspection along with my interview and observational data over the course of this research project. In some cases, I also made introspective comments in the interviews, which appeared in the transcripts. I maintained two journals: a research journal and a personal journal. In my research journal I recorded thoughts, feelings, experiences and anxieties more or less related to the research experience. Maintaining a personal journal is an ongoing activity in my life but one about which am more diligent during foreign travel. In this journal I record experiences, events and feelings of a more general nature about the experience of living in Ireland. I drew upon both journals in developing my narrative account. I endeavored to achieve authenticity in my analysis through triangulation, member checking and breakdown resolution.

3.3.1   Triangulation

Triangulation refers to checking inferences drawn from one set of data sources with those collected from others. The use of multiple sources in this way enabled me to provide corroborating evidence -- evidence other than my own -- to support my interpretations (Creswell, 1998; Fetterman, 1998; Jick, 1979; Miles and Huberman, 1994; Silverman, 1993; Yin, 1989). The term, borrowed from navigational language, was first used in relation to research methods by Denzin (1978). I used participant observation, documentary analysis and interviews with people outside the information sector to triangulate the interpretation of my information-sector interview transcripts. A fallacy associated with triangulation is that multiple sources will result in convergent data. This is not always the case, however. An example was the topic of union participation in information technology firms. Both management and workers told me that unions were not necessary in high tech firms. But from my colleagues at the University, I was told that American multinationals are actively antiunion. Given these two different points of view, I was motivated to seek data from additional sources. This data came from interviews with union personnel, reading published materials about unions in the electronics industry, and viewing a documentary film about multinational companies and unions in Ireland (*Trouble the Calm,* 1989). While two different perspectives on unions remained, this triangulation resulted in a much more textured rendering of the topic.

Another example of triangulation not resulting in convergent data but rather helping me to understand the meaning behind the apparent contradictions had to do with the class system in Ireland. In the corporate interviews I was told that Ireland did not have a rigorous class system. That is, most of Irish society consisted of the same -- middle -- class. Yet through other methods of data collection, I received the opposite viewpoint. Through participant observation, I noted the existence of class system with strong borders, particularly between the working and the middle classes. This came out in discussions with my students. I also experienced the presence of class distinction in discussions about where I should live in Dublin. The existence of a class system was further reinforced in a series of articles that appeared in *The Irish Times* about the class system in Ireland (O'Toole, 1990). The point was made in these articles that one's family background was a significant aspect of one's social class. Rather than resolve the question of whether a rigid class system did or did not exist, multiple methods of data collection provided me with more information about how individuals perceive movement between classes. Those working in the information technology firms, those who did not believe in a rigid class structure, saw education, employment, and income as the basis of class position. The other sources of data suggested that one's class position is determined more by factors out of one's control such as family background. Rather than resulting in convergence, triangulation provided me with other types of information.

3.3.2   Member Checking

Another method used to establish authenticity was member checking. This meant going back to check interpretations with those who were being studied (Cresswell, 1998; Ely et al.,1991; Lincoln and Guba, 1985; Miles and Huberman, 1994; Silverman, 1993; Trauth, 1997). In member checking the researcher solicits the *inside* perspective on the credibility of the interpretations by reviewing the data, analyses, and interpretations with the participants. The object is to determine whether those familiar with the context can recognize in the results their own world of experience, whether the story being told rings true to them. I employed member checking in the following ways. My objective was to gain feedback on my interpretations of Irish socio-cultural characteristics as they related to the Irish information economy. Therefore, I did not limit myself to the respondents only. In this research "those familiar with the context" included several groups of people: representative respondents, colleagues in Ireland who have professional expertise in the topics I was exploring, Irish scholars in the American Irish Studies community, and members of the information systems community with expertise in global informatics.

Following the extensive period in the field, I returned to Ireland four times. During these visits I met with some of the respondents and Irish colleagues to gain feedback on my developing interpretations. I also gave six presentations to the Irish studies community and published one paper in an Irish Studies journal to elicit reaction to my developing interpretations. Finally, I gave five presentations to the information systems community and published six papers to elicit feedback from this community.

Over the course of this project, members of these groups provided valuable reactions to my interpretations. In general, this was a very positive experience. There was one occasion, however, that raised the issue of what to do when the "members" disagree with your interpretation. This occurred when I presented a paper at an Irish Studies conference about women in the Irish information sector (Trauth, 1994). When I delivered the paper one Irish woman in the audience had a strong and negative reaction to my interpretations. Her response caused me to rethink what I had written. I went back to my transcripts and observational data and retraced the process by which I reached the interpretations presented in my paper. In the process of doing this I discussed this experience with some of those who had witnessed it (there was a large group in attendance). In these discussions I received help in understanding why this audience member might have reacted as she did. I also made a point of talking with this woman later in the conference. In the end I remained with my original interpretation. But while I did not change my interpretation, the insights I gained did influence the way I presented the topic in this book. In the Irish Studies community I had a support group who read my work and offered critical commentary. I found their comments to be invaluable in my efforts to establish confidence in my interpretations.

3.3.3 Breakdown Resolution

The final method that I employed to achieve authenticity was breakdown resolution. As described above, this is the iterative process of resolving anomalies. It is achieved by considering particular data in relation to the larger context and revising interpretations accordingly. Triangulation and member checking were employed to help me understand anomalies. One such anomaly occurred with respect to the Irish attitude toward education. I was having some difficulty in understanding the nature of responses to this question until I was able to place them in a larger context that included emigration patterns. When I did this, I could see the logic in the responses.

Anomalies sometimes arose in relation to participant observation. When my observations differed from what I was hearing in the interviews, I needed to explore the reasons. In some cases I was able to resolve the anomaly. When I couldn't I presented the contradiction as part of the rich fabric that is Irish culture. Sometimes the anomaly was that the answers were *too* consistent. A problem with too much consistency is that respondents might be giving a "party line," what they want you to believe or what *they* want to believe. This happened with respect to religion. Despite evidence to the contrary, they told me that the Catholic Church exerted little influence over people. Resolving this anomaly was not so much a process of understanding difference as it was the rationale for sameness. Through triangulation I was able to probe beneath the surface of some of these "pat" responses.

I engaged in a dialectic process of considering multiple sources of data, returning to the field and the people being studied, and examining individual information within the context of the whole. In this way I was able to establish the authenticity of my interpretive analysis of socio-cultural factors that were interacting with Ireland's information economy.

4.   RESEARCH ISSUES ENCOUNTERED AND LESSONS LEARNED[xii]

In the course of reaching a decision about the methods I would use in this study, and then later when I was engaged in applying them, certain issues related to the use of qualitative research methods arose. These issues are considered in this final section of the Appendix. Some of these issues arose from reviews of papers I have written about this research. Others have come from questions and comments during conference presentations. Still others were the result of my own self-education in qualitative research methods. In many respects these issues are about a single theme: the unstable ground of subjectivity. In conducting this research I learned significant lessons, not only about Ireland and its emerging information economy but about research methods as well. These issues and lessons are organized around five themes.

4.1   Self-consciousness

My own training in positivist thinking and quantitative methodologies was an obstacle I had to overcome. I was taught that objectivity was the hallmark of good science, that standing apart and conducting consistent measurements was the proper way to ensure validity. But a dilemma I faced was how to cope with the subjectivity that is an inherent part of qualitative methods. Part of this challenge was learning to be comfortable in my dual role. On the one hand, I needed to fully participate in my context in order to collect and interpret information. Yet I also felt the need to remain apart from this context in order to be able to note and process what I was experiencing and learning. I had to maintain some psychic space around myself for reflection and analysis. I had to learn how to get close to my context and yet remain *strange.*[xiii]

Knowing that my presence as the researcher was influencing the data collection, I sometimes wondered about the extent to which the respondents were simply telling me what they thought I wanted to hear. I wondered about the extent to which they were "packaging" their responses.[xiv] I wondered how much I could believe what they were telling me. My response to this issue was to employ triangulation in order to ensure multiple perspectives on each topic.

One source of alternative viewpoints came through my social network. I found myself turning to various Irish and American friends and colleagues as a sounding board for the interpretations I was developing about the socio-cultural factors. Even though -- or perhaps because -- these individuals tended not to work in the information sector, they had a different perspective from the respondents. As I formalized my findings, once again I relied upon member checking.

A related issue was about questioning myself as a source of data, and questioning my own assumptions. This heightened sensitivity to context helped me to develop a posture of being self-conscious -- to use the words of a British respondent working at an American firm in the West of Ireland. He was self-conscious in that he reflected on his reactions. Since he had only recently come to the Republic from Northern Ireland he was very attuned to the cultural experiences I was having. He quite often stopped by my interview room to share his thoughts with me.

Halfway through the year in which I conducted the interviews, I was asked to give a seminar on my research at the University. I reluctantly agreed. I hesitated because I felt that I had barely begun to conduct my interviews and felt that I had little by way of coherent conclusions or insights to offer. The experience drove home to me the importance of questioning my own assumptions. The first assumption to be questioned was that giving a seminar would be a one-way communication event. Instead, the experience became an opportunity for me to articulate some of my assumptions and initial perceptions, and to receive feedback on them. While the audience of Irish faculty and students wasn't hostile, neither was it overtly supportive of what I was doing.[xv] It was not until they learned more about the thrust of my research, that they began to set aside their own assumption that the purpose of my research was to uncritically glamorize the presence of American multinational firms in Ireland. Their challenging questions influenced me to question what I was thinking, assuming and perceiving as much as I may have influenced them.

4.2   Emotional Proximity

During the initial stages of my research, I noted in my journal my concern that I seemed to be enjoying myself too much. I wondered whether I was staying strange (aloof was how I termed it) enough. As the year wore on I became more comfortable with the idea of enjoying myself during my research and even becoming friendly with some of the respondents in my study. However, as I became more comfortable with the people and the country, I continued to be aware of the issue of how familiar I *should* become.

During the last month of the year I spent in Ireland, I had two occasions on which I wondered if I had crossed the line and become too familiar in my surroundings. In both instances I had engaged in a lively discussion about such charged topics as gender, contraception, abortion and religion with some respondents with whom I had spent a fair amount of time over the course of the year. In noting their reactions to my views when we differed, I was brought back once again to the issue of balancing strangeness and familiarity. I concluded that achieving the proper balance had both ethical and methodological dimensions.

When I reflected upon my interactions with people whose views were different from mine I noted that when these others controlled the flow of information, when I was primarily a passive listener our interactions were fine. But as I became more comfortable with these people and began to open up and share more of my own personality with them I felt a tension develop. As I was becoming closer to these people as friends I wanted to reveal more of myself to them. In reflecting on these two situations I wondered (methodologically) whether I had been too much my own person and not enough the researcher. As a result, I wondered if I were running the risk of alienating my informants. But I also wondered (ethically) whether it was proper to be so much the researcher in my interactions that these aspects of my persona had not emerged sooner.

4.3   Control

Two months into my year in Ireland I noted in my research journal that I was moving about aimlessly and had yet to establish a coherent research design. I was frustrated and anxious that my research project seemed to be so out of control. The important lesson I eventually learned was that when conducting interpretive research, the more alien the context the more important flexibility becomes. I learned that as a researcher I had to be prepared to embrace the data whenever it was presented regardless of the location, intention or source. For example, I was frequently invited on Sunday afternoons to the houses of some of Irish families who had befriended me. When I would arrive I never quite knew what things about Ireland I would learn or how I would be learning them. I just began to expect the unexpected.

By giving up control over the circumstances of data collection, I soon recognized that I was always working. In one journal entry I noted that during a dinner party I had obtained valuable background information about a particular firm I wanted to include in my study. In wishing that I had brought along my tape recorder I was recognizing that my research was going on continuously. I learned to be prepared to take advantage of all opportunities to learn more about the topic of my study. During my initial visit to one multinational firm the Irish human resources manager was stiff and formal during our conversation in his office. I had difficulty during the interview getting him to open up and talk about cultural differences. His reply to every question seemed to be a quote out of the corporate policy manual. But at the end of the conversation over coffee in the canteen he loosened up considerably when I was not taking notes.

I came to see that conversations in a restaurant or a pub or at a dinner party were important sources of data. One day an Irish faculty colleague invited me to join her and a guest speaker in her class at the local pub. The man was an Irish filmmaker and I was invited not because of my research project but simply because I was friendly with this colleague. But as it turned out, this man was a source of invaluable cultural insights. I learned to take advantage of social networks both to find contacts for interviews and to obtain feedback on my evolving interpretations. One rich source of research contacts materialized quite unexpectedly through my participation in the American Women's Club. Through this organization's monthly dinner parties I had additional opportunity to interact with managers of several of the American firms in my study.

I learned to accept that I was not totally in control during my on-site interviews. Entries in my research journal at the beginning of the interview process registered some anxiety about wanting to control the interview process, to make certain I was covering all the topics during each interview. I was feeling obsessed about the methodology. I was struggling with the difference between the published descriptions of qualitative research and the experience of actually doing it. I came to learn that the qualitative data collection process was not something over which I had complete control. I would need to go back and reassess the data over and over again. If I tried to control the responses too much I would perhaps get *data I sought* but I would not have the *information I needed*. I would be missing the opportunity to gain unplanned insights. Indeed, the respondents themselves initially introduced several socio-cultural factors that became part of my study.

Allowing the respondent rather than the interview protocol to drive the discussion was very useful particularly before I had a complete list of the socio-cultural factors I wanted to focus on. I had to remind myself that I was interviewing enough people to ensure coverage of all of the important topics. Nevertheless, at times I had to resist the urge to have breadth of treatment at the expense of depth.

4.4   Metadata

Early into my round of interviews at the firms I had an experience that pointed out the importance of sensitivity to contextual metadata. It brought home to me the importance of being vigilant and responsive to the exigencies of context. In this particular situation the respondent was -- at age 48 -- one of the oldest workers at this American plant. He was nervous upon first meeting me. As the human resource manager introduced me and briefly explained my research project, the man stood there shifting his weight from one leg to the other, pulling out of the back pocket of his jeans and fumbling with a rolled up copy of a three-page research summary that I had sent to the managing director. As I watched this man I tried to put myself in his place. He had been made redundant three times at other multinational firms and had only been at this particular firm a matter of months. And now here he was being asked by senior (American) management to talk with this American woman! A quick assessment of the situation told me that I should not to even *ask* if I could use a tape recorder, something I normally did at the beginning of each interview.

A similar situation that called for heightened sensitivity to context occurred at another American firm. This firm was experiencing financial difficulties, and redundancies were a distinct possibility. I recognized that it was important to keep this atmosphere in the foreground as I was conducting my interviews and interpreting the data. Diminished resources and the possibility of layoffs were generating considerable insecurity, which in turn, would be reflected in respondents' comments during the interviews.

My interactions with female respondents were quite often a rich source of metatdata. As I mentioned earlier in this book, the type of interaction I had with these women was both a surprise and a puzzlement. As a rule, I found the interviews to be more difficult than those with men. Some women were merely abrupt and not inclined to be introspective about the socio-cultural factors we were discussing. But a few bordered on resistant. One woman bristled when I asked, in the course of collecting background demographic data, what part of Ireland she was from: "I thought this wasn't going to be anything personal!" she replied. I had to work extremely hard to get her to open up to me. I believed myself to be successful when she began to smile part way through the interview. By the end, she said maybe she would be in Boston some day and I could sign a copy of the book I was going to write. Through all of these interactions I came to recognize that observing the respondent and the context during the interview process provided a rich source of metadata to accompany the words I was hearing.

4.5   Beginning

The final lesson I learned was about the parameters of the research project. Early in my career I had a conversation with a more senior colleague about a research project I had in mind that had to do with studying the relationship between information policy at the national level and its implementation at the corporate level. He began to quiz me about how I would measure the "relevant variables." When I told him that I didn't know how to think about this project in terms of measurable variables, he replied, "Well, then you're not yet ready to begin the research."

This admonition haunted me in Ireland. A few months into my research project I was feeling frustrated with myself that so much time had gone by and I was just then starting my research. I was thinking that the "research" would begin when the on-site interviews commenced. I held this view because I defined research as the conduct of the formal interviews. What I was not recognizing was that the research began the moment I conceived of this project. I gradually came to understand that generating the questions in grounded fashion through participating in and observing the culture was also part of the research.

Half of the lesson was recognizing that while different phases of the project required different methods, the research began at the very beginning. The other half of the lesson was realizing that the research did not end with the analysis of interview data. The final piece was returning to the field for member checking. My assumptions, biases and motivations all influenced the meanings that I developed from the data. Going back to the context to receive feedback on my interpretations served to enhance the authenticity of my narrative.

5. CONCLUSION

As the limitations of quantitative methods for social science research in the information systems field have come to be recognized, increased attention is being paid to the richness and variety available from the alternative approaches offered by qualitative methods. While qualitative methods address some of these limitations, they are not without their own issues that can impede the research effort. In the interests of contributing to our understanding of the benefits and challenges of qualitative research, I have provided detail about both my methods and some of the issues that I faced in employing them. The issues associated with using qualitative methods illustrate the ways in which research methodology can sometimes interfere with rather than enhance the research effort. Certain aspects of the process which should be a means by which research is conducted and communicated, can exert considerable pressure on the research direction itself; in some cases it can move it away from its original intent.

After systematic reflection on my methodology in this study, I cannot say I have derived definitive answers about the rules of proper behavior in every situation. However, I have come to some conclusions, which have influenced subsequent research. One is that as a researcher I cannot be removed from the context, nor should I want to be. I cannot be totally outside the setting and yet be successful in my research. Several of the respondents in this study have become close acquaintances; a few have become friends. To generalize from my own experience, I believe the answer is not for me to remain apart from the context but rather to embrace it. At the same time, however, I should constantly be conducting self-examination with respect to assumptions, biases and motivations being used to interpret data. I should make use of multiple perspectives and sources of data, and be open as to the source. Finally, I should obtain feedback while in the process of both collecting the data and interpreting it. Collecting and analyzing the data in this way shows the iterative nature of interpretive research. The neat linear outline must be replaced with the metaphor of an evolving mosaic. I have learned that these approaches have been necessary if I am to achieve the goal for which the research was undertaken.

Both the challenges and the rewards associated with interpretive research are, for me, embodied in the interview experience I had with Nuala. I first met her at the company site to introduce myself and schedule an interview. First, she wanted to think about my interview questions in advance of meeting with me so I gave her a copy of the interview form. Then she suggested we meet outside work. I said, "OK" and asked where she would like to meet and when, thinking she would suggest some hotel coffee shop. Instead, she suggested a pub in Temple Bar, an emerging bohemian section of Dublin, at six o'clock the following week. Her final comment was something about three professors at the University where I taught and their left-of-center political views.

As I prepared for my interview with her I tried to sort through all the metadata contained in that initial conversation. One interpretation was that I was being tested. Perhaps her comment about the left-leaning tendencies of the professors was a test of my willingness and ability to set aside my American-business-professor persona and accommodate to a different setting. Alternatively, the interview-in-a-pub could have been an *acknowledgment* of my acceptance, given the focal point of pubs in Irish culture. Not knowing for sure, I substituted my business attire for blue jeans, entered the pub and waited with a glass of Guinness in hand for my respondent to arrive. When she did, her sister and two young men who had been her classmates in university accompanied her. Then, for the next five and a half hours I listened while the four of them talked quite frankly about Ireland, the culture, gender, the information sector and themselves. I ran the tape recorder with Irish music playing in the background until the tape ran out. In the semi-light with my Guinness glass continuously topped off I took notes furiously until my notepaper ran out and I had to resort to writing on the back of my interview form! As I left that pub I was certain that I had not worked as hard in any other interview, yet it was also one of the most rewarding experiences and clearly one the richest interviews of the entire project.

Conducting this research has given me the opportunity to engage in personal as well as professional growth. I received considerable practice in questioning my assumptions and challenging my approaches. Because the ethnographic researcher cannot be removed from the phenomenon under study, conducting this cross-cultural research study required that I constantly examine my own biases, motivations and interpretations. It has made me much more aware of the organic nature of change in general and learning in particular. Above all, I have been reminded that as a researcher not only do I not have all the answers, I don't know all the questions either.

---

[i] An earlier discussion of data collection methods is presented in Trauth and O'Connor (1991).

[ii] Those with whom I conducted ad hoc interviews are not included in this number.

[iii] There was one exception to this. One Irish firm was quite small and I interviewed only the entrepreneur/ managing director of the firm.

[iv] See, for example, Jorgensen (1989), Becker and Geer (1969), and Spradley (1980).

[v] The American Conference on Irish Studies (ACIS) and the Irish American Cultural Institute.

[vi] Triangulation is the use of multiple sources to provide corroborating evidence of the researcher's interpretations. It is considered in more detail later in this chapter.

[vii] The database software that was used is Foxpro.

[viii] See Glaser and Strauss (1967) and Strauss (1987).

[ix] Agar (1986) refers to these as "strips." A strip could be an observable act, an interview, an experiment, a document, a comment or any other bounded phenomenon against which an ethnographer tests his or her understanding.

[x] See Trauth and Jessup (2000) for another analysis of the open coding process and a discussion of the implications of employing preset coding categories.

[xi] The italicized headings are not among the coding categories. They merely serve as an organizing aid.

[xii] Earlier versions of these lessons are presented in Trauth (1996b and 1997)

[xiii] For further discussion of this notion see, for example, Hammersly and Atkinson (1983).

[xiv] Kirk and Miller (1986, p. 41) explain that this "quixotic reliability" occurs when respondents provide rehearsed responses and, consequently, information that is of questionable value.

[xv] At the time, a sentiment in some quarters of Irish society was critical of the multinationals and this viewpoint was represented in the audience in attendance at my seminar.

REFERENCES

Department of the Taoiseach. 1996. "Action towards a New Focus on Equality." In *Partnership 2000, for Inclusion, Employment and Competitiveness.* <www.irlgov.ie/taoiseach/publication/p200/chpt5.htm> (April 15, 1999).

American Engineering Association (AEA) Manpower Committee. 1998. *Information Technology Workforce Findings and Recommendations.* American Engineering Association, Inc.

Agar, M.H. 1986. *Speaking of Ethnography.* Newbury Park, CA: Sage Publications.

Ang, A.Y. and S. Jiwahhasuchin. 1998. Information systems education in Thailand: A comparison between the views of professionals and academics. *Journal of Global Information Management* 6, no. 4: 34-42.

Barnes, J. and D. Lamberton. 1976. The growth of the Australian information society. In *Communication economics and development,* edited by M. Jussawalla and D.M. Lamberton. New York: Pergamon.

Becker, H. and B. Geer. 1969. Participant observation: A comparison. In *Issues in participant observation,* edited by G. J. McCall and J.L. Simmons. New York: Random House.

Behar, R. 1996. *The Vulnerable Observer: Anthropology That Breaks Your Heart.* Boston: Beacon Press.

Behr, A. 1994. On the trail of Leopold Bloom in Dublin. *The Boston Sunday Globe,* 12 June, C13.

Bell, D. 1973. *The Coming of Post-industrial Society: A Venture in Social Forecasting.* New York: Basic Books.

-----. 1980. The information society. In *The microelectronics revolution,* edited by T. Forester. Oxford: Basil Blackwell Publishers.

Bilmes, L., K. Wetzker, and P. Xhonneux. 1997. Value in human resources. *Financial Times,* 10 February, 12.

Boyle, P. P. and C. O'Grada. 1986. Fertility trends, excess mortality, and the great Irish famine. *Demography* 23:542-562.

Braa, J. and E. Monteiro. 1996. Infrastructure and institutions: The case of public health in Mongolia. In *Information technology development and policy: Theoretical perspectives and practical challenges,* edited by E.M. Roche and M.J. Blaine. Aldershot, UK: Avebury Publishing, Ltd.

Breathnach, P. 1998. Exploring the 'Celtic Tiger' phenomenon: Causes and consequences of Ireland's economic miracle. *European Urban and Regional Studies* 5, no. 4:305-316.

Breen, R., D. H. Hannan, D. B. Rottman, and C. T. Whelan. 1990. *Understanding Contemporary Ireland: State, Class and Development in the Republic of Ireland.* Dublin: Gill and Macmillan.

Brennan, J. 1990. The journey has begun. In *Integrated manufacturing in the nineties: Producing for profit.* Proceedings of the 7th National Conference of the Irish Production and Inventory Control Society.

Buckholtz, T.J. 1995. *Information Proficiency: Your Key to the Information Age.* New York: Van Nostrand Reinhold.

Buckley, P. 1974. Some aspects of foreign private investment in the manufacturing sector of the economy of the Irish Republic. *Economic and Social Review* 24:301-321.

Building on Reality: 1985-1987. Pl.2648. Dublin: The Stationery Office.

Burke, A. E., ed. 1995. *Enterprise and the Irish Economy.* Dublin: Oak Tree Press.

Burn, J. M., E. M. W. Ng Tye, and L. C. K. Ma. 1995. Paradigm shift -- cultural implications for development of IS professionals. *Journal of Global Information Management* 3, no. 2:18-28.

Callan, T. and B. Farrell. 1991. *Women's Participation in the Irish Labour Market.* December. Dublin: National Economic and Social Council.

Callan, T., B. Nolan, D. O'Neill, and O. Sweetman. 1998. "Female Labour Supply and Income Inequality in Ireland," *Department of Economics, NUI Maynooth, Working Papers.* <http://www.may.ie/academic/economics> (June 9, 1999).

Carey, T. 1999. "Distributing the Benefits of the Information Age on the Islands of West Cork - an Introduction," *SWITCH -- South West Islands' TeleCommunications Hub.* May. <http://www.sleeping-giant.ie/islandit> (21 October 1999).

Carr-Gomm, P. 1991. *The Elements of the Druid Tradition.* Shaftesbury, Dorset: Element Books, Ltd.

Cash, J. I., F. W. McFarlan, J. L. McKenny, and L. M. Appelgate. 1992. Multinational IT issues. In *Corporate Information Systems Management,* edited by J. I. Cash, F.W. McFarlan, and J.L. McKenny. Homewood, IL: Richard D. Irwin, Inc.

Castells, M. 1996. *The Rise of the Network Society*, Vol. 1. Cambridge, MA: Blackwell Publishers, Inc.

Central Statistics Office (CSO). 1991. *Census of Population of Ireland*. Pl. 8248. Dublin: The Stationery Office.

-----. 1992. *Labour Force Survey*. Pl. 9007. Dublin: The Stationery Office.

Chrystal, A. 1990. Making world class manufacturing a way of life. In *Integrated manufacturing in the nineties: Producing for profit*. Proceedings of the 7th National Conference of the Irish Production and Inventory Control Society.

Claffey, C. E. 1988. The vision of Edna O'Brien. *The Boston Globe,* 27 November, B1, B10, B13.

Clancy, P. 1988. *Who Goes to College: A Second National Survey of Participation in Higher Education*. Dublin: Higher Education Authority.

Clancy, P., S. Drudy, K. Lynch, and L. O'Dowd, eds. 1988. *Ireland: A Sociological Profile*. Dublin: The Institute of Public Administration.

Commission on the Status of Women, 1972.

Coogan, T. P. 1987. *The Disillusioned Decades: Ireland 1966-1987*. Dublin: Gill and Macmillan.

Coopers and Lybrand. 1988. *A Study of the Irish Software Industry*. Dublin: Information and Computing Services Association.

Corkery, S. 1990. Demand driven manufacturing. In *Integrated manufacturing in the nineties: Producing for profit*. Proceedings of the 7th National Conference of the Irish Production and Inventory Control Society.

Coulter, C. 1997. 'Hello divorce, goodbye Daddy.' In *Gender and sexuality in modern Ireland,* edited by A. Bradley and M.G. Valiulis. Amherst: University of Massachusetts Press.

Creswell, J. W. 1998. *Qualitative Inquiry and Research Design: Choosing among Five Traditions*. Thousand Oaks, CA: Sage Publications.

Cronin, M. 1993. Fellow travellers: Contemporary travel writing and Ireland. In *Tourism in Ireland: A critical analysis*, edited by B. O'Connor and M. Cronin. Cork: Cork University Press.

Crowley, N. 1998. Partnership 2000: Empowerment or co-option? In *In the shadow of the tiger: New approaches to combating social exclusion,* edited by P. Kirby and D. Jacobson. Dublin: Dublin City University Press.

Cuddy, M. P. and M. J. Keane. 1990. Ireland: A peripheral region. In *The single European market and the Irish economy,* edited by A. Foley and M. Mulreany. Dublin: Institute of Public Administration.

Cullen, P. 1999a. Ireland is listed lower on quality of life index. *Irish Times,* 12 July, 5.

-----. 1999b. Ireland's poverty level is rated second-worst in industrialized world. *Irish Times,* 12 July, 1.

-----. 1999c. Staying Irish may become an art. *Boston Globe,* 17 January, C1, C3.

Cummings, M. L. and J. L. Guynes. 1994. Information system activities in transnational corporations: A comparison of U.S. and Non-U.S. subsidiaries. *Journal of Global Information Management* 2, no. 1:12-26.

Daly, M. E. 1992. *Industrial Development and Irish National Identity, 1922-1939.* Syracuse, NY: Syracuse University Press.

Davenport. T. H. 1997. *Information Ecology: Mastering the Information and Knowledge Environment.* New York: Oxford University Press.

Deans, C. 1991. International concerns of MIS executives in US-based multinational corporations. In *Managing information technology in a global society.* Proceedings of the 1991 Information Resources Management Association International Conference, edited by M. Khosrowpour. Hershey, PA: Idea Group Publishing.

Delaney, F. 1989. *The Celts.* London: Grafton Books.

Dell recruits abroad. 1999. *Irish Times,* 15 July, 2.

Denzin, N. 1978. *The Research Act.* 2nd ed. New York: McGraw-Hill.

Department of Foreign Affairs. "Economic Development." *Facts about Ireland.* <http://www.irlgov.ie/iveagh/facts/economy.htm> (14 April 1999).

Dordick, H. S. and G. Wang. 1993. *The Information Society: A Retrospective View.* Newbury Park, CA: Sage Publications, Inc.

Drucker, P. 1950. *The New Society: The Anatomy of the Industrial Order.* New York: Harper and Brothers.

-----. 1959. *Landmarks of Tomorrow.* New York: Harper and Brothers.

-----. 1969. *The Age of Discontinuity: Guidelines to Our Changing Society.* New York: Harper and Row,

-----. 1993. *Post-capitalist Society.* New York: HarperBusiness.

-----. 1994. The age of social transformation." *The Atlantic Monthly,* November, 53-80.

-----. 1999. Beyond the information revolution. *The Atlantic Monthly,* October, 47-57.

Dunsford, C. 1999. Dramatis persona. *Boston College Magazine* (Winter): 38-47.

Dyson, E. 1997. Education and jobs in the digital world. *Communications of the ACM* 40, no. 2:35-36.

Economic and Social Development, 1969-72.

Economic and Social Research Institute (ESRI). 1997. *Medium Term Review: 1997-2003.* Dublin: Economic and Social Research Institute.

The Economist Intelligence Unit. 1998. *Country Profile Ireland 1998/1999.* The Economist Intelligence Unit Limited (January 4).

Ely, M., M. Anzul, T. Friedman, D. Garner, and A. M. Steinmetz. 1991. *Doing Qualitative Research: Circles within Circles.* New York: The Farmer Press.

Enterprise Ireland. 1998. *Briefing Document: Millennium Entrepreneur Fund.* November. Dublin: Enterprise Ireland.

-----. 1999. "Ireland in the 1990's - Increasing Exports," *Economic Data Ireland.* <http://194.106.146.103/ECONOMIC_DATA/ECONOMIC_DATA_03.HTML> (14 April 1999).

Feldman, M. S. 1995. *Strategies for Interpreting Qualitative Data.* Thousand Oaks: Sage Publications.

Fetterman, D. M. 1998. *Ethnography: Step by Step.* 2nd ed. Thousand Oaks: Sage Publications.

Financial Services Industry Association. 1988. *Financial Services Industry Manpower and Training Needs: Report of Focus Group.* Dublin: Financial Services Industry Association.

Finnegan, P. and J. Murray. 1999. Between individuals and teams: Human resource management in the software sector. *Journal of Global Information Management* 7, no. 2:4-12.

Fitz Gerald, J. 1995. *The Republic of Ireland after 2000 - The Icarus Complex.* ESRI Working Paper, no. 88. Dublin: Economic and Social Research Institute.

Fitzpatrick, J. and J. Kelly, eds. 1985. *Perspectives on Irish Industry.* Dublin: Irish Management Institute.

Foley, A. and B. Griffith. 1994. Irish banks and the development of small and medium sized enterprises. *The Irish Banking Review* (Autumn): 30-47.

Foley, A. and T. Hogan. 1998. Start-ups and closures in indigenous manufacturing: An analysis of the census of industrial production, 1986-1995. *Irish Banking Review* (Autumn): 43-56.

Foley, A. and D. McAleese, eds. 1991. *Overseas Industry in Ireland.* Dublin: Gill and Macmillan, Ltd.

Foster, R. F. 1988. *Modern Ireland: 1600-1972.* London: Allen Lane, The Penguin Press.

Freeman, P. and W. Aspray. 1999. *The Supply of Information Technology Workers in the United States.* Washington, D.C.: Computing Research Association.

From humble beginnings. 1997. *The Sunday Business Report,* 26 October.

Fukuyama, F. 1999. The great disruption: Human nature and the reconstitution of social order. *The Atlantic Monthly* (May): 55-80.

Gan, S. 1998. An overview of information technology and education in Malaysia. *Journal of Global Information Management* 6, no. 1:27-32.

Gannon, M. J. 1994. Irish conversations. In *Understanding global cultures: Metaphorical journeys through 17 countries.* Thousand Oaks, CA: Sage Publications, Inc.

Garavan, T. N., B. O'Cinneide and P. Fleming. 1997. *Entrepreneurship in Ireland.* Vol. 1, *An Overview.* Dublin: Oak Tree Press.

Garvin, T. 1989. Wealth, poverty and development: Reflections on current discontents. *Studies* 78, no. 311:312-325.

Geertz, C. 1973. *The Interpretation of Cultures,* New York: Basic Books.

Girvin, B. 1982. Irish industrial policy: The constraints and opportunities of an open economy. *Journal of Public Policy* 3, no. 1:81-96.

Glacken, B. 1999. Diary of a telecom wife. *Irish Times,* (16 July): 16.

Glaser, B. and A. Strauss. 1967. *The Discovery of Grounded Theory.* Chicago: Aldine Publishing Co.

Golden-Biddle, K. and K. Locke. 1993. Appealing work: An investigation of how ethnographic texts convince. *Organization Science* 4, no. 4:595-616.

Gray, A. W., ed. 1992. *Responses to Irish Unemployment: The Views of Four Economists.* Dublin: Indecon International Economic Consultants.

Grimes, S. 1992. Exploiting information and communication technologies for rural development. *Journal of Rural Studies* 8, no. 3:269-278.

-----. 1995. The implications of information technologies for regional development in Ireland. Paper presented at Regional Studies Association Conference on Regional Development: An All Ireland Perspective. St. Patrick's College, Maynooth, Ireland, September 14-15.

Grimes, S. and G. Lyons. 1994. Information technology and rural development: Unique opportunity or potential threat? *Entrepreneurship and Regional Development* 6:219-237.

Hall, E. T. 1994. *West of the Thirties: Discoveries Among the Navajo and Hopi.* New York: Doubleday.

Hammersly, M. and B. Atkinson. 1983. *Ethnography Principles in Practice.* London: Tavistock Publishers, Ltd.

Harris, L. 1989. Women's response to multinationals in County Mayo. In *Women's employment in multinationals in Europe,* edited by D. Elson and R. Pearson. London: Macmillan Press, Ltd.

Harris, R. A. 1994. *The Nearest Place that Wasn't Ireland: Early Nineteenth-Century Irish Labor Migration.* Ames: Iowa State University Press.

Harris, R. A. and E. O'Keeffe, eds. 1993. *The Search for Missing Friends, Irish Immigrant Advertisements Placed in the Boston Pilot, 1854-1856.* Vol. 3. Boston: The New England Historic Genealogical Society.

Hayes, R. H. and G. P. Pisano. 1994. Beyond world-class: The new manufacturing strategy. *Harvard Business Review* 72, no. 1: 77-86.

Heeks, R. 1996. Promoting software production and export in developing countries. In *Information technology development and policy: Theoretical perspectives and practical challenges,* edited by E. M. Roche and M. J. Blaine. Aldershot, UK: Avebury Publishing Ltd.

Hernandez, D., R. Gibson, and E. G. McGuire. 1996. Informatics in Uruguay: Evolution and implications. *Journal of Global Information Management* 4, no. 1:23-31.

Higher Education Authority, 1988. *First Destination of Award Recipients in Higher Education (1987).* Dublin: Higher Education Authority.

Hill, C. E., K. D. Loch, D. W. Straub, and K. El-Sheshai. 1998. A qualitative assessment of Arab culture and information technology transfer. *Journal of Global Information Management* 6, no. 3:29-38.

Hodgetts, R. M., S. M. Lee and F. Luthans. 1994. New paradigm organizations -- From total quality to learning to world-class. *Organizational Dynamics* 22, no. 3: 5-19.

Hofstede, G. 1983. The cultural relativity of organizational practices and theories. *Journal of International Business Studies* (Fall): 75-89.

-----. 1984a. *Culture's Consequences: International Differences in Work-Related Values.* Beverly Hills, CA: Sage Publications.

-----. 1984b. Cultural dimensions in management and planning. *Asia Pacific Journal of Management* (January): 81-99.

Hogan, T. and A. Foley. 1996. *Fast Growth Firms in Ireland: An Empirical Assessment.* Dublin City University Business School Research Papers Series, no. 5. Dublin: Dublin City University.

Houston, E. 1999. *Working and Living in Ireland.* Dublin: Oak Tree Press.

IDA Ireland. 1997a. *Briefing Document: Ireland*, Dublin: Industrial Development Authority.

-----. 1997b. *Facts about Ireland, 1997.* January. Dublin: Industrial Development Authority.

-----. 1998. *Economic Brief.* August. Dublin: Industrial Development Authority.

-----. 1999. *Ireland: Vital Statistics.* February. Dublin: Industrial Development Authority.

Industrial Development Act of 1969.

Industrial Development Act of 1986.

Industrial Development Authority (IDA). 1982. *IDA Annual Report.* Dublin: Industrial Development Authority.

-----. 1992. *Ireland as a Cost Competitive Location for Back Office Data Processing and Remote Software Development Operations.* Presentation to Taylorix AG.

-----. "Electronics." <http://www.ida.ie.elec.htm> (21 October 1997a).

-----. "Financial Services." <http://www.ida.ie.fs.htm> (21 October 1997b).

Industrial Policy Review Group. 1992. *A Time for Change: Industrial Policy for the 1990s.* Dublin: The Stationery Office.

Information Technology Association of America (ITAA). 1998. *Help Wanted: A Call for Collaborative Action for the New Millenium. Executive Briefing of a Study on It Workforce Shortages.* Blacksburg: Virginia Polytechnic Institute and State University.

Institute of Public Administration (IPA). 1989. *1990 Administration Yearbook and Diary.* Dublin: Institute of Public Administration.

Ireland shines. 1997. *The Economist,* 17 May, 16.

The Irish Software Association. 1998. *To Boldly Go . . . The Irish Software Industry: A Strategy for Growth.* Dublin: The Irish Software Association.

Ito, Y. 1981. The 'johoka shakai' approach to the study of communication in Japan. In *Mass Communication Review Yearbook,* edited by G. C. Wilhoit and H. de Bock. Beverly Hills, CA: Sage Publications.

Ives, B. and S. Jarvenpaa. 1991. Applications of global information technology: Key issues for management. *MIS Quarterly* 15, no. 2:33-49.

Jackson, P. and U. Barry. 1989. Women's employment in the Republic of Ireland: The creation of a new female labour force. In *Women's employment in multinationals in Europe,* edited by D. Elson and R. Pearson. London: Macmillan Press, Ltd.

Jacobson, D. 1996. *New Forms of Work Organization in Ireland: An Annotated Bibliography.* Dublin City University Business School Research Papers Series, no. 9. Dublin: Dublin City University.

Jacobson, D. S. and R. S. Mack. 1995. *Core - Periphery Analysis: A Tale of Two Nations.* Dublin City University Business School Research Papers Series, no. 8. Dublin: Dublin City University.

Jacobson, D. and D. O'Sullivan. 1994. Analyzing an industry in change: The Irish software manual printing industry. *New Technology, Work and Employment* 9, no. 2:103-114.

Jick, T. 1979. Mixing qualitative and quantitative methods: Triangulation in action. *Administrative Science Quarterly* 24, no. 4:602-611.

Johnston, W. B. 1991. Global work force 2000: The new world labor market. *Harvard Business Review* (March-April): 115-127.

Jordan, D. 1992. The Ireland-Silicon nexus. *Journal of the West* 31, no. 2:79-84.

Jorgensen, D. L. 1989. *Participant Observation: A Methodology for Human Studies.* Newbury Park, CA: Sage Publications.

Katz, R. L. 1986. Explaining information sector growth in developing countries. *Telecommunications Policy* 10, no. 3:209-228.

Kedia, B. L. and R. S. Bhagat. 1988. Cultural constraints on transfer of technology across nations: Implications for research in international and comparative management. *Academy of Management Review* 13, no. 4:559-571.

Keen, P. G. W. 1992. Planning globally: Practical strategies for information technology in the transnational firm. In *The global issues of information technology management,* edited by S. Palvia, P. Palvia and R. Zigli. Harrisburg, PA: Idea Group Publishing.

Keidel, R. W. 1985. *Game Players.* New York: E. P. Dutton.

Klein, H. K. and M. Myers. 1999. A set of principles for conducting and evaluating interpretive field studies in information systems. *MIS Quarterly* 23, no. 1:67-93.

Kluckholn, F. and F. Strodtbeck. 1961. *Variations in Value Orientations.* Evanston, IL: Row, Peterson.

Kirk, J. and M. L. Miller. 1986. *Reliability and Validity in Qualitative Research.* Beverly Hills, CA: Sage Publications.

Kling, R. 1990. More information, better jobs? Occupational stratification and labor market segmentation in the United States' information labor force. *The Information Society* 7, no. 2:77-107.

-----, ed. 1996. *Computerization and Controversy: Value Conflicts and Social Choices.* 2nd ed. San Diego: Academic Press.

-----. 1999. What is social informatics and why does it matter? *D-Lib Magazine* 5, no. 1.

Kwan, S. K., E. M. Trauth, and K. C. Driehaus. 1985. Gender differences and computing: Students' assessment of societal influences. *Education and Computing* 1, no. 3:187-194.

La Rovere, R. L. 1996. Diffusion of IT and the competitiveness of Brazilian banking. In *Information technology development and policy: Theoretical perspectives and practical challenges,* edited by E. M. Roche and M. J. Blaine. Aldershot, UK: Avebury Publishing Ltd.

Lally, L. 1994. The impact of environment on information infrastructure enhancement: A comparative study of Singapore, France and the United States. *Journal of Global Information Management* 2, no. 3:5-12.

Lange, W. and R. Rempp. 1977. *Qualitative Aspects of the Information Sectors.* Karlruhe, Germany: Karlruhe Institut fur Systemtechnil und Innovationsforschung.

Leavy, B. 1993. Managing the economy of a newly independent state. In *Management in Western Europe: Society, culture, and organization in twelve nations,* edited by D. J. Hickson. New York: Walter de Gruyter.

-----. 1999. Strategy - - but not as we know it. *World Link* (July/August): 30-35.

Lee, D. M. S., E. M. Trauth, and D. Farwell. 1995. Critical skills and knowledge requirements of the IS profession: A joint academic/industry investigation. *MIS Quarterly*19, no. 3:313-340.

Lee, J. J. 1989. *Ireland 1912 - 1985: Politics and Society.* Cambridge: Cambridge University Press.

Lincoln, Y. and Guba, E. 1985. *Naturalistic Inquiry.* Beverly Hills, CA: Sage.

Lopez, E. J. and M. Vilaseca. 1996. IT as a global economic development tool. In *Information technology development and policy: Theoretical perspectives and practical challenges,* edited by E. M. Roche and M. J. Blaine. Aldershot, UK: Avebury Publishing Ltd.

Machlup, F. 1962. *The Production and Distribution of Knowledge in the United States.* Princeton: Princeton University Press.

Mahon, E. 1991. Women and equality in the Irish civil service," in *Equality, politics and gender,* edited by E. Meehan and S. Sevenhuijsen. London: Sage Publications.

McAleese, D. and A. Foley. 1991. The role of overseas industry in industrial development. In *Overseas Industry in Ireland,* edited by A. Foley and D. McAleese. Dublin: Gill and Macmillan, Ltd.

McBride, S. and R. Flynn, eds. 1996. *Here's Looking at You, Kid!* Dublin: Wolfhound Press.

McCabe, R. 1984. New technology -- the investment crisis. *Technology Ireland* (January): 26-28.

McCall, B. 1989. Industry from education. *Management* (February).

McCann, C. 1995. *Who Cares? A Guide for All Who Care for Others.* Dublin: The Columba Press.

McCarthy, A. 1995. Family and work in the large public sector organisation. Presentation to Families and Work Conference, Brussels, November.

McCormack. 1998. "Telework Ireland's ADAPT Programme." *Telework Ireland.* <http://www.telework.ie/OldTWISTE/adapt_project1.htm> (2 September 1999).

McDonagh, E. 1989. Europe, the faith and Ireland. *Studies* 78, no. 311:255-261.

McEvoy, M. 1998. Gender equality in the partnerships: Confronting power. In *In the shadow of the tiger: New approaches to combating social exclusion,* edited by P. Kirby and D. Jacobson. Dublin: Dublin City University Press.

Miles, M.B. and A. M. Huberman. 1994. *Qualitative Data Analysis: An Expanded Sourcebook.* 2nd ed. Thousand Oaks, CA: Sage Publications.

Mokyr, J. 1980. The deadly fungus: An economic investigation into the short-term demographic impact of the Irish famine, 1846-51. *Research in Population Economics,* no. 2.

Monks, K. 1992. Models of personnel management: A means of understanding the diversity of personnel practices. *Human Resource Management Journal* 3, no. 2:29-41.

-----. 1996. Global or local? HRM in the multinational company: The Irish experience. *International Journal of Human Resource Management* 7, no. 3:721-735.

Monks, K. and Barker, P. 1995. *The Glass Ceiling: Cracked but not Broken? Evidence from a Study of Chartered Accountants.* Dublin City University Business School Research Paper Series, no. 1. Dublin: Dublin City University.

Moynihan, M., ed. 1980. *Speeches and Statements by Eamon de Valera 1917-1973.* Dublin: Gill and Macmillan, Ltd.

Murray, J. A. 1981. In search of entrepreneurship. *Journal of Irish Business and Administrative Research* 3:41-55.

Murray, P. and J. Wickham. 1982. Technocratic ideology and the reproduction of inequality: The case of the electronics industry in the Republic of Ireland. In *Diversity and decomposition in the labour market,* edited by G. Day et al. Aldershot, UK: Gower Publishing Co.

Naisbett, J. 1982. *Megatrends: Ten New Directions Transforming our Lives.* New York: Warner Books, Inc.

National Development Plan, 1989-1993. Pl. 6343. Dublin: The Stationery Office.

National Economic and Social Council (NESC). 1981. *Irish Social Policies: Priorities for Future Development,* no.61. Dublin: National Economic and Social Council.

-----. 1982a. *A Review of Industrial Policy: A Report Prepared by the Telesis Consultancy Group,* no. 64. Dublin: National Economic and Social Council.

-----. 1982b. *A Review of Industrial Policy: Summary,* no. 64. Dublin: National Economic and Social Council.

-----. 1986. *A Strategy for Development, 1986-1990,* no. 83. Dublin: National Economic and Social Council.

-----. 1992. *The Association between Economic Growth and Employment in Ireland,* no. 94. Dublin: National Economic and Social Council.

National Software Directorate (NSD). 1992. *The Software Industry in Ireland: A Strategic Review.* Dublin: IDA Ireland.

-----. 1995. *Survey of the Irish Software Industry.* Dublin: IDA Ireland.

-----. 1998a. "Companies and Employment," *Industry Information.* <http://www.forbairt.ie/nsd/infsur.html> (14 June 1999).

-----. 1998b. "Ireland as an Offshore Software Location," *Industry Background.* <http://www.nsc.ie/inflitof.html> (30 April 1999).

National Telecommunications and Information Administration. 1999. *Falling Through the Net: Defining the Digital Divide.* A Report on the Telecommunications and Information

Technology Gap in America. July. Washington, D.C.: U.S. Department of Commerce, National Telecommunications and Information Administration.

Nelson, K. G. and T. D. Clark. 1994. Cross-cultural issues in information systems research: A research program. *Journal of Global Information Management* 2, no. 4:19-29.

Neo, B. S. 1991. Information technology and global competition. *Information & Management* 20:151-160.

Nic Ghiolla Phadraig, M. 1988. Religious practice and secularisation. In *Ireland: A Sociological Profile,* edited by P. Clancy, S. Drudy, K. Lynch, and L. O'Dowd. Dublin: Institute of Public Administration.

Nonaka, I. and H. Takeuchi. 1995. *The Knowledge-creating Company: How Japanese Companies Create the Dynamics of Innovation.* New York: Oxford University Press.

Norman, A. L. 1993. *Information Society: An Economic Theory of Discovery, Invention and Innovation.* Dordrecht: Kluwer Academic Publishers.

Norton, R. 1999. The luck of the Irish. *Fortune,* 25 October, 193-220.

NSF Informatics Task Force. 1993. *Educating the Next Generation of Information Specialists.* A Framework for Academic Program in Informatics. Task Force Report. Lafayette, LA: The Center for Advanced Computer Studies, The University of Southwest Louisiana.

O'Colla, S. 1967. Development of small industries in Ireland. *Eire-Ireland* 2, no. 2: 86-93.

O'Connor, B. 1993. Myths and mirrors: Tourist images and national identity. In *Tourism in Ireland: A critical analysis*, edited by B. O'Connor and M. Cronin. Cork: Cork University Press.

O'Connor, J. 1983. Issues in enterprise development: Business owners perceptions and experiences. *Irish Business and Administrative Research Journal* 5 (April-December): 649-662.

O'Connor, O. 1999. UN ranking is of little real meaning. *Irish Times,* 16 July, 6.

Odedra-Straub, M. 1993. Critical factors affecting success of CBIS: Cases from Africa. *Journal of Global Information Management* 1, no. 3:16-31.

O'Donnell, S. 1979. The multinationals justified? *Eire-Ireland* 14, no. 1:118-121.

-----. 1980a. The silicon revolution in Ireland. *Eire-Ireland* 15, no. 2:128-131.

-----. 1980b. Alcan: New jobs, lost work. *Eire-Ireland* 15, no. 4:135-138.

O'Farrell, P. 1986. *Entrepreneurs and Industrial Change.* Dublin: Irish Management Institute.

O'Gadhra, N. 1973. The economic development of the Gaeltacht. *Eire-Ireland* 8, no. 1:124-130.

O'Hearn, D. 1987. Estimates of new foreign manufacturing employment in Ireland, 1956-1972. *The Economic and Social Review* 18, no. 3:173-188.

-----. 1989. The Irish case of dependency: An exception to the exceptions? *American Sociological Review* 54: 578-596.

-----. 1998. *Inside the Celtic Tiger: The Irish Economy and the Asian Model.* London: Pluto Press.

O'Malley, E. 1987. *The Irish Engineering Industry: Strategic Analysis and Policy Recommendations.* Paper 134. Dublin: The Economic and Social Research Institute.

-----. 1989. *Industry and Economic Development: The Challenge of the Latecomer.* Dublin: Gill and Macmillan Ltd.

Organisation for Economic Cooperation and Development (OECD). 1981. *Information Activities, Electronics and Telecommunications Technologies.* Paris: OECD.

-----. 1999. "Economic Survey of Ireland," *Economic Surveys* (May). <http://www.oecd.org/eco/surv/esu-ire.htm> (May 10, 1999).

O'Riain, S. 1997. The birth of a Celtic tiger. *Communications of the ACM* 30, no. 3:11-16.

O'Toole, F. 1990. Ireland -- A class-ridden society? *Irish Times*, 2-6 April.

O'Toole, F. 1990a. A middle class losing its confidence. *Irish Times,* 6 April, 15.

O'Toole, F. 1990b. Where all the odds favor the rich. *Irish Times*, 2 April, 17.

Palvia, S., P. Palvia, and R. Zigli, eds. 1992. *The Global Issues of Information Technology Management.* Harrisburg, PA: Idea Group Publishing.

"Partnership 2000 for Inclusion Employment & Competitiveness," 1996. <http://www.irlgov.ie/taoiseach/publication/p2000/default.htm (15 April 1999).

Pettigrew, A. 1987. Context and action in the transformation of the firm," *Journal of Management Studies* 24, 6:649-670.

Pettigrew, A. 1990. Longitudinal field research on change: Theory and practice. *Organization Science* 1, 3:267-292.

Pollak, A. 1998. OECD forecasts drop of a fifth in children aged from five to 14. *Irish Times,* 24 November, 9.

Pollak, A. 1999. Equality an issue for men also -- justice official. *Irish Times,* 16 July, 10.

Porat, M. 1977. *Information Economy: Definition and Measurement.* Washington, D.C.: Office of Telecommunications.

Porter, M. E. 1990. *The Competitive Advantage of Nations.* New York: Free Press.

Power, C. 1990. *1992: A New Dawn for Knowledge-based Industries in Ireland.* Paper presented at the Bolton Trust international seminar, "1992: Its Impact on Technological Education," Dublin, February.

Prendiville, P. 1988. Divorce in Ireland: An analysis of the referendum to amend the constitution, June 1986. *Women's Studies International Forum* 11, no. 4:355-363.

Preston, P. 1998. 'Content' matters: The media and cultural industries in Ireland's national information strategy. *Irish Communication Review* 7.

Price Waterhouse. 1989. *Doing Business in the Republic of Ireland.* Dublin: Price Waterhouse World Firm Ltd.

Programme for Economic Expansion. 1958. 12 November. Dublin: The Stationery Office.

Programme for National Recovery. 1987. Pl.5213. Dublin: The Stationery Office.

"Programmes," 1999. *Information Age Town.* (28 October) <www.ennis.ie/iat/programmes.html> (28 October 1999).

Punset, E. and G. Sweeney, eds. 1989. *Information Resources and Corporate Growth.* New York: Pinter Publishers.

Pyle, J. L. 1990. *The State and Women in the Economy: Lessons from Sex Discrimination in the Republic of Ireland.* Albany: State University of New York Press.

Rabinow, P. 1977. *Reflections on Fieldwork in Morocco.* Berkeley: University of California Press.

Rea, R. 1988. Business study scheme backed. *Belfast Telegraph,* 6 January.

Redlich, P. 1999. We have failed our tribe of lost children. *The Irish Independent,* 18 July, 5.

Reich, R. B. 1991. Who is them? *Harvard Business Review* (March-April): 77-88.

Review of Industrial Performance, 1986.

Rifkin, J. 1995. *The End of Work: Technology, Jobs and Your Future.* New York: G.P. Putnam's Sons.

Roche, B. 1982. Social partnership and political control: State strategy and industrial relations in Ireland. In *Power, conflict and inequality,* edited by M. Kelly, L. O'Dowd, and J. Wickham. Dublin: Turoe Press.

Rottman, D. B., D. F. Hannan, N. Hardiman, and M. M. Wiley. 1982. *The Distribution of Income in the Republic of Ireland: A Study of Social Class and Family Cycle Inequalities.* No. 109. Dublin: Economic and Social Research Council.

Sanday, P. R. 1979. The ethnographic paradigm(s). *Administrative Science Quarterly* 24, no. 4:527-538.

Schement, J. R. and T. Curtis. 1995. *Tendencies and Tensions of the Information Age: The Production and Distribution of Information in the United States.* New Brunswick, NJ: Transaction Publishers.

Schmidt, D. 1973. *The Irony of Irish Democracy: The Impact of Political Culture on Administrative and Democratic Political Development in Ireland.* Lexington, MA: D.C. Heath and Company.

Schultz, U. 2000. A confessional account of an ethnography about knowledge work. *MIS Quarterly* 24, no. 1:3-41.

Second Programme for Economic Expansion, 1964-1970.

Sen, A. 1999. *Development as Freedom.* New York: Knopf.

Silverman, D. 1993. *Interpreting Qualitative Data: Methods for Analyzing Talk, Text and Interaction.* Thousand Oaks, CA: Sage Publications.

Singer, H. W. 1970. Dualism revisited: A new approach to the problems of the dual society in developing countries. *Journal of Development Studies* 7:60-75.

Smyth, J. 1990. Partners in business. In *Integrated manufacturing in the nineties: Producing for profit.* Proceedings of the 7th National Conference of the Irish Production and Inventory Control Society.

Spradley, J. 1980. *Participant Observation.* New York: Holt, Rinehart and Winston.

Strauss, A. L. 1987. *Qualitative Analysis for Social Scientists.* New York: Cambridge University Press.

Steinbart, P. J. and Nath, R. 1992. Problems and issues in the management of international data communications networks: The experiences of American companies. *MIS Quarterly* 16, no. 2:55-76.

Sweeney, P. 1998. *The Celtic Tiger: Ireland's Economic Miracle Explained.* Dublin: Oak Tree Press.

Tapscott, D. 1996. *The Digital Economy: Promise and Peril in the Age of Networked Intelligence.* New York: McGraw-Hill.

Tapscott, D. 1998. *Growing Up Digital: The Rise of the Net Generation.* New York: McGraw-Hill.

Thurow, L. 1999. Building wealth: The new rules for individuals, companies and nations. *The Atlantic Monthly,* June, 57-69.

Toffler, A. 1973. *Future Shock.* New York: Random House, Inc.

-----. 1981. *The Third Wave.* New York: Bantam Books, Inc.

Trauth, E. M. 1979. *An Adaptive Model of Information Policy.* Ann Arbor, MI: University Microfilms.

-----. 1986. An integrative approach to information policy research. *Telecommunications Policy* 10, no. 1:41-50.

-----. 1993a. Educating IT professionals for work in Ireland: An emerging post-industrial country. In *Global information technology education: Issues and trends,* edited by M. Khosrowpour and K. Loch. Harrisburg, PA: Idea Group Publishing.

-----. 1993b. The position of women in Ireland's information economy: An illustration of technology-society interaction. Presentation to Boston Irish Colloquium, Boston, November.

-----. 1994. The position of women in Ireland's post-industrial society. Paper presented at American Conference on Irish Studies, Omaha, NE, April.

-----. 1995a. Irish cultural influences on women in the workplace. Presentation to The Irish Ancestral Research Association, Boston, February.

-----. 1995b. Women in Ireland's information economy: Voices from inside. *Eire-Ireland* 30, no. 3:133-150.

-----. 1996a. Impact of an imported IT sector: Lessons from Ireland. In *Information technology development and policy: Theoretical perspectives and practical challenges,* edited by E.M. Roche and M. J. Blaine. Aldershot, UK: Avebury Publishing Ltd.

-----. 1996b. Issues with ethnographic research across cultures: The dilemma of staying 'strange' during participant observation. Paper presented at Annual Meeting of the American Conference on Irish Studies, Carbondale, IL, April.

-----. 1997. Achieving the research goal with qualitative methods: Lessons learned along the way. In *Information systems and qualitative research,* edited by A. S. Lee, J. Liebenau, and J. I. DeGross. London: Chapman and Hall.

-----. 1999a. Leapfrogging an IT labor force: Multinational and indigenous perspectives. *Journal of Global Information Management* 7, no. 2:22-32.

-----. 1999b. Who owns my soul: The paradox of pursuing organizational knowledge in a work culture of individualism. In *Proceedings of the 1999 ACM SIGCPR Conference,* edited by J. Prasad. New York: Association for Computing Machinery.

Trauth, E. M., F. E. J. M. Derksen, and H. M. J. Mevissen. 1993. The influence of societal factors on the diffusion of electronic data interchange in the Netherlands. In *Information systems development: Human, social and organizational aspects,* edited by D. Avison, J. Kendall, and J. I. DeGross. Amsterdam: North-Holland.

-----. 1998. Societal factors and the diffusion of EDI. In *EDI and data networking in the public sector: Governmental action, diffusion and impacts,* edited by K.V. Andersen. Boston: Kluwer Academic Publishers.

Trauth, E. M., D. Farwell, and D. Lee. 1993. The IS expectation gap: Industry expectations versus academic preparation. *MIS Quarterly* 17, no. 3:293-307.

Trauth, E. M. and L. Jessup, L. 2000. Understanding computer-mediated discussions: Positivist and interpretive analyses of group support system use. *MIS Quarterly* 24, no. 1:43-79.

Trauth, E. M. and O'Connor, B. 1991. A study of the interaction between information technology and society: An illustration of combined qualitative research methods. In *Information systems research: Contemporary approaches & emergent traditions,* edited by H. E. Nissen, H. K. Klein and R. Hirschheim. Amsterdam: North-Holland.

Trauth, E. M. and Pitt, D. C. 1992. Competition in the telecommunications industry: A new global paradigm and its limits. *Journal of Information Technology* 7:3-11.

Trouble the Calm. 1989. Produced and Directed by D. Fox. London: Faction Film.

Turkle, S. 1984. *The Second Self: Computers and the Human Spirit.* New York: Simon and Shuster.

Van Maanen, J. 1988. *Tales of the Field: On Writing Ethnography.* Chicago: University of Chicago Press.

Van Ryckeghem, D. 1996. Computers and culture: Cases from Kenya. In *Information technology development and policy: Theoretical perspectives and practical challenges,* edited by E. M. Roche and M. J. Blaine. Aldershot, UK: Avebury Publishing Ltd.

Wall, S. D. 1977. *Four Sector Time Series of the U.K. Labour Force, 1841-1971.* London: Post Office Long Range Studies Division.

Walsham, G. 1993. *Interpreting Information Systems in Organizations.* Chichester, UK: Wiley.

Walsham, G. and S. Sahay. 1999. GIS for district-level administration in India: Problems and opportunities. *MIS Quarterly* 23, no. 1:39-65.

Walsham, G., V. Symons, and T. Waema. 1988. Information systems as social systems: Implications for developing countries. *Information Technology for Development* 3, no. 3:198-204.

Walsham, G. and T. Waema, T. 1994. Information systems strategy and implementation: A case study of a building society. *ACM Transactions on Information Systems* 12, no. 2:150-173.

Waters. J. 1993. Creating a caricature out of de Valera's 'dream speech.' *Irish Times* 16 March, 10.

The Way Forward: National Economic Plan 1983-1987. 1982. Pl.10161. October. Dublin: The Stationery Office.

Webster, F. 1995. *Theories of the Information Society.* London: Routledge.

Wickham, J. 1989. Women in the Irish electronics industry: A presentation of research findings. In *Women in technology in Ireland,* edited by S. Lynam. Dublin: Irish Advisory Group, European Network on the Diversification of Vocational Choice for Young and Adult Women.

Wickham, J. and P. Murray. 1987. *Women in the Irish Electronics Industry.* August. Dublin: Employment Equality Agency.

Whitaker, T. K. 1958. *Economic Development.* 22 November. Dublin: The Stationery Office.

Whitaker, T. K. 1987. Ireland: Land of change. *Eire-Ireland* 22, no. 1:4-18.

White Paper on Industrial Policy. 1984. Pl. 2491. 12 July. Dublin: The Stationery Office.

Whyte, W. F. 1996. On the evolution of street corner society. In *Journeys through ethnography: Realistic accounts of fieldwork,* edited by A. Lareau and J. Schultz. Boulder, CO: Westview Press.

Wilson, R. E. and C. J. Meadows. 1998. Tele-teaching: Australia's competitive question. *Journal of Global Information Management* 6, no. 1:15-26.

Woodham-Smith, C. 1962. *The Great Hunger, Ireland 1845-1849.* New York: Harper and Row.

Wolf, M. 1992. *A Thrice-Told Tale: Feminism, Postmodernism and Ethnographic Responsibility.* Stanford: Stanford University Press.

Wong, P. 1998. Leapfrogging across the millennium: Information technology in Singapore schools. *Journal of Global Information Management* 6, no. 1:5-13.

Yin, R. K. 1989. *Case Study Research: Design and Methods.* Newbury Park, CA: Sage Publications.

Index